CRAIG CASTER

PARENTING
DISCIPLESHIP
WORKBOOK

Therefore go and make disciples of all nations,
baptizing them in the name of the Father and of the Son and of the Holy Spirit,
and **teaching them to obey everything I have commanded you.**
And surely I am with you always, to the very end of the age."

MATTHEW 28:19-20

FAMILY DISCIPLESHIP MINISTRIES

561 N. Magnolia Avenue

El Cajon, CA 92020

Phone: (619) 590-1901

Fax: (619) 590-1905

Email: info@parentingministry.org

www.parentingministry.org

Parenting Discipleship Workbook
By Craig Caster
ISBN 10: 1-60039-210-5
ISBN 13: 978-1-60039-210-8

Published By:

LAMP POST INC.

www.lamppostpubs.com

Preface

All parents would agree on at least two things - raising children can be wonderful, and difficult. Adjustments must be made for the uniqueness of each personality, and keeping children entertained can be a challenge. But the real bugger is discipline. Couples have to work as a team, single parents are working without back-up, and every parent faces the challenge of protecting and training each child from birth to adulthood. *When, where, how, how much, how often, how long* and *is this really working* are just a few of the questions crowding the thoughts of a parent staring into the face of a precious, disobedient child. The truth is, most parents today are not sure where to turn, probably believe that their own parents did just an OK job, and really feel pretty poorly equipped themselves.

But there is help for those who will listen. God, the creator of all things, has not left us without guidance. He is the creator of the institution we call family, and has given us clear instructions in His Word on how to be successful. We need to take this seriously because we have an enemy. The Bible tells us that the Devil, or Satan, is working against us and would love to break down the strength of the family, which is also an attack against the church, society, and our Christian witness to a lost world. But God, knowing all our needs, gives us both His Word and the Holy Spirit, which is enough to win any battle.

Sadly, most Christians are not aware that the Bible is *relevant* for raising children, so they turn to past experience or worldly philosophy for help. But now is the time to listen, and seek God's wisdom and guidance to strengthen our families. If we are not willing to submit to our Creator, then what can we expect for the future? When we operate outside of God's will, the result is chaos and destruction. It may come slowly, so we hardly notice, but the end is pain.

I know our parenting course will help you learn God's plan for raising children. Whether you function as a traditional family, blended family, single parent family, or grandparents raising grandchildren, God's parenting principles are effective and conclusive. We are all God's children, parent and child alike, and He would never leave us without the possibility of a joy-filled, successful life. May God bless you through His wonderful, life-changing principles, and bless your family as you allow Him to transform you into the parent He knows you can be.

Table of Contents

Week 10: Starting Over

Prologue

His Precious Gifts

I have three children, and I love them all and want the best for them, but I have fallen so short in love as compared to God's love for me. There were times, while raising my children, that I did not always have the best attitude toward them. In ignorance I thought, *Oh my gosh! God, I think you made a mistake. This one is defective.* I have come to understand that God does not make mistakes, and not one of my children is defective. In fact, each unique child is a gift that God knew I needed.

We learn in Psalm 127 that our children are a gift from God. So, my question to you is not, "What are the gifts that God has given you, but *who* are the gifts? And what have you done with those gifts? Think about how you have valued them, and realize that God has seen the way you have handled, or mishandled, the gifts that He has given to you.

In the past, I thought that God was always very disappointed with me. Every time I would consider what God must be thinking about me, I feared that He was thinking, *Craig, you ding-dong. When will you get it together? And then, Ok, that's it. That's the last time Craig.* I had a terrible idea of how God viewed me because of the things I had done in my life. I thought He was downright upset and angry with me all the time. Eventually, I learned that this thinking was a lie from Satan.

If you went to the beach and scooped up sand with both hands, the grains in your grasp would outnumber all the seconds you would live for the rest of your natural life. In His Word, God says that all His thoughts toward us are good, and they outnumber all the grains of sand in the entire earth (Psalm 139:17-18). With all of these good thoughts, when can our Creator have a bad thought about us?

God predestined all of our days, including the "bad days" and the difficult trials that will touch our lives. God knows that people are not perfect and, as such, parents make mistakes. But He uses all our mistakes, trials and difficulties to reveal Himself and bring us into a closer relationship. Within His providential permission, God allows us to do some foolish things, and there will always be consequences. We see this in many families today, non-Christians and Christians alike, because parents have been leaning on their own understanding to raise children. This has created such pain and confusion, and resulted in a lack of peace, joy and other blessings for both parents and children.

But, praise God! He does not leave us or forsake us when we do such foolish things with His precious gifts (Hebrews 13:5). It is so important to remember that God will never leave or forsake (abandon) His children (us). So, let us receive the discipline of our Lord so that we can experience His peace and righteousness in our homes. Remember, God knew every single one of us before time itself began, including the good, the bad, and the ugly (Psalm 139:1-18), and He still chose us to be His children. Thank God for that!

In the Gospel of Luke, chapter 15, Jesus speaks to a mixed group of believers and non-believers, commoners and elitists, about a relationship with His children. He says to them (and to us), "Listen to me and I will teach you how My Father in Heaven looks upon His children." It is glorious when we really come to know and understand our relationship to the living God.

In Luke 15:4-7, Jesus begins with the parable of the lost sheep, telling how God lovingly pursues us when we go astray. In Luke 15:8-10, Jesus tells us the parable of the lost coin, which reveals the value that God places upon each one of us, how precious and unique we are to Him. In the parable commonly known as The Prodigal Son, in Luke 15:11-24, Jesus teaches us about the gifts that God has given to His children. God has given each one of us gifts that He says are uniquely personal. This is the perspective that He tells us to have about our spouse and children, to consider them very special gifts from God.

A prodigal son is someone who takes the inheritance his father gives to him, then misuses and abuses it according to his own desires. Even when we foolishly abuse God's gifts, just like the prodigal son, He is not condemning us as, "Oh you stupid idiot." In His foreknowledge, God already knew we would do the things we have done. Truly we cannot understand His love and mercy; the Word tells us that *"His ways are above our ways"* (Is 55:8-9). We also are told to listen, believe in the love that God has shown us in Jesus, and to follow His wisdom rather than our own understanding. Jesus came so that we could know the Father, and begin to experience the miracle of His lovingkindness toward us.

In Luke 15:11-13, Jesus tells us that, *"A certain man had two sons and the younger of them said to his father, 'Father, give me the portion of goods that fall to me.' So he divided to them his livelihood. And not many days after, the younger son gathered all together and journeyed to a far country and there wasted his possession with prodigal living."* Notice it was the prodigal son speaking to his father, asking for his portion of goods and then going his own way. As God's sons and daughters, this message is meant as an example to us.

When the prodigal son says, *"Give me the portion of goods that fall to me,"* he is asking his father for all that is legally coming to him. He is not asking for more, just what's coming to him. In a sense, this is us saying to our Heavenly Father, "I want it all, God. Give me those blessings you promised me." Do you want all of the gifts He has for you? It is not wrong to ask, "God, give me all that You have for me." In fact, He loves it when we want it all. The sad reality is that most of us treat the gifts He gives to us recklessly. When we don't look upon all His gifts as blessings, we treat them incorrectly.

How many of us have treated our spouse, or our children, who are God's gifts to us, carelessly and inappropriately? How many of us do not know what to do with the gifts He has given to us? By the time my oldest son was three, I wanted to wrap that gift up and send it back. Even at such a young age, there was no other human being on the earth who could make me so angry. He was a mere eighteen pounds to my two hundred, and I was praying, "God where can I go and trade this one in? I think you made a mistake! This one is broken."

Praise God, much has changed since then. One of the greatest transformations in me is my attitude toward this strong-willed child. God penetrated my frustrated mind with the understanding that my son is His gift to my wife and me. My anger problem was not my son's fault, or responsibility; the problem was within *me*. God used this strong-willed child to reveal my selfish, foolish heart, and to bring me to my knees. As I began to pray and fast, pleading, "God, help me," He began to transform me according to His promise.

That's the purpose of having trials in raising our children. God brings us to the point where we say, "Lord, I need help. I don't know what I'm doing here. You say that my son (daughter) is a gift, but he (she) doesn't seem like a gift." That's when God says, "He (She) is a very special gift, and, if you come to Me, I'll show you how to treat him (her). I'll show you how to take care of him (her)." God had to do some real surgery to transform my heart and mind, and teach me how to properly value and treat *His* precious gift.

We read in Luke 15: 12-13, where the son said to his father, *"give me all that is coming to me."* What he was saying in essence was, "OK, I'm ready father. I'm ready to take care of all the things that I own. I do not need your help or support to take care of them anymore. I can do it on my own." Then he went out on his own and wasted his possessions with prodigal (reckless, wasteful, selfish) living. This son did not value his father's blessings; rather he wasted them according to *his own desires*. He took the gifts that were coming to him and foolishly said, "You know what? I am not going to follow your way, dad. I don't want your help anyway. I don't need your support. I am going to take these gifts and use them the way I want to."

This is the first part of the message of the prodigal son. When somebody receives gifts from God and then treats or uses those gifts in a different way than God intended, they are living as the prodigal son; recklessly, wastefully, selfishly and foolishly. Why are so many within the body of Christ living as prodigals? I believe that many are blind to their spiritual condition; living by their own understanding or following worldly advice, plus many are neglecting the gifts God has offered us through His Word. And some of us are simply in *rebellion*.

PARENTING DISCIPLESHIP WORKBOOK

Have you ever looked at your spouse and children as gifts from God? The divorce rate in America is staggering, but did you know that some have reported that approximately one-half of all divorces occur in churched couples claiming to believe in Jesus as their Lord and Savior? Divorce is terribly painful and devastating for children. If we do not look to Jesus for wisdom and strength, then we will begin to think and act selfishly, becoming foolish like the prodigal and possibly lose our gifts. Numerous Christians today are even now on the statistical path to divorce, while others are living in a strained, unfulfilling relationship where all are suffering continuously.

Tension can enter the marriage relationship when dad and mom do not agree on methods for parenting. Friction with the children also develops through frustration because the church and or other believers do not make parents aware of the biblical instruction God has provided on this very topic. Or maybe dad and mom do know the facts, yet continue to indulge in yelling, disrespecting one another, arguing, manipulation and inconsistency. When I finally realized the presence of an angry, selfish condition in myself, I cried out, "Lord, please help me!" And in His mercy He did not turn me away.

Going back to the prodigal son, what does he eventually realize in the midst of his circumstances? In verse 17 we read, *"...but when he came to himself, he said, 'how many of my father's hired servants have bread enough to spare, and I perish with hunger'?"* There are some very important principles in this verse. The son came to his senses (yielded to the conviction of the Holy Spirit) and thought to himself, "Of course I should go to my dad. He's the one who had the gifts. He's the one who gave them to me. He knows how to take care of them. I need to go back to him." This shows that he had come to the end of himself, or his *self-will*, doing things his own way.

There are many people on plan number 999 that refuse to admit they are at the end of themselves. Their marriage lacks true companionship, love and unity. And their relationship with the children is strained and out of order. Instead of coming to the Lord, they devise yet another inferior plan. They decide on their own, get "help" from a friend, read some book giving worldly counsel, and embark on their "new" surefire plan without God, the One who gave them the gifts. The prodigal son went to the world and the world had nothing for him. When will we also realize the world cannot help us? There is only One who can! The prodigal son had to come to the end of himself before he would return to his father. What crisis will it take before we admit to being at the end of ourselves, and go to our Father in Heaven for help?

Why, for so many, does it take a huge *crisis* before we go to our Savior and say, "Lord, help me"? God wants us to come to Him, but Satan is working on believers to convince them that the Word of God is not applicable to these areas of our lives. Satan has convinced many that God is uninterested, unconcerned, unable or unwilling to help us. Few would outright admit this, but look at the condition of the body of Christ. We are saying it with the choices we make in our daily lives.

It's by *God's grace alone* that we are able to take care of His gifts. Did you know that in every area of your life where you are not experiencing the power, peace and understanding of God, it is because you have not truly brought it to God? What will it take before you turn to Him for the information and power that will enable you to take care of your spouse and children? Proverbs 3:5-6, tells us to *"Trust in the Lord with all your heart and lean not on your own understanding. But in <u>all</u> your ways acknowledge Him and He shall direct your path."* Do you know what the word "all" means? Nothing is excluded. Everything is included. Are you ready to look to Him and say, "God, please help me," and then be willing to follow His instructions?

The prodigal son wakes up to reality in Luke 15:18 – 19, and declares, *"I will rise and go to my father and I will say to him, 'Father, I have sinned against heaven and before you and I am no longer worthy to be called your son. Make me like one of your hired servants.'"* This is important to understand. When some of us come to Christ, we try to make a deal. But repentance is not about negotiating with God. For example, "Ok God, I'll love my husband, but *if* he does not do this or that…forget it!" or "Lord, *if* you don't give me what I want, *then* you know what I don't have time for You." When you examine your attitudes and behaviors, are they telling God, "I'll go to church on Sunday, *but* I am to busy to spend time with you each day." or "When my son or my daughter quits acting this way, *then* I will quit screaming and yelling at them or *if* they start obeying everything I say, *then* I will quit acting this way."

Sinful behavior can never be justified. We cannot rightfully say to any other person, "You made me sin." Why do you think God gives such a complete definition in His Word of what love is, and is not? When parents hear how this love applies to raising children, they often begin weeping over their sin. Able to look honestly at themselves, they see the unloving acts committed against their spouse and/or children every day. Do you know the opposite of love? It is hate, which God calls sin. You cannot practice sin by ignoring God's instruction and still reap His blessings (Gal 5:7). God is pure and cannot condone or reward sin.

As we look again to Luke 15:, verses 20 – 24, we see how the prodigal's father responds to his return. The Bible says that, *"…when he was still a great way off, his father saw him and had compassion and ran to him, fell on his neck and kissed him. And the son said to his father, "I have sinned against heaven and in your sight and I am no longer worthy to be called your son."* But the father said to his servants, *"Bring out the best robe and put it on him. And put a ring on his finger, and sandals on his feet. And bring the fatted calf here and kill it and let us eat and be merry, for my son was dead and is alive again. He was lost and he is found, and they began to be merry."*

Father was *not* sitting in the house thinking, "My jerk son is ruining my name out there and making me look like a dirt bag. He's taking my gifts and throwing them away and wasting them. You know what, I hope he never comes back!" He was *not* complaining, whining and fretting over the foolishness of his son. Instead, the father was *waiting* for his prodigal son to come home to him. This is a picture of your heavenly Father. He is waiting and hoping that you will come to Him every day to receive wisdom and grace to take care of the spouse and children He gave to you. He knows your mistakes. Remember that He knows you better than you know yourself. He chose you, and gave you these gifts.

God is not going to come to you and take them back. We can abuse them so much that we lose them and, yes, He allows us the freedom to choose. But your God is waiting for you to come to Him so He can wrap His arms around you and kiss you and bless you. He never intended us to do anything by relying on our own wisdom and strength. He is waiting and hoping that you will come to Him. He is not waiting for you to quit being angry. He knows you cannot change on your own. He wants you to come to Him and receive all the blessings and all the power that He so lovingly desires to give.

God knows our sins and weaknesses better than we do, and that we have been trying to do things our own way. He knows that we have turned to worldly, sinful things to help us deal with the pain of not looking to Him. But His love is amazing. His grace and mercy are wonderful gifts. When you come, God will meet you right where you are now, and begin to fill you with the wisdom, strength and power needed to do His will. He can and will enable you to treat your gifts the way He desires.

I hope that when you have completed these materials, you will see your children through God's eyes, as His gifts to you. And that you will be better prepared to love and care for them as He desires. I pray that you will cast aside all of your *traditional* views about parenting, and learn through God's Word, by the Holy Spirit, what He would have you do with His gifts. By fulfilling His promises in my family, God has shown me that no matter what is in the past, or how you have previously treated your gifts, that He is eagerly waiting for you to embrace Him and His ways. God's desire is to see you victorious, to see you as the parent He calls you to be. His Word reveals that these are His children He has given to you and His Word is the instruction manual.

Follow Him and He will bless you.

Craig Caster

Are you really ready to follow Him now? Jesus encourages us, *"Take My yoke upon you and learn from Me, for I am gentle and humble in heart, and YOU WILL FIND REST FOR YOUR SOULS. For My yoke is easy and My burden is light."* (Matthew 11:29 – 30).

Prayer:
Father, thank You for Your grace and mercy to me. Thank You for Your Word. Thank You for Your patience, and that you wait for me, with arms stretched out, to come to You every day. I believe that You want to

bless me. I believe that You want to give me wisdom. I believe that You want to empower me, Lord, with the grace that I need to love and train my children. Thank You that I can come into Your presence anytime and anyplace. Please help me to hear Your voice, to know Your will in caring for the children You have given me. Help me, Lord, to be willing to invest time in learning what Your Word has to say. And I pray that Your Holy Spirit will guide me and give me understanding. Lord, I repent of my ways, and I am willing to denounce all worldly wisdom. I ask Your forgiveness for turning to these things in the past. I pray that You would be glorified by my life. I ask these things in Jesus' name. Amen.

Introduction to Parenting Discipleship Workbook

This workbook is designed to bring you onto the path of discipleship, which really means walking in God's principles. And when we use words like "walk", we hope you understand that living in these principles is just as fundamental as learning to walk. The goals of our workbook are: 1) To show you that God provides principles for parenting, 2) To equip you with tools and applications for applying these principles, and 3) To guide your family into the forgiveness, healing and unity that comes through obedience to God. Family Discipleship Ministries exists because we believe that failure in discipleship is directly related to failure in parenting. And how do we know this? By what we have seen, experienced and what is proven by statistics today.

The Process

The study is divided into weeks, with five lessons each week. It is important to work toward completing one lesson each day for five days. Building daily study with consistency is a key to spiritual success. We encourage you to start with Week One and continue through Week Two and Three, etc.; skipping to a section that sparks your interest is tempting, but not efficient because one-week builds upon another. For example, you really want to master disciplining your child so move ahead to that study, but there are biblical principles that must be learned before you can discipline in a godly way.

The principles we are presenting have been tried and proven successful. I have experienced it in my own life, my own family, and also through the lives of countless people in counseling and parenting classes. Please understand, this is NOT a "Five Easy Steps to Parenting" manual. *Biblical Discipleship* is **challenging work** and will require that you change some of your attitudes and behaviors. The process will require commitment and sacrifice to successfully implement the principles as you learn them.

Remember:

- This work is a new priority and will require dedicated time. The lessons are spread over five days, and to be done daily. If you miss a day, DO NOT skip it, but work to complete all days in order within the week. If you miss often, pray about your priorities and what you are placing ahead of this commitment.

- At times we start projects and do not finish. Consider the importance of your responsibility in the area of parenting and make a decision to faithfully complete this study. Enlist the help of an accountability partner for prayer and study if necessary.

- If married, your spouse is an essential partner in this effort. Study together or separately, but always discuss what you have learned as it relates to marital and parenting issues and changes.

Starting Each Day

1. View each daily study as time spent with your God, and expect Him to speak to you through His Word.

2. Start each day with prayer, asking God to reveal where you need to change, and to empower you to apply what you are learning.

3. Have a reflective mindset; do not rush through the material just to say you finished it. Give God time to speak to you, and meditate on what you learn.

Things to note:

- Studies may vary in the amount of information presented. After you complete each day, look ahead to the next so you can plan your time with God and get the most out of it.

- Space is provided for writing answers to questions, and also for relevant thoughts and prayers. If you have downloaded and printed this manual from our website, we suggest you put it in a three-ring binder, and include additional paper for personal journaling and notes.

- Please take advantage of the Appendices at the end of the workbook. They are there for your growth and we refer to them throughout the workbook.

Important Markers

FACT FILE

When you see this, you will find the definition of a word and/or phrase from the Bible. We have taken great care to use well-known and theologically sound biblical dictionaries and commentaries for biblical clarity, referenced when possible. Many of these definitions appear in the glossary, located in the Appendix.

DIG DEEPER: *FURTHER STUDY*

This marks an opportunity to read a text of Scripture and relate it to the subject that is being presented. During this discipleship process, you will become more familiar with the Bible, biblical principles of parenting, and what God expects from you as a parent.

SELF-EXAMINATION

As you study and learn biblical principles, there will be times for self-examination, finding areas where personal improvement is needed. Space is provided for listing insights, confessions, and prayers for strength and wisdom to make those changes. One aspect of the discipleship process is personal accountability; if God reveals that you have sinned against your spouse and/or children, we encourage you to confess your sin to them and ask their forgiveness. Make this a regular practice even if it is not noted to do so.

✓ACTION PLAN

After you have studied the biblical principles of that day or week, take action and apply what you have learned to your life. To be true disciples, we must understand that God not only desires that we grow in knowledge, but He also requires that we use it, or "live it out".

All the materials on our website www.parentingministry.org, focus on discipleship and are provided free of charge.

A Leader's Guide for small or large group class settings is available at www.parentingministry.org under Free Ministry Downloads.

Week 1: God's Purposes for Parenting

WEEK 1: DAY 1

Where Do We Turn?

Parenting is a little like learning the computer, only harder, because the confusion is greater, the frustration stronger and the learning curve a lot longer. When we bring home our first bundle of computer technology, it is accompanied by instructions and a phone number for tech support, because we know sooner or later we will need help. We must learn how to navigate through a screen filled with pictures and information to our desired destination. And we also soon learn that typing without periodically hitting the Save feature can result in the frustrating disappearance of our hard work. But in spite of it all we persist, because we will not be beaten, and eventually using the computer becomes a rewarding and enjoyable experience!

May we say that learning to parent is similar? Take note of the word "learning," because successful parenting requires instruction and application. Within hours of bringing that precious infant home from the hospital, the mystery begins to unfold. Why the crying? What is the need? And so it goes as the child grows, and so does the anxiety, until we realize that there is more to this than love. The only constant is that what works today won't work tomorrow, and so on. This continues from infancy to adolescence. And if you raise more than one child, you discover that God really has a sense of humor. Being unique really means that techniques working with one child will have a completely different result with another. Every child needs training and guidance, and finding that routines and plans are not enough, we reach for wisdom.

But the news is good; there is wisdom available and, despite the challenges, parenting can be incredibly rewarding! Whether you have one child or several, you already realize that parenting is an enormous responsibility, fraught with potential difficulties, but also filled with much joy and delight. Just watching your children grow, seeing the dynamics as they interact, and noticing the change in their personalities is so interesting. And the best news of all; effective parenting is not a mystery. We can parent with confidence when we draw from the wisdom of Biblical concepts and an understanding of God's will. When we do it God's way, our efforts will not be lost. God wants us to understand our role and purpose as parents, and to successfully escort our children to that desirable destination of Godly maturity.

As you begin this study on parenting, God wants you to be fully assured that He can provide whatever you need. Read the following verses and notice what He promises.

2 Peter 1:3-4 *"As His divine power has given to us all things that pertain to life and Godliness, through the knowledge of Him who called us by glory and virtue, by which have been given to us exceedingly great and precious promises, that through these you may be partakers of the divine nature, having escaped the corruption that is in the world through lust."*

It says that God gives us *"all things that pertain to life"*, which includes biblical parenting. Our instructions are in God's Word, and it is by HIS divine power that we can do it (v 3).

FACT FILE

Our source is "**His divine power**": power is *dunamis* (Greek), which translates as dynamic strength, or ability to do what only God can do.

When we are born again by faith in Jesus Christ, we receive the Holy Spirit (Eph 1:13-14) and the power that raised Jesus from the dead begins working in us (Eph 1:19-20). But notice that all this can only be accessed "through the knowledge of Him."

FACT FILE

We partake of the divine nature and promises "**through the knowledge of Him**": knowledge is *epignosis* (Greek), which means thorough participation in acquiring knowledge.

Knowledge of Christ powerfully affects the believer, and comes only through salvation and abiding in His Word. To abide means "to dwell in," and indicates more than just head knowledge. It means receiving the Word as truth and then being obedient.

It is important to understand that as we abide in Christ, we not only gain knowledge that can change us, we also qualify for **"great and precious promises"** from a God who is 100 percent faithful. And, as **"partakers of the divine nature,"** we truly have access to supernatural wisdom and strength for parenting according to His principles.

DIG DEEPER: *FURTHER STUDY*

Write out what God promises in these Scriptures:

Psalm 84:11 *"For the LORD God is a sun and shield; The LORD will give grace and glory; No good thing will He withhold From those who walk uprightly."*

_____

_____

_____

Matthew 6:33 *"But seek first the kingdom of God and His righteousness, and all these things shall be added to you."*

_____

_____

_____

_____

⌕ SELF-EXAMINATION

How have these truths affected your attitude/disposition as a parent?

_____

_____

_____

_____

What are the main principle(s) that are promised to you?

_____

_____

_____

_____

Past Experience Is Not Enough

Looking back at life with your parents, do you believe that they really knew what they were doing?

❑ Yes   ❑ No   ❑ Hit and Miss

Most of us are suspicious that our parents used a "hit-and-miss" philosophy for child rearing, and were probably not confident about their effectiveness.

In view of your current parenting methods, how do you know what you are doing is right? Typically, people copy the good things their parents did, throw out the bad and make up the rest. And most of this is based upon their own personality and past experiences. Since it is rare that both husband and wife had exactly the same type of upbringing, each brings a past into the present, and then both must cooperate to work out a mutually acceptable approach to parenting. But this method can be confusing as parents soon learn that children are uniquely different from them, and that their best techniques are not bringing the desired outcome.

Understanding all this, we are ready for the first key to effective parenting: **it is essential to depend on God's Word**. Such logic as, "I thought if I was doing the job better than my parents, my kids would turn out at least as good as me," or, "At least I'm not screaming and beating them - I had it much worse than they do," is not uncommon, yet it is not a foundation for success. The foundation on which parents must build, the only guide, is the Bible. God wants parents to succeed and He has provided *all* the necessary information.

DIG DEEPER: *FURTHER STUDY*

Read the following verses and write out what God is saying about following your own wisdom.

Proverbs 3:5-6 *"Trust in the LORD with all your heart, and lean not on your own understanding; in all your ways acknowledge Him, and He shall direct your paths."*

Proverbs14:12 *"There is a way that seems right to a man, but its end is the way of death."*

_____
_____
_____
_____
_____
_____

Read the following Scriptures. In verse 6 Paul gives a command for them to WALK.

Colossians 2:6-7 *"As you therefore have received Christ Jesus the Lord, so walk in Him, (7) rooted and built up in Him and established in the faith, as you have been taught, abounding in it with thanksgiving.*

How are we supposed to walk? And if you walked that way, how would it affect your parenting?

_____
_____
_____
_____
_____

Paul makes an important comparison in verse 8. He says BEWARE, which translated literally means be-aware and continue to be-aware.

Colossians 2:8 *"Beware lest anyone cheat you through philosophy and empty deceit, according to the tradition of men, according to the basic principles of the world, and not according to Christ."*

What is the danger? What is the source of this danger? According to this Scripture what do we need to beware of?

_____

_____

_____

_____

_____

Where should we be getting our information, or instruction?

_____

_____

These verses are filled with examples of possible consequences. Identify and list them, both the good and the bad.

> **Ephesians 5:6** *"Let no one deceive you with empty words, for because of these things the wrath of God comes upon the sons of disobedience."*

_____

_____

_____

_____

_____

> **Colossians 1:10** *"that you may walk worthy of the Lord, fully pleasing [Him], being fruitful in every good work and increasing in the knowledge of God..."*

_____

_____

_____

_____

_____

> **Colossians 3:17** *"And whatever you do in word or deed, [do] all in the name of the Lord Jesus, giving thanks to God the Father through Him."*

_____

_____

_____

_____

_____

1 Corinthians 3:18-19 "Let no one deceive himself. If anyone among you seems to be wise in this age, let him become a fool that he may become wise. For the wisdom of this world is foolishness with God. For it is written, "He catches the wise in their own craftiness"

✓ACTION PLAN

We have learned in this lesson that apart from God's Word, power and wisdom we are unable to be the parents God desires us to be. If you have any reservation about being a child of God turn to the **Appendix C** and follow the instructions of how to be one laid out in God's Word.

WEEK 1: DAY 2

The Original Blueprint

In order to follow God's plan for parenting, we must first look to the original blueprint. It was God, not man, who created the institution of family. And it was the first, therefore a foundationally important institution.

> *Genesis 2:18, 21-22, 24; 1:28:*

> "And the LORD God said, "It is not good that man should be alone; I will make him a helper comparable to him." And the LORD God caused a deep sleep to fall on Adam, and he slept; and He took one of his ribs, and closed up the flesh in its place. Then the rib which the LORD God had taken from man He made into a woman, and He brought her to the man. Therefore a man shall leave his father and mother and be joined to his wife, and they shall become one flesh. And Then God blessed them, and God said to them, "Be fruitful and multiply; fill the earth and subdue it; have dominion over the fish of the sea, over the birds of the air, and over every living thing that moves on the earth."

Legal marriage in the United States, for the most part, consists of one husband and one wife. This is due to the Christian perspective of those who founded this country, although currently that definition of marriage is under attack. In some other areas of the world man's wisdom has prevailed resulting in polygamy. Women are considered possessions to be dominated, abused and even killed, and have few rights as wives and even as mothers of their own children. The true God is the creator of marriage and has much to say about proper behavior as husbands and wives, and also about the training of children.

In Genesis 1:28, God says, "A husband and wife will come together and have children." (paraphrase). This is God's design for the family, but just a starting point. The majority of couples soon discover that "togetherness" of heart and mind is difficult. And, as children are added, frustrations and unfulfilled *expectations* can multiply. We put demands on each other and on our children, and when these needs are not met, the result is anger and other sins of the flesh such as resentment, bitterness, betrayal and so on.

It would be a dirty trick for God to leave us with such challenging responsibilities as marriage and parenting, and not provide clear guidelines for success. And God, of course, does not play dirty tricks. Scripture tells us, *"The Lord is righteous in all His ways, gracious in all His works."* (Ps. 145:17). Unfortunately, a 1998 survey shows that fewer than 11 percent of Christians believe the Bible has relevant or significant information about parenting.[1] In truth, children are a gift from God, and He has greater love for them than we do. Therefore, He provides in His Word all that we need to know about parenting and godly living. He wants our actions to *glorify Him* and bless the children he has put into our care. Again, it is imperative we understand that God's Word contains what we need for success, and that God's desires for the family are not hidden from us.

Read the following Scripture:

> **2 Timothy 3:16-17** *"All Scripture is given by inspiration of God, and is profitable for doctrine, for reproof, for correction, for instruction in righteousness, that the man of God may be complete, thoroughly equipped for every good work."*

FACT FILE

"Thoroughly equipped for every good work" means it is God's intention for us to both understand His will and be empowered to follow through in obedience.

⌕ SELF-EXAMINATION

How does this verse apply to learning how to be a parent?

_____

_____

_____

_____

_____

---

1   Churches Have Opportunity to Help Parents, Barna Group, January 15, 1998

Read 1 Thessalonians 2:13:

> *"For this reason we also thank God without ceasing, because when you received the word of God which you heard from us, you welcomed it not as the word of men, but as it is in truth, the word of God, which also effectively works in you who believe."*

Examine your attitude toward the Word of God: Do you believe it is the truth, and that following God's Word will lead to success?

_____

_____

_____

_____

DIG DEEPER: *FURTHER STUDY*

According to James 1:22-25, there are right and wrong ways to receive the Word of God. Please identify the two different approaches, and the characteristics of each.

> *"But be doers of the word, and not hearers only, deceiving yourselves. For if anyone is a hearer of the word and not a doer, he is like a man observing his natural face in a mirror; for he observes himself, goes away, and immediately forgets what kind of man he was. But he who looks into the perfect law of liberty and continues in it, and is not a forgetful hearer but a doer of the work, <u>this one will be blessed</u> in what he does."*

What should be our attitude toward the Word of God?

_____

_____

_____

_____

What are the positive consequences when we obey and do the Word of God?

_____

_____

_____

_____

_____

Read the following verses and explain what is said about the Word of God and you?

Joshua 1:8 *"This Book of the Law shall not depart from your mouth, but you shall meditate in it day and night, that you may observe to do according to all that is written in it. For then you will make your way prosperous, and then you will have good success."*

_____

_____

_____

_____

Psalm 19:7–11 *"The law of the LORD is perfect, converting the soul; The testimony of the LORD is sure, making wise the simple; The statutes of the LORD are right, rejoicing the heart; The commandment of the LORD is pure, enlightening the eyes; The fear of the LORD is clean, enduring forever; The judgments of the LORD are true and righteous altogether. More to be desired are they than gold, Yea, than much fine gold; Sweeter also than honey and the honeycomb. Moreover by them Your servant is warned, And in keeping them there is great reward."*

_____

_____

_____

_____

1 Peter 2:2–3 *"as newborn babes, desire the pure milk of the word, that you may grow thereby, if indeed you have tasted that the Lord is gracious."*

_____

_____

_____

_____

In Genesis 18:19, God said to Abraham:

"For I have known him, in order that he may command his children and his household after him, that they keep the way of the LORD, to do righteousness and justice, that the LORD may bring to Abraham what He has spoken to him."

Just as Abraham was told to command his children, we also must teach our children with intention – be intentional about our ways, and intentional about following God's Word. Once we understand that, as parents, we are truly ministers to our children, and that our relationship to Christ is the source of needed wisdom and strength, we can begin to walk the path of successful parenting.

Also notice that God says He has "known" Abraham personally, "in order that he may command his children and his household." This implies that God knows Abraham's strengths and weaknesses, but *promises* to teach and strengthen him for the responsibility of training his children.

SELF-EXAMINATION

Are you confident at this point in your parenting journey that you know how to command your children according to God's Word?   ❏ Yes ❏ No

How comforting is it to you to know that God knows your strengths and weaknesses and promises to give you the wisdom and strength to do His will as a parent. Write out a few thoughts telling God how grateful you are for His help.

_____

_____

_____

_____

_____

> **2 Corinthians 5:9** *Paul says, "Therefore we make it our aim, whether present or absent, to be well pleasing to Him."*

Paul made it his *aim* to be well *pleasing to God*; he was very intentional about it. Write out a prayer below, telling God that your aim is to please Him by completing this workbook.

_____

_____

_____

_____

_____

WEEK 1: DAY 3

The Ministry of Parenting

When we hear the word "minister," we commonly think of a pastor or person who works for a church. But the word includes more than those descriptions?

FACT FILE

The word *minister* is derived from the Greek word *diakonos* which means a *servant*.

Minister - *(noun) A servant or waiter, one who oversees, governs and fulfills.*

Minister - *(verb) To adjust, regulate and set in order; to serve, render service to another; to labor for the Lord as a servant.*

So how does this apply to us as Christian parents? It means that we are under the care and authority of Jesus Christ, who is one with God the Father, and that we receive our instructions from Him. God has given us our children and He desires for us to execute His purposes as we raise them. You and I *are* ministers over our children, under God. This mindset should completely change our disposition and approach to parenting.

Have you seen your role in the home as that of a minister?   ❏ Yes ❏ No

As parents, depending totally on the Lord Jesus Christ is essential. We are not to promote our own will and wishes, but we are responsible to follow the Lord's will and desire in raising our children. Matthew 20:28 (King James Version) says, *"Even as the Son of man came not to be **ministered** unto, but to **minister**..."* The same verse in the New King James reads, *"Just as the Son of Man did not come to be **served**, but to **serve**..."* Clearly, ministering and serving are the same, and Jesus is our example. Do not mistake "serving" as the worldly view of indulging children, but serve by raising them according to God's instructions. In serving, we also are not to be harsh with our children, but model the loving kindness of the Lord. When we begin to see parenting as serving God and ministering to our children for His purposes, we are headed in the right direction.

DIG DEEPER: *FURTHER STUDY*

Read the following Scripture describe in your own words how Paul and his companions ministered to people. What attitudes did they display?

1 Thessalonians 2:7-8 *"But we were gentle among you, just as a nursing mother cherishes her own children. 8 So, affectionately longing for you, we were well pleased to impart to you not only the gospel of God, but also our own lives, because you had become dear to us."*

_____

_____

_____

_____

_____

_____

The Right Blueprint

As *ministers* of God, we must know His *purposes*, what He wants us to accomplish and how we are to proceed. Understanding His purposes helps us recognize our daily need for God's wisdom and strength.

FACT FILE

Purpose - means an intended, or desired, result or goal.

If two hundred parents are asked what they believe God's purpose is for them as ministers and parents, it will likely produce many different answers. This is an indication of the lack of unity between husbands and wives in this area. To a certain extent, this is the problem: when two people with the same task are going in different directions, confusion results. And the Bible shows us that this is **not** God's plan!

1 Corinthians 14:33 *"For God is not the author of confusion but of peace."*

Regrettably, the body of Christ has not given preference to training or discipling people in parenting. Many churches have never conducted a parenting class! During our teen years, we undergo fifty hours or more of training to get a driver's license, yet how many hours of training is required for parenting children? None! Which is more important, driving a car or raising children? The answer is obvious. And due to that lack of training, many parents, even Christian parents, can be a very negative influence on their children, more even than that of the world.

Counseling Christian families in distress has revealed that, in most cases, it is not music, drugs, or influences at school that most affect children – it is what occurs within the four walls of home. Of course, these couples did not marry and decide together that "we want to mess up our kids." It results when two people are just doing things their own way, with no firm foundation to build on, and no common wisdom to guide them. What happens when a husband and wife disagree and are not clear in their God-given purposes? Problems arise followed by tension, strife, and division. This, in turn, puts a strain on marriage and family, which is a devastating problem today in the body of Christ.

In Matthew 12:25, Jesus revealed a self-evident truth:

> *"Every kingdom divided against itself is brought to desolation, and every city or house divided against itself will not stand."*

SELF-EXAMINATION

Take time right now to write out a prayer. Ask God, as husband and wife, to give you the grace to begin again with your parenting. Ask Him for the mercy to forgive each other for past mistakes, and for not working in harmony while parenting your children and to open your hearts to receive His instruction and work together as a team.

Husband:

_____

_____

_____

_____

_____

_____

_____

_____

Wife:

_____

_____

_____

_____

_____

_____

_____

_____

Read the following Scripture meditating on the attitudes that God desires for us:

> **Colossians 3:12-16** *"Therefore, as the elect of God, holy and beloved, put on tender mercies, kindness, humility, meekness, longsuffering; bearing with one another, and forgiving one another, if anyone has a complaint against another; even as Christ forgave you, so you also must do. But above all these things put on love, which is the bond of perfection. And let the peace of God rule in your hearts, to which also you were called in one body; and be thankful. Let the word of Christ dwell in you richly in all wisdom, teaching and admonishing one another in psalms and hymns and spiritual songs, singing with grace in your hearts to the Lord."*

It is clear that the foundation for all we do must be an understanding of the purposes and plans that God has *for us*. This will be the topic of the following section. Once we embrace God's authority, it is essential to follow through in practical ways. God is the architect, but it is our job to build the house according to His blueprint. When we understand what God is trying to do *through us*, and *within us*, when we follow His design, we then understand why it is so vital that we have a right relationship with Christ.

Read the following verse and in your own words, explain how this verse can relate to you as a parent/minister.

> **Ephesians 2:10** *says, "For we are His workmanship, created in Christ Jesus for good works, which God prepared beforehand that we should walk in them."*

_____

_____

_____

_____

WEEK 1: Day 4

God's Purposes for Parents

God's purpose for us as parent/ministers can be broken down into four areas:

First Purpose: God's Glorification

> **Glorify –** To reflect, to honor, praise, to give esteem or honor by putting him into an honorable position.[2]

Our primary purposes as believers is to glorify God. In 1 Corinthians 6:20, scripture says, *"For you were bought at a price; therefore glorify God in your body and in your spirit, which are God's."* The word glorify translates "to reflect". As believers and ministers of God to our children, we are to act as His reflection to them.

> **Matthew 5:16** *"Let your light so shine before men, that they may see your good works and glorify your Father in Heaven."*

Remember, God is changing us from the *inside*, which is evident by our attitudes and behavior. Our transformation becomes real as we exhibit the very nature of Christ to those around us.

⌕ SELF-EXAMINATION

Consider the attitudes that you are demonstrating to your children. Write out what words and behaviors do not reflect God?

---

2   *Spiros Zodhiates, The Complete Word Study Dictionary: New Testament* (Chattanooga, TN: AMG Publishers, 2000), 481.

_____

_____

_____

_____

_____

_____

_____

The story of Moses, in Numbers 20:8-13, provides an example of a person challenged under the pressure of responsibility. Moses wandered through the desert with two to three million people for forty years. The people were rebellious whiners, despite the fact that they had the evidence of God right in front of them as a cloud by day and a pillar of fire by night and provided food and water! When Moses left them and went to meet with almighty God on the mountain, they created and worshipped an idol!

Although God allowed consequences to occur, and He administered discipline, He patiently endured and led these stiff-necked children. When the Israelites complained to Moses about needing water, he turned to God again for help. God told Moses to "speak to the rock." But Moses became so frustrated with the people and their constant complaining, that he did not say, "Water, come forth!" as God has instructed him. Instead he grabbed his rod and struck the rock in anger.

The Lord was not pleased with Moses because he disobeyed and *misrepresented* God's nature and attitude to the people. Moses failed because he exhibited his angry nature rather than God's mercy when he struck the rock. God does not condone our sin, but He does promise to supply our needs, and the people needed water for themselves and their animals. God is perfectly just, and will guide his servants into the proper response for every situation. We need to be cautious not to put the heavy burdens of our selfish expectations and frustrations on the children trusted to our care. But as we grow closer to God, understanding how He transforms us, we then can better *represent* Him to our children.

SELF-EXAMINATION
Write down any incidents in the last week in which you have misrepresented God, and then ask for His forgiveness.

_____

_____

_____

_____

_____

_____

_____

God has given principles in His Word that, if followed, are linked to a promise.

> **Proverbs 20:7** *"The righteous man walks in his <u>integrity</u>; His children are blessed after him."*

FACT FILE

Integrity here indicates singleness of heart, not double-minded - one who walks according to His will and exemplifying God's righteousness.

Write out how you believe this applies to parenting. How can this bless your children both now and in the future?

_____

_____

_____

DIG DEEPER: *FURTHER STUDY*

Timothy was pastor of the church at Ephesus when Paul wrote to him:

> **2 Timothy 1:5** *"When I call to remembrance the genuine faith that is in you, which dwelt first in your grandmother Lois and your mother Eunice, and I am persuaded is in you also."*

According to this verse, who influenced Timothy in righteousness? What was the outcome for Timothy?

_____

_____

_____

WEEK 1: DAY 5

Second Purpose: Our Transformation

1 John 2:5 *"But whoever keeps His word, truly the love of God is perfected in him. By this we know that we are in Him."*

Being transformed into Christ's image is God's plan and purpose for every believer. The word perfected translates "to make complete," which indicates that something is in process. This process involves our responses to everyday experiences and situations, including the challenges of home life where we interact with spouses and children. We like to tell ourselves when we are angry, "Another made me act this way." But can we find that in God's Word? No! God says that out of the abundance of the heart, the mouth speaks (Matt. 12:34). That ungodliness is inside you and God is using a child to bring it out, yet you imply your innocence by not taking responsibility. It is vitally important that you and I understand as ministers that God is using the dynamics of our families to purge us and transform us into the likeness of Christ.

2 Corinthians 3:18 *says, "But we all, with unveiled face, beholding as in a mirror the glory of the Lord, are being transformed into the same image from glory to glory, just as by the Spirit of the Lord."*

FACT FILE

Transformed is *metamorphóō* (Greek), from which we derive our English word metamorphosis: to change into something entirely different, as a caterpillar to a butterfly.

Here it represents the thorough change as a Christian gradually transforms into the likeness of Christ, and comes to desire God's will in all things.

This verse gives assurance that God is at work in you, changing you. Can you thank Him for the work already done, and ask Him to reveal areas where you still need improvement?   ❏ Yes ❏ No

Write in the space below a commitment to accept His perfect way in revealing the lack of Christlikeness in you.

_____
_____
_____
_____
_____

DIG DEEPER: *FURTHER STUDY*

Read the following Scripture and write out what God promise to do in you?

Philippians 1:6 *"Being confident of this very thing, that He who has begun a good work in you will complete it until the day of Jesus Christ."*

_____
_____

This good work is the process of becoming like Christ. Do you still have room to grow in this area?
❏ Yes ❏ No

In my own life, God particularly used my oldest son, Nicholas. In the beginning, because of my ignorance to God's ways, I was so disturbed by Nicholas' miss behaving that I took everything he did the wrong way, and very personal. God often used him to reveal anger and impatience within me.

When Nicholas was five years old, God finally got my attention. He said, "Craig, that's Me. That's not Nick. I'm just using him to bring about this transformation in you." I have discovered, over the years, that God has used my son Nicholas, my little mule, as one of the most powerful tools to reveal those areas that needed to be transformed. In the same way God is using the mule He has blessed you with!

Isaiah 29:16 New Living Translation, says:

> *"How foolish can you be? He is the Potter, and He is certainly greater than you, the clay! Should the created thing say of the one who made it, "He didn't make me"? Does a jar ever say, 'The potter who made me is stupid'?"*

Ouch! So many times in a heated moment, when God is trying to bring about transformation, we tell Him through our actions, "Take Your hand off of me, Lord! I don't want to be shaped, I don't want to be transformed. I'm not going to look at this child right now, whose head I want to take off, and believe that is You!" We must remember, however, that it *is* God who brings about, or permits, these circumstances, and that *He* uses them to reveal things *in us* that are ungodly and do not glorify Him.

God is not allowing these circumstances so He can find out what is within us, He already knows and sees all, and still loves us. Praise Him! He is doing it so that we will see ourselves, and seek His help for change.

> **Proverbs 17:3** *says, "The refining pot is for silver and the furnace for gold, But the LORD <u>tests</u> the hearts."*

SELF-EXAMINATION

As God is testing your heart, what are some of the ungodly attitudes and actions being revealed to you through your child, or children?

_____
_____
_____
_____
_____
_____

> **Isaiah 48:10** *"Behold, I have refined you, but not as silver; I have tested you in the furnace of affliction."*

Jeremiah 17:10 *"I, the L*ORD*, search the heart, I test the mind, Even to give every man according to his ways, According to the fruit of his doings."*

When we believe God is in control, it helps us to stop and think, "Oh! Wait a minute, how is God using this trial for me?" I don't want to tell God to get Your hands off of me. Parenting can be difficult because of the overwhelming feeling that we give, give, give and get very little appreciation in return. In fact, it feels like children take, take, take and we are often the enemy when giving them our best. But look at Jesus - people rarely walked up to Him and said, "Thanks Jesus! I'm so glad you're here." Consider the trials of Moses. No matter how God provided for the Israelites, they complained to Moses and rebelled. *Ministry* is oftentimes a selfless task, with delayed or little thanks.

We need to understand that God has a purpose in the trials that He brings through our children. It will be impossible to embrace these trials as lessons, and transformation will not occur, if our eyes are not fixed on the goal of becoming more like Christ. When our hope is not in Christ and these circumstances come about, we react from our flesh and exhibit such sins as anger, pride, self-pity and more. People tend to interpret their sinful attitudes and responses in relation to external causes, such as a difficult child. But listen for the voice from God, saying, "No, that's your sin, own it!"

Hebrews 12:2 *says, "Looking unto Jesus, the author and finisher of our faith, who for the joy that was set before Him endured the cross, despising the shame, and has sat down at the right hand of the throne of God."*

SELF-EXAMINATION

Notice that Jesus endured the pain of the cross because of the joyous result, the salvation of our souls. What joy do you see that makes the pain of transformation worthwhile? Name at least two areas: "God is revealing within you that He wants to change such things as anger, impatience...

_____

_____

_____

_____

The verse also says to "look unto Jesus." Write out a prayer of commitment to look to Him when a challenging parenting issue comes up in your home?

_____

_____

_____

_____

_____

Third Purpose: To Love Them

Certainly a primary purpose of parents is to love our children. Remember that we are being transformed into the image of Christ, and that the Bible tells us that "God is love." Our attitudes should be guided by the example of Jesus, who acted with love and forgiveness. Remember, even as adults we are considered by God to be His "children". How do we want to be treated by God? As parents we must view our children through God's Word first, *not* according to their personalities, stages of life, or their failures. God has determined the value of our children, and *He* dictates how we must treat them.

> **Psalm 127:3** *"Behold, children are a gift of the LORD, the fruit of the womb is a reward."* *(NAS)*

SELF-EXAMINATION

Do your children feel that you consider them a *gift* from God, by the way you treat them?
❏ Yes ❏ No ❏ Sometimes

> **Reward** – a great precious value.

How should we treat a valuable gift from God?

_____
_____
_____
_____
_____

(We will study this topic in Weeks 3, 4 and 5.)

Fourth Purpose: To Train Them

Finally, our fourth and most obvious purpose is to train our children. *"And you, fathers, do not provoke your children to wrath, but bring them up in the training and admonition of the Lord"* (Eph. 6:4). To *"bring them up"* is to raise our children to maturity, to educate them. Sometimes during this process, parents are more concerned about the opinions of strangers than they are about the impression they make within the walls of home. This type of pride comes off as hypocrisy and can be the cause, especially during the teen years, of your children becoming rebellious and walking away from the Lord. When they see us at home doing things that are contrary to what we teach, or expect of them, they become confused and disillusioned. We must be concerned with glorifying God at all times, especially to those within our home! Even those who are serving in ministry as a career must remember that their first ministry is family.

(We will study this topic in Weeks 6 - 9)

No Exceptions

The principles and promises covered in this material apply to every parenting situation – single parent, blended family, perhaps grandparents – whoever is in charge. God's Word applies equally to all. And He understands that raising children, especially for those who are single, is one of the most difficult challenges in this world.

Divorce has devastated many families, causing children to be hurt and confused which complicats an already daunting responsibility. But God promises: "*A father of the fatherless, a defender of widows, is God in His holy habitation*" (Ps. 68:5). The Bible refers to the fatherless forty-one times, and mentions the widow seventy-four times. This shows us that God's heart is upon the single-parent family!

We think the word *widow* means a wife who has lost her husband by death, but in Christ's day it meant much more than that. The Greek word *chera*, translated "widow," is derived from the word *casma*, meaning the deficiency or vacancy of somebody. A widow was a woman who was simply minus a husband.

We also tend to think of single-parenting as a rather recent problem. This is not true - in Christ's day, all it took to put away a wife was a certificate bearing the signature of a priest. It was a big problem then, as it is now, and God knows and cares. James 1:27 says, "*Pure and undefiled religion before God and the Father is this: to visit orphans and widows in their trouble, and to keep oneself unspotted from the world.*"

Again, if you are a single parent or in a blended family, *all* of the instructions and principles contained in this book apply to you. Thankfully, God's Word promises that He will help you apply each of these principles to your unique situation.

> **Matthew 11:28** "*Come to Me, all you who labor and are heavy laden, and I will give you rest*"

> **Psalm 10:14** "*. . . The helpless commits himself to You; You are the helper of the fatherless*"

As a single parent take a moment and meditate on the passages above. Find God's promises, write them down, and then prayerfully thank Him for what He has done, and will continue to do for you.

Week 2 : Having a Strong Foundation

WEEK 2: DAY 1

A Strong Foundation

God wants His instructions to be clear, so scripture often includes examples and comparisons that people can easily understand. In Matthew 7:24 – 27, Jesus tells the parable of the two builders: one man who built his house upon rock and another who built on sand. Eventually *"the rain descended, the floods came, and the winds blew and beat on that house..."* and, as expected, the house on rock remained while the house on sand fell. Jesus had been teaching many things to His followers over time, and Matthew 7:24 reveals His point: *"Therefore, whoever hears these sayings of Mine, and does them, I will liken him to a wise man who built his house on the rock."*

We always have a choice to follow the path of *wisdom*, or the path of *folly*. There is no third alternative. One path leads to success, the other to failure. For example, many years ago, I was a land developer who built industrial parks, shopping centers and storage facilities. A piece of property was purchased for the construction of an office building, based on a cost analysis that looked profitable. But when the architect finished the plans, the foundation was much larger than expected, adding additional expenses. The foundation footings required were seven foot in diameter and used four times the usual amount of steel!

When questioned, the architect explained that about 30 feet under the crust of this land was a fault line resulting in a level of mud. In his expert opinion, the only way to build safely required a massive foundation to support the building. By this time in my career, I had completed various projects representing more than 3,000,000 square feet of construction, and I could have chosen to follow my own experience rather than the architect's advice. Imagine what would have happened, however, if I had taken those plans and decided to build according to my past experience.

If I chose to shrink the foundation to what I thought would be adequate, the problems would have been devastating. As storms and earthquakes hit, the foundation would have cracked. The deterioration would go like this: the slab would eventually break, and cracks begin to appear in the windows, then the door jambs would get to the point where the doors did not close, and the staircase would begin cracking, and the elevator shaft would not line up. Eventually, the building would be condemned as unsafe because of the inadequate foundation and resulting damage.

Obviously, I would have been foolish to ignore the architect for any reason, be it greed, pride or even putting faith in my past experience. To follow anything but the architect's plan for a strong foundation would have resulted in disaster and greater loss. And so it is for us as believers when we are ignorant of, or ignore the instruction of God and do not follow them. It is not enough for us to be "**hearers**", but we must be "**doers**" if we are to build a strong foundation for our life (James 1:22). It is always *foolish* for us to question or ignore the architect of our faith, Jesus Christ.

Scripture reveals information on God's design for a strong foundation that we need to study and follow, because a building is only as good as the foundation it stands on. Your life can look good for a while, but how strong are you really? The storms of trouble will eventually reveal the true nature of your foundation.

Priorities in Place

Jesus told us, *"But seek first the Kingdom of God and His righteousness, and all these things shall be added to you"* (Matt. 6:33).

> ### FACT FILE
>
> **Seek first** – is a command to do and never stop. The promise is that if we do, *"all these things shall be added to you."* When interpreting "all these things" you need to take into account that this sermon starts at 5:1, known as the Sermon on the Mount. The immediate context (v 31) speaks of food, drink and clothing, if Christ will take care of those needs if we seek Him first, how much more will He give us all things to parent His children.

Seeking God and His kingdom is to be our priority as believers, and as such it is the foundation for life. Remember, as parents we also are ministers of God to our children, and face the added challenge of fulfilling His will in all things pertaining to family. We accomplish this by putting the issues of life in perspective, and by prioritizing our choices according to what God says is important. To truly fulfill God's purposes in and through us, we must look to Him *daily* for strength to accomplish this task.

We would all agree that it is important for a pastor to have a strong, intimate relationship with the Lord. We would expect him to get up every day and spend time studying and praying, seeking wisdom and guidance from God to lead his congregation and family. If he did not, we would question his dedication as we recognize the need for God's empowerment and direction in order to fulfill his responsibilities.

You can easily put those expectations on your pastor, but now consider yourself. If God looks upon ministering to your children with the same importance that he places on a pastor's relationship to his congregation, is it not just as urgent for you to seek God's face every day? Is it not necessary for you to build that strong foundation, that relationship with Christ where you get the strength and wisdom needed to lead a family? Experience, and scripture, tells us all that if we do not read the Word and pray daily, the old sin nature begins to show up, bringing chaos and destruction into our lives.

When we look at families throughout the world, we can see that they are in trouble. Our kids are killing one another, abusing drugs, experimenting with sex, and many are walking away from the faith. "Somewhere between eighty and ninety percent of kids in America are abandoning their parents' faith once they reach adulthood. At that tragic rate, the fifty million children who are growing up in church today would die out to fewer than *seven thousand* in only ten generations time. That's sadly where current Christian families in America are headed without a radical change."[3]

Christian counselors that see families experiencing major trials often find that the foundations for strong and enduring faith have been neglected. In many cases this is due to ignorance, parents acting from experience and worldly advice rather than Biblical truth. Because the parents have not been taught how to build this strong foundation in their own lives, the influence they should have on their children for good is weak at best, and at times actually turning their children away from God.

Intimacy with God

In Deuteronomy 6, Moses fulfilled God's will by teaching the Israelites what was expected of them when they entered the Promised Land. Within these instructions, God reveals *His* heart regarding the close relationship He wants to have with us. This *intimate* relationship with God is the foundation, the strength of our faith, upon which we build.

> **Deuteronomy 6:1-6** *"Now this is the commandment, and these are the statutes and judgments which the LORD your God has commanded to teach you, that you may observe them in the land which you are crossing over to possess, that you may fear the LORD your God, to keep all His statutes and His commandments which I command you, you and your son and your grandson, all the days of your life, and that your days may be prolonged. Therefore hear, O Israel, and be careful to observe it, that it may be well with you, and that you may multiply greatly as the LORD God of your fathers has promised you—'a land flowing with milk and honey.' "Hear, O Israel: The LORD our God, the LORD is one! You shall love the LORD your God with all your heart, with all your soul, and with all your strength. And these words which I command you today shall be in your heart."*

Verses three and four begin with, *"Hear, O Israel,"* to emphasize the importance of listening to God's voice. Whenever that phrase appears, the message is, "Listen up!" God is really on our side; He wants us to

---

3   Stephen & Alex Kendrick with Randy Alcorn, *The Resolution for Men*, ed by Lawrence Kimbrough (Nashville, TN: B&H Publishing, 2011), 115.

succeed. In these verses, the information was actually essential for Israel to survive as a nation. And what God said in Deuteronomy 6 is relevant to us today. These verses reveal truths that also are fundamental to our success as believers and ministers to our children.

In Deuteronomy 6:5, it says, *"Love the LORD your God with all your heart, with all your soul, and with all your strength."* **This means that you show your love for Him by *choosing* to have an intimate relationship with Him.** Spending time with Christ is a daily choice. Being closely acquainted, familiar and personal, and abiding in Him *"with all your heart, soul and strength"* means the involvement of your total being – body, soul, and spirit. We recognize that our spouse, our children need love from us and we have some idea of how to do that. God asks for individual attention, time, as you build a loving relationship with Him. In fact, God promises that if you put Him first, other relationships will also improve.

Verse six tells us God's words must be first in our hearts. This means not only reading it regularly, but also obeying. To exemplify Christ and teach others, you must have intimate knowledge of God's will. That, combined with dependence upon Christ's wisdom and strength, is the foundation needed to fulfill the difficult responsibilities of guiding your children to Godly maturity. And your *daily* practice of devotion and communication with God is directly related to success.

FACT FILE

Heart: Hebrew *lebab*, meaning heart, mind, inner person. The primary usage of this word describes the entire disposition of the inner person.[4] Greek *kardia*, is the seat of the desires, feelings, affections, passions, impulses, i.e., the heart or mind.[5]

DIG DEEPER: *FURTHER STUDY*

Describe in your own words what the following Scripture says about God's Word and what we are to do with it?

Psalm 119:10-11 *"With my whole heart I have sought You; Oh, let me not wander from Your commandments! Your word I have hidden in my heart, that I might not sin against You."*

_____

_____

_____

_____

_____

---

4   Warren Baker, *The Complete Word Study Dictionary : Old Testament* (Chattanooga, TN: AMG Publishers, 2003), 537.

5   Spiros Zodhiates, *The Complete Word Study Dictionary : New Testament, electronic ed.* (Chattanooga, TN: AMG Publishers, 2000).

Read the following Scriptures and write out the main principles. What principles can you draw from this Scripture to be a better parent? List two ways you can do this.

Deuteronomy 32:46 *"and he said to them: 'Set your hearts on all the words which I testify among you today, which you shall command your children to be careful to observe—all the words of this law.'":*

_____
_____
_____
_____

Deuteronomy 11:18-19 *"Therefore you shall lay up these words of mine in your heart and in your soul, and bind them as a sign on your hand, and they shall be as frontlets between your eyes. You shall teach them to your children, speaking of them when you sit in your house, when you walk by the way, when you lie down, and when you rise up."*

_____
_____
_____
_____

Deuteronomy 30:14 *"But the word is very near you, in your mouth and in your heart, that you may do it."*

_____
_____
_____
_____

Psalm 37:31 *"The law of his God is in his heart; None of his steps shall slide".*

_____
_____
_____
_____

Psalm 40:8 *"I delight to do Your will, O my God, And Your law is within my heart."*

_____
_____
_____
_____

Sadly, many people in the body of Christ have never been discipled in the truth that intimacy with God (the Father, the Lord Jesus Christ, and the Holy Spirit) is proportionate to the amount of effort put into seeking Him. That requires time in His Word, praying and fellowshipping with other believers. The word "discipled" indicates that one Christian (or several), perhaps more mature in the faith, has come alongside to help another develop intimacy with the Lord. Without a guide, the pathway can be difficult to follow. We may think, *How is it possible to develop a relationship with an invisible God?*

And many may also think, *I go to church on Sunday. I'm a Christian because I prayed the prayer of salvation. I remember the emotion of that decision. Haven't I quit smoking and drinking and changed some of my bad habits? Is there something more?* Yes, there is.

SELF-EXAMINATION
How have you been maintaining a daily relationship with God, in prayer and the reading of His Word?

_____

_____

_____

_____

✓ACTION PLAN
After learning these principles, is confession and asking forgiveness needed? If so use the space below to write out your prayer and commitment to start each day with Him.

_____

_____

_____

_____

WEEK 2: DAY 2

Three Essential Ingredients

Luke 6:46-49 *But why do you call Me "Lord, Lord," and not do the things which I say? Whoever comes to Me, and hears My sayings and does them, I will show you whom he is like: He is like a man building a house, who dug deep and laid the foundation on the rock. And when the flood arose, the stream beat vehemently against that house, and could not shake it, for it was founded on the rock. But he who heard and did nothing is like a man who built a house on the earth without a foundation, against which the stream beat vehemently; and immediately it fell. And the ruin of that house was great.*

Again we see the importance that Jesus put on having a strong foundation. In this passage, He breaks it down into three essential ingredients. *First*, He says *"whoever comes to Me,"* which indicates **where** we are to build. The Bible is clear that Jesus is our foundation, I Corinthians 3:11 reads: *"For no other foundation can anyone lay than that which is laid, which is Jesus Christ."* There must be a time in life when you sought forgiveness for your sins and asked Jesus Christ to come into your life as Lord and Savior. Merely being born in America and/or attending a church does not make you a Christian. That requires a decision to repent from sin and turn the control of your life over to God, through Jesus Christ.

> **John 1:12** *speaks of Jesus, "But as many as received Him, to them He gave the right to become children of God, to those who believe in His name."*

The *first* ingredient is receiving Jesus Christ.

Second, the passage in Luke says, "(whoever)... **hears** My sayings" which refers to the **tools** we use for building, God's Word and prayer. You must decide to regularly spend time reading and meditating on God's Word, really listening to what God is saying. Through God's Word and prayer, we get to know Him and understand His love; and how to live correctly. Galatians 2:20 says, *"I have been crucified with Christ: it is no longer I who live, but Christ lives in me; and the life which I now live in the flesh I live by faith in the Son of God, who loved me and gave Himself for me."*

The *second* ingredient is your daily relationship with Christ through reading and mediating on His Word and prayer.

The *third* ingredient essential to building a strong foundation involves follow-through. Jesus says, *"(whoever)...hears my sayings and **does** them,"* describing the person who is doing God's will. This process of hearing and doing means to obey, or apply His Word to life. 1 Peter 1 22-23 says, "Since you have purified your souls in **obeying** the truth through the Spirit...through the Word of God which lives and abides forever."

The *third* ingredient is living out, or obeying, God's Word

Scripture tells us that it is important to continually examine our intentions and actions: *"Let us search out and examine our ways, And turn back to the LORD"* (Lamentations 3:40).

SELF-EXAMINATION

So how would you describe the **quality** of your spiritual foundation?

_____

_____

_____

Let's look at the following areas and inspect the three ingredients that Jesus emphasized in Luke 6:46-49.

The first ingredient is either "yes" or "no". Have you agreed with God that you are a sinner, received Christ's death on the cross as payment for those sins, and asked Jesus into your heart as Lord and Savior? This is the first essential step for building a strong foundation. You cannot skip this one, because Christ is the foundation for our faith. If this is still confusing, hopefully Romans 10:9-10 will help. **(Look at Appendix B for receiving Christ.)**

> **Romans 10:9-10** *"...if you confess with your mouth the Lord Jesus and believe in your heart that God has raised Him from the dead, you will be saved. For with the heart one believes unto righteousness, and with the mouth confession is made unto salvation."*

You also can pray:

> *Lord Jesus, I know that I am a sinner. I am sorry for my sin. Thank You for dying on the cross for me and paying the price for my sin. Please come into my heart. Fill me with Your Holy Spirit and help me to be Your disciple. Thank You for forgiving me and coming into my life. Thank You that I am now a child of God and that I am going to heaven. Amen.*

After choosing to build your life on faith in Jesus Christ, the next two ingredients refer to "following" Christ by establishing priorities. *First*, let's consider the practice of prayer. Prayer is often considered an attempt to enlist God's power to alter circumstances, but God is more interested in having constant mental communion with us. Prayer is a function of thought, but more than that, it is an open channel of communication with God that involves both speaking and listening. God wants you to know that He is available for all things at all times.

> **Philippians 4:6** *says, "Be anxious for nothing, but <u>in everything</u> by prayer and supplication, with thanksgiving, let your requests be made known to God."*

God desires constant awareness of His presence and continuous communication. He also wants you to spend some quiet, private time with Him each day. In Psalm 5:3, David said, *"My voice You shall hear in the morning, O Lord; In the morning I will direct it to You, And I will look up."*

Prayer and study of the Bible are essential elements for growth in the Christian life. This time of study and communication is often referred to as a "devotional" time. To become truly engaged beyond the written word requires an aspect of imagination called faith - to believe though we cannot see. In John 20:29, Jesus said, *"...because you have seen Me, you have believed; blessed are those who have not seen and yet have believed."* In Matthew 6:9-13, often called "the Lord's prayer," Jesus Himself gives us an example of how He prayed and some basic aspects to be considered in prayer.

The following prayer is an example of simple, heartfelt communication inspired by elements of the Lord's Prayer to be said prior to beginning your devotional time:

Lord Jesus, I praise You for desiring to be close to me, for wanting to spend time with me. I praise You for Your love and Faithfulness, and praise You, for You are God, the creator and sustainer of all things. I am asking for the grace to walk in obedience today, to love my spouse and children, and to tend to them according to Your Word. Help me to forgive anyone who hurts me today, and give me the grace to ask for forgiveness when I fail to represent You, Jesus. And Jesus, please open my heart to receive Your Word this morning. I'm asking for understanding to know You more and for Your grace to obey. AMEN

It is important to begin your devotional time with prayer, perhaps one similar to this. You may be tempted to use prepared prayers, but God's greatest desire is to just talk with you. After all, He already knows what is in your heart, and loves you in spite of what you have done. Romans 5:8 says, *"...God demonstrates His own love toward us, in that while we were still sinners, Christ died for us."* As you spend time each day with God, you will begin to feel comfortable in His love, and praying will become "talking to God" about everything.

☑ ACTION PLAN

Take a moment and write out a prayer to God, asking for help in developing an intimate, open prayer life with Him. (And remember that it is only by faith in Christ that we are given access to the Father. In John 14:6, Jesus says, *"I am the way, the truth, and the life. No one comes to the Father except through Me."*)

_____

_____

_____

_____

_____

Now, please pray through this prayer that Paul offered for the Ephesians, and make it personal by putting yourself in each spot where the space _____ appears.

Ephesians 3:14-21 *"For this reason I___ (your name) bow my knees to the Father of our Lord Jesus Christ, from whom the whole family in heaven and earth is named, that He would grant you___, according to the riches of His glory, to be strengthened with might through His Spirit in the inner man, that Christ may dwell in your___ hearts through faith; that you___, being rooted and grounded in love, may be able to comprehend with all the saints what is the width and length and depth and height— to know the love of Christ which passes knowledge; that you___ may be filled with all the fullness of God. Now to Him who is able to do exceedingly abundantly above all that we___ ask or think, according to the power that* *works in us___, to Him be glory in the church by Christ Jesus to all generations, forever and ever. Amen."*

Make a list of some specific requests, or praises, Paul included in his prayer.

_____

_____

_____

_____

_____

Along with personalizing this prayer, you can also use it regularly to pray these things into the lives of your spouse and children, and other loved ones, just put their names in there instead.

You have learned that God desires relationship, which requires that you first receive Jesus as Lord and Savior, and then choose to set aside time for prayer and Bible study. Living the Christian life, sometimes referred to as "abiding in Christ," involves listening to God through reading and meditating on His Word. In Matthew 4:4, Jesus says, *"...Man shall not live bread alone, but by every word that proceeds from the mouth of God."* Perhaps your pastor is an extraordinary teacher, but living for a week on a Sunday morning message alone will lead to being spiritually feeble.

Many Christians put "daily devotional" booklets, such as *Daily Bread,* in the bathroom, or beside the bed, to grab a quick dose of spiritual energy. They pull it out, read a little, and think, *OK, I did my thing. I got into the Word today, praise the Lord.* But a quick meal like this wears off soon, as does the memory of what we read. In our culture, we have so many gadgets to help us "multi-task," with our cell phones, radios, TV, Kindles, etc, that often our time with God becomes just part of the daily mix. If we do not *actively* pursue daily time alone with God, including focused study, meditation and prayer, then we may fall into the "grab a quick bite" category, which surely will lead to poor spiritual health.

DIG DEEPER: *FURTHER STUDY*

Study the following verses and write down what they say about the attitude we should have when reading the Word and seeking wisdom from God.

> **Proverbs 18:15** *"The heart of the prudent acquires knowledge, And the ear of the wise seeks knowledge."*

_____

_____

_____

_____

Proverbs 23:23 *"Buy the truth, and do not sell it, Also wisdom and instruction and understanding."*

_____

_____

_____

_____

Colossians 1:10 "That you may walk worthy of the Lord, fully pleasing Him, being fruitful in every good work and increasing in the knowledge of God;"

_____

_____

_____

_____

To avoid the quick study, cultivate the habit of "meditating" on the Word of God. When people hear the word meditation, many think of Hindu prayers, but meditation is a term used in the Word of God. We are to meditate upon the things that we read, which indicates that we are listening responsively in thought to what God is saying.

FACT FILE

<u>Meditate:</u> in the Biblical world meditation was not a silent practice; it meant to moan, utter or growl. It had the idea of muttering sounds like reading half aloud or conversing with oneself so that you would so interact with the text that it would soak into your mind. As a tea bag soaking in water permeates the liquid, so meditating on Scriptures permeates our minds.

Psalm 119:15 *"I will meditate on Your precepts, And contemplate Your ways."*

DIG DEEPER: *FURTHER STUDY*

What did God tell Joshua to do in this verse, and why was this so important to God, and to Joshua's success?

Joshua 1:8 *"This Book of the Law shall not depart from your mouth, but you shall meditate in it day and night, that you may observe to do according to all that is written in it. For then you will make your way prosperous, and then you will have good success."*

_____

_____

_____

_____

Do you want to have good success? ❑ Yes ❑ No

Read the following passage and then write out the meaning of these verses, in your own words, and how they would affect your parenting if you did this.

> **Psalm 1:1-3** *"Blessed is the man Who walks not in the counsel of the ungodly, Nor stands in the path of sinners, Nor sits in the seat of the scornful; But his delight is in the law of the Lord, And in His law he meditates day and night. He shall be like a tree Planted by the rivers of water, That brings forth its fruit in its season, Whose leaf also shall not wither; And whatever he does shall prosper"*

_____

_____

_____

_____

_____

_____

WEEK 2: DAY 3

When children are young, their dependence on mom and dad can make them uncomfortable or fearful when left in another's care, and when mom or dad returns, there is great affection and rejoicing. As they mature, the excitement cools and parents may be given a greeting like "Hi Mom," "Hey Dad," or maybe not much at all. By this time, the presence of parents is somewhat taken for granted, and or is not acknowledged at all.

Beware, because we can do the same thing to the Lord. When we first come to Christ, we cannot wait to pray and get into the Word. When we read it, we feel God speaking right to our hearts. Oftentimes we experience wonderful emotions, and even share our good news with friends and loved ones.

Over time, if we are not watchful, our attitude can become, "Yeah, yeah, studying Matthew again. Been there, done that." Sadly, we lose the attitude "Daddy's here!" We cannot stay in this state of mind! Just think: you have the blessed privilege of going into the Holy of Holies, with a God who wants you to call Him "Daddy" (Romans 8:15 *"...Abba, Father"*), to hear Him whisper awesome truths and tell you how wonderful and important you are to Him!

⌕ SELF-EXAMINATION

When was the last time you sat quietly with the living God, excited for Him to speak to you?

_____

_____

_____

The first event recorded in the Bible after Jesus Christ gave up His spirit on the cross was the ripping of the veil, from top to bottom, which covered the entrance to a temple chamber called the Holy of Holies (Matt 27:51). It meant that Christ's death on the cross had ended our separation from God. Before that, only the high priest could enter once a year bearing sacrificial animal blood. A great price was paid when Christ offered His own blood for our deliverance. Hebrews 10:19 says, *"Therefore, brethren, having boldness to enter the Holiest by the blood of Jesus,"* So Jesus' death was not only to defeat the power of sin, but to buy a way for the Father to have intimate fellowship with us. We must not *"neglect so great a salvation,"* (Hebrews 2:3).

For those who have grown children, how blessed are we when they want to spend time with us? Do you think God is any different? He loves it when you and I call "time out" and say, "Daddy, this is Your time, mine and Yours, right now, and I'm not going to let anything get in the way. I'm going to protect this, God."

And it is interesting, and revealing, that when we make this commitment to set time aside for God, that distractions seem to come "out of the woodwork". If not interruptions from family and phones, then your mind floods with thoughts – a problem at work, the bills, your spouse, your kids, etc., etc. Many times Satan sends those distractions because he knows that our firm foundation, the strength of our faith, does not come from good works, or just desiring to be the best dad, mom, or spouse, but from our relationship to Christ. Everything good grows out of this relationship.

DIG DEEPER: *FURTHER STUDY*

Read 2 Corinthians 10:3-5, and write in your own words what this Scripture says about the battle we are in, and what we are supposed to do about it.

> **2 Corinthians 10:3-5** *"For though we walk in the flesh, we do not war according to the flesh. For the weapons of our warfare are not carnal but mighty in God for pulling down strongholds, casting down arguments and every high thing that exalts itself against the knowledge of God, bringing every thought into captivity to the obedience of Christ."*

_____

_____

_____

_____

When Jesus explained the parable of the sower to His disciples (Mark 4:13-20), He wanted them to know what Satan and his demons are up to. How would this Scripture relate to your time in the Word: What is the battle?

Mark 4:15 *"And these are the ones by the wayside where the word is sown. When they hear, Satan comes immediately and takes away the word that was sown in their hearts."*

_____

_____

_____

When Paul wrote 2 Corinthians 11:3, he referred to Genesis 3:1-7 which describes how sin entered the world when Eve listened to Satan's lies. Paul's fear was that Satan, in the same way, would *corrupt* (spoil, subvert or destroy) the new believers' minds from the *simplicity* (purity, sincerity, "singleness of heart"),[6] that they had in their relationship with Christ.

2 Corinthians 11:3 *"But I fear, lest somehow, as the serpent deceived Eve by his craftiness, so your minds may be corrupted from the simplicity that is in Christ."*

Eve was *deceived* (led into error) by Satan's *craftiness* (cunning shrewdness), so that she believed a lie to be the truth. Satan's plan is always the same.

SELF-EXAMINATION

Are there any lies you have believed regarding God's desire to be in a close relationship with you?

_____

_____

_____

_____

_____

What are some common thoughts that come when starting or doing your devotions? Write them out.

_____

_____

_____

_____

_____

_____

6   Spiros Zodhiates, *The Complete Word Study Dictionary : New Testament*, electronic ed. (Chattanooga, TN: AMG Publishers, 2000).

But Satan cannot be blamed for everything; sometimes we are at fault ourselves. When Jesus prayed in the garden as He faced going to the cross, His disciples slept when they should have been praying also. Jesus warned them about the weakness of the flesh:

> **Matthew 26:41** *"Watch and pray, lest you enter into temptation. The spirit indeed is willing, but the flesh is weak."*

Jesus' command is to "watch and pray", and the result is for our good – that we are not overwhelmed by temptation and our laziness. Praying is an essential discipline so we must fight the battle against such thoughts as, *I just don't feel like it, I'm tired, or I just don't care or have time.* Complacency must be replaced by non-negotiable priorities in seeking the Lord.

DIG DEEPER: *FURTHER STUDY*

Write out in your own words what these verses are instructing you to do.

> **1 Peter 5:8** *"Be sober, be vigilant; because your adversary the devil walks about like a roaring lion, seeking whom he may devour."*

_____

_____

_____

> **Ephesians 6:11** *"Put on the **whole armor** of God, that you may be able to stand against the wiles of the devil"* [emphasis added].

_____

_____

_____

All your success, including the power to minister as a parent, comes from a continuous relationship with Christ. Mark 4:34 says, *". . . And when they were alone, He explained all things to His disciples."* We will receive great insights and understanding from Scripture, as well as power and wisdom that we need as a parent as long as we are spending time with Jesus in daily devotions and Bible study. God loves each of us the same, and He longs to commune with us. There is no parenting book written that will cover every situation you face. That is why God wants you to depend on Him each day, looking to His Word for understanding and guidance.

DIG DEEPER: *FURTHER STUDY*

Read the following Scripture and notice the disciples' attitude when they did not understand Jesus' teaching. What did they do?

Matthew 13.36 *"Then Jesus sent the multitude away and went into the house. And His disciples came to Him, saying, 'Explain to us the parable of the tares of the field'."*

_____

_____

_____

_____

Remember, God is always waiting for us to come to Him, wanting us to seek the wisdom we need to deal with life. Knowing this, how can we be too busy to spend time with the living God? We need to keep this continuously in mind, guarding against our tendencies to become independent, or take God's goodness to us for granted.

In 2 Timothy 2:15 (KJV), Paul writes: *"**Study** to show thyself approved unto God, a workman that needeth not to be ashamed, rightly dividing the Word of truth."*

FACT FILE

Study: this word is an imperative verb, meaning it is a command to do and to continue to do. The word denotes a zealous persistence in accomplishing a goal.

Rightly dividing: has the idea of cutting something straight as you would in carpentry, masonry or with cutting a piece of cloth to be sewn together.

What grade would you give yourself in your *Bible study*? What do you think God means here by the word "ashamed"?

_____

_____

_____

_____

✓ACTION PLAN
Take a moment and meditate on what you just read and learned and write out a prayer to the Lord asking Him for specific help in following His instructions.

_____

_____

_____

_____

What is the exhortation in this verse?

2 Peter 1:10 *"Therefore, brethren, be even more diligent to make your call and election sure, for if you do these things you will never stumble."*

_____

_____

_____

_____

Obedience Is Action

The *third* ingredient of building a strong foundation is the decision to act upon what we hear, or learn from God.

> **Luke 6:47-48**, *Jesus says, "whoever...hears My sayings and **does** them...He is like a man building a house, who dug deep and laid the foundation on the rock. And when the flood arose, the stream beat vehemently against that house, and could not shake it, for it was founded on the rock."*

We need to treat the Bible, the Word of God, as the words of **GOD**. In the Old Testament, the Jews considered the very name of God so sacred that they dared not to speak it. It is by God's grace alone in the sacrifice of Jesus Christ that you are considered righteous, and given the indwelling presence of the Holy Spirit as a teacher and guide. Your part is to desire to do His will, and respond in thankfulness and obedience. If you treat the Word of God as suggestions, then you may find yourself picking and choosing what best suits your will. This is not wise and will not result in the success that comes from building on a strong foundation.

> **Luke 14:33** *"So likewise, whoever of you does not <u>forsake</u> all that he has cannot be My disciple."*

FACT FILE

The word "forsake," means to deny. This verse is telling us to daily align our priorities to God's Word, which places His will over ours.

There were many who considered Jesus' teaching too difficult to follow, so they turned and walked away from God. There will be instructions in these lessons that may be different from the way you do things currently. Some may seem hard, but remember that by God's grace you are able to do His will, not by your own strength.

> **John 6:66-67** *"From that time many of His disciples went back and walked with Him no more. Then Jesus said to the twelve, 'Do you also want to go away?'"*

WEEK 2 : HAVING A STRONG FOUNDATION

☑ACTION PLAN

Write out a commitment to God, to depend on Him for the grace, or power, to both desire and follow His instructions on parenting.

_____

_____

_____

Take a moment and consider your priorities with God, spouse, children, work, church, leisure time, and fellowship? Do you believe they are in proper order? If not write out a prayer of commitment to change.

_____

_____

_____

God shares His heart regarding our priorities,

> **1 Timothy 3:1-13** *"This is a faithful saying: If a man desires the position of a bishop, he desires a good work. **2** A bishop then must be blameless, the husband of one wife, temperate, sober-minded, of good behavior, hospitable, able to teach; **3** not given to wine, not violent, not greedy for money, but gentle, not quarrelsome, not covetous; **4 one who rules his own house well, having his children in submission with all reverence 5 (for if a man does not know how to rule his own house, how will he take care of the church of God?); 6** not a novice, lest being puffed up with pride he fall into the same condemnation as the devil. **7** Moreover he must have a good testimony among those who are outside, lest he fall into reproach and the snare of the devil. **8** Likewise deacons must be reverent, not double-tongued, not given to much wine, not greedy for money, **9** holding the mystery of the faith with a pure conscience. **10** But let these also first be tested; then let them serve as deacons, being found blameless. **11** Likewise, their wives must be reverent, not slanderers, temperate, faithful in all things. **12** Let deacons be the husbands of one wife, ruling their children and their own houses well. **13** For those who have served well as deacons obtain for themselves a good standing and great boldness in the faith, which is in Christ Jesus.*

This passage makes it clear that your home must have first priority in order for you to be a good minister. Many homes are out of order; where people are more concerned about leisure, work, or even service in the church.

One author says concerning this passage:

> *"Paul indicated that the experience the leader gained in the home would develop sensitive*

WEEK 2: DAY 3 | 39

compassion ("take care of")—(tending to [our emphasis]) for his role in the church. The verb "manage" appeared in v. 4. The development of proper leadership skills in the home was a prerequisite for using them in the church.[7]

SELF-EXAMINATION

Since a pastor must have his family in order before qualifying in God's eyes, then he is able to set an example for the congregation. If you where in a church, and you saw that the pastor had many problems with his family, and that he did not tend to His family correctly, would you respect him and his leadership? Why?

_____

_____

_____

Genesis 18:19, says: "For I have known him, in order that he may command his children and his household after him, that they keep the way of the Lord, to do righteousness and justice, that the Lord may bring to Abraham what He has spoken to him."

We mentioned this Scripture earlier, but it is excellent example of God's attitude on parenting. God is telling Abraham, the father, that He has *known him* for a <u>purpose</u>, *in order* to <u>instruct</u> his family in the ways of the Lord. These are priorities. Notice that God does not say, "you need to work all the time to bring in the cash" (although we know if we do not provide for our family we have denied the faith, 1 Tim. 5:8), nor does He say "do more ministry", or "why don't you mount that camel and head on down to Egypt to relax, take it easy". Even though work, ministry and leisure time are important, and even Biblical, none are first priority. A balance must be reached, but your priority relationship is with God first, and then family next.

SELF-EXAMINATION

Take a moment and write down what has been the priority in your life. Has God been first, then family, then work or...? If you are married, ask your spouse if they agree with your assessment. If you have kids you can ask them, they will usually give you a straight answer if you ask in a gentle way.

_____

_____

_____

DIG DEEPER: *FURTHER STUDY*

Read the following Scripture and write down what is says about the Biblical concepts of *choosing*, *serving* and the *family*?

_____

7   Thomas D. Lea and Hayne P. Griffin, *vol. 34, 1, 2 Timothy, Titus, The New American Commentary* (Nashville: Broadman & Holman Publishers, 2001), 112.

Joshua 24:15 *"And if it seems evil to you to serve the Lord, choose for yourselves this day whom you will serve, whether the gods which your fathers served that were on the other side of the River, or the gods of the Amorites, in whose land you dwell. But as for me and my house, we will serve the Lord."*

_____

_____

_____

_____

1 Kings 18:21 *"And Elijah came to all the people, and said, 'How long will you falter between two opinions? If the Lord is God, follow Him; but if Baal, follow him.' But the people answered him not a word."*

_____

_____

_____

_____

Matthew 6:24 *"No one can serve two masters; for either he will hate the one and love the other, or else he will be loyal to the one and despise the other. You cannot serve God and mammon."*

_____

_____

_____

_____

Finally, are you practicing Godly principles in your home? The fruit of the Holy Spirit is *". . . love, joy, peace, patience, kindness, goodness, faithfulness, gentleness, self-contol..."* (Gal. 5:22-23 NIV). Are these the qualities that your children see growing in you and increasing in your home environment? How would you evaluate yourself? Doing Great?   ❑ Sometimes   ❑ Lots of room to grow?

What is most important to you, other than your relationship with Christ? If anything else becomes more important, you will suffer and so will your family. God blesses obedience. Disobedience, on the other hand, puts us outside God's provisional grace that we need day by day, and causes us to begin to operate in our flesh.

Do you see any room for improvement? These are not trick questions. God gives us these instructions, and He makes them clear enough to understand. He also says that we are to encourage one another continuously. We all need God's power and grace every single day. *But we must never forget that God will not do by miracle what He has called us to do by obedience.*

What are the three ingredients for a Strong Foundation?

1. _____
2. _____
3. _____

WEEK 2: DAY 4

The Chief Cornerstone

The most significant aspect of building on a strong foundation is selection of the proper chief cornerstone. Let's look at what Scriptures say about that in relation to Christ, and also our relationship to Him:

> **Ephesians 2:19-20** says: *"Now, therefore, you are no longer strangers and foreigners, but fellow citizens with the saints and members of the household of God, having been built on the foundation of the apostles and prophets, Jesus Christ Himself being the chief cornerstone."*

> **1 Peter 2:6-8** *"Therefore it is also contained in the Scripture, 'Behold, I lay in Zion A chief cornerstone, elect, precious, And he who believes on Him will by no means be put to shame.' Therefore, to you who believe, He is precious; but to those who are disobedient, 'The stone which the builders rejected Has become the chief cornerstone,' and 'A stone of stumbling And a rock of offense.' They stumble, being disobedient to the word, to which they also were appointed."*

It is important to notice that there is an order of spiritual progress presented in these verses: 1) accept Jesus Christ, 2) abide in Him, and 3) obey. Most Christians become preoccupied with the third step. Perhaps you have found your thoughts dwelling on, *Oh, I've got to quit doing this; or I have to do something better; or Why can't I stop doing these wrong things?* Fortunately, accomplishing the first two steps brings success for the third – we find ourselves with the power, grace and desire to be obedient believers.

When people come in for counseling, struggling with sinful behaviors or even addictions, the first question should be, "How's your abiding relationship with Christ?" The most common response often is, "What does that mean?" The answer is that our relationship with Christ is the connection that gives us the power to obey. Our intimacy with God is what gives us the power, the grace for that day, to have victory over sin. And He only gives us grace for the day. He does not give us grace for a week. We need to see this connection and understand this spiritual principle.

Read **John 15:4-5**:

> *"**Abide** in Me, and I in you. As the branch cannot bear fruit of itself, unless it **abides** in the vine, neither can you, unless you **abide** in Me. 5 I am the vine, you are the branches. He who **abides** in Me, and I in him, bears much fruit; for without Me <u>you can do nothing</u> "[emphasis added].*

Jesus is concentrating on the idea of abiding, as He uses the word four times.

FACT FILE

Abide means, *"To stay, remain, to continue in a place, to endure without yielding."*

When Jesus gave this instruction to His disciples, it was only a short time before He would go to the cross and then on to be with the Father in Heaven. He wanted to make sure that His disciples knew that their relationship with Him would continue, even after He was not physically there.

DIG DEEPER: *FURTHER STUDY*

According to the following Scriptures, where are we to abide? What is the result?

> **John 8:31-32** *"If you abide in My word, you are My disciples indeed. And you shall know the truth, and the truth shall make you free."*

_____

_____

_____

_____

> **John 15:7** *"If you abide in Me, and My words abide in you, you will ask what you desire, and it shall be done for you."*

_____

_____

_____

_____

Notice how the following Scriptures relate to us abiding in Christ, our dependence upon Him, and the outcome.

> **2 Corinthians 3:5** *"Not that we are sufficient of ourselves to think of anything as being from ourselves, but our sufficiency is from God."*

2 Corinthians 4:16 *"Therefore we do not lose heart. Even though our outward man is perishing, yet the inward man is being renewed day by day."*

Our devotional life is so like the foundation under a house. You cannot see it, but the strength of it will be revealed as natural disasters occur. We may spend most of our time and money making the house look good, but a weak foundation can quickly bring all that time and money to nothing. If we spend our time on mere image of success instead of growing in righteousness, our home will be built on "sand" and will "fall" just as Jesus predicted in Matthew 7. It is the foundation that holds up the house, not the frills and attractive paint job.

In the following chapters, you will find Biblical tools for raising children. However, if you skip this spiritual principle, ignore your foundation, you will go right back to your old habits. The strength of your relationship to God, in Christ, is the only foundation on which you will build successfully

Rebellion and Choices

When you hear the word *rebellion,* what comes to mind? Teenagers? The word *rebellion* often is associated with adolescents, however, *rebellion* means *any* resistance to authority.[8] When you choose to do things your own way, including setting priorities according to your desires instead of God's instruction, that is rebellion. So, choosing to not set aside time for an intimate relationship with the Lord is rebellion.

Developing intimacy and abiding in Christ are *choices*, and God clearly tells us in Scripture, "Do it." He said it to the Israelites before they went into the Promised Land: *"Love God with all your heart, mind, body and soul"* (Deut. 6:1-6). We spend time with the people we love, and we must choose every day to love God by spending time to know Him better by searching the Bible for spiritual truth, then work it into our lives through prayer and obedience.

The erosion of our spiritual foundation, our connection to God, begins with neglecting our devotional life and usually leads to the following:

1. We stop giving of ourselves and start asking, *"What about me, my feelings and my needs?"*

2. We begin to wallow in selfishness and exhibit *conditional*, rather than unconditional, love.

3. We stop hungering (seeking) for holiness.

---

8   *Webster's New International Dictionary of the English Language; Second Edition Unabridged*; G & C Merriam Company, Publishers, Springfield, MA 1944

4. We begin to justify our sinful attitudes, behavior and selfishness toward others and our children.

5. We start blaming others for our misery, and sinful attitudes and behaviors.

⌕ SELF-EXAMINATION

Are you exhibiting any of these types of thoughts, or behaviors? If so, write down which ones. Then take a moment and confess it to the Lord and ask His forgiveness. Remember 1 John 1:9 says, *"If we confess our sins, He is faithful and just to forgive us our sins and to cleanse us from all unrighteousness."*

_____

_____

_____

_____

_____

How can we combat our natural tendency towards neglect, which leads to apathy and sin? The answer is that we must train ourselves. In 1 Corinthians 9:27, Paul the Apostle wrote, *"I discipline my body and bring it into subjection."* He understood that he needed to work, that he needed to train his own body to make it do what it normally did not want to do.

FACT FILE

The word "discipline" is *hupopiazo* (Greek), which was used to describe boxers giving knock out blows—punches to the part of the face right under the eyes, until they were black and blue. (Related passages: 1 Timothy 4:7-8; Jude 3; 2 Peter 1:5-6.)

What are your first thoughts in the morning? When you are lying in bed, when you become conscious, what is your first thought? Train *yourself* this way: first thing in the morning—focus your mind on Christ and remember or acknowledge to yourself and God how much you need His strength to battle your natural sinful desires. The great thing is that God already knows your struggles. And remember, when you were still a sinner, Christ died for you. Now, in Christ, God can get through to you with, "Here I am; I want to bless you, I love you."

DIG DEEPER: *FURTHER STUDY*

What do the following Scriptures teach us about the Psalmist's thoughts in the morning? What was he doing? How can you remind yourself to think of God first thing, before you get out of bed?

Psalm 5:3 *"My voice You shall hear in the morning, O Lord; In the morning I will direct it to You, And I will look up."*

_____

_____

_____

Psalm 119:147 *"I rise before the dawning of the morning, And cry for help; I hope in Your word."*

_____

_____

_____

God knows everything; He knows how weak and foolish we can be, already knew all the "junk" that we had inside when He adopted us as His children. He knew, *and chose us anyway*! He is not here to condemn us, but He desires to bless us. *We* must train our minds. When you wake up, let your first thoughts be, "God here I am. Thank you that I am one of Yours! I know there are so many areas in my life that need improvement; God, I need Your strength!" The Lord is longing to hear you say that every day.

Train yourself to put your mind upon Jesus in the first moments of the morning; not on your bills, your spouse, your kids, or your job, no matter how pressing those things may seem. Pray and ask Him for His grace to love your family and to walk in His will today. Now, this is before you begin or do your personal devotional time with Him. *"Do not be deceived, God is not mocked; for whatever a man sows, that he will also reap"* (Gal. 6:7). If we put God first, before all things, we will reap all the promises waiting for us in Him.

So, you set your mind on God first, have your devotional time, but you must also return to Him in thought during the day. God is the One we depend on, and obey, when we face difficulties, including problems with our children.

Notice how God encourages us to think in the follow verse:

Colossians 3:1-2 *"If then you were raised with Christ, <u>seek</u> those things which are above, where Christ is, sitting at the right hand of God. <u>Set</u> your mind on things above, not on things on the earth"* [emphasis added].

FACT FILE

"Seek" and "set your mind," are imperative verbs, indicating the action is a continual process. "*Seek*" means to look for and strive to find. "*Set your mind*" refers to the will, affections and conscience.

What are you to set our mind on?

_____

_____

✓ ACTION PLAN

Write out a prayer asking God to quicken your mind to think upon Him.

_____

_____

_____

Our Sovereign God

As God's children and His ministers, we must always remember that God is in control, and that He has a purpose in the trials we face. Psalm 139:1-18, tells us our days are predestined, every one of them. They were written in His book before time was created, before the earth even existed.

The Bible says, *"For we are His workmanship, created in Christ Jesus for good works, which God prepared beforehand that we should walk in them"* (Eph. 2:10). We can take comfort in the knowledge that in every situation, God has already been there. He knows all things; He is never surprised. So when you get up Saturday morning to find your three-year-old has spilled orange juice and cereal all over the floor and is making a little goulash, you can walk in and calmly think, *OK, God, You were already here. What is this about?* And on Friday night when your teenager comes home later than allowed, you can remind yourself, *OK, God, You have been here already. You knew this was going to happen to me. You said in all situations You have prepared me for good works.* We can learn to glorify Christ in all our circumstances!

Here is a catchy motto that you can write down, and use as a guide to developing a good attitude: "If I put my eyes on others, I get stressed. If I put my eyes on myself, I get depressed. If I put my eyes on Jesus, I get blessed." Post that on your refrigerator, or on your mirror, so you see it each morning to remind you to do your devotion. Or better yet, memorize it!

DIG DEEPER: *FURTHER STUDY*

According to this verse, what is God doing behind the scenes? Who do we have to trust?

> **Ephesians 1:11** *"In Him also we have obtained an inheritance, being predestined according to the purpose of Him who works all things according to the counsel of His will."*

_____

_____

_____

Read the following Scriptures and write out what they reveal about God's nature.

Deuteronomy 29:29 *"The secret things belong to the LORD our God, but those things which are revealed belong to us and to our children forever, that we may do all the words of this law."*

_____

_____

_____

Isaiah 14:24 *"The LORD of hosts has sworn, saying, "Surely, as I have thought, so it shall come to pass, And as I have purposed, so it shall stand:"*

_____

_____

_____

Isaiah 25:1 *"O LORD, You are my God. I will exalt You, I will praise Your name, For You have done wonderful things; Your counsels of old are faithfulness and truth."*

_____

_____

_____

Proverbs 19:21 *"There are many plans in a man's heart, Nevertheless the LORD's counsel— that will stand."*

_____

_____

_____

2 Timothy 1:9 *"who has saved us and called us with a holy calling, not according to our works, but according to His own purpose and grace which was given to us in Christ Jesus before time began,"*

_____

_____

_____

WEEK 2: DAY 5

Your Amazing Transformation

Again, our primary goal as believers, and as parents, is to be *transformed* into the image of Christ and doing His will. Simply put, to become more and more like Him in thought and action. God has a plan and purpose in the trials that you face. As God works, He will use these challenges to reveal the areas we need to be transformed in.

DIG DEEPER: *FURTHER STUDY*

Read the following Scriptures and write out the positive consequences.

James 1:2-4 *"My brethren, count it all joy when you fall into various trials, knowing that the testing of your faith produces patience. But let patience have its perfect work, that you may be perfect and complete, lacking nothing."*

_____

_____

_____

1 John 2:5 *"But whoever keeps His word, truly the love of God is perfected in him. By this we know that we are in Him."*

_____

_____

_____

An illustration of this transforming process can be found in **Matthew 14:22-31**. Jesus had been ministering to people. He fed thousands, healed and preached, and at the end of the day, He was exhausted. He walked down to the Sea of Galilee and told the apostles, *"Get in the boat, go to the other side; I'll meet you over there."* So the apostles jumped in the boat and began to sail across, while Jesus remained behind to pray.

"Immediately Jesus made His disciples get into the boat and go before Him to the other side, while He sent the multitudes away. 23 And when He had sent the multitudes away, He went up on the mountain by Himself to pray. Now when evening came, He was alone there. 24 But the boat was now in the middle of the sea, tossed by the waves, for the wind was contrary. 25 Now in the fourth watch of the night Jesus went to them, walking on the sea. 26 And when the disciples saw Him walking on the sea, they were troubled, saying, "It is a ghost!" And they cried out for fear. 27 But immediately Jesus spoke to them, saying, "Be of good cheer! It is I; do not be afraid." 28 And Peter answered Him and said, "Lord, if it is You, command me to come to You on the water." 29 So He said, "Come." And when Peter had come down out of the boat, he walked on the water to go to Jesus. 30 But when he saw that the wind was boisterous, he was afraid; and beginning to sink he cried out, saying, "Lord, save me!" 31 And immediately Jesus stretched out His hand and caught him, and said to him, "O you of little faith, why did you doubt?"

When they were halfway across the sea, a storm came up. But Jesus had sent His disciples out into that storm, knowing full well it was coming. He purposefully put them out there, just like He often does to us. Seeing Jesus walking on water, Peter cried heroically, *"Lord, if it is You, command me to come to You on the water."* At Jesus invitation to *"come,"* Peter began to walk on the water! But then took his eyes off Jesus and put them on the storm, he began to sink. When Peter cried *"Lord, save me,"* the Word says that Jesus *"immediately"* extended his hand and caught him.

When Jesus asked Peter to step out of the boat, it is important to recognize that He was testing Peter's faith. Was Peter going to keep his eyes on Christ and have faith that He had it all under control, giving him the ability to do something he could not do on his own? Peter had the faith to begin, but then wavered in fear and began to sink. Peter *learned* the importance of keeping his eyes upon the Lord. Some 30 years later, when Peter wrote the following words, you can see the transformation in his perspective.

> **1 Peter 1:6-7** *"In this you greatly rejoice, though now for a little while, if need be, you have been grieved by various trials, that the genuineness of your faith, being much more precious than gold that perishes, though it is tested by fire, may be found to praise, honor, and glory at the revelation of Jesus Christ."*

FACT FILE

The word **"genuineness,"** *dokimion* (Greek), means something that has been tested and approved. It was used of metals that had been through a purifying process to remove all impurities.

Peter is encouraging the church, assuring them that trials are necessary to develop sincere, pure faith. If you see trials this way, and cooperate with God, you will be able to rejoice.

DIG DEEPER: *FURTHER STUDY*

Look up the following scriptures and write down what they say about trials, testing, and how God works in the midst of them.

> **Psalm 17:3** *" You have tested my heart; You have visited me in the night; You have tried me and have found nothing; I have purposed that my mouth shall not transgress."*

_____

_____

_____

> **Psalm 66:10** *" For You, O God, have tested us; You have refined us as silver is refined."*

_____

_____

_____

Proverbs 17:3 *" The refining pot is for silver and the furnace for gold, But the LORD tests the hearts."*

_____

_____

_____

James 1:3–4 *" knowing that the testing of your faith produces patience. But let patience have its perfect work, that you may be perfect and complete, lacking nothing."*

_____

_____

_____

As parents in crisis, *we* often take our eyes off of Christ and His promises, put them on circumstances, and become overwhelmed. So often, turning to Jesus is our last move. We need to remember that God is waiting to prove Himself faithful and more powerful than our circumstances! We must keep our hope fixed upon Him (Heb. 12:2), and remember He sends us into storms because He has a plan (Eph. 1:11).

Just as Christ showed power over nature when He walked on water, and His power over death, man's greatest fear, so God wants to perform miracles for us as we raise our children. We need to live each day seeking to please God alone, keeping our eyes on Him, not on the storms and the difficulties. Sadly, because we do not develop intimacy with Christ, peace disappears. We become agitated, angered, and lose our joy and strength when the going gets tough. Peter wrote, *"Yet if anyone suffers as a Christian, let him not be ashamed, but let him glorify God in this matter."* (1 Pet. 4:16). No one enjoys suffering, but for parents it is part of the job. Rather than think, *God, why is this happening to me*? turn your thoughts to: *God, what are You revealing in me through this circumstance?*

SELF-EXAMINATION

Over the next 7 days, write down as many things as you can that qualify as your trials. It can even be a disagreement you have with your spouse. This will become a beginning list of areas that God can transform *in* you. Many parenting and marriage problems stem from not viewing trials God's way. Also write out what was revealed to be *in* you – anger, impatience, etc. - attitudes that you believe fall short of God's nature. I encourage you to start taking responsibility for those failures by asking for forgiveness from God, spouse and kids.

_____

_____

_____

_____

_____

_____

_____

_____

_____

_____

Suffering is part of God's plan and can lead to *inner transformation* and His glorification. Our struggles come from three sources: the world, the flesh and the Devil. Yes, even Satan has the freedom to trouble us, as He did with Job, (chapters 1-2). If you are not totally dependent upon God's daily strength (Ps 88:9), and His wisdom in every situation (James 1:5), the temptation is to trust in yourself. Moving away from God gives strength to our sin nature (Gal. 5:16). Fleshly reactions and attitudes are not a reflection of God's nature (Gal. 5:19-26), and these most often trouble us when we are out of fellowship (Heb 10:24-25), or when reject the fact that God uses our children to transform *us* spiritually.

DIG DEEPER: *FURTHER STUDY*

Read the following verse and write out how this verse changes your attitude toward non-glorifying and or sinful behavior.

> **1 Corinthians 10:13** *"For no temptation (no trial regarded as enticing to sin), [no matter how it comes or where it leads] has overtaken you and laid hold on you that is not common to man [that is, no temptation or trial has come to you that is beyond human resistance and that is not adjusted and adapted and belonging to human experience, and such as man can bear]. But God is faithful [to His Word and to His compassionate nature], and He [can be trusted] not to let you be tempted and tried and assayed beyond your ability and strength of resistance and power to endure, but with the temptation He will [always] also provide the way out (the means of escape to a landing place), that you may be capable and strong and powerful to bear up under it patiently." — (Amplified Bible)*

_____

_____

_____

_____

It is true that, in Christ, no trial is beyond our ability to be victorious, but God is not saying that you and I must be perfect. All of us will fail at times. But you must accept responsibility for your actions and ask God for help. In this way you cooperate with God to change, grow, and mature in Christ. The moment that you and I accept Jesus Christ as Savior, the journey of *transformation* begins. We will travel this road until we die. There will never be time when we can think, *OK, I'm done,* until we are with Him in heaven (Rom. 8:22-23; 1 John 3:2-3).

Read this as a prayer, from you to God, asking Him to do this work in you.

Hebrews 13:20-21 *"Now may the God of peace who brought up our Lord Jesus from the dead, that great Shepherd of the sheep, through the blood of the everlasting covenant, make you complete in every good work to do His will, working in you what is well pleasing in His sight, through Jesus Christ, to whom be glory forever and ever. Amen."*

After meditating on these Scriptures and praying, what principles do you see that relate to your transformation? How can these also relate to your parenting?

_____

_____

_____

_____

Laborers Together

In the first verse of Psalm 127, the author wrote, *"Unless the LORD builds the house, they labor in vain who build it; unless the LORD guards the city, the watchman stays awake in vain."* God so wants to protect our families. Can you see from this passage that you and God are to be working together, with Him in the lead position? He wants to intercede in your child's life, showing Himself both faithful and powerful, but you must first allow Him to be the Lord over your family.

God's Word tells us that He blesses obedience (Josh. 1:8; Ps. 18:20-21). When we are disobedient in the areas of intimacy and relationship with Christ, will God be able to intercede on our behalf (John 9:31; Heb. 11:6)? He is faithful, but we need to do our part (Phil. 2:12-13). In order for you to glorify God, you must stay *connected* to Him each day. It is then that you will experience transformation, and stand on a solid foundation. *Remember*, God will not do by miracle what He has called you to do by obedience.

As a parent and minister of Christ, the mainspring for service is not love for your children, but love for Jesus Christ. If you are devoted to the cause and or outcome of raising children, you will become discouraged and brokenhearted looking to them for your reward. Parents often receive less gratitude from their children than they do from the family house pet. But if *love* and *service* toward God is your motive, no ingratitude or outcome will hinder you from serving your children and fulfilling His will and wishes. Christ Himself came to earth with one desire - to serve and please His Father in Heaven. Matthew 20:28 says, *" just as the Son of Man did not come to be served, but to serve, and to give His life a ransom for many."*

Clever methods are not the key to accomplishing *God's purposes*; the key is your relationship with Him. God will foil the best of man's plans if He is left out of them. The tools we will cover in the remainder of this book will be extremely useful in helping you raise your kids. Remember: tools are the means, but the meaning comes from commitment to God and fulfilling His will and plan. And God has a plan for each child and we are to study, pray, train, discipline and enjoy them, but the day will come when they also will be fully accountable to God for themselves.

The integrity of the foundation on which we build our homes, and raise our children, is directly related to the strength of our relationship with Jesus Christ. Through daily prayer, Bible study, and a desire to obey we are working with God as He purifies and changes us, enabling us to become Godly parents to our children. We must be disciplined, devoted, and as always, God has a glorious promise waiting for us.

> **2 Peter 1:1-4** *"To those who have obtained like precious faith with us by the righteousness of our God and Savior Jesus Christ: grace and peace be multiplied to you in the knowledge of God and of Jesus our Lord, as His divine power has <u>given to us all things</u> that pertain to <u>life</u> and <u>godliness</u>, through the knowledge of Him who called us by glory and virtue, by which have been <u>given to us exceedingly great and precious promises</u>, that through these you may be partakers of the divine nature, having escaped the corruption that is in the world through lust."*

If you could get up every morning and take a pill for peace, knowledge, divine power, and wisdom for every situation of the day, would you do it? Clearly, that is what God promises to us if we will simply seek Him first.

DIG DEEPER: *FURTHER STUDY*

What are the promises in the following verses? Write them below.

> **Luke 11:9-13** *"So I say to you, <u>ask</u>, and it will be given to you; <u>seek</u>, and you will find; <u>knock</u>, and it will be opened to you. For everyone who asks receives, and he who seeks finds, and to him who knocks it will be opened. If a son asks for bread from any father among you, will he give him a stone? Or if he asks for a fish, will he give him a serpent instead of a fish? Or if he asks for an egg, will he offer him a scorpion? If you then, being evil, know how to give good gifts to your children, how much more will your heavenly Father give the Holy Spirit to those who ask Him!"*

_____

_____

_____

_____

_____

_____

To help you better understand this all-important truth—when Jesus Christ died on the cross, He made a deposit of grace, power, knowledge and wisdom in each one of our names (Eph. 1:3). But you can only make a withdrawal from your account if you use His name, and He only gives His name to those who receive and trust Him. How often have you gone to the bank lately? Have your efforts to have a devotional life, to be alone with the Lord for even a few minutes, ended in distraction? Never let failure turn you away from your Lord. Ask for His help and keep at it. Don't be robbed by discouragement, or let your account go dormant due to lack of use.

Keep Building!

If God reveals that your relationship with Him has become weak, or stale, the first thing to do is ask forgiveness (1 John 1:9), saying "I'm sorry. I forgot. I've lost my first love. I've allowed life's duties, desires and troubles to turn me from the very reason that I exist - to have fellowship with You."

Then commit to begin anew. Start with fifteen minutes; tell yourself you are going to read one chapter, or read until He speaks to you. Start first with prayer, putting yourself in His presence, praising Him, with the *expectation* that God is going to reveal Himself to you. When you are finished, meditate on what you have read.

Finally, get a journal. Keeping a record of your devotional time is telling yourself and the Lord, *I'm expecting You to say something to me today.* This is very important. Wait upon the Lord, and whatever He gives you, write it down and date it. He may give you some direction or a prayer, or simply remind you of His promises.

Keeping a journal enables us to go back and see what God has already done, what He has shown us, and maybe renew our strength for a present trial. Sometimes I go back and read through my journal, and usually, by the third or fourth page, I am brought to tears because of the things written there that God spoke to me about my life, my kids, my wife, and for the ministry.

Intimacy is a *process*. Begin with fifteen minutes daily, and it will grow. You will learn how to abide in Christ, pray without ceasing, and be in fellowship with Him throughout the day. On this strong foundation you will be able to build a solid family.

See back of book for more devotional instructions. See Appendix D and E.

Week 3: Loving Communication - Part 1

WEEK 3: DAY 1

Introduction: What's Love Got to do With It?

Surprisingly, as a family counselor I hear many kids make the statement, *"I feel my parents don't love me,"* despite the fact that virtually any parent questioned would emphatically state that they *do* love their kids. The problem is, parents sometimes *act* without love. The frustrations and difficulties of parenting can bring out the worst in us; we do and say things that are the opposite of love. Over time, if a parent is not taking responsibility, asking for forgiveness, a child will *not* feel loved.

As we look at the subject of Biblical love, Jesus gives us insight into what He expected of His disciples, which still applies to us today. Notice that Jesus is not making a suggestion, but a commandment.

> **John 13:34-35** *"A new commandment I give to you, that you love one another; as I have loved you, that you also love one another. ³⁵ By this all will know that you are My disciples, if you have love for one another."*

⌕ SELF-EXAMINATION

According to verse 35, how does the fulfillment of this commandment relate to your relationship with Christ and others, especially your children?

_____

_____

_____

_____

_____

God tells us that we cannot express this love without His help. In the following verses, notice the connection between God's Word and the working of the Holy Spirit in our lives.

> **1 Peter 1:22-23:** *"Since you have purified your souls in <u>obeying the truth through the Spirit in sincere love</u> of the brethren, love one another fervently with a pure heart, ²³ having been born again, not of corruptible seed but incorruptible, through the word of God which lives and abides forever"* [emphasis added].

In this instance, the word *sincere* means without hypocrisy. This *sincere* love is made possible only by abiding in Christ, and obeying the truth through the power of the Holy Spirit who dwells in every Believer. In a previous study, we learned that 2 Peter 1:3 says of Jesus, *"His divine power has given us knowledge of all things...through the knowledge of Him."* And that knowledge comes through God's Word.

DIG DEEPER: *FURTHER STUDY*

Read the following Scriptures and <u>describe</u> the 4 ways God is telling us to love others including our children.

Romans 12:9 *"Let love be <u>without hypocrisy</u>. Abhor what is evil. Cling to what is good."*

_____
_____
_____

1 Peter 4:8 *"And above all things <u>have fervent love</u> for one another, for "love will cover a multitude of sins."*

_____
_____
_____
_____

Hebrews 6:10 *"For God is not unjust to forget <u>your work and labor of love</u> which you have shown toward His name, in that you have ministered to the saints, and do minister."*

_____
_____
_____
_____

1 John 4:7 *"Beloved, let us <u>love one another</u>, <u>for love is of God</u>; and everyone who loves is born of God and knows God."*

_____
_____
_____
_____

What is biblical love?

Biblical love is not based on feelings, nor does it come naturally. We are naturally selfish and self-centered. Biblical love is an action, based on choice. This type of love is supernatural and can only come from a heart that is yielded to God, because it comes from Him. So it follows that to truly, sincerely love our children, we must first love God and yield our hearts to Him! In our culture today, the word *love* is tossed around so much that the meaning has been cheapened. We use the same word to describe how we feel about God, our children, and certain foods! Most parents will eagerly testify that they love their children. But the *only* standard by which we can measure real love is the Word of God.

In the original Greek version of the New Testament, the following two words translate to *love*, in English:

FACT FILE

Phileo – *The response of the human spirit to what appeals to it as pleasurable. "Phileo seems to be clearly distinct (from agape) and speaks of esteem, high regard, and tender affection and is more emotional."[1] Phileo is friendship love, determined by the pleasure that one receives from the object of that love. Phileo is conditional love.*

Agape –*The response of God's heart toward unworthy sinners. Agape is God's love demonstrated in self-sacrifice for the benefit of the objects of His love. "God's essential quality that seeks the best interests of others regardless of the others' actions."[2] "It involves God doing what He knows is best for man and not necessarily what man desires...His son to bring forgiveness to man."[3] It is choosing to love.*

We have this *agape* love because *"...the love of God has been poured out in our hearts by the Holy Spirit who was given to us" (Rom. 5:5).*

God has called us to love His children with *agape* love, a sacrificial love that is not withdrawn if the one loved fails to live up to demands or expectations. *Agape* love is based on the value God has placed upon our children, not on their personalities, strengths, weaknesses, or failures.

You have most likely come to the realization that it is *impossible* in our own strength to love with God's love! But praise God, when we receive Christ, the Holy Spirit comes to live in our hearts. If we yield (die to self-will), the Holy Spirit will love our children through us! Because *Biblical* love is not based on feelings, or emotions, it is something that you do (a verb, not a noun) and can only be described by seeing it in action.

Therefore, it is essential that we *learn* to show God's love to our children. The good news is, if our foundation of intimacy with Jesus Christ is properly laid, we are capable, in God's strength, of building the

---

1   J.D. Watson, *A Word for the Day* (Chattanooga, TN: AMG Pub, 2006), 21.

2   Richard L. Pratt, Jr, vol. 7, *I & II Corinthians, Holman New Testament Commentary*; Holman Reference (Nashville, TN: Broadman & Holman Publishers, 2000), 447.

3   Spiros Zodhiates, *The Complete Word Study Dictionary : New Testament*, (Chattanooga, TN: AMG Publishers, 2000), 66.

"supports of love" that our children need. Failure is not an option, we can all start somewhere and that point comes when we realize that loving our children comes from a heart surrendered to God. It is a behavior that we have to choose, seek, learn and grow into. We all love our children to a certain extent, but what we want to pursue is *excellence* in love.

Paul knew that the people in Philippi loved each other, but he encouraged them to press on further:

> **Philippians 1:9-11** *"And this I pray, that your love may abound still more and more in knowledge and all discernment, ¹⁰ that you may approve the things that are excellent, that you may be sincere and without offense till the day of Christ, ¹¹ being filled with the fruits of righteousness which are by Jesus Christ, to the glory and praise of God."*

Notice that Paul did not pray for them to *feel* like loving, which will be discussed more in the next chapter. This is a prayer of action that we can use to pray for ourselves. Let me help you think through how you can use this as a prayer.

1. "That your love may abound still more and more in knowledge and all discernment" (v 10). To *abound* means to have excess—more than enough - in this case, love. *Knowledge* in the Greek *epignosis*, means to know something intellectually, but then act upon it. It is a prayer to know how to love Biblically and then live it out. *Discernment* means to have insight, or the capacity to understand, and make a decision concerning behavior that flows from your knowledge.

2. "That you may approve the things that are *excellent*" (v 11). *Approve* in this context means to continually put to the test, examine prior to the approval of your action. In other words, does it meet the qualification of being *excellent agape,* or love that meets the standard of God's Word, which will then be a *sincere* love.

Our prayer is that God would fulfill this in you as you study His Word. Perhaps you have not done this before, take a few minutes and use the above passage of Scripture to write out a personal prayer on a 3x5 card and ask God to make it true in *your* life. For the next few weeks use the card to begin your study times by praying about these principles. For example:

> *"Lord Jesus, I am asking for this love to flow through me at all times. I want to overflow with Your love in all the situations I face each day. Lord, help me to never make an excuse for an unloving thought, word, or deed toward my children. Please give me Your discernment on how to share this love in all situations I face as a parent. Jesus, please be glorified in all I do in front of and to my children, Amen.*

DIG DEEPER: *FURTHER STUDY*

Read the following Scriptures and write out what are the main exhortations.

Colossians 1:9 *"For this reason we also, since the day we heard it, do not cease to pray for you, and to ask that you may be filled with the knowledge of His will in all wisdom and spiritual understanding."*

_____

_____

_____

_____

Romans 12:2 *"And do not be conformed to this world, but be transformed by the renewing of your mind, that you may prove what is that good and acceptable and perfect will of God."*

_____

_____

_____

_____

Ephesians 5:10 *"finding out what is acceptable to the Lord."*

_____

_____

_____

WEEK 3: DAY 2

The Uniqueness of Our Children

An important principle, sometimes overlooked, is that God creates each child to be *unique*. For example, my daughter Katie was so shy, from the time she was able to walk until she was about five years old, if we were in a public place away from the house, she had to be physically connected to either my wife or me. She would not leave our side. Thankfully, with age she became much more confident. But during those younger years, even at a place like church where she knew so many people, she would literally run a distance of 10 feet just to switch from my hand to her mom's. It was a little weird at times.

On Fridays, when Katie was in kindergarten, they had praise and worship for the whole school, some three to four hundred students. Fridays were definitely very difficult! Each week when worship started, the kids would be screaming, "Oh, praise the Lord!" It was like a nightmare for Katie; she would cover her ears and put her head down, fighting the feelings of panic.

Even the daily routine on the playground, with fifty kids throwing balls around and yelling, was too difficult for Katie. So she would sit at a table, coloring and talking with the teachers. When she was about 5 years old, we took her to Disneyland and it was anything but the "happiest place on earth." Katie did not like it at all. It took nearly five hours for her to relax in such a crowd of people. That is just the way Katie was as a child.

Yet my boys were completely different, nothing like Katie. My son Nick, in particular, was the complete opposite. We had to chase him around all the time, calling "Get over here young man!" because he always wanted to be so independent.

Many friends and family members noticed Katie's behavior and it seemed strange to them. What if my wife and I had become embarrassed, or impatient, and ignored her needs by saying, "Will you stop it? Let go of me! Stand over there. The boys never did this." If we had shunned her, what would have happened? We could have hurt Katie deeply and caused possible long-lasting damage simply because we refused to accept her *unique* emotional needs.

In order to have a deep appreciation for each child, we must always keep in mind *Who* created them. Yes, we are participants in the creation of our children but, from the beginning, God is the actual Creator. Genesis 1:26 says, *"Then God said, "Let Us make man in Our image, according to Our likeness…"* and verse 27, *"So God created man in His own image; in the image of God He created him; male and female He created them."* God formed man out of the dust (Gen. 2:7), and afterward He said that it was *"very good"* (Gen 1:31). Our children are created in God's image and we need to value them that way, even with all their imperfections and unique personalities. It does not matter if you are a traditional, blended, single-parent, grandparent or even foster family, we all share the responsibility of having God's children in our homes and need to value them as He does.

We must also keep in mind that God makes each of us with a unique personality. Ever notice how one child learns faster than another? One may be sensitive, another energetic, and yet another very kick-back and relaxed. You notice this in the Bible with Jesus' twelve disciples. Peter was brash, always speaking up, while John, known as the apostle of love, was depicted leaning on Jesus' breast.

In Psalm 139:13-14, David says to God:

> *"For You formed my inward parts; You covered me in my mother's womb.* [14] *I will praise You, for I am fearfully and wonderfully made; Marvelous are Your works, And that my soul knows very well."*

One commentator writes concerning this passage:

> David now turns to consider *His power and skill.* And the particular phase of divine omnipotence he chooses is the marvelous development of a baby in his mother's womb. When conception is made, it is like a speck of watery material smaller than the dot over this i, and all the future characteristics of the child are programmed—the color of their skin, eyes and hair, the shape of their facial features, the natural abilities they will have. All that the child will be physically and mentally is contained in that fertilized egg.[4]

This cannot be clearer. God has made each of us who we are, from birth, and He loves us. And yes, our children are born sinners just like us, and they need to be lovingly trained and disciplined, but it will always be in the context of who they are, and always with love.

DIG DEEPER: *FURTHER STUDY*

Read the following Scriptures and write down how the Psalmist's attitude toward God's creation (including our children) could help you embrace your child's uniqueness. What should your attitude be?

Psalm 92:4 *"For You, LORD, have made me glad through Your work; I will triumph in the works of Your hands."*

_____

_____

_____

_____

Psalm 104:24 *"O LORD, how manifold are Your works! In wisdom You have made them all. The earth is full of Your possessions."*

_____

_____

_____

_____

Psalm 111:2 *"The works of the LORD are great, Studied by all who have pleasure in them."*

_____

_____

_____

_____

4   William MacDonald and Arthur Farstad, *Believer's Bible Commentary : Old and New Testaments* (Nashville: Thomas Nelson, 1997), Ps 139:13–14.

According to the following Scriptures, when does God's plan for His children begin?

Jeremiah 1:5 *"Before I formed you in the womb I knew you; Before you were born I sanctified you; I ordained you a prophet to the nations."*

_____
_____
_____

Galatians 1:15 *"But when it pleased God, who separated me from my mother's womb and called me through His grace."*

_____
_____
_____

So the conclusion that we can make from all this is that each of us is unique! It should now be no surprise that our children are very different from us, and from each other. In order to love them properly, we need to become students of our children; to accept their personalities, understand their needs, and learn to communicate with them in a loving way. And never to forget to show affection to them, which can even be according to their personality. If we do not apply ourselves to these areas of parenting, serious problems can occur.

Many parents, without knowing or recognizing it, can grieve a child's spirit and damage their self-worth. Also by misrepresenting the Lord, by *not* loving a child and *adapting* to their emotional needs, parents can prematurely erode their own influence, or power, over that child.

✓ACTION PLAN

Take some time right now and write down a list of characteristics that are unique to each of your children and take it to God in prayer, and discuss if married. For example:

"Lord, my child is shy and at times she is very fearful. I know You have made her that way, so please give me Your wisdom, show me (us) how to minister to her in a way that will honor You and meet her needs."

_____
_____
_____
_____
_____
_____

As we move through these studies, you will learn more about how to love your children God's way. Commit it to prayer, and He will be faithful to provide the wisdom and strength you need to make needed changes.

Loving Communication Takes Time

Another important aspect of loving a child is to spend time with them. In today's world, we are pulled in so many directions by jobs, ministries, hobbies, and recreation, little time is left for the children. Even parents whose kids are in soccer, softball, or other sports can be at risk. Sports are good, but some people take them to the extreme. If you have one child who is a sports "nut," but the other three are not, what are you communicating to those three when you spend all day Saturday and Sunday, like a taxi cab, driving the "sport" around while they stay home? Worse yet is when you drag them along and make them sit in the bleachers. We must find a *balanced* way to love each of our children, with their own particular interests.

Today, in our society, many mothers are at work. Please understand that I am not putting down working moms. The area where you live can dictate the need for a two-parent income. But the question is: When working parents come home, where are their hearts and minds? "Kids, leave me alone for a while. I need my space." We can be tired, so be honest with yourself about being available to them. If you are not, there are going to be problems.

Loving our kids is not necessarily affected by the fact that we are working, but by *our* behavior and attitude when we are home with them. Recent statistics show that an average working mother spends 11 minutes a day in one-on-one communication with her child. For those with multiple children, that time per child decreases even further. On an entire weekend, a working mom spends about 30 minutes per day in one-on-one communication with her child. A father today spends about eight minutes a day communicating one-on-one with his child, and about fourteen total minutes of one-on-one communication with his kids on a weekend.[5]

Within these same statistics, we find that children today are watching between three and four hours of TV a day. Is it any wonder that the media is proselytizing and infecting our children's minds with worldly views? Loving our children and meeting their emotional needs means sacrifice, giving of ourselves and being available for them. Adapting to their interests may be reading a book to them, playing catch, or walking the dog. It takes time, but parents will also reap the new rewards of really getting to know their children, and enjoying them!

The Most Powerful Motivator

It is my observation through study that there are four basic forces that motivate all humans. First is love, the most powerful motivator. The second is physical needs: food, security, warmth. Number three is pleasure: our jobs, car, house, or other things that please us. Fourth, and least powerful, is pain and fear.

---

5   http://www.findarticles.com/p/articles/mi_m1175/is_v20/ai_ 4433362

When it comes to motivating children, parents often lean most heavily on pain and fear. Isn't that interesting? The reality is, however, that a far more powerful motivator is *love*. Love will motivate our children to make right decisions when they are not in our presence, especially when they become adolescents. Our love is the most powerful motivation for them to say, "No, I don't want that" or "I won't do that." Our love for them is the key. God is our example, as discussed earlier, and it is "knowing that the goodness (loving kindness) of God leads you to repentance," (Rom 2:4) that we need to embrace. Since it was God's love and goodness that brought us to the point of repentance, should we not do the same with our children? What was the motivation that caused Jesus to come down and die for us? John 3:16 tells us it was His love for us that motivated Him to die on the cross.

DIG DEEPER: *FURTHER STUDY*

Write down what the following verses say about acting out of love. What are the reasons, and the results, and how can you apply this to parenting?

Romans 5:8 *"But God demonstrates His own love toward us, in that while we were still sinners, Christ died for us."*

_____

_____

_____

_____

_____

2 Corinthians 12:15 *"And I will very gladly spend and be spent for your souls; though the more abundantly I love you, the less I am loved."*

_____

_____

_____

_____

1 John 4:7 *" Beloved, let us love one another, for love is of God; and everyone who loves is born of God and knows God."*

_____

_____

_____

_____

_____

In our next section, you will learn to train your children by establishing rules, discipline and punishment. But remember, effective training must be done in love and motivated by love if we are doing it God's way. This is difficult for parents because it requires sacrifice. For love to be genuine, it must be demonstrated. Aren't you thankful that God didn't just *feel* love for us? Aren't you glad He *demonstrated* that love? He asks us to follow His example by going beyond *feeling* love to *demonstrating* love!

WEEK 3: DAY 3

Love: Reaction or Response?

Reacting in the Flesh

> **FACT FILE**
>
> **React**: The dictionary defines the word *react* in the following way: "to act in response to a stimulant or to stimulus, to act in opposition."[6]

So, to react is not a purposeful or proactive state of mind, and as such, can surely turn out to be a **negative** action. We can take that further by saying that *loving* someone will not be of great quality if we are merely *reacting* to that person.

> **Reacting in the Flesh** can be defined as a Christian reacting to a situation in a sinful manner, in the habit of their old fallen nature, or reacting in their strength and understanding rather than the power and wisdom of the Holy Spirit.

As Christian parents, as ministers, *reacting* in a negative way is sin and a misrepresentation of God. We should not be negatively reacting to our children in any circumstance. Reacting takes no thought, is a "no-brainer" response when the mind is motivated by the flesh. In other words, whatever comes to mind, we simply go with it. Reacting is from our sin nature, or flesh, and is not a demonstration of self-control, which is included in the fruit of the Spirit (Gal. 5:22). When kids do something wrong, parents can react in the wrong way with the first thing that comes to mind, which is often shouting harsh words, using disgusted or frightening facial expressions, or even physical violence. Other tactics are silence, rejection, and alienation. The list of sinful and fleshly reactionary expressions toward our children can get pretty lengthy. These are not loving and do not qualify as godly training.

---

6   *Webster's New International Dictionary of the English Language; Second Edition Unabridged*; G & C Merriam Company, Publishers, Springfield, MA 1944

It is so important that we remember *every day* that we are the most powerful influence in our children's lives! Every time we get angry, or react to our kids in a negative way, we should visualize pulling a sword out and slicing their hearts. Of course, we do not see the damage immediately, but it is truly taking place. In addition, when we do not deal properly with that damage, infection sets in and brings bitterness, then resentment, and when our kids become teenagers, we pay the price.

As a counselor, I have seen hundreds of Christian boys and girls with broken hearts. They are so infected and full of pain. Sadly, the parents who raised these kids never even realized the damage they were doing to their children, over and over again, by reacting in the flesh instead of responding in love.

Reacting to circumstances with a burst of emotions takes no time or effort, it is instantaneous. Proverbs 15:1 tells us, *". . . a harsh word stirs up anger."* The Bible also tells us that we are to eliminate harsh actions from our behavior: *"But now you yourselves are to put off all these: anger, wrath, malice, blasphemy, filthy language out of your mouth"* (Col. 3:8). We are to accept this truth and make a conscious decision to stop every sinful reaction towards our children. Sadly, it is quite common for Christian parents to react in the flesh towards their children, yet never take responsibility for their behavior.

DIG DEEPER: *FURTHER STUDY*

Read the following Scriptures. Write down each negative quality and cause, relating it to the habit of "reacting". Do you see commands?

Psalm 37:8 *"Cease from anger, and forsake wrath; Do not fret—it only causes harm."*

_____
_____
_____
_____

Ephesians 4:22 *"that you put off, concerning your former conduct, the old man which grows corrupt according to the deceitful lusts."*

_____
_____
_____
_____

James 1:20 *"for the wrath of man does not produce the righteousness of God."*

_____
_____
_____

Proverbs 20:3 *"It is honorable for a man to stop striving, Since any fool can start a quarrel."*

_____

_____

_____

_____

Proverbs 27:3 *"A stone is heavy and sand is weighty, But a fool's wrath is heavier than both of them."*

_____

_____

_____

_____

Responding in Love

FACT FILE

Respond: According to the dictionary, when we *respond* to someone, we "react positively or favorably."[7]

When we are responsive, the Thesaurus tells us that we are being acceptant, persuadable, or in other words, we are behaving in a positive way, which is the opposite of reacting.

Responding in Love – A Christian responding to a situation with the inward guidance, love, wisdom and power of the Holy Spirit.

Responding takes *thought;* we have to use our mind and will. Scripture commands that we *". . . bring every thought captive unto God's Word"* (2 Cor. 10:5). Responding also takes *self-control*. We must bring our will under subjection to the power of God, which allows the fruit of the Holy Spirit to blossom. *"But the fruit of the Spirit is love, joy, peace, longsuffering, kindness, goodness, faithfulness, gentleness, self-control"* (Gal. 5:22-23). In addition, Scripture tells us we must add self-control to our foundation of faith:

2 Peter 1:5-7 *"But also for this very reason, giving all diligence, add to your faith virtue, to virtue knowledge, to knowledge self-control, to self-control perseverance, to perseverance godliness, to godliness brotherly kindness, and to brotherly kindness love."*

---

7   *Webster's II New Riverside Dictionary Revised Edition, Office Edition*, Houghton Mifflin Company, 1996

⚲ SELF-EXAMINATION

Take a moment and list some of the negative facial or verbal reactions you use with your children.

_____
_____
_____
_____

Finally, responding rather than reacting takes *time*. It may take as long as counting to ten, it may take much longer. In a later chapter we will discuss discipline, including the importance of never doing it in anger. Sometimes the ability to respond with appropriate discipline requires that a parent take "time out". Do you need to walk away from the situation and pray? Ask God for the wisdom to respond in a way that honors Him and lovingly encourages your child.

Proverbs 15:28 *"The heart of the righteous studies how to answer . . ."*

James 1:19-20 *"So then, my beloved brethren, let every man be swift to hear, slow to speak, slow to wrath; for the wrath of man does not produce the righteousness of God."*

Clearly, Scripture tells us not to react in the flesh; but to respond thoughtfully with love. Remember, our purpose is to glorify God, even during discipline, even when our kids are failing, even when they do not want to listen, even when they are challenging us - even then, we need to respond in love. Remember that it is God's will we are fulfilling, not our own.

DIG DEEPER: *FURTHER STUDY*

Read the following verses and list our responsibilities concerning love.

John 13:34 *"A new commandment I give to you, that you love one another; as I have loved you, that you also love one another."*

_____
_____
_____
_____

Colossians 3:14 *"But above all these things put on love, which is the bond of perfection."*

_____
_____
_____
_____

Ephesians 4:15 *"But, speaking the truth in love, may grow up in all things into Him who is the head—Christ."*

_____

_____

_____

1 Peter 1:22 *"Since you have purified your souls in obeying the truth through the Spirit in sincere love of the brethren, love one another fervently with a pure heart."*

_____

_____

_____

1 Peter 4:8 *"And above all things have fervent love for one another, for "love will cover a multitude of sins."*

_____

_____

_____

Working with the Strong-Willed Child

Proverbs 14:29 says, *"He who is slow to wrath has great understanding, but he who is impulsive exalts folly."* In other words, reacting rather than responding demonstrates a lack of understanding in us, as well as promoting continued foolish behavior in our children. This is especially true with the strong-willed child.

As I shared previously, during the first four or five years of my oldest son's life, I frequently *reacted* to his strong-willed behavior like a raving maniac. I was angry, and I abused my authority. Finally, God got through to me, "Hey Craig, would you ever put gasoline on a fire when you're trying to put it out?" I thought, "Of course not!" Then, again I heard God's voice, "Well, every time you get angry and your son knows it, you are provoking him to continuous folly in his behavior."

Scripture reveals that when we exasperate a child, those with a strong will push right back. Ephesians 6:4 says, *"And you, fathers, do not provoke your children to wrath, but bring them up in the training and admonition of the Lord."* This verse says "fathers" because they are given responsibility to govern the home, but the principle is for moms, too. The command is "do not provoke." There is no exception clause here, or elsewhere. The acceptable option is to *train* them, which will be discussed later, in depth. To "provoke to anger," *parorgizo* (Greek), means to move someone to the point of anger, or "to provoke to anger, irritation or resentment."[8]

---

8   Zodhiates, 1122.

When God commands us not to do something, and we do it anyway, it is a *sin*. No parent likes it when a strong-willed child refuses to listen, or obey. But the Bible encourages us to always *respond* in love, or Christ-likeness. Hebrews 10:24 presents "provoke" in a positive way, *"And let us consider one another in order to stir up love and good works."* Stir up, sometimes translated stimulate, or provoke, is *paraxusmos* (Greek), and refers to the act of encouraging someone to good behavior. What we really want to do is "stir up" love, which stimulates good behavior in your child. This I call using the "fire-extinguisher" of love.

We have to remember that personality comes from the way God wires us. Those strong-willed individuals are the Peter's and Paul's of the world. We need people like them in our lives, in the kingdom! They are the people who, when they are trained right, cannot only press on through great opposition, but also bring others through with them. Victory comes by *responding* to **truth**, using self-control, and not being driven by our feelings and emotions. For us as parents, *truth* means that our response comes from a heart and conscience trained by the Word of God. Deut. 27:26 says, *"Cursed is the one who does not confirm all the words of this law by observing them. And all the people shall say, 'Amen!'"* To *confirm* means God's Word has come into our hearts and dictates our behavior.

> **Matthew 22:36-39** *"'Teacher, which is the great commandment in the law?' Jesus said to him, 'You shall love the LORD your God with all your heart, with all your soul, and with all your mind.' This is the first and great commandment. And the second is like it: 'You shall love your neighbor as yourself.'"*

In this passage, God emphasizes the importance of love and the value of human life. When we love and value someone, we treat him or her accordingly. Obviously, we can choose to fail by not loving, even though we are called to serve as a *minister* and example of Christ to our children. Here is an example of acting in the opposite of love: It is a heated moment after your child just did something really foolish, and you are having an intense debate. The phone rings, and you stop to answer (it's a friend of yours): "Hello. Hi, oh hey, everything's OK. I'm fine, how are you?" You seem happy to hear from them and your tone of voice turns instantly pleasant. What did you just communicate to your child? The person on the phone is more valuable.

Sadly, we frequently do that, never even thinking twice. Especially when our kids are little, before their cognitive skills are developed, they see it so plainly: *Mom or Dad likes other people more than me.* This common occurrence, even in Christian homes, is one reason we find so many kids struggling with self-worth.

Love Is a Choice

The Bible says that we are to *"put on love."* It is a *choice*, not a *feeling*. Feelings may follow, but first we must act in obedience to the Word of God. *"But above all these things put on love, which is the bond of perfection"* (Col. 3:14). The word translated "love" here is *agape.* The Nelson Illustrated Bible Dictionary says this about *agape love:* "contrary to a popular understanding, the significance of 'agape' is not that it is unconditional love, but that it is primarily a love of the *will* rather than of the *emotion.*"[9]

Agape love means *responding* to my children as if I love and value them, even when I am upset with their choices. I may have negative thoughts, but still *respond* with love and patience. I am learning *self-control,* the art of quenching my flesh, so that I avoid saying something foolish, judgmental, mean, or unkind. This is the fruit of the Spirit, not the fruit of Craig. This love does not come naturally. Plus, Biblical love is not based on feelings; it is a choice to submit, or yield to the conviction of the Holy Spirit. We all recognize it – the conviction telling us when we are out of control (Eph 4:30). Agape love is the decision to value another person, perhaps a child, when our own comfort is disturbed. Romans 13:8 says, *"Owe no one anything except to love one another, for he who loves another has fulfilled the law."*

Communicating love starts in the heart. Learning to respond in love rather than react from the flesh is a process. Today, I no longer react in anger to my children but *respond* in love. Praise God, my oldest son has not held any un-forgiveness toward me for the many mistakes during his first six years of life. It is because God has healed his memory of my angry, sinful behavior.

If you are trapped in a reactive, sinful pattern of behavior, take heart. You and your child can experience similar healing. In the next chapter we will deal with changing that reactive behavior to a loving response. It is important to understand, however, if you choose to continue *reacting* negatively, you will pay dearly later, and so will your children.

WEEK 3: DAY 4

What Love Is Not: Part 1

All of us believe that we know how to love our children. But we can only prove it by comparing our type of love with the love described in God's Word. The most complete passage on this topic is found 1 Corinthians 13, which describes both what love is and is not. While we study the principles in this chapter, we will be evaluating our knowledge and behavior in relation to God's revealed wisdom on love.

As we go through this process, please keep in mind that God loves you, and His instruction is meant to encourage, not condemn. It is Satan, our enemy, who wants us to feel condemned. The Holy Spirit ministers to us by revealing areas where we need change, and our job is to receive that conviction. God wants us to

9   *The Nelson Illustrated Bible Dictionary*

understand the difference between conviction and condemnation, and that *"there is no condemnation for those who are in Christ."* (Rom. 8:1).

Think about it: there is a reason you are reading this material right now. God has been waiting to share these things with you. Tell Him, "OK, God, I am ready. As You reveal truth to me, where I am doing something wrong, I pray that You would bring conviction, and place a desire in my heart for change."

In 1 Corinthians 13, God uses **verbs** to explain love, not adjectives. This is because "agape" love can only be described by observing it in action. Love is not something that we merely *define;* it is something that we *do.* It is not just a feeling, or an attitude; it is an action that centers on others, not on self.

> **1 Corinthians 13:4-8a** *"Love suffers long and is kind; love does not envy; love does not parade itself, is not puffed up; does not behave rudely, does not seek its own, is not provoked, thinks no evil; does not rejoice in iniquity, but rejoices in the truth; bears all things, believes all things, hopes all things, endures all things. Love never fails.. "*

As we look at ourselves in relation to these aspects of love, giving special attention to the way we love our children, it will be helpful to look at both what love is, and is not.

1) LOVE IS NOT IMPATIENT.

> **FACT FILE**
>
> **Longsuffering, or patience**: means to be long-tempered, the opposite of hasty anger, instead it involves exercising understanding and patience toward people. It also requires that we endure circumstances, not losing faith or giving up.[10]

The Scripture tells us that love *"suffers long,"* (patient NASB, NIV) and commands us to do so. The opposite of long-suffering, or being patient, is *impatience*. **Love is not impatient**. If we put selfish, unrealistic expectations on our children, and then become angry when they fail, we are being impatient and failing to love them properly by God's standard.

I hear parents complain, "My three-year-old constantly leaves messes, and doesn't want to obey." My response is, "Really? What do you expect of a three-year old?"

Others reveal, "My teenager never wants to do chores and it makes me so angry. It's hard to be patient

---

10   Spiros Zodhiates, *The Complete Word Study Dictionary : New Testament* (Chattanooga, TN: AMG Publishers, 2000) 939.

when he (she) won't do what I ask!" I respond by asking, "Is that a surprise? How have you trained your child?" And often the response is, "What do you mean 'trained'? I just expect obedience."

Then I reply, "No wonder he's fourteen and acts like he's six. You place expectations on him, yet you have no idea how to train him to meet those expectations." By reacting in anger, you are actually creating an angry person within your child (Prov 15:1), and you are influencing him to go out and do the same (Prov 22:24-25). So, who should break this cycle? Who is really responsible, your fourteen-year-old child, or you?"

The love we show our kids *must* be longsuffering. Whether it is the "terrible twos", or the "challenging teens," love means dying to self as we patiently teach them and guide them into maturity. From the time we bring them home from the hospital, it seems that they just *want, want, want*. Everything is, "Mine, mine, mine." But we cannot be impatient! Love requires patience.

This is a good place to stop and reflect on your relationship with the Lord. Before you came to Christ, God was very patiently leading you to a place where you would surrender to Him, and even now God is being patient with your ignorance and disobedience.

> **Romans 2:4** *says, "Or do you despise the riches of His goodness, forbearance, and longsuffering, not knowing that the goodness of God leads you to repentance?"*

The Scripture also says in 1 Corinthians 13:4 that love "*suffers-long,*" which is derived from the above word "*longsuffering*". Notice that the longsuffering and goodness of God leads us to repentance, not God's anger and impatience. Should we not demonstrate the same attitudes to our children?

> *The Bible says in 2 Peter 3:9, "The Lord is not slack concerning His promise, as some count slackness, but is <u>longsuffering toward us</u>, not willing that any should perish but that all should come to repentance."*

Oh, how truly looooooooongsuffering God is toward us!

✅ACTION PLAN

Write down three areas where you are impatient with your children, then ask God to forgive you. Now, ask your child/children to forgive you (be specific to each area). Follow up by committing these areas to prayer, asking God for strength and wisdom to change.

_____

_____

_____

_____

_____

_____

_____

_____

Keep in mind, some children will require much more patience than others. My son Nicholas was a strong-willed child. He required much time from my wife and I, and ten times the amount of energy compared to my son Justin and our daughter Katie. It was constant! He would wake up in the morning, and by 9:00 a.m. my wife and I would think, "Oh, my gosh, he's beating to a drum, but it sure is not ours." Sometimes we would have to discipline him ten, even twenty times in one day. Justin or Katie, meanwhile, might have required one or two.

Loving Nicholas was indeed hard work during these times! Often, our thoughts were, "I'm sick of this! Why can't he just obey the rules? Why doesn't he just grow up?" We would stay up until all hours of the night discussing him, "What are we going to do tomorrow? God give us strength!" Loving Nicholas properly *required* a tremendous amount of patience.

> **Romans 15:4** *"For whatever things were written before were written for our learning, that we through the patience and comfort of the Scriptures might have hope."*

DIG DEEPER: *FURTHER STUDY*

Paul prayed concerning the quality of love and patience we need in our hearts. What is the source of this love?

> **2 Thessalonians 3:5** *"Now may the Lord direct your hearts into the love of God and into the patience of Christ."*

_____

_____

_____

ADD/ADHD

At this point, I want to say something about attention deficit disorder (ADD). This is a genuine disorder causing inability to focus, take direction, put commands in order, respond, and so on.[11] I do work with some children who truly have ADD, or attention deficit/hyperactivity disorder (ADHD), but I would say that over 85 percent of the ADD and ADHD diagnoses today are false. This is especially obvious when considering the questions a therapist, or physician, typically asks parents about their child's behavior, while never asking

---

11   http:www.cdc.gov/ncbddd/adhd/symptom.htm

about the parents' *method* of training. In addition, they never consider how often the parents *react* to a child with anger, exasperating them and provoking his/her behavior to continuous folly.

It is questionable why the number of children diagnosed with ADD or ADHD is increasing. Current reasons seem to be that they do not sit in class and listen to the teacher, or have had zero training at home other than yelling and screaming. With no consistent loving discipline, it is no wonder children act the way they do. After closely examining their discipline style, I have told many parents, "It's not that your child has ADD, or ADHD, but the problem is your ignorance and/or unwillingness to love and train them according to God's will."

When parents are *blessed* with a strong-willed child, they can be led to believe that treating the child medically is the solution. In most cases, the greatest problems are parental ignorance and/or unwillingness to *yield* and *obey* God's commands. Have you heard the terms "battle of the wills", or "power struggle" in relation to parenting? This can all lead to a disorder in children that we have named *UADD,* or unwilling-attention-deficit disorder. And, if a child does not have UADD, then it is often what we call *LOPD,* lack-of-parenting disorder, or a combination of both.

If your child has been diagnosed with ADD or ADHD, however, please do not think you must immediately take them off medication. Instead, apply the principles that you are learning throughout this study. You might find that ninety days from now, you will be able to wean them off that medication, and perhaps you will discover he/she never needed it in the first place. We have witnessed this many times! I encourage you to pray about this.

DIG DEEPER: *FURTHER STUDY*

Read the following Scriptures and write down what they say about longsuffering patience, love, or both.

> **Romans 15:5** *"Now may the God of patience and comfort grant you to be like-minded toward one another, according to Christ Jesus,…"*

_____

_____

_____

_____

> **Galatians 5:22** *"But the fruit of the Spirit is love, joy, peace, longsuffering, kindness, goodness, faithfulness,…"*

_____

_____

_____

_____

WEEK 3: LOVING COMMUNICATION - PART 1

Hebrews 6:12 *"That you do not become sluggish, but imitate those who through faith and patience inherit the promises."*

_____

_____

_____

_____

1 Thessalonians 5:14 *"Now we exhort you, brethren, warn those who are unruly, comfort the fainthearted, uphold the weak, be patient with all."*

_____

_____

_____

_____

WEEK 3: DAY 5

2) LOVE IS NOT UNKIND

FACT FILE

Kind: the word *chrestos (Greek)*, to do good; denotes being gentle, merciful, sympathetic, gracious and good natured in contrast to harsh, hard, sharp, bitter or cruel. The term also expresses the idea of moral excellence.

A good illustration of this word is when Christ used it of Himself, saying, *"... My yoke is easy (chrestos), and My burden is light."* (Matt 11:30). True love motivates us to act in merciful goodness toward our children, so that they can see Christ in us, an example of a loving and kind *minister* of God.

"Love is . . . kind." (1 Cor. 13). The opposite of kindness is being unkind. ***Love is not unkind***. Unkindness is allowing oneself to be provoked and angry, then yelling, judging, ignoring, comparing our children to their siblings, and acting as if their failures are a threat against our parental authority. God will use our children's mistakes and failures to accomplish His will in our lives, to *transform* our character as needed. He will use our child's weaknesses to reveal our *own* weaknesses. If we refuse to accept and work with God in those difficult areas, we will also miss opportunities for God to work on our own weaknesses!

We must remember that our homes are a training ground. Children are born without Godly character, as we were also. They do not arrive with traits of maturity. The Word tells us *"foolishness is bound up in the*

WEEK 3: DAY 5 | 77

heart of the child" (Prov 22:15). The emphasis here is that all children are born with a *sinful bent*; understanding this, we can learn to discipline them in a loving way.

Proverbs gives us a picture of their lack of maturity, which puts a big responsibility upon the parents (22:6; 19:18). They lack judgment (10:21); enjoy foolishness (10:23); are gullible (14:15); avoid the wise (15:12); are proud and haughty (21:24); despise good advice (23:9); make truth useless (26:7); repeat their folly (26:11); trust in themselves (28:26); vent their anger (29:11); cause strife and quarrels (22:10); stir up anger (29:8); go their own way (15:21); lash out when they are discovered in folly (17:12); are endangered by their words (18:6, 7); walk a troublesome path (22:5); must be guided by hardship at times (26:3); persist in foolishness (27:22); show propensity for laziness (22:13); and are lustful (22:14), and greedy (22:16), just to name a few. This does NOT mean all these negative character traits will manifest themselves, but it does give us a description of immaturity—foolishness. Are you beginning to get the picture? Good. Now you are ready for the assistance you need to Biblically help your children develop character and maturity through *proper* teaching and Godly discipline.

Why do we act surprised at childish behavior? And why do we think that *anger* makes our discipline more effective? Many people were raised this way, and are just repeating behavior learned from their own parents. That is the way I was raised. There was a time that I believed if I wasn't twisting my face and raising my voice, my discipline was not working. However, where is that behavior commended in the Bible? Nowhere. In fact, James 1:20 states the exact opposite, "*...for the wrath of man does <u>not</u> produce the righteousness of God.*" What are you trying to produce?

I was in a restaurant restroom washing my hands years ago when an extremely agitated man came bursting through the door. He was herding his nine- or ten-year-old son, who was obviously on the verge of losing his dinner. The dad threw open a stall door and pushed the boy inside, all the while yelling,

> *"Hurry, hurry, hurry. Are you going to throw up? What's wrong with you?"*

Apparently the sick boy supported himself by leaning his hands on the toilet seat. The dad yelled, "Don't touch the toilet seat!" grabbed his son, ran him over to the sink and began frantically washing his hands, complaining, criticizing and judging the poor boy. This *out-of-control* father, upset because his dinner was interrupted, made a big, embarrassing scene in front of me, an absolute stranger. I could only imagine what went on in the privacy of his own home!

I felt like handing the guy my card and telling him that, in the near future, he would have an angry adolescent on his hands and probably need some counseling!

We must *learn* how to discipline with no sinful expression, without our hair standing up, or our veins popping out of our neck. The good news is, as we submit to the Lord we will be able to do it. I want to remind you again, acts of love and kindness are to be done out of obedience to the Lord; we love Him, abide in Him, and He empowers us to do these things. It is NOT about feelings, because at times we do not FEEL like loving.

The sad reality in many Christian homes is that parents show more contempt and more unkindness toward their own children than they do anyone else on earth—*reacting* in the flesh instead of *responding* in love (truth). We must *cooperate* with God by allowing Him to first train us, and then take responsibility when we are unloving.

Paul gives some pointed instruction in Ephesians 4:31-32:

> *"Let all bitterness, wrath, anger, clamor, and evil speaking <u>be put away</u> from you, with all malice. And <u>be kind</u> to one another, tenderhearted, forgiving one another, even as God in Christ forgave you."* [emphasis added].

Notice what needs to be put away. There also is the command to *"be kind"*, *"chrestos"* (Greek), which is a behavior that we are to pursue and continue to pursue.

✓ACTION PLAN

Take some time and write down those things that you need to "put away", ask forgiveness from God and then ask God to show you how to *proactively* be kind to your children. Pray for the faith to trust Him and keep at it, even though you sometimes fail. Ask for His grace to <u>always</u> ask for forgiveness when you fail. This is the only way you will experience godly change.

_____

_____

_____

_____

_____

_____

DIG DEEPER: *FURTHER STUDY*

What are the following verses instructing us to do toward others and our children?

Romans 12:10 *"Be kindly affectionate to one another with brotherly love, in honor giving preference to one another."*

_____

_____

_____

_____

Colossians 3:12 *"Therefore, as the elect of God, holy and beloved, put on tender mercies, kindness, humility, meekness, longsuffering;"*

_____

_____

_____

_____

Galatians 5:22 *"But the fruit of the Spirit is…longsuffering, kindness, goodness…"*

_____

_____

_____

_____

Proverbs 19:22a *"What is desired in a man is kindness…"*

_____

_____

_____

_____

_____

Week 4: Loving Communication - Part 2

WEEK 4: DAY 1

What Love is Not [Continued]

3) LOVE DOES NOT ENVY.

> **FACT FILE**
>
> **Envy:** this is discontent or uneasiness at the sight of another's excellence or good fortune, accompanied with some degree of hatred and a desire to possess equal advantages; malicious grudging.

Love does not envy. Parental jealousy, or envy, can result when a parent had a painful childhood, and his/her child has an easier life, or is excelling in areas in which he/she did not excel. For example, a young daughter has a great relationship with her mother. Once in high school, she becomes a cheerleader, very popular, and is receiving much attention from guys. Gradually she pulls away from Mom, while gaining many friends her own age, which is entirely *normal*. Mom begins to feel loss, then regret, as she looks back on her own teenage years. As she compares her life to her daughter's, jealousy and resentment begin to surface until mom's attitude becomes full-blown envy.

Another common example is a dad whose son is getting bigger; he's a football player, and feeling pretty cocky about himself, a *typical* teenager. Excitedly, he reports to his father, "I bench pressed 150 pounds today, Dad!" Dad callously *reacts*, "So what. At your age, I was doing more." Amazingly, we behave like that when we envy our kids. We must *guard our hearts* against these things.

Are you blessing and encouraging your children in all their gifts and talents? Are you excited about their accomplishments? Are you cheering them on? Are you talking about their successes, or are you only pointing out the negatives, the bad things? We need to recognize the gifts our kids have, and exhort them often.

⌒ SELF-EXAMINATION

Is there a particular child to whom you have shown contempt, or envy?   ❏ Yes ❏ No

If so explain:

_____

_____

_____

_____

_____

DIG DEEPER: *FURTHER STUDY*

Instead of turning to envy, we need to act according to God's *wisdom*:

> **James 3:17-18** *"But the wisdom that is from above is first pure, then peaceable, gentle, willing to yield, full of mercy and good fruits, without partiality and without hypocrisy. Now the fruit of righteousness is sown in peace by those who make peace."*

Write down some of the characteristics of wisdom from this Scripture.

_____

_____

_____

_____

_____

Read the following verses and write down what kinds of actions result from envy.

> **Acts 17:5** *"But the Jews who were not persuaded, becoming envious, took some of the evil men from the marketplace, and gathering a mob, set all the city in an uproar and attacked the house of Jason, and sought to bring them out to the people."*

_____

_____

_____

_____

> **Mark 15:9-10** *"But Pilate answered them, saying, 'Do you want me to release to you the King of the Jews?' 10 For he knew that the chief priests had handed Him over because of envy. 11 But the chief priests stirred up the crowd, so that he should rather release Barabbas to them."*

_____

_____

_____

_____

✓ACTION PLAN

Write out the natural gifts and talents each of your children have. Then ask God for His grace to praise your children for these gifts this week.

_____

_____

_____

_____

_____

_____

4) LOVE DOES NOT PARADE ITSELF, OR BRAG.

FACT FILE

Brag: to talk about oneself, or things pertaining to oneself, in a boastful manner; to boast.

Love does not parade itself, or brag, saying things like, "You know, when I was your age I had it much harder than you. I didn't even have a dad!" Or, "My dad used to beat me with a belt." "I never got a ride to school. I had to walk both ways, uphill, in the snow." "I had to do all the chores…"

These types of statements often occur when we are disciplining our children, or when they are complaining. But these testimonials do not motivate, as they are bragging. A synonym for the word brag is "windbag."[1] Is that what we want to be? Of course not. Bragging is not discipline, nor should it be part of it. Do we honestly think our teenagers can relate to our childhood? They cannot. So do not brag; it is wrong.

Truthfully, it is hard not to pull this card when our children are complaining and whining, "Ohhhh, I've got to walk to school," when school is two blocks away. Most kids are lazy; this has not changed. Socrates made a statement around 400 BC that says in part, _"Children today are tyrants. They contradict their parents, gobble their food, and tyrannize their teachers."_[2] Some things never change! But, no matter how tempting, we must _choose_ not to brag, but to encourage them.

The Bible says of bragging, _"Let another man praise you, and not your own mouth; a stranger, and not your own lips"_ (Prov. 27:2). We do not ever need to impress our children with how great and wise we are, nor belittle them in order to show them how important we are, saying things like, "I never talked to my parents

---

1   Thesaurus.com
2   William L. Patty and Louise S. Johnson, _Personality and Adjustment_, p. 277 (1953).

that way when I was your age," etc. *"For not he who commends himself is approved, but whom the Lord commends"* (2 Cor. 10:18).

SELF-EXAMINATION

Is bragging a technique that you use during discipline, or a way to try and motivate your children?
❏ Yes ❏ No

If yes, explain

_____
_____
_____
_____

DIG DEEPER: *FURTHER STUDY*

Read the following Scriptures and write down what they have to say about exalting ourselves in front of others-our children.

Romans 12:3 *"For I say, through the grace given to me, to everyone who is among you, <u>not</u> to think of himself more highly than he ought to think, but to think soberly, as God has dealt to each one a measure of faith."*

_____
_____
_____
_____

Galatians 6:3 *"For if anyone thinks himself to be something, when he is nothing, he deceives himself."*

_____
_____
_____
_____

Philippians 2.3 *"Let nothing be done through selfish ambition or conceit, but in lowliness of mind let each esteem others better than himself."*

_____
_____
_____
_____

5) LOVE IS NOT PUFFED UP OR ARROGANT.

FACT FILE

Arrogant or proud: means to be conceited; feeling or showing self-importance, disregard for others. Prideful; giving oneself high rank, or an undue degree of significance.

Love is not puffed up or arrogant. We are not to be dictators, brutally, or arrogantly ruling others. God wants us to *train* up our children, *not* control them. Our attitude must reflect that we are acting in their best interest in every situation, helping them *mature* and develop godly character. Our children should feel like they are part of a team, working together with us in this journey of raising them, not soldiers in an army.

Some parents miss this point; many men who have been in the military, or were raised in a military family often try to implement a drill Sargent type leadership. Godly leadership is not a Gestapo approach, such as maintaining an attitude of secret police and looking for a way to trap or catch a child doing something wrong. When parents tell their kids, "I know you're lying. I'm going to catch you" and then they plot and plan how to succeed, this is not a biblical approach and will cause resentment and drive your children away.

I have been told by many teenagers, "I think my parents are always trying to just catch me." That is not teamwork, but more like a dictator, the police, or an enemy, hoping to be the victor in battle. Can you imagine a quarterback saying to a lineman, "I'm watching you," or the lineman to the quarterback, "You'd better throw the ball to the guy I want, or I'm going to let this defender cream you"? What kind of teamwork is that?

We must always remember a primary principle of Godly parenting, we are *ministers*. We have to view our position in the family as a *divine calling* from the Lord, and do all for His glory, not ours. Jesus was with His disciples when two of them asked if they could sit one on His right hand and the other on His left in God's kingdom.

Jesus said to them in Matthew 20:25-28:

"You know that the rulers of the Gentiles lord it over them, and those who are great exercise authority over them. 26 Yet it shall not be so among you; but whoever desires to become great among you, let him be your **_servant_**. *27 And whoever desires to be first among you, let him be your* **_slave_**— *28 just as the Son of Man did* **not** *come to be* **_served_**, *but to* **_serve_**, *and to give His life a ransom for many."* (emphasis added).

The words *servant, served,* and *serve* are derived from the Greek word *diakonos*, translated **minister** in some verses of the New Testament. A *slave* was someone who had no rights of his own, but was devoted to the will of another. Jesus was not condemning authority, but emphasizing the *proper* use of authority. Jesus had all the authority in the world, but His attitude was to *serve* and fulfill the *"Father's* will." Parents have God-given authority, but how we exercise that privilege is of the utmost importance to God, as we are *His ministers.*

To put it another way, God tells pastors to minister, not as *". . .being lords over those entrusted to you, but being examples to the flock"* (1 Pet. 5:3). In the same way, we should be ministering to, not ruling over, the flock that God has committed to our care. God has not charged us with a task, but *entrusted* us with a great responsibility. We must be concerned that we exemplify Him, not become some tyrant. *"An arrogant man stirs up strife, but he who trusts in the LORD will prosper."* (Prov. 28:25 NASB).

⌕ SELF-EXAMINATION

Are you a dictator at times, talking down to your children instead of to them, making Gestapo-like comments?   ❏ Yes ❏ No

Write out what the LORD has revealed to you.

_____

_____

_____

_____

_____

DIG DEEPER: *FURTHER STUDY*

Read the following Scriptures and write down what the Bible says about pride and arrogance, and how this could affect our parenting.

> **Proverbs 8:13** *"The fear of the LORD is to hate evil; Pride and arrogance and the evil way, And the perverse mouth I hate."*

_____

_____

_____

_____

> **Proverbs 11:2** *"When pride comes, then comes shame; But with the humble is wisdom."*

_____

_____

_____

_____

Proverbs 13:10 *"By pride comes nothing but strife, But with the well-advised is wisdom."*

_____

_____

_____

_____

James 4:6 *"But He gives more grace. Therefore He says: "God resists the proud, But gives grace to the humble."*

_____

_____

_____

_____

WEEK 4: DAY 2

6) LOVE DOES NOT BEHAVE RUDELY, IS NOT UNBECOMING.

FACT FILE

Rude: *characterized by roughness; harsh, severe, ugly, indecent, or offensive in manner or action.*

Love does not behave rudely, or act unbecomingly, as to embarrass and/or demean a child. Parents can do this by discussing a child's failures or shortcomings with others, or by being angry or critical when disciplining. This would include scolding, lecturing, and/or spanking in front of other people, including siblings. Many parents give themselves permission to *openly* discuss a child's behavior without regard to who is listening. Moms, not to pick on you, but this is common when you get on the phone with your friends, saying, "Oh you won't believe the day I had. First my son did this, then he did that, then he did this." All the while your child is in the other room listening as you expose his sins and failures to whomever. But Paul exhorts us to, *"Let no corrupt word proceed out of your mouth, but what is good for necessary edification, that it may impart grace to the hearers."* (Eph. 4:29).

FACT FILE

Edification, *oikodome* (Greek), means to build up for the spiritual profit or advancement of someone else, and also used to indicate building up a house or structure.

We must see that there are times to exercise constraint, *"let no corrupt word proceed out of your mouth."*

Why? Because it does *not* build up, rather brings our children down. It really qualifies as gossip, which is rude, harsh, unkind, and is the opposite of building up. We must keep in mind, *"are my next words going to build my children up, draw them to Christ and impart the grace of God to their ears?"* Now, that's LOVE!

It is so painful when, even at church, I hear people going on and on about a child's mistakes while the child is sitting right there! Yes, there is a time and place for us to seek counsel, but we must never casually expose their sinful behaviors publicly to anyone. Never!

DIG DEEPER: *FURTHER STUDY*

How do you think the following passage relates to this subject? Meditate on it.

> **Proverbs 17:9** *"He who covers and forgives an offense seeks love, but he who repeats or harps on a matter separates even close friends."* (Amplified)

_____

_____

_____

_____

To *cover* means to put a lid on it, conceal it. Why would we want to do that? Because loving a child seeks the *best* for that individual. To quote a noted Christian scholar, "Someone has said, that, if tempted to relate unsavory things of an absent person, it is well to ask mentally three questions: Is it true? Is it kind? Is it necessary?"[3] And I would add one more question: Would it edify the person we are talking about and those who are listening?

This caution never means that we ignore, or overlook, our children's sin and/or failure to obey by covering it up. Read from an analysis of Proverbs 17:9, how one author explains covering a transgression:

> *"To cover a transgression, however, does not mean to make light of sin and allow iniquity to go unrebuked in another. It is, on the contrary, to go to the erring one personally in tenderness and brotherly kindness; to seek to exercise his conscience as to that in his course, which is bringing dishonor upon his Lord. If such a mission is successful, the sin should never again be mentioned. It is covered, and none other need know of it."[4]*

Our children know our faults, don't they? They have seen and heard things that you and I have done wrong at home. Could you imagine if one Sunday morning at church the teachers that were watching your

---

3   H. A. Ironside, *Notes on the Book of Proverbs* (Neptune, NJ: Loizeaux Bros, 1908), 212.

4   H. A. Ironside, 211.

beautiful little children said to them, "We're going to have prayer time, so anyone who wants to come up and pray, come on up." So your little eight-year-old boy goes up and says, "Lord, I pray for my mom and dad. They yell, they argue, they scream, and they use bad language." How would you feel if you heard that had happened? You would be so embarrassed, you would probably quit going to that church! If we do not want our children to expose us like that, it stands to reason they do not want us to do it either.

SELF-EXAMINATION

Are there times that you are rude, or harsh to your children?   ❏ Yes ❏ No

What behavior has the Lord revealed that needs changing? Write out your confession.

_____
_____
_____
_____
_____
_____
_____
_____
_____

7) LOVE DOES NOT SEEK TO HAVE ITS OWN WAY.

FACT FILE

Seek your own way: this is a person who pursues what best fits their own interests, without any concern of how their actions or ways affect others. This person is unwilling to receive input, which includes instruction from God's perspective.

Love does not seek to have its own way. In other words, we cannot *insist* that our children do only what we think they should do, or not do, when it comes to *non-moral* issues. For example, a couple came in for counseling and right from the start, it was obvious that the mother was trying to control the family, which included the children's interests. She sat in my office venting about how angry she was with her fourteen-year-old son. In the process of her venting, she brought up the subject of paintball, and she said, "My son wants to play paintball. Paintball is so bad; I think it's so wrong."

I asked the father, "Dad, what do you think about it?"

He replied, "Well, I think it's OK."

She jumped in, "Well, I think it is wrong. You shoot at people in paintball!"

I then said to her, "I play paintball and have shot my kids many times! It's great fun, we love playing paint-ball. Your son is different from you, have you noticed?"

This same mom did not want her son to have a skateboard because "all skaters are bad, they wear their hats backwards and have sagging pants." I explained to her "I know you don't like it, but it's not about you!" I then said to the father, "If you think it's OK, you need to step up and *lead*; tell your wife you believe this is OK, and that she needs to *trust* you and not treat your son with contempt because he wants to enjoy things boys *naturally* like to do."

Now, I know that my wife would never play paintball with our boys and me; it is not her "thing". As a help-mate, a wife can *lovingly express her concerns* without trying to feminize her husband, or son. Many times I took my shirt off after playing paintball and would have bruises on my body, so she asked, "You liked that? Didn't it hurt?"

And I replied, "Oh yeah, it hurt. But if it didn't hurt a little, then it wouldn't be so fun. I think it's great fun, and so do the boys."

My older son is a surfer. When he got his driver's license, he could not wait to drive to the beach and surf. My wife was naturally very concerned about him driving there on his own. Her input was, "I think he should not drive outside our city for at least the next six months."

I replied, "Well, let's give him a couple of months. After he has some experience, I will let him drive me to the beach and see how he does. If he does fine, I will let him drive to the beach alone."

Husbands, in the *spirit of teamwork*, it is important to let your wife express her concerns and to *involve* her in family decisions. Husbands and wives need to work together to come up with plans and solutions, but the *final* decision lies with the father in these situations.

Part of not seeking to have one's own way is that the parents are seeking to get each other's input. Proverbs 20:18 states, *"Plans are established by counsel; By wise counsel wage war,"* and *"Without counsel, plans go awry, But in the multitude of counselors they are established"* (Prov. 15:22).

We have to be careful not to let *our* selfish opinions, fears, or what we like and dislike dictate what we al-low our kids to do. They are different than we are. We need to let them pursue their interests, within the context of morality and safety.

DIG DEEPER: *FURTHER STUDY*

How can the following Scriptures illustrate adapting to the interests of our children?

WEEK 4: LOVING COMMUNICATION - PART 2

Philippians 2:4 *"Let each of you look out not only for his own interests, but also for the interests of others."*

_____

_____

_____

_____

Philippians 2:3 *"Let nothing be done through selfish ambition or conceit, but in lowliness of mind let each esteem others better than himself."*

_____

_____

_____

_____

Galatians 5:13c *"...but through love serve one another."*

_____

_____

_____

_____

I have heard parents say, "Well, I don't let my kids listen to that 'rock junk.' I know it's Christian, but it has an evil beat." Is there really such a thing as an evil beat? There are even people who put on conferences regarding the "evil of rock music"; people pay to go see them. I challenge you to find that in the Bible! There is no such thing as an evil beat. There are evil lyrics and evil actions, but there is no evil beat. My point is that there is a wide variety of music that kids like that may be very different from our taste. If it is Christian and the lyrics are OK, then fine, what is the problem? *Try* to find a way to compromise, without compromising your faith.

DIG DEEPER: *FURTHER STUDY*

How can the following Scriptures relate to evil, unwholesome lyrics?

Ephesians 4:29 *"Let no corrupt word proceed out of your mouth, but what is good for necessary edification, that it may impart grace to the hearers."*

_____

_____

_____

_____

WEEK 4: DAY 2 | 91

Colossians 3:8 " *But now you yourselves are to put off all these: anger, wrath, malice, blasphemy, <u>filthy language</u> out of your mouth.*"

_____

_____

_____

_____

Psalm 19:14 " *Let the words of my mouth and the meditation of my heart Be acceptable in Your sight, O LORD, my strength and my Redeemer.*"

_____

_____

_____

_____

We should not be *inflexible* about the things we allow our kids to do, controlling them for the wrong reasons. Instead, we should *help* them enjoy their interests, paying very close *attention* that we never *compromise* our faith, or what the Bible stands for, by letting them pursue activities that are morally wrong.

It is good to participate with our kids in their interests when possible. My son Nicholas loves surfing. During his adolescence, I remember so many times going out with him in the wintertime, fifty-four-degree water, six-foot waves. On many occasions, just getting out past the waves nearly killed me. I was freezing half the time and I was exhausted, but praise the Lord, I was out there with my boy having fun. On some of these surf outings, I would rather have been doing something else, *but* he asked me to join him. So we went *together*.

Each child is different. My daughter, when she was young, liked to jump on the trampoline, or take our dog for a walk . . . not activities I would choose for enjoyment, but that wasn't the point. We were just spending time with each other, doing what she wanted to do.

When my daughter was ten years old, she wrote me a Father's Day card, explaining why she loved her daddy:

"These are the reasons I love you, Daddy.

Number one, you go on the trampoline with me. Number two, you take me to Dairy Queen. [OK, I like that one—that's no sacrifice for me!] *Number three, you take my dog for walks with me. Number four, you play soccer with me. Number five, you take me on bike rides. Number six, you take me on a motorcycle ride. Number seven, you read with me. Number eight, you make me breakfast. Number nine, you play cards with me.*"

Notice that every reason my daughter listed was an *action*. I was giving her *my* time. *Love* is all about ac-tion, which includes the *amount* of time spent. Every one of our kids needs it; and we need to remember and practice this continuously. The best *defense* against our kids pulling away from us too soon is to launch a strong offense by spending *time* with them, both individually and as a family.

Another important aspect of relating to children is showing proper affection. Often, dads tell me, "Well, I'm not a hugger." I respond to them with, "Well, it's not about *you*. It really doesn't matter if you're a hugger. True love is a sacrifice and is all about the other person. You have a child who loves you and needs to be hugged. Do something about it."

Dads, you may tell yourselves that Mom has been making up for your lack of attention, but it does not work that way. You need to get rid of whatever fear or stubbornness you have, and say, "I am going to become a hugger." Then ask God to *change your heart* and make you a hugger for your hugger kid.

Sometimes moms also have a problem with hugging, but the same principles apply. Moms usually have a natural affection toward their children, but past issues (especially unresolved ones) can have an effect on freedom to show love in this way. If so, this needs to *change*, and can change with God's help.

DIG DEEPER: *FURTHER STUDY*

Read about Paul's actions toward the people in Thessalonica:

> **1 Thessalonians 2:7-8** *"But we were gentle among you, just as a nursing mother cherishes her own children. 8 So, affectionately longing for you, we were well pleased to impart to you not only the gospel of God, but also our own lives, because you had become dear to us."*

What was his attitude and actions toward this church?

_____

_____

_____

_____

_____

Read about Jesus' action toward children and what He expected others to do:

> **Mark 9:36-37** *"Then He took a little child and set him in the midst of them. And when He had taken him in His **arms**, He said to them, 37 "Whoever receives one of these little children in My name receives Me; and whoever receives Me, receives not Me but Him who sent Me."*

What was Christ exhorting His disciples to do with children?

_____

_____

_____

_____

My older son, Nicholas, was never much of a hugger. His way of receiving affection was to jump on my back and wrestle with me. So we wrestled often. My son Justin, as a teen, would still lie on my lap, pleading, "Scratch my back." Many nights after we would say our prayers, Justin would lay right next to me for twenty minutes so I could rub his head, scratch his back, or rub his feet. He loved it.

Each child is _different_ and it is important to _treat_ them that way, but all need some kind of special affection. Most parents who struggle with this have never prayed about it. They have never asked God to change them, or they have put off examining themselves to understand why it is so difficult.

SELF-EXAMINATION
If that is you—stop right now and ask God to help you in this area. Write down what He revealed to you.

_____

_____

_____

_____

_____

_____

_____

We must remember that it is _not_ about us; if you feel uncomfortable, begin pleading, "God, change me." It is _not_ your will, but God's will. We need to glorify Him, even when it comes to showing affection to our kids. Past issues may be the cause of your difficulty; perhaps you had parents who did not show affection, or even abused you physically in some way. If you are harboring bitterness and or have unhealed wounds caused by a parent(s) and have not forgiven them, trusting the Lord with your past, then this issue can be a "grace clogger" in your life.

> **Hebrews 12:15** _"Looking carefully lest anyone fall short of the grace of God; lest any root of bitterness springing up cause trouble, and by this many become defiled."_

God can _heal_ the pain, and wants to deliver you from the emotional damage. If you do not trust this to Him in prayer and, in obedience, seek a new attitude, your negative behavior will become a destructive force to all around you.

See Appendix U concerting Forgiveness and Reconciliation for more help in this area.

God wants to pour *His* transforming power into our lives; make us tenderly affectionate toward the children He gives us. But, if we do not obey the Lord by forgiving our parents, this will *block* our ability to change. This is a very common problem. We must die to our flesh and let go of the offenses that cripple us, for the love of God and our children. Only then will we be able to freely give them affection in all ways they need to receive it.

DIG DEEPER: *FURTHER STUDY*

Read these verses, write out what they mean, and how they could apply to parenting.

Matthew 16:25 *"For whoever desires to save his life will lose it, but whoever loses his life for My sake will find it."*

_____
_____
_____
_____
_____

1 Corinthians 10:24 *"Let no one seek his own, but each one the other's well-being."*

_____
_____
_____
_____
_____

Have you been seeking to have your own way at home? ❑ Yes ❑ No

If you answered 'yes', write out your commitment to change, asking God for strength to follow through.

_____
_____
_____
_____
_____
_____
_____
_____

WEEK 4: DAY 3

8) LOVE DOES NOT THINK EVIL.

FACT FILE

Thinks no evil: *logizomai* (Greek), is used as an accounting term, meaning to put things together in one's mind, to count or add up, to occupy oneself with calculations.

Love thinks no evil. We cannot keep score of our children's *failures* with a mind to harass them with it later. Sadly, this is a common method many parents use during discipline. Failure is part of a child's life and many parents, instead of just disciplining them for that failure, place the incident in their "back pocket," only to pull it out and use it against them later.

An example would be when your teen asks if he can go with a friend to the school football game, and your response is, "No! Remember what you did last Tuesday? Sorry. You aren't going anywhere." This method of discipline is *wrong* and can promote resentment. It is the opposite of love; love keeps no record of wrongs.

Wrongs need to be dealt with immediately, and with explanation. What happened last Tuesday should have been covered then, handled with Godly wisdom and discharged. Developing feelings of anger and resentment that remain over time will be destructive to relationships and result in ineffective discipline. Feelings are good passengers, but poor drivers. We must let truth, not our feelings dictate how we *respond* to our children, even when it comes to disciplining them.

> **Hebrews 12:14-15** *"Pursue peace with all people, and holiness, without which no one will see the Lord: looking carefully lest anyone fall short of the grace of God; lest any root of bitterness springing up cause trouble, and by this many become defiled."*

To *"become defiled"* means that because we have harbored bitterness about something our child has done, we begin to spill poison that infects and hurts those around us. Parents, who entertain thoughts of evil towards their children, and stew upon their failures, often begin to ignore them. Or, the parent may pout, stay angry for days, use unkind words or compare them to siblings etc. These practices are the *opposite* of love. Many parents never consider the fact that they are practicing the opposite of love. We must choose not to think evil, but meditate on what is good.

The NASB version of 1 Corinthians 13:5 says that love *"does not take into account a wrong suffered,"* NIV *"keeps no record of wrongs."* NKJV says that love *"thinks no evil.";* but I especially like the way The Living

Bible says it: love *"is not irritable or touchy. It does not hold grudges, and will hardly even notice when others do it wrong."* That is the real meaning of 1 Corinthians 13:5, and that is how we must behave. Love forgives and releases the past issues.

Unforgiveness is a poison that one takes, hoping to hurt the other person. Truly, unforgiveness is like a cancer. If we allow it to, it will devour us from the inside and infect everyone around us in a negative way.

As a parent, we have opportunities to *forgive* our children, sometimes *daily*. Many parents have the wrong perspective when it comes to their children breaking a rule, or disobeying. God want us to see a child's foolish act or failure as an opportunity to train them, not for us to become personally angry or hurt.

When someone wrongs us, God says, *"You ought rather to forgive and comfort him, lest perhaps such a one be swallowed up with too much sorrow. Therefore I urge you to reaffirm your love to him"* (2 Cor. 2:7-8). Notice the process, forgive and then reaffirm you love.

How often should we forgive? Always...seventy times seven (Matt. 18:22). God's Word is clear on this.

DIG DEEPER: *FURTHER STUDY*

Read the following verse and write down how we should forgive others.

> **Ephesians 4:32** *"And be kind to one another, tenderhearted, forgiving one another, even as God in Christ forgave you".*

_____

_____

_____

_____

✓ACTION PLAN

Have you been following Christ's example of forgiving, forgetting and thinking good thoughts toward your children?   ❏ Yes ❏ No

If not, write down the areas where you are failing to forgive your child/children. Ask God's forgiveness and pick a time to ask your children's forgiveness.

_____

_____

_____

_____

_____

DIG DEEPER: *FURTHER STUDY*

What does the following verse mean, and how can you apply it to parenting?

> **Philippians 4:8** *"Finally, brethren, whatever things are true, whatever things are noble, whatever things are just, whatever things are pure, whatever things are lovely, whatever things are of good report, if there is any virtue and if there is anything praiseworthy—meditate on these things."*

_____

_____

_____

_____

_____

_____

_____

9) LOVE DOES NOT REJOICE IN UNRIGHTEOUSNESS.

FACT FILE

Not rejoicing in iniquity: this means that when you see someone fall into sin, or make a mistake, you are not happy and/or vindictive toward him or her.

Love does not rejoice in iniquity. This is a *command.* It is like God is saying, "Don't even think about it." That is the emphasis. Have you ever said to your child, "I told you so! You deserve what you got. I told you that you would get in trouble. I was right!" When a child makes a mistake and is caught, we should never act *happy* that they are in trouble or hurt. God does not want us to *react* to our children in the flesh; He wants us to *respond* in love, even when they deliberately do some foolish thing.

Let's face it, because of our fallen nature there is a mean streak in us that sometimes takes pleasure when someone is suffering because of foolish choices. In fact, all we have to do is turn on the T.V. and watch the latest reality show where people are laughing at, or at least being entertained by, the foolishness of others. "Well that person - mother, father, daughter, son, friend - deserved what they got." When this attitude creeps into our homes it has devastating effects upon our children, and us, because we are *misrepresenting God*. It totally blurs and corrupts what love is. As parents, we have to deal with the foolishness of our children on a daily basis. The question is, "How are you going to represent God during these times?" Really, to put the focus back on ourselves, how do we want God to treat us when we fail to glorify Him and or *not* do things His way?

The Bible gives us strict warning concerning how we handle sin. Proverbs 14:9 says, *"Fools mock at sin, but among the upright there is favor."* To *mock* means to boast, to scorn, deride or be inflated. The word *favor* has the root meaning of delight, pleasure or acceptance. As parents, we need to adhere to the latter part of the verse so that when our children fall into sin, they *find favor* with us from a heart of compassion that lovingly disciplines them.

When a woman was caught in the act of adultery, the Jews brought her to Jesus and asked, *"Teacher, this woman was caught in adultery, in the very act. Now Moses, in the law, commanded us that such should be stoned. But what do You say?"* (John 8:4-5). Verse 6 says the Jews were testing Jesus, but they also were rejoicing that she was caught in the act (note: where was the offending man?), and were looking forward to stoning her. Many times we will catch our children in the act of sinning, perhaps lying to us, or _____ (you fill in the blank), and what should be our response? Jesus answers this for us in verse 7, *"He who is without sin among you, let him throw a stone at her first."* Jesus then started writing on the ground and it is believed that He was pointing out the accusers sins. One by one they all left because their hearts where convicted (v 9). Then, Jesus spoke directly to the woman, saying that He did not condemn her, and that this was her opportunity to go and sin no more (v 11).

There were times when, in my heart, I was happy that Nick got what he deserved, but I did not show it. We need to exercise *self-control*. Proverbs 24:17 says, *"Do not rejoice when your enemy falls, and do not let your heart be glad when he stumbles."* Since we are not to rejoice when our enemy falls how much more should we not when are children fall.

When you read the story of the *prodigal son* (Luke 15:11-32), you get a glimpse of a father's heart toward a son who falls into sin, which is a picture of our heavenly Father's heart. When his son finally made a decision to return home, the Bible says, *"And he arose and came to his father. But when he was still a great way off, his father saw him and had compassion, and ran and fell on his neck and kissed him"* (v. 20). There was not any superior morality over his son's fall, instead he embraced his son and kissed him. Many parents still need to *develop* this type of *compassion*.

When we ignore God's Word, or resist the guidance of the Holy Spirit, and fall into sin and error, God does not rejoice. Instead, His heart is broken over our foolishness and rebellion. When we find ourselves not practicing love with our children, we must *confess* this to God, asking Him to forgive us, then *repent* and turn from this sin. God *will* change our hearts as we confess and obey Him. Remember to always keep in mind that God is using our children to transform us into His image.

The Biblical explanation of *mercy* is that we do not receive the penalty for our sin because of the work of Christ and His grace. But the Bible also tells us that God disciplines His children, meaning you and me. Showing mercy does not indicate a lack of discipline, which is necessary, but means that we discipline with love for the best interest of the child. So, discipline done *properly* is an expression of love.

DIG DEEPER: *FURTHER STUDY*

Write down what the following Scriptures say about mercy and compassion and how they could relate to parenting.

Luke 6:36 *"Therefore be merciful, just as your Father also is merciful."*

_____
_____
_____
_____

Matthew 5:7 *"Blessed are the merciful, For they shall obtain mercy."*

_____
_____
_____
_____

Lamentations 3:22-23 *"Through the LORD's mercies we are not consumed, Because His compassions fail not. They are new every morning; Great is Your faithfulness."*

_____
_____
_____
_____
_____

Colossians 3:12a *"Therefore, as the elect of God, holy and beloved, put on tender mercies."*

_____
_____
_____
_____
_____

Proverbs 3:3 *"Let not mercy and truth forsake you; Bind them around your neck, Write them on the tablet of your heart."*

_____
_____
_____
_____

WEEK 4: DAY 4

10) *NOT* REJOICING IN THE TRUTH

FACT FILE

Rejoicing in the truth: this means that you have great joy, or you are able to rejoice at what is true based on God's promises.

Love rejoices in the truth. When we fail to praise our children and instead constantly point out their faults, we are not rejoicing in the truth. When parents come in for counseling, I ask them, "If your teenager was here and I asked him, on an average day, how much of your conversation with your parents is *positive* versus *negative*, what would he say?"

Positive communication is, "How are you doing? You look nice. What happened at school today?" *Negative* is, "Stop that, leave your sister alone! Do your homework! Take out the trash!" or any form of lecturing.

Quite often parents respond, "Oh, that's an easy one. It's 90 percent negative. Every day." Days turn into weeks, and weeks turn into months, all the while we are poisoning our kids, sinning against them, not loving them, because we are consumed with pointing out what they are *not* doing right, and not thinking about praising them for their successes. We parents need to be *actively* thinking about the good things in our kids. I know it can be hard with those strong-willed children. I remember telling Nick many times, "You're strong-willed, that's good." That's all I could come up with! There were days I turned to prayer to come up with something good to say.

If this *negativity* is sending your family in the wrong direction, turn it around. When you have your family prayer time, take a moment and say, "OK everyone, say something good about each other." Make it a fun thing. Get the whole family started on looking for the good things in each other. It is so important that we work together as a team; Dad or Mom—you start it off.

Personally, I sometimes have a tendency to micro-manage. The minute I walk into the house, I begin to notice what's out of place, correct everyone's faults. "Who left that on the floor?" True, the faults need to be fixed, but we must do it with loving discipline and training. Making sure *we* are keeping *ours0elves* in check in this area is so important.

My wife has been such a blessing to me in this area. She encouraged me to walk into the house and relax without saying a word about what is out of place or what didn't get done. This allows me to let the kids come around and visit for a while before I begin pointing out what needs to be done. I also have found that my drive home from work is a wonderful opportunity to turn the radio or music off, and turn to God, so that I can *prepare my heart* to meet the needs of my family. Remember, home is our first priority and we live this out by being *ministers of the Lord* to them.

Imagine really *rejoicing* in your child, and being creative about finding ways to do that. Writing to them is a great way to communicate love! My wife was putting away some clothes in my older son's drawer and found every letter that I had ever written to him. Praise God they were good letters! I did not say, "You little brat . . ." Instead, the letters were filled with, "I love you. You're making me so proud. I am so happy to see your gifts and your talent in music." My wife and I cried as we read through them. He had saved every one, and so had my son Justin. God has given us such powerful influence as dads and moms! We need to use that power to bless and praise our children. It makes such a difference!

We need to *study* our children, to learn their strengths, and to praise them for their qualities and good deeds.

SELF-EXAMINATION
Do you struggle in this area? ❏ Yes ❏ No

If you do struggle in this area take some time right now and write down at least three strengths that you have seen in your children. Ask God to show you the best time and way to communicate this. It could be through a letter, or a conversation out on a special dinner. *Make it a point* in your devotional time to ask God to help you be observant of your children, and how to praise them.

_____
_____
_____
_____
_____

✓ACTION PLAN
Work together as husband and wife to encourage each other in this practice. Also, discuss some ways you can help each other in those challenging parenting moments. Write them down.

_____
_____
_____
_____
_____

DIG DEEPER: *FURTHER STUDY*

Look up the following Scriptures; write down what it says about rejoicing in the truth; what is good and how the principle(s) could apply to parenting.

Psalm 139:17-18 *"How precious also are Your thoughts to me, O God! How great is the sum of them! If I should count them, they would be more in number than the sand; when I awake, I am still with You."*

_____

_____

_____

Romans 12:9 *"Let love be without hypocrisy. Abhor what is evil. Cling to what is good."*

_____

_____

_____

1 Thessalonians 5:15 *"See that no one renders evil for evil to anyone, but always pursue what is good both for yourselves and for all."*

_____

_____

_____

3 John 4 *"I have no greater joy than to hear that my children walk in truth."*

_____

_____

_____

_____

11) NOT BEARING ALL THINGS

FACT FILE

Bears all things: bears, *stego* (Greek), means to hide, to conceal. Love hides the faults of others, or covers them up.[5] It keeps out resentment as the ship keeps out the water, or the roof the rain.[6]

---

5   Zodhiates, 1310.

6   Marvin Richardson Vincent, *Word Studies in the New Testament* (Bellingham, WA: Logos Research Systems, Inc., 2002), 1 Co 13:7.

Love bears all things, meaning we avoid criticizing or neglecting our children because they have failed to meet *our* expectations. Ever notice that we parents have certain expectations when raising our children? We expect them to talk, act and perform the way we want them to, so that they are not such an inconvenience. Parenting takes *time*, it is *work*, it takes *sacrifice*, and it is a "God" given task. Have you truly accepted this yet? If we are not careful, resentment can creep into our parenting style. Bearing all things in love means accepting our ministry as parents – the good, the bad, and the challenging – and behaving with godly love. This includes seeing our children's failures and faults as *opportunities* to train them, not to criticize or deliver harsh, self-righteous lectures.

True, it is hard work being a parent. But we must ask, does our difficult child know through our daily actions toward him/her that we accept them? Do we show a willingness to love them and work through that strong will? Do they see a willingness to give the extra time and energy? Or does he/she believe that "Mom and Dad don't like me, or like me less than my brother/sister"?

Does a five-year-old strong-willed child understand why he thinks and processes situations the way he does? Of course not. He does not understand why, when a parent says, "Don't cross that line," his thought is, "My parent doesn't think I am able to, so I must show them I can." They do not know why they are wired the way they are. When we are constantly getting angry, start resenting the way *God* made them and the extra work it takes to parent that child, the message is you love them less. Period. That is their perception.

Instead, we have got to say, "OK, God, You brought me this mule. I've got to accept this and endure this in Your power and might, not mine." Remember your transformation.

⌕ SELF-EXAMINATION

What has the Lord been revealing *in* you through this child that is not of God, how do you need to change?

_____

_____

_____

_____

Remember, our children are born foolish. It is the parents' *responsibility* to actively love, guide, teach, and discipline them through the different stages of life, without becoming resentful of their natural growth process and/or the personality God gave them. As this study progresses, we will give you Biblical tools to help lead your children to maturity, all to the glory of God.

DIG DEEPER: *FURTHER STUDY*

What principles can we gain from the following Scriptures that would help us with our parenting?

Romans 15:1 *"We who are strong have an obligation to bear with the failings of the weak, and not to please ourselves." (ESV)*

_____

_____

_____

_____

Galatians 6:2 *"Bear one another's burdens, and so fulfill the law of Christ".*

_____

_____

_____

_____

SELF-EXAMINATION

Do you have resentment because of the personality God gave your child/children?   ❑ Yes ❑ No

If so, write down the issues and then make a plan for responding to them in love.

_____

_____

_____

_____

_____

_____

_____

12) *NOT* BELIEVING OR HOPING ALL THINGS

FACT FILE

Believing: is *pisteuo* (Greek), and means having faith in, or to be firmly persuaded in something. It indicates that there is an attitude of expectant hope.

Love believes and hopes all things. The Biblical principle here is that love has a way of believing the best in people even when your feelings tell you otherwise. Believe is a verb, which calls for *action* no matter how we feel. The last principle we learned was to bear, or be willing to cover, our children's mistakes with love. Now we must believe and hope the best for them and maintain a hopeful attitude. We need a willingness to always *pursue* a trusting relationship, even when there has been dishonesty. Too often, I see parents doubting what their child says before they know the facts. I have heard from many parents, "My kid's a liar. I can put up with anything, but when they lie, ohhh."

I often will ask that parent, "Do you always ask for forgiveness from your spouse or child when you misrepresent God in your behavior toward them?" Jesus said, *"He who has My commandments and keeps them, it is he who loves Me. And he who loves Me will be loved by My Father, and I will love him and manifest Myself to him"* (John 14:21).

The perspective that lying is "the mother of all bad things to do" can exasperate our children and *provoke* them to continue that behavior. Yes, lying is a sin and needs to be corrected, but we cannot elevate lying above all other sins. Instead, we must simply unemotionally discipline them. You can have a rule that states, "If you lie, the consequences are double."

I have found that in cases where kids are constantly lying, the parents need to make the first changes. They must quit getting angry, being judgmental, and saying things like, "I don't trust you" or "I know I'm going to catch you." Love hopes *all* things, **not** doubts all things. Your mental attitude can actually influence you to constantly doubt your child, and even want to give up trying to help them. Entertaining thoughts like *"How many times will I have to correct them concerning this behavior?"* does not come from hoping all things, but comes from wanting to give up. This attitude, a love that believes and hopes all things, can only come from *God* through your *abiding relationship* with Him.

DIG DEEPER: *FURTHER STUDY*

What principles from the following Scriptures will help us parents to have hopeful and believing faith? Write them down and be specific.

Matthew 19:26 *"But Jesus looked at them and said to them, "With men this is impossible, but with God all things are possible."*

_____
_____
_____
_____
_____
_____

2 Corinthians 5:7 *"For we walk by faith, not by sight."*

_____
_____
_____
_____
_____
_____

Romans 5:5 *"Now hope does not disappoint, because the love of God has been poured out in our hearts by the Holy Spirit who was given to us."*

_____

_____

_____

_____

_____

✔ ACTION PLAN

Are there ways in which you have given up believing and hoping in your child?   ❑ Yes ❑ No

If so, write out the issues and take time with the Lord, asking Him to heal your unbelief and help you with a *plan* to reassure your children that God is going to work these things out.

_____

_____

_____

_____

_____

_____

_____

_____

WEEK 4: DAY 5

13) *NOT* ENDURING ALL THINGS

FACT FILE

Endure all things: to endure, *hupomeno* (Greek), means to abide under, to bear up under, suffer, as a load of miseries.[7] Also patient acquiescence, holding its ground when it can no longer believe nor hope.[8]

Love endures all things. This verb indicates that love abides, stays strong and holds its ground. This is not only important for the parent, but the parent must be able to encourage the child to stay strong.

---

7   Zodhiates, 1424.

8   Marvin Richardson Vincent, *Word Studies in the New Testament* (Bellingham, WA: Logos Research Systems, Inc., 2002), 1 Co 13:7.

Love does *not* give up, or tell a child that "we just can't take it anymore!" and then let the house run amuck. We cannot do that. We need to be faithful to support our children in all seasons of life. We should not play "head games," or treat them with contempt. We must maintain our responsibility as ministers, continuously exercising patience and disciplining them properly in love.

My son Justin never seemed to mind spending hours doing homework. Neither my wife nor I could relate to that; we both disliked homework when growing up. Nick, on the other hand, hated homework and tried to avoid it like the plague. From the time Nick hit junior high, all the way through the end of high school, if we did not sit down with him while he did his homework, he would never do it. So, every night my wife and I shared this often-unpleasant homework time with Nick; one of us would either finish the dinner, or do the dishes, while the other sat down and did homework with Nick.

A single mother came into my office complaining about the same situation. She said to me, "Every night when I come home from work, I'm so tired, but if I don't sit down with my son, he just dillydallies and takes one hour's worth of homework and makes it three hours. Every night I'm yelling and screaming at him and he won't change. It is ridiculous." Then she made a comparison which we should *never* do as parents, she said, "I've never had to sit down with my older son; he comes home and just does it. I'm so upset, what do I do to fix it?"

I calmly replied, "Sit down and do his homework with him." She said, "But aren't I supposed to train him?" My answer was, "Yes, but right now he needs you.

His actions are saying, 'Mom, I need you to sit down with me, I need your help, I need your structure in this area.'" I also told her, "You can't compare him to your older son. Instead, remind yourself every night 'this is my time with my son' and do his homework with him. What else are you doing that is more important?" The poor woman had spent the first eight years of this kid's life comparing him to his brother and being angry every night, instead of just sitting down and helping him with his homework.

We must endure these situations with our kids. Children who struggle academically and/or are strong-willed take *more* time and energy. The question for us parents is, "Do you accept the child God gave you and the ministry He has put before you to do?" He will give you the strength to do it if you ask Him and quit complaining.

Another way to endure with our children is spending *quality* time. How much one-on-one do you get with each child? This area takes creative effort, especially as they get older. When my children were teenagers, I learned to actively pursue them. It was easy when they were younger because they would pursue me. As a family, we often went camping, fishing and enjoyed other outdoor activities. But, as my children matured, their sphere of activity widened into activities that didn't include parents! Beware of taking this *personally*, being offended, and pulling away. Parenting is not a popularity contest; we will always be their parents, which will never change, but the *relationship* does change.

In order to spend time with our kids, we have to meet them where they are, and be willing to join the activities that they individually enjoy. Nick and I are both very physical, so finding activities we enjoy doing together was easy. But with Justin, it was a different story. I have always been active: riding motorcycles, surfing and diving. Justin likes to read, do puzzles, play video games, and enjoys acting. I had to adapt to Justin's interests in order to spend time with him. I *endured* his differences and *learned* to appreciate his interests. Years ago, I took up the hobby of sailing and Justin began to go with me. At first, he wasn't real excited, but we spent many hours doing it together. I had to make an effort to plan trips tailored to the interests of each unique child. Most of the time, these types of activities don't just happen. That puts the responsibility on us. And remember, *love* reaches out expecting nothing in return; we do these things for our children because we love them. Jesus is our example.

> **Matthew 20:28** *says, "...just as the Son of Man did <u>not</u> come to be served, but to <u>serve</u>, and to <u>give</u> His life a ransom for many.".*

My daughter, Katie, liked to jump on the trampoline. In the beginning I could do flips and twirls, however, by the time she was 7 years old, about fifteen minutes of jumping and bouncing was all my old knees could handle. But I endured and adjusted for her. If we love our children we need to <u>make</u> <u>time</u> to be with them.

✅ACTION PLAN

Take a moment, write out some of the activities that each of your children enjoys, see list below for ideas.

_____

_____

_____

_____

_____

_____

_____

_____

_____

How much time do you spend enjoying these activities with them? If you aren't write down a day that you are going to spend with him/her, make a commitment.

_____

_____

_____

Are you pursuing spending time with your children?   ❑ Yes ❑ No

Are you willing to participate in, and enjoy, activities that you would not ordinarily choose for the sake of spending time with your children?   ❑ Yes ❑ No

Stop right now and pray, asking God for His insight and help. If married, discuss this with your spouse and write down the things you can do to spend more one-on-one time with your children. You can use the suggested activities list below to get started.

_____

_____

_____

_____

_____

_____

_____

Suggested Activities:

Hiking	Kayaking	Flying kites
Swimming	Sewing or crafts	Diving
Bicycling	Walking the dog	Boating
Mountain biking	Board games	Canoeing
Window shopping	Card games	Fishing
Rock climbing	Computer games	Surfing
Sporting events	Skiing	Tea Parties
Jumping on a trampoline	Movies, plays, concerts, etc	

These are examples from my own family, as well as from my counseling with others. You must let the Lord speak to you personally about how the Biblical truths of 1Corinthians 13 should and can be lived out in your own home. Observe your children and their unique talents and interest, and I'm sure you can add your own activities to this list. Remember, this together time is for love and, as such, may be geared more to your child's interests than your own!

Do What Comes Unnaturally

Much of the time, problems raising our children come from ignorance and disobedience; we do not know how to discipline them properly, or how to view their failures, foolishness, and the choices they make. But, once we learn how to relate to them with godly love, apply principles of godly discipline, and work together as a team, much of our frustrations will be alleviated.

Love never fails. When someone mistreats you, God can empower you to do what comes *supernaturally,* not naturally. When someone does not live up to our expectations, we want to *react* in the flesh, the natural way. But God says, "No, as **My** *ministers,* I want you to *respond* in a supernatural way." Our example is in Christ, and the way He has and will always respond to us.

> **Ephesians 4:29-32** *"Let no corrupt word proceed out of your mouth, but what is good for necessary edification, that it may impart grace to the hearers. And do not grieve the Holy Spirit of God, by whom you were sealed for the day of redemption. Let all bitterness, wrath, anger, clamor, and evil speaking be put away from you, with all malice. And be kind to one another, tenderhearted, forgiving one another, even as God in Christ forgave you."*

This passage describes the kind of love that God has called us to, as parent ministers. Remember, if God gave us a command that He could not enable us to fulfill, that would make Him a liar. But He does not lie. If we are discouraged, fail, or find all this very difficult, God does not want us to feel condemned. Rather, He wants us to pray, and ask Him for the power to love our children the way we should. He tells us, *"Whatever you ask in My name, I will give you."* (John 16:23).

It is true that God chose us to be parents, knowing how foolish and selfish we are. But He does not do it with the idea that we will stay that way. He gives us His supernatural Word, but we must dig into it and build a strong foundation of faith, so the Word can *transform* our hearts. And God is always present to help us succeed, to guide and empower us. He declares our victory, through His promise, when He says, "I will give you the ability, through the power of the Holy Spirit, through your intimate relationship with Jesus, and faithfully taking responsibility when you fail to glorify Him through forgiveness, to accomplish every single command." (Philippians 4:13, paraphrased).

Praise God!

Week 5: Loving Communication - Part 3

WEEK 5: DAY 1

Introduction: Communication is Essential

FACT FILE

Communication: the act of communicating is the exchange of thought, message, or information.[1]

It is possible to communicate without saying a word; however, it is impossible to truly communicate without listening. When God gave us two ears, he had more in mind than just framing our faces. We have two ears and one mouth for a good reason.

If communication requires listening, then it also involves being attentive. So, to achieve loving communication with our children we must really listen to them attentively. Because situations requiring disciplinary action can produce strong emotions in both parent and child, it is very important to consider the effects of different types of communication.

Ways We Communicate

1. VISUALLY

The most powerful communication is expressed through facial expressions, or the messages that kids see on our faces. Statistics state that this accounts for 55 percent of our communication,[2] so we must be very aware of facial expressions when we are relating to our children.

Let me give you an example: driving home one night with your children in the back seat, somebody cuts in front of you, nearly causing you to swerve off the road. You speak out in frustration, "Oh, you stupid . . . blank, blank, blank," while your face reflects the anger you feel.

When you arrive home, the kids are buzzing from eating cookies and candy and do not want to get in bed.

---

1   *Webster's II New Riverside Dictionary Revised Edition, Office Edition*, Houghton Mifflin Company, 1996.

2   See Albert Mehrabian's Rule, http://www.businessballs.com/mehrabiancommunications.htm.

You tell them once, "Go to bed," and they will not, so you put on the same angry facial expression that appeared when the guy cut you off and yell, "I told you to get in your bed right now!" Your children's perception at that moment is that you see them, or value them, the same way you did that stranger who nearly ran you off the road. Ouch! Our facial expressions can be sinful and unloving, and are a major part of what we communicate: the stare, the glare, etc. We need to watch what "we say" with our faces.

FACT FILE

Countenance: (Hebrew) *paniym*, does have the literal meaning of *face* (Gen. 43:31; 1 Kings 19:13), but also means the reflection of a person's mood or attitude, such as being defiant (Jer. 5:3); ruthless (Deut. 28:50); joyful (Job 29:24); humiliated (2 Sam. 19:5); terrified (Isa. 13:8). The Scripture gives us examples of a bad countenance in (Matt. 6:16), and a good one in (Psalm 4:6).

Is an angry countenance common for you during discipline?　　❑ Yes ❑ No

DIG DEEPER: *FURTHER STUDY*

Read the following passages and write out how they may relate to you personally. Then write out a prayer to each one asking God to help you change this. Remember to be specific.

Proverbs 25:23 *"The north wind brings forth rain, And a backbiting tongue an angry countenance."*

_____
_____
_____
_____

Proverbs 14:29 *"He who is slow to wrath has great understanding, But he who is impulsive exalts folly."*

_____
_____
_____
_____

James 1:19–20 *"So then, my beloved brethren, let every man be swift to hear, slow to speak, slow to wrath; 20 for the wrath of man does not produce the righteousness of God."*

_____
_____
_____
_____

Proverbs 29:22 *"An angry man stirs up strife, And a furious man abounds in transgression."*

_____
_____
_____
_____

2. VOCALLY

Tone of voice comprises 38 percent of our communication.[3] When we raise our voice during or for discipline, we are communicating anger. Think about this: if we add together facial expressions and tone of voice, we get 93 percent! So, when we are twisting our faces with anger, resentment, or disappointment and elevating our voices, we are communicating at 93 percent in an unloving, sinful way. Why do you believe so many parents do this, and even make it a part of their discipline? Where does that come from? Let me tell you where it comes from: it comes from our flesh and the devil. This type of communication from parents has destroyed many a life. Remember, James 1:20 says, *"...for the wrath of man does not produce the righteousness of God."* If you think about it, there is an attitude (i.e., the state of mind toward something) behind your tone of voice and your facial expressions. Anger surfaces when you are *reacting* with your feelings and emotions, instead of *responding* in love.

⌕ SELF-EXAMINATION

Is raising your voice common during discipline?   ❏ Yes ❏ No

If so, take a moment and write out a prayer of repentance to the Lord.

_____
_____
_____
_____
_____

3. VERBALLY

Surprisingly, verbal communication accounts for only 7 percent of all communication.[4] For those who have picked up the bad habit of lecturing, may this fact help you quit. If you lecture all your children hear is blah, blah, blah, blah, blah. This bad habit erodes both your good relationship and your influence.

It is important for children to know what they did wrong and what the discipline is, but lengthy explanations of what you perceive their motives were or how it may affect their future is not effective discipline,

---

3   Mehrabian's Rule.

4   Mehrabian's Rule.

it is lecturing. In most cases parents are just blowing off steam or seeking revenge toward their child for making them do their job of parenting their child but these are wrong sinful motives.

As I stated before, a common question I ask parents when counseling is, *"On an average day, what percentage of one-on-one communication with your child is positive, and what percentage is negative?"*

Negative communication sounds like...
> *"Don't do that...Why did you do this?...I told you to clean your room...Pick up after yourself... Leave your sister alone...Take out the trash..."*

If a parent is communicating one-on-one with a child ten minutes per day, and 75% is negative, how much positive communication is taking place?

Positive communication sounds like...
> *"You look nice...How was school today...How are your friends...What would you like for dinner tonight..."*

Parents are the most *influential* people in a child's life. If the most influential person in your life primarily gave you orders, or lectured you, accused you, and talked down to you, how would you begin to perceive yourself?

As I said earlier, many teens tell me, "My parents don't love me, and they don't care about me." Many believe this because their parents are communicating negatively or sinfully on an ongoing basis. It is no wonder that so many kids are struggling with self-worth. A child's self-worth comes from how their parents show love, care, and value to them. When you and I misrepresent God on a daily basis, we create what I call the EDTNI syndrome: Emotionally Deprived Through Negative Input. So many kids are struggling with this. And those who are affected most negatively give in to all types of sinful temptations as they deal with their hurt. Eventually, when they become parents, they often repeat the same negative behavior with their own children.

SELF-EXAMINATION

Take a moment to consider your relationship with your children. Write out how many minutes of one-on-one communication you have with each child per day, and what percentage of that communication is negative and positive.

_____

_____

_____

_____

_____

_____

_____

_____

_____

Many adults are still struggling with emotional scars due to the negative treatment they received from their parents. If this is striking a cord with you, take a moment and turn to Appendix U, *Biblical Principles of Forgiveness and Reconciliation,* where you will learn about Biblical forgiveness and how to put the past behind you permanently.

WEEK 5: DAY 2

LOVING COMMUNICATION
1. IT STARTS WITH THE HEART

Read the following Scriptures a couple of times slowly noting what is being said about the heart.

> **Matthew 15:18** *"But those things which proceed out of the mouth come from the heart, and they <u>defile</u> a man."*

> **Matthew 12:35** *"A good man out of the good <u>treasure</u> of his heart brings forth good things, and an evil man out of the evil <u>treasure</u> brings forth evil things."*

There are valuable Biblical principles that we can learn from Jesus' teaching in these passages. In Matthew15:18, Jesus says that the words which proceed from your mouth can *defile* both you and others.

> **FACT FILE**
> **Defile:** means to pollute, render impure; or corrupt.

God is very concerned about what comes out of our mouths, but the bigger issue is the source of evil. In Matthew 15:19, God reveals a number of evil thoughts and deeds that may come from the human heart. What we need is a transformation of heart (Rom 12:1-2), so that what comes out of our mouths will then be good.

> **Romans 12:1–2** *"I beseech you therefore, brethren, by the mercies of God, that you present*

your bodies a living sacrifice, holy, acceptable to God, which is your reasonable service. And do not be conformed to this world, but be transformed by the renewing of your mind, that you may prove what is that good and acceptable and perfect will of God."

Matthew 12:35, states that we each have a treasure in our heart, which can be either good or evil. In this context, treasure means the storehouse of the mind; where thoughts and feelings are kept. Many of us have *"evil treasures,"* or issues that have not been resolved. Yes, when we get saved we have a new heart (Eze. 11:19; 18:31; 36:26; 2 Cor. 5:17), but this does not mean that the old habits of evil communication have vanished. There is a *process* of change as we reject the bad and develop "good treasure". This goes back to the idea of building on our strong foundation. As we seek God's will by putting the Word of God in our hearts, guess what is going to come out? Good things. *Day by day*, as we fellowship with God through study and prayer, we are building up our *"good treasure."* Only the Word can give us a definition of what is good and evil, and only God can truly change our hearts.

DIG DEEPER: *FURTHER STUDY*

Read the following passages, noting the examples of good and evil treasure, and the result of each.

Psalm 119:11 *"Your word I have hidden in my heart, that I might not sin against You."*

_____

_____

_____

_____

_____

Psalm 37:30 *"The mouth of the righteous speaks wisdom, and his tongue talks of justice."*

_____

_____

_____

_____

_____

Proverbs 10:20 *"The tongue of the righteous is choice silver; the heart of the wicked is worth little."*

_____

_____

_____

_____

_____

Proverbs 12:6 *"The words of the wicked are, 'Lie in wait for blood,' but the mouth of the upright will deliver them".*

_____
_____
_____
_____

✅ACTION PLAN

Since the beginning of this study, how has your daily devotional time been? Is it meaningful? ❏ Yes ❏ No
Consistent?   ❏ Yes ❏ No

If not write out a commitment and plan to change.

_____
_____
_____
_____
_____
_____

2. IT COMES FROM OUR VALUE OF OTHERS

Loving communication is Christ-centered, not self-centered. It is the decision to place value on another person. *"Behold, children are a gift of the Lord"* (Ps. 127:3 NASB). The word *gift* is also translated *heritage* (NKJV, ESV), which suggests something that is passed down by a will, or legal document, as an inheritance (i.e. property) (Ez 48:29). In this case, it is children that have been given to us by the Lord. This means that toddlers are a gift, and teens, and also children that are not biologically yours.

Let me give you an example of valuing others. If you invited your pastor over for dinner, would you find out what his favorite dish is before he came? Would you make sure your house is clean? Would you be very careful not to say the wrong thing so you didn't offend him? Would you make sure that your kids were going to behave? How would you dress? Of course, you would put your best foot forward because you value your pastor. I am sure your pastor is a good guy, and is worth valuing—but not more than your children.

Our kids are not dumb; they know when you are devaluing them. Sadly, many parents do not even consider their actions. This is not OK. Valuing someone is a *choice*, and God's Word says this child is a gift from God. Because He has placed high value upon our kids, we must choose to always treat them that way, and take responsibility when we don't by asking for forgiveness.

DIG DEEPER: *FURTHER STUDY*

Read the following Scriptures and write down the parental attitudes about children.

> **Genesis 33:4-5** *"But Esau ran to meet him (Jacob), and embraced him, and fell on his neck and kissed him, and they wept. 5 And he lifted his eyes and saw the women and children, and said, 'Who are these with you?' So he said, 'The children whom God has graciously given your servant'."*

_____

_____

_____

_____

> **Genesis 48:8-9** *"Then Israel saw Joseph's sons, and said, 'Who are these?' 9 Joseph said to his father, 'They are my sons, whom God has given me in this place.' And he said, 'Please bring them to me, and I will bless them'."*

_____

_____

_____

_____

SELF-EXAMINATION

Are there times or situations that you are devaluing your children by your behavior?   ❑ Yes   ❑ No

If so write down the times or situations this happens and then ask God to help you change, to change *your* perspective to be godly.

_____

_____

_____

_____

3. IT IS A LEARNED SKILL.

Loving communication is a choice to be Christ-centered. The Bible instructs us to *"Put on the Lord Jesus Christ..."* (Rom. 13:14). It is a command and a responsibility. Putting on Christ is a conscious decision we have to make ALL the time whether we feel like it or not. This type of love can only come from Him, which takes us back to our strong foundation. 1 John 2:10, says, *"He who loves his brother abides in the light, and there is no cause for stumbling in him."* Abiding in the light means abiding in Christ, which means dying to self will and becoming more alive to Christ's will.

Many parents know that they need to stop sinful communication with their children, yet do nothing about it. It is God's will that we communicate love, so asking Him to change us is a guarantee that He will work to bring it about. The Scripture says, *"The heart of the righteous studies how to answer..."* (Prov. 15:28), indicating that righteous communication is **learned** and deliberate. *"The heart of the wise teaches his mouth, and adds learning to his lips"* (Prov 16:23), also confirms that communication skills are **progressive** and can be learned. Notice again that the mouth reveals what is in the heart. God's blessing comes through righteous communication because we are being obedient to His will (Eph. 4:29). And this communication will be persuasive, accomplishing its purpose. It is through loving communication and proper training that we will successfully persuade our children to do what is right.

⌕ SELF-EXAMINATION

Take a moment to ponder the Scriptures above. Write down what these verses mean to you personally in communicating with your children?

_____

_____

_____

_____

_____

In order to establish loving communication, we must begin to look at our children through a different set of lenses. God wants us to see our children through His eyes (as a gift) and through what His Word says. I love this statement from Christian author, Warren Wiersbe, "Ministry takes place when divine resources meet human needs through loving channels to the glory of God."[5] Parenting is a ministry, and our communication needs to come from the divine resources that God has given us. But it must always be with the intent of glorifying Him, reflecting His character. Our divine resource is that abiding relationship in Christ, the rock-solid foundation upon which we build.

Dedicate Your Children to God

"Train up a child in the way he should go, and when he is old he will not depart from it" (Prov. 22:6). Many people think this passage offers some type of guarantee, but it does not always work out that way. When interpreting Proverbs, we must understand that phrases like this are probabilities, not guarantees; however, we must put forth maximum effort to raise our children in the will of God, and pray without ceasing for their development in righteousness.

---

5   *On Being a Servant of God*, by Warren Wiersbe; Thomas Nelson Publishers, 1993.

You can be working the principles faithfully and a child could still choose to live a sinful or immoral lifestyle. Why? Because God gives them free will, or choice, just like He gives us.

There is **no** guarantee that our children will turn out right. That is not the emphasis of what God's Word says here.

> ### FACT FILE
>
> **Train up:** in the original Hebrew is *chanak,* which means to dedicate or set aside for Divine service.

It was used of Solomon and Israel dedicating the house of the Lord (1 Kings 8:63). In other words, we need to be *mindful* at all times that our children are not our own, but the Lord's, and we need to *treat* them that way—always. We must dedicate them back unto the Lord.

When we bring our babies up on Sunday mornings to dedicate them, it is an important event. We stand before the entire congregation, saying, "We are publicly dedicating this child back unto You, Lord. He/she is not mine, they are Yours. I believe this and want to treat them that way as long as they are in my care." That is what God is saying in this passage found in Proverbs 22:6: dedicate your children unto the Lord, and remember they are His, not yours. But this dedication is not a disclaimer, as in, "Here Lord, they are Yours now." Within this dedication is the awareness of a *God-given responsibility* to love, guide and train our children. As Ephesians 6:4 states, we parents are to *"...bring them up in the training and admonition of the Lord."*

We will not be held responsible for the choices our children make, but for the choices **we** *make in raising them.* We are often so concerned about the mistakes our kids are going to make, and how they will embarrass us, that it dictates the way we treat them—or should I say, do not love them. We must understand that the value of our children comes from what God has said, not their personalities, failures, or their stage of life. God said, "This is My gift to you."

Many times I felt like wrapping up my oldest son and sending him back with a note: "God, I don't want this one. He is too much work." But I didn't have a choice in the matter, did I? Neither do you. God knew exactly what we needed. There is no exchange policy.

Does this change if you are a single parent, blended family, foster parent, or grandparent raising kids? No, it does not.

Let's pause for a reality check.

Did you know that your children are gifts from God? ❏ Yes ❏ No

Do you always treat them that way? ❏ Yes ❏ No

That is our battleground. It is as if God is saying, "Here's My gift to you, complete with instructions on how I want you to handle it. Follow my directions because I'll be watching you." Should we try our best, and desire to do what God says? Absolutely!

The instruction manual that God gives us on how to treat our children is the Holy Bible. And the Scriptures say, "Love them; treat them as a gift *always*."

Respect Each Unique Personality

The second part of Proverbs 22:6 says, *". . . in the way he should go."* "The way he should go" is a Hebrew idiom that literally means, "upon the mouth of his ways," or according to the demands of his or her personality, conduct, stage of life, or natural bent. What this means is that we are to treat each one of our kids as a unique gift, embracing their individual personality. God wants us to adapt to the personalities He has given them.

Beginning with Adam and Eve, the first family, we see evidence of different personalities. Cain was self-willed and determined to go his own way—a strong-willed mule. Abel, on the other hand, loved the Lord and was a sensitive, more compliant child.

Isaac's sons, Jacob and Esau, were twins—same mom, same dad. Jacob was a momma's boy, smooth skinned, and often in the kitchen. Esau was a man's man, rough, a hunter, a really gruff guy. They were twins with different personalities, very different interests. God has been doing this from the beginning of time.

It is interesting that parents who receive a strong-willed, or handicapped, child often feel that they have gotten the short end of the stick. God knows what He is doing, and He does not make mistakes. Do you believe that?

I want to review this again so it is cemented into your minds. The Bible says, *". . . As the LORD lives, who made our very souls . . ."* (Jer. 38:16). God is the creator of the soul, which is the seat of the mind, will, and emotions. You and I had something to do with the color of our child's eyes, hair, their size, and the color of their skin, but when it comes to their mind, will, emotions, and personality we had nothing to do with it. Yes, they will pick up our traits, but their mind, will, and emotions are given by God, and He does not make mistakes.

We must quit blaming ourselves, our spouse, or our parents. Instead, blame God for the bent that your child has, for his/her personality, because God is the one and only Creator. Psalm 139:13 says, *"For You formed my inward parts; You covered me in my mother's womb."*

God created your soul; He breathed life into you. The Word says that *all* of us are *"fearfully and wonderfully made"* (Ps. 139:14). When we get angry and resentful at our kids, and begin to misrepresent Christ, we are acting like He made a mistake. Colossians 3:21 says, *"Fathers, do not provoke your children, lest they become discouraged."* Yet many parents provoke their children by not practicing biblical love, and not considering them to be a gift from God.

FACT FILE

Discouraged: *athumeo* (Greek), is a very insightful word. The root of this word is *thumos,* which means violent motion or passion of mind, such as anger, wrath or indignation. By putting the *"a"* (alpha) in front of the word, it becomes a negative, means "without". So it means without passion, despondent, disturbed in mind, and indicates loss of courage.

God gives us a clear picture of the natural consequences when we parents practice unloving communication with our children. If your child is discouraged, one of the most common reasons is our negative influence. We have the ability to drive them to despair. This is NOT to blame everything on parents, but we do play a key role in their lives as they are growing up, for good or evil.

WEEK 5: DAY 3

Different Seasons

There is a time and season for all things, (Ecclesiastes 3:1), which includes the "terrible twos" and even the difficult season of adolescence. God designed these seasons, it is not a mistake. Even though Proverbs 22:6 is not a guarantee of success, it clearly indicates that we need to study each child, adapting to their unique personality, being willing to accept the fact that one may need more instruction, discipline, and time than another. Some are going to take a lot more time and energy. When we follow the will of God in our parenting, we are not provided a guarantee, but a promise to receive all the grace we need to do it correctly.

SELF-EXAMINATION

Take a moment and reflect on this truth. Perhaps you believe that God made a mistake by giving you that child. So I urge you to stop now, before you continue with this study, and write out your confession to the Lord. Ask God for the strength to see your child's unique personality as His perfect will.

_____

_____

_____
_____
_____
_____
_____

We must always keep in mind the influential power God has given us over our kids, especially us dads. Our influence is like no one else's. Always remember that.

Our children's minds are like tape recorders, and for the first twelve or thirteen years they are on "record." But when they hit adolescence, they switch to "playback". At that point, we are often just reaping what we sowed over and over during previous years.

If we truly love God and our desire is to serve Him, we will pay no attention to the distinctions of a child's individuality, personality, failures, or stages of life. If our desire is to please the Lord and do it His way, these things will not dictate how we react to them. As a minister for the Lord, we must not be ruled by our natural temperament, but by God's Word and the Holy Spirit.

DIG DEEPER: *FURTHER STUDY*

Take a moment and carefully read James 3:17-18. How do these truths relate to your communication with your child?

> **James 3:17-18** *"But the wisdom that is from above is first pure, then peaceable, gentle, willing to yield, full of mercy and good fruits, without partiality and without hypocrisy. Now the fruit of righteousness is sown in peace by those who make peace."*

_____
_____
_____
_____
_____

My son, Nick, was a strong-willed child from the day of his birth. I still remember watching my wife deliver him. The pregnancy and even the delivery were so hard, it was scary. He was even stubborn about being born! I could just imagine him in there screaming, "No, I'm not ready to come out!"

My wife struggled for almost nine hours, then finally the doctor picked up some scary-looking forceps; I immediately began getting queasy. He started to pull really hard, and all the while I was thinking, "Hey Doc, you're going to pull his head off!" Suddenly I heard, "Pop!" and there was Nick's head. There was no spanking needed; he came out screaming, telling everybody right from the start, "I'm in control and I am angry at you all."

I cut his umbilical cord, then the nurse picked him up and I will never forget what happened next; as she placed him on the scale, my son thrust his arms, arched his back and almost flipped over. The nurse cried out, "Oh my gosh!" and jumped back. That was the first sign we were in trouble!

From the time he was one year old, he would not take a nap. Unless he was really sick, he did not sleep during the day. The minute the sun was up, he was up. He had more energy than any human being I ever knew. He was also bent and determined, "I'm gonna rule and do what I want, when I want." That is the way God wired him. He is a true strong-willed child.

Yes, parenting *is* a ministry. It is not always easy, or convenient, and can be downright exhausting. Sometimes the daily grind can push a parent to the edge of insanity, but raising our children is one of the most important and rewarding things we will do in this lifetime. Our obedience to the Lord, and the sacrifices we make, will be turned into blessings.

To be a minister means to go beyond our natural selves - our weaknesses, prejudices and selfish expectations – and to operate by the power of the Holy Spirit.

- How can we love our children who don't always show love in return?

- How do we keep our own temperaments from clashing with our kids' temperaments when they disobey?

- How do we trust God's perfect plan in our transformation when He is using our children's personality or failures?

Apart from a parent's submission to Christ, this is absolutely impossible!

REASONS WE FAIL TO LOVE

Parents beware: "**The battle is on**"! God designed the family unit and desires to use it for His glory; therefore, Satan has made families a target for destruction. As parents, it is vital that we understand the battleground, a place where Satan would like to stop the godly transformation of parents as well as the rearing of godly children. We may erroneously believe that it is *'them'* (the kids) against *'us'* (the parent), rather than being alert to the tactics of our real enemy.

The Bible teaches that our battle is spiritual, and our enemy is Satan (Eph. 6:12), not our children or our spouse! Let us look at four common reasons why parents fail in the area of loving communication:

1. **Unforgiveness:** Not forgiving someone that has offended or sinned against you.
2. **The Set Up:** Not realizing that the source of many negative thoughts is satanic.
3. **Persecution:** Feeling self-pity, rather than seeing trials (with our children) as part of our growth in righteousness.
4. **Selfishness:** Shirking responsibility by not being a minister (servant for Christ) to your family.

1. UNFORGIVENESS

Among the ways that we fail to love, the most common is unforgiveness. We do this by storing hurts, or voids from our past.

FACT FILE

Voids: something that has been left out. For example, a child has certain developmental emotional needs that must be nurtured through loving authority, with consistent proper discipline. If these needs are compromised and/or not provided, a void is created within the child. This often occurs because parents do not understand their God-given responsibilities, or the extent of their influence for good or bad. Most children cannot identify what is missing, what the void is, but they will instinctively try to fill it with something. For example, a lack of real love and proper discipline can make a child vulnerable to addictions and/or emotional and psychological problems that lead to destructive behavior. As you move through these lessons, you will receive biblical instruction which, *when followed*, can produce a healthy relationship with your child and also an emotionally healthy person in your child.

FACT FILE

Hurts: As explained in a previous chapter, harboring bitterness toward parents, an ex-spouse, children, current spouse, or whomever, blocks the transformation of character that God desires for you. Bitterness cuts us off from the grace of God needed to walk and grow spiritually, and causes us to contaminate others. Hebrews 12:15 says, "*...looking carefully lest anyone fall short of the grace of God; lest any root of bitterness springing up cause trouble, and by this many become defiled.*"

Just as God created physical laws to govern the universe, such as gravity, the Bible contains God's spiritual laws designed to govern all mankind, believers as well as non-believers. We do not think about it, but all these forces are at work every single day. And God's spiritual laws are as absolute and non-negotiable as His physical laws. Just as we understand gravity, and would not jump from a ten-story building, when we follow spiritual principles, there is safety on the paths of righteousness, and we experience God's blessings by living in His promises.

DIG DEEPER: *FURTHER STUDY*

Read the following passages of Scripture and describe (write out) the consequences God brings.

Romans 2:8–9 *"but to those who are self-seeking and do not obey the truth, but obey un-righteousness—indignation and wrath, 9 tribulation and anguish, on every soul of man who does evil, of the Jew first and also of the Greek."*

_____

_____

_____

_____

Hebrews 12:5–6 *"And you have forgotten the exhortation which speaks to you as to sons: "My son, do not despise the chastening of the LORD, Nor be discouraged when you are rebuked by Him; 6 For whom the LORD loves He chastens, And scourges every son whom He receives."*

_____

_____

_____

_____

Galatians 6:7 *"Do not be deceived, God is not mocked; for whatever a man sows, that he will also reap."*

_____

_____

_____

_____

Forgiveness is one of God's spiritual laws. I have found that the most common way a parent fails to love a child, or communicate love, is by UN-forgiveness. Often, parents are still suffering from the negative experiences of their own childhood. They were treated in an unloving, angry way, and may still be harboring bitterness or hurt. But deliverance is available, as in 2 Corinthians 5:17, *"Therefore, if anyone is in Christ, he is a new creation; old things have passed away; behold, all things have become new."* We are given this wonderful promise that once we are saved, our life becomes new. This means new abilities, new potential for righteousness and in no way indicates that past issues no longer have any affect upon us. Growing spiritually is work, and a process of applying Biblical principles, plus depending on Christ's nature within us will be our strength.

I say *biblical* principles because we deal with hurt in various ways. For instance, a natural self-defense mechanism is to repress the memory of past hurts, and act like they never happened. We try to follow that old adage that says, "time heals all wounds". But the Bible teaches that to *be healed,* we must *forgive* those who offended us; face the truth and release others from blame. When we do not forgive, a root of bitterness settles into our heart, which troubles us and defiles those close to us, including our children! When parents yell, judge, lecture, and or do not follow through with discipline, it is often an indication that they have forgiveness issues with their own parents or, if they are treating their children with the same harshness, or abuse that they received.

Because we live in a fallen world, we are *sinners* who were *parented by sinners*. Many adults in the body of Christ carry hurts, or voids from homes where there was drug use, abuse, divorce, rejection, molestation, mistreatment, neglect and/or abandonment, and lack of proper loving discipline. In fact, many will testify that it was the trauma of childhood that caused them to seek Christ.

When we are hurt emotionally, especially by a parent who has tremendous influence over us, it can create various negative and destructive, even addictive, behaviors. Many adults I have worked with have confessed that from adolescence, they became involved with drugs, alcohol, pornography, and unhealthy relationships while trying to cope with hurts and voids. Most had no idea why they were doing it, or what was the root cause.

Many youth today, when they hit adolescence, are struggling due to lack of love, affection, and correct parenting; this has created voids and hurts, which many are attempting to fix with drugs, pornography, unhealthy relationships, anorexia, bulimia, overeating, and the many other counterfeit *"antidotes"* that Satan provides. All too often, counselors focus on correcting bad behaviors and choices, instead of looking to God's provision of forgiveness to take the pain away. It is possible to become a Christian, and repent of destructive behavior, still not understanding or addressing the root cause and allowing the stronghold to remain.

If you are stuck in this rut, unable to grow in Christ, repeating the sinful, unloving habits of your parents, then examine yourself and ask the Lord to help you work through the pain in your past. This is not to blame anyone for our behavior, but to find understanding as to why we are stuck, in this "stronghold."

Thankfully, there is a Biblical antidote for past hurts or voids in our lives, it is found in God's Word. First of all, to *forgive* means to let go or send away; this is what Christ has done with our sins (2 Cor. 5:21). He paid the price to redeem us, and paid the price for our sins at the cross (Eph. 1:7). When God forgives, He casts *"all our sins into the depths of the sea"* (Micah 7:19); and *"As far as the east is from the west, So far has He removed our transgressions from us"* (Ps. 103:12); and He says, *"I, even I, am He who blots out your transgressions for My own sake; And I will not remember your sins"* (Isaiah 43:25, cf. Jer. 31:34). He no longer holds our sins against us. He does NOT meditate upon them because He makes a choice to remember them no more. God is omniscient (all-knowing); He does not forget, but He makes a choice to cast our sins into the sea - true forgiveness.

The Bible commands that we forgive others as God forgives us. Colossians 3:13 says, *"bearing with one another, and forgiving one another, if anyone has a complaint against another; even as Christ forgave you, so you also must do."* *Forgiving* is an imperative and, therefore, we have the command to forgive. *Complaint* means faultfinding, blaming or holding grudges. Our human nature is to hold grudges and/or "stuff" bad memories (meaning to hold down, suppress, or ignore), and make excuses for our parent's behavior: "I know they loved me and did the best they could", or "it's better now and I don't want to rock the boat by bringing this old stuff up." But only through forgiveness can we be freed from what was done or not done. The standard for our forgiveness is *"as Christ forgave you,"* we are to forgive. We must choose to cast the offence into the sea of forgetfulness. If bitter thoughts return, we refuse to meditate on them, rather dismiss them as already forgiven.

This principle is laid out in what is traditionally known as the Lord's Prayer (Matt. 6:9-13). Verse 12 says, *"... forgive us our debts, as we forgive our debtors."* We are to pray, *"Lord forgive me my sins as I forgive those who sin against me."* This prayer provides a pattern for us when communing with the Lord, and is right in the middle of Jesus' teaching of the Sermon on the Mount (Matt. 5-7). When we are asking God for His grace and to forgive our sins, to have mercy and compassion on us, there is a direct connection to us receiving and having mercy and compassion on those who have sinned against us. We must be willing to forgive.

FACT FILE

There are basically two types of ways we carry out sin, the sin of,

Commission: which means that we sin acting out of our own authority. God says, "No, do not do that," and we do it anyway. Example: God says, "Don't steal" (Eph 4:28), but we steal.

Omission: which means that we sin by not doing what is right by God, He commands us to do something, and *we* decide not to do it or, out of ignorance we treat our children according to what *we* feel is best, NOT doing God's will. Another example: God says to forgive, but we refuse to.

Note: For the Christian, ignorance of sin is no excuse, whether it is the sin of commission, or the sin of omission. God has given us His Word so we may know what God's will is, and what is not. This is why it is so important to be in His Word, abiding in Christ.

But what if <u>we make a choice</u> not to forgive? Verses following the Lord's Prayer state, *"For **if** you forgive men their trespasses, your heavenly Father will also forgive you. But **if** you do not forgive men their trespasses, neither will your Father forgive your trespasses"* (Matt. 6:14-15). This is a fundamental principle in Christianity, and many times it is overlooked. Please notice the "if" clause, this means there is a condition to forgiveness, both positive (v 14) and negative (v 15). The *positive* is that "if" we make a choice to forgive others, He will forgive us. That is a promise. Romans 4:7 says, *"Blessed are those whose lawless deeds are forgiven, and whose sins are covered."* The *negative* is that "**if**" we make a choice not to forgive, God will not forgive us. This also is a promise, but what does it mean?

You must understand that this is *not* a condition for salvation. It does NOT mean "If you forgive someone else, God will forgive and save you; if you do not, He will not." Jesus is talking about *believers* coming to Him and asking to forgive their sin. If they chose not to obey, it will affect their fellowship with God, His empowering grace, and their sense of feeling forgiven them-selves. The Bible says, *"If we confess our sins, He is faithful and just to forgive us our sins and to cleanse us from all unrighteousness"* (1 John 1:9). Once we confess and obey we are restored to fellowship.

So we see, an unforgiving heart hinders our fellowship with God and man, and will bring chastisement. The unmerciful response of the unforgiving servant (Matt 18:21-35) is an example. A king called a servant to pay a debt so large it was virtually impossible; the servant fell down before the king and begged for mercy. The king had compassion and forgave him the whole amount. Then, the same servant went out and demanded payment from a servant who owed him. When this servant begged for patience, the forgiven servant cast his debtor into prison. When the king heard about it, he was so angry at the unthankful, hardhearted man that he delivered him to the torturers for chastisement until he would pay all. Jesus said, *"So My heavenly Father also will do to you if each of you, <u>from his heart</u>, does not **forgive** his brother his trespasses* (Matt 18:35)." When God forgives our sins in Christ, we are forgiven an unpayable debt, so we must forgive others or chastisement will follow.

There are beliefs about forgiveness with no biblical basis, but are more related to emotions. When God speaks about "forgiveness," He commands us to forgive in spite of our feelings. Feelings are unstable and will not lead to true forgiveness. Let's face it, going to a parent and telling them God has revealed some hurts and voids from your childhood may be extremely difficult. When you have been hurt by someone and/or harbor bitterness towards that individual, it may seem that bringing up something negative will jeopardize the current relationship. But you need to remember, you are not going with a "complaint", but with a heart of forgiveness (a gift). It can be challenging, but we need to be obedient and trust God.

Read the following verses.

> **Luke 14:26-27** *"If anyone comes to Me and does not hate his father and mother, wife and children, brothers and sisters, yes, and his own life also, he cannot be My disciple. 27 And whoever does not bear his cross and come after Me cannot be My disciple."*

It is important to understand what Jesus is saying here. The word *hate*, simply means, "to love less"; the command is to love Jesus above everyone. These verses apply to situations just like this. When the Lord reveals that we need to forgive someone, our alliance to Jesus is tested. If we love Jesus supremely, then our bitterness, stubbornness or human sentiments for how it may affect that person now will NOT hinder us from being obedient to God's desire to set us free. It is a FAITH issue.

God does not say that the offender will acknowledge, take responsibility and/or ask forgiveness after you have approached them. Many times people go with the expectation that the offender will fess up and admit wrongdoing. But they cannot be *expected* to be of the same mind; they may still be blinded and or hardened. Your offender may want to argue, deny and or justify their actions. You must remember it is Jesus alone that is going to heal and fill those voids not your offender. The offenders words or actions is not what brings the healing, it is your obedience to God by His grace alone that you are healed. I have witnessed many people getting saved through this process, and/or entire families entering a reconciliation process.

God says that in spite of a person's disposition and or circumstances, we simply must forgive. Romans 12:18 says, *"If it is possible, as much as depends on you, live peaceably with all men."* It is our responsibility to be the reconciler, to live at peace as best as we can.

You can do it in a letter, by telephone, via email, or you can do it in person.

It is hard to forgive, but it is harder not to forgive. A readiness to forgive others indicates that we have truly repented and received God's forgiveness. A broken heart toward God cannot be a hard heart toward others. Pride, fear and loving God less are the real reasons we will not forgive others. Refusing to repent, demanding rights, and defending yourself are indications that selfish pride is ruling your life, rather than the Lord. If fears and "what-ifs" are controlling you, pray for the faith to trust and obey God. Matthew 18:21-35 warns that an unforgiving heart will put us in an emotional prison.

See Appendix U for more detail on Forgiveness and Reconciliation.

 ACTION PLAN

Write out your plan and commitment to forgive someone if this applies to you.

_____

_____

_____

_____

_____

Set a date here to when you will get this done. Date: _____

WEEK 5: DAY 4

2. THE SET UP

Another common reason we fail to love our children is persecution/ opposition from Satan, or one of his demons. Ephesians 6:11 says, *"Put on the whole armor of God, that you may be able to stand against the **wiles** of the devil."*

> **FACT FILE**
>
> **Wiles-** is *methodia* (Greek), which comes the English word *method*, indicating craftiness, cunning, and deception. The term was often used of a wild animal that cunningly stalks and then unexpectedly pounces on its prey. Satan's evil schemes are built around stealth and deception.[6]

The enemy has been around since before time began; remember he tempted the first family (Adam and Eve) to fall into sin, and it worked (Gen. 3:1-7). His plan has not changed; the enemy is devising ways to attack us, and to bring distractions, dissensions and divisions into the home. This is what I call **The Set Up**. He is in the business of "setting us up" for failure.

DIG DEEPER: *FURTHER STUDY*

Read the following Scripture and tell in your own words what kind of war we are fighting, and what WE are supposed to do about it.

> **Ephesians 6:12-13** *"For we do not wrestle against flesh and blood, but against principalities, against powers, against the rulers of the darkness of this age, against spiritual hosts of wickedness in the heavenly places. Therefore take up the whole armor of God, that you may be able to withstand in the evil day, and having done all, to stand."*

---

6   John MacArthur, *Ephesians* (Chicago: Moody Press, 1996), 338.

_____
_____
_____
_____
_____
_____
_____

Be constantly aware that you are in the midst of warfare, and your heart and mind is the battleground. We must weigh every thought that comes into our minds against God's Word, *"...bringing every thought into captivity to the obedience of Christ"* (2 Cor. 10:5). *Bring captive* means to capture or subdue a prisoner and lead him away into captivity. In this context, it is capturing our ungodly thoughts, and making them obedient to Christ and His Word. Satan hates us, and hates our kids, and the last thing he wants us to do is successfully represent Christ to our children.

Satan wants us to be mean and harsh, and to use our God-given influence for his evil will. When a Christian man or woman misrepresents Christ at home, and shows contempt towards their kids, they can become a tool to push them right into the hands of Satan. Sadly, many Christians are doing just that without realizing it.

What we must do is find God's heart in the midst of our thinking and put to death anything that is not of Him. Once we become a Christian, the Bible says, *"we have the mind of Christ"* (1 Cor. 2:16). In other words, we now have the Spirit of God dwelling in us (Rom. 8:9), which guides us through the Word to be like Christ.

⌕ SELF-EXAMINATION

So, why is it important to be IN the Word each day?

_____
_____
_____
_____
_____

Remember this: our mind receives thoughts from three sources. The first source is our own soul, psyche or self. These are thoughts related to our own needs, feelings, opinions, etc. We know when our thoughts originate from our own soul because they are dominated with words like *I, me or myself*. For example, *"I don't like having to deal with my strong willed child," "I want to have my own time," "I _____,"* you fill in the blank. These are our own thoughts and feelings. The Bible clearly says that our mind has to be transformed

(Rom. 12:2), renewed (Eph. 4:23), and guided by the Word of God, because it *"is a discerner of the thoughts and intents of the heart"* (Heb. 4:12).

Our minds can also receive thoughts or messages from the Holy Spirit. God's Word teaches us in 1 Corinthians 2:12 that, *"Now we have received, not the spirit of the world, but the Spirit who is from God, that we might know the things that have been freely given to us by God."*

As we walk in an abiding relationship with Christ, He fills our hearts with the truths of His Word. As we meditate on His righteousness, our minds become open to the Holy Spirit and we hear words of guidance, encouragement, wisdom and instruction. We can know when we have received a thought from the Holy Spirit because it is *scriptural*, *true*, *edifies* and *draws us to the Lord* and is *never contrary* to His Word. How comforting to know that, as children of God, we are not left to our own understanding. God desires to speak to us and will speak to us through His Word and by the ministry of the Holy Spirit.

Finally, our minds receive thoughts from *demons*. Even believers who love the Lord Jesus can experience spiritual oppression, having demonic thoughts bombard their minds. Peter is a perfect example.

> **Matthew 16:22-23** *"Then Peter took Him aside and began to rebuke Him, saying, 'Far be it from You, Lord; this shall not happen to You!' But He turned and said to Peter, 'Get behind Me, Satan! You are an offense to Me, for you are not mindful of the things of God, but the things of men.'"*

Please notice that Jesus rebuked Peter because he was *"not mindful of the things of God."* Peter wanted to stop Jesus from going to the cross, but Jesus recognized that these thoughts originated from Satan and needed to be dealt with immediately.

We know that a thought has demonic origin when it falls into one of the following categories:

Pray right now and ask God to reveal if any of these categories are affecting your thought life.

SELF-EXAMINATION

1. Lies
"...the devil...does not stand in the truth because there is no truth in him. Whenever he speaks a lie, he speaks from his own {nature} for he is a liar and the father of lies." John 8:44.

What was revealed to you?

_____

_____
_____
_____
_____

2. Condemnation, or accusations against ourselves and/or others

"...the devil and Satan...the accuser of our brethren, has been thrown down, he who accuses them before our God day and night." Revelation 12:9,10.

What was revealed to you?

_____
_____
_____
_____

3. Temptations to sin

"And the tempter came and said to Him, "If You are the Son of God, command that these stones become bread." Matthew 4:3.

What was revealed to you?

_____
_____
_____
_____

When we are tempted with lying thoughts (opposed to Biblical truth), condemnation, or invitations to sin against God and others, it is certain that we are experiencing spiritual warfare. We cannot avoid the fiery darts of the evil one (See Ephesians 6:16); however, we can control what we do with those thoughts. Again, God says that we must take every thought that comes into our mind and weigh that thought against the Word of God. If a thought does not *pass the test*, God says we must purge it from our mind immediately.

Bringing *every* thought captive is a *discipline* that must be practiced continually. Sin is conceived in your mind before you act upon the temptation; therefore, you must, if you are pursuing holiness, practice this discipline. God gives us a very specific checklist in the following Scripture.

Philippians 4:8 *"Finally, brethren, whatever things are **true**, whatever things are **noble**, whatever things are **just**, whatever things are **pure**, whatever things are **lovely**, whatever* *things are of **good report**, if there is any **virtue** and if there is anything **praiseworthy**—medi-tate on these things."*

If we are ignorant of this battle and or not *actively* fighting it, it will be the enemy's opportunity to come against our families. Keep in mind; the enemy is always scheming, plotting to find some method to make us fall as parents.

The following story illustrates this truth. As you read, highlight or underline where ungodly thoughts come in, how the enemy is working. We have studied the difference between *reacting* to a circumstance, or *responding* in love. Remember *responding* takes *thought* (think first), *self-control* (bending our will to the Holy Spirit), *time*, and is not dictated by feelings, or emotions. Try to note when reacting, or responding occurs.

Years ago, I went to pick up Nick from a junior high youth group he was attending. I got there early and was waiting in the church parking lot when an old friend arrived to pick up his son. When he saw me, he jumped out of his car and ran up to my window.

> *"Hey Craig, did you hear what happened? A group of kids, including your son and mine, ditched youth group tonight and are down the street at some girl's house playing basketball. Man, when my son gets here, I'm gonna really let him have it!"*

When I asked him how he got this information, he went on to tell me that his wife's friend, who lives next door to the house where the kids were playing basketball, saw his son and called his wife. He continued,

> *"Can you believe our kids? I'm a lay pastor at my church. Can you believe how embarrassing this is for me? The whole church will know! He's really gonna pay for this!"*

Now, I had counseled this man-years earlier, and lead him to the Lord. As this man went back to his car before I knew it, I had these thoughts coming into my head:

> *"Gosh, I'm a pastor. What does this guy think of me? I can't believe Nick would do this. What about my reputation? Does he think he can get away with sneaking off? He thinks I won't find out? This is it! When he gets here, I'm gonna let him have it!"*

Satan was bombarding my mind with judgmental, evil accusations and temptations. I didn't know the truth about the situation, only hearsay from an upset father. Before I knew it, I was agreeing with Satan's accusations against my son, and I was tempted to *let my son have it.* My own prideful concerns about what this guy thought of me were fueling my anger. My carnal nature was having a field day! This situation was the *set up,* and Satan was trying to capitalize on it. Satan had set me up! He dangled the hook in my face, I took it and he was reeling me in!

Thank God for His grace and mercy. The Holy Spirit brought to remembrance of my own youth:

> *"Craig, how many church groups did you get kicked out of when you were a kid? What things were you doing when you were 13? When you were Nick's age, did you even go to youth group?"*

I took some time and prayed for strength and wisdom to deal with this situation correctly.

Nick finally arrived and came up to the car asking if I could give his friend a ride home. I agreed, knowing that I shouldn't confront him in front of another kid. Within a few seconds, Nick told me,

> *"Hey, Dad, I have to tell you what happened tonight. We didn't go to youth group because they were having a graduation ceremony and the leader said we didn't have to attend if we didn't want to, but we needed to call our parents. One of the kids lives down the street and asked if we wanted to play basketball at her house, so we did."*

I played dumb, as if I didn't know what had happened, then responded,

> *"You know, Nick, we've never had this happen before. Next time you decide not to be where you are supposed to be, we want a phone call. Let your mom and me make that decision. You don't have the authority to make those decisions yet."*

He didn't give me any excuses, but agreed that he would call next time. That was it. It was over. He learned to call next time, and I had another *victory* in bringing my thoughts captive to Christ.

The following day, one of the mothers of the kids from the youth group called my wife. She told her that her daughter was one of the kids in this group that left to go play basketball. Her daughter told her that as they were walking back to the church, they began discussing among themselves how they were going to lie to their parents. Nick said to them,

> *"Don't lie, you guys. Why would you lie? Just tell the truth. Our parents will find out anyway!"*

I can only imagine if I had let Satan have the victory, *reacted* to my son in anger and embarrassed him in front of his friends, how I would have felt after learning how my son encouraged the other kids to tell the truth. This is how it works. Satan loves to get in the midst of our daily interaction, flinging his fiery darts of lies, condemnation and temptations that divide our homes. Parents, when we are not obedient to bringing our thoughts captive, we can open the door for Satan's oppression.

⌕ SELF-EXAMINATION

Take a moment and reflect upon what you have learned about The Set Up, Satan attacks our minds. What are some of the lies or fiery darts that the enemy has shot at you regarding your children?

_____

_____

_____

_____

_____

WEEK 5: DAY 5

3. PERSECUTION

Another common reason that we fail to love our kids is persecution, or opposition. Matthew 5:43-45 tells us how to respond to opposition:

> You have heard that it was said, "You shall love your neighbor and hate your enemy." But I say to you, **love** your enemies, **bless** those who curse you, **do good** to those who hate you, **pray** for those who spitefully use you and persecute you, that you may be sons of your Father in Heaven.

What does *loving*, *blessing*, *doing good* and *praying* for our enemies have to do with parenting? As you will see, the principles laid out in this verse have everything to do with our mindset toward our children.

Sometimes it seems like our kids are the enemy. We feel like they are deliberately going out of their way to irritate us but even if they are, God tells us how to respond to them. Proverbs acknowledges that children can have a negative effect on us, *"a foolish son is the grief of his mother"* (10:1); *"A foolish son is a grief to his father, And bitterness to her who bore him"* (17:25); *"He who begets a scoffer does so to his sorrow, And the father of a fool has no joy"* (17:21). As discussed earlier, foolishness is bound up in the heart of a child" (Prov 22:15), so we should *expect* to have opposition at times, which feels like persecution, when raising our children.

FACT FILE

Persecute - *To pursue in a manner to injure, grieve, or afflict; to oppress; to set upon with cruelty; to cause to suffer.*

This feeling of persecution comes when our children challenge us, refuse to respond to our correction and training, rebel against our authority, or resist our love. They often act like enemies, and treat us like we are their enemies. Naturally, most parents take this personally and, in time can become discouraged or even harden their hearts. Instead of responding in love, parents can react and love is lost in negative feelings and attitudes. But God gives us a way to overcome these sinful reactions by following the principles in Matthew 5:43-45. Each of these instructions is a command to do, and continue to do. As depicted here, enemies are people you would not naturally want to be around.

✓ACTION PLAN

Write your personal commitment to do this under each one:

1. *"**Love** your enemies."* Love here is *agape* (Greek), and as explained earlier this type of love is primarily of the will instead of emotions. No one really "feels" like loving an enemy. One author says, "It is not the same as natural affection because it is not natural to love those who hate and harm you. It is a supernatural grace and can be manifested only by those who have divine life."[7] This can only come through your strong foundation, abiding in Christ.

_____

_____

_____

_____

2. *"**Bless** those who curse you."* Blessing is the idea of bestowing a gift, and what gift could be better than love. Cursing is using words that hurt. We cannot let words cause us to *react* and strike back in anger, but we must *respond* in love. As we move through the manual we will give you tools to discipline in love.

_____

_____

_____

_____

7   William MacDonald and Arthur Farstad, *Believer's Bible Commentary : Old and New Testaments* (Nashville: Thomas Nelson, 1997), 1223.

3. **"Do good** to those who hate you."* There may be a time that your child tells you, "I hate you," or puts on a defiant face when you discipline, or say "no" to something they want to do. Again, you must not lash out, but look and pray for a way to "do good." *Responding* in love may take a little time, but shows you have self-control and that you are committed to glorifying God.

_____
_____
_____
_____

4. **"Pray** for those who spitefully use you and persecute you."* Spitefully has the sense of misusing, insulting or falsely accusing. It does not take long in parenting to see this dark side come out in our children. Jesus gives the command to pray because many times it will be the last thing we do. Why prayer? Here are three reasons: 1) Prayer means you are asking God to bring change to you and your children, that He would open their eyes and empower them to be obedient. 2) Prayer means that you are dependent upon God and not your own strength and wisdom, but you are asking for His wisdom in the situation (James 1:5-8). 3) Prayer changes your heart. The best way to change your attitude to *agape* love is to bring a child before the Lord in prayer. And since it is a command to pray and continue to pray, God slowly softens your heart so that you start loving them like He does.

_____
_____
_____
_____

Pray this now,

Dear Lord, I thank you so much for the children you have given me. I know that you created them and they are a gift from you. I ask you to help me to know how to love them the way you do even when I do not feel like it. Lord, I need Your strength and Your wisdom to respond with 1 Corinthians love to each opposition my children will bring. Help me know how to bless and do good to them; transform my heart. And Lord, give me a heart to pray for my children daily and even minute-by-minute. I pray that You would change my children from the inside out, that they would have a heart of wanting to be obedient to Your Word, and as I instruct them biblically they would embrace You. In Jesus' name, AMEN.

As a parent, as a minister, this is the way God wants us to respond to our kids.

1 Peter 2:20-21 *"For what credit is it if, when you are beaten for your faults, you take it patiently? But when you do good and suffer, if you take it patiently, this is commendable before God. For to this you were called, because Christ also suffered for us, leaving us an example, that you should follow His steps."*

God says that we are blessed when we are persecuted for Christ's sake, or for our obedience to Christ. We are stewards entrusted by God to carry His message and plan to our children by word and by deed (our actions). Parenting can include suffering; at times, it is difficult, but the Word tells us: *"For it is better, if it is the will of God, to suffer for doing good than for doing evil."* (1 Pet. 3:17). God will bless us as we remain consistent and faithful to obey Him. **We are stewards, entrusted by God to carry His message to our children.**

FACT FILE

Steward - *Overseer; manager; one who acts as a custodian, administrator or supervisor.*

Paul gives us some encouraging words to keep the focus off of ourselves, and instead focusing on pleasing God.

1 Thessalonians 2:4 *"But as we have been approved by God to be entrusted with the gospel, even so we speak, not as pleasing men, but God who tests our hearts."*

As God's stewards over our families, we must examine our hearts and motives daily, with pleasing the Lord as our main objective. Our motive should not be to succeed at being *good* parents or even to raise *good* kids, but (to please God). As He examines our hearts, God is faithful to reveal to us what He sees!

4. SELFISHNESS

Finally, another common reason we fail to love is selfishness. Again, 1 Corinthians 13:5 tells us that love *"does not seek its own."* But because we are sinners, we are selfish by nature and we love conditionally.

We do not realize how selfish and conditional we are until our children come home from the hospital and we begin to raise them. If they do not live up to our *expectations*, what do we do? "Oh, that's it; you crossed the line now, Buddy." You react.

But God tells us we must **not** put selfish expectations upon our kids. Even though our children do not want to listen and they do not want to be trained, we need to train them faithfully without our anger and selfishness dictating how we respond to them. Perhaps your first child was a wonderful, easy, pleasing kid. Then the next one you believe is a Tasmanian devil, and you spend so much time comparing the two. "Why can't you just be like your sister?" Remember, one will never be the same as the other. We cannot put selfish demands upon our kids.

Scripture tells us that God tests us; He examines our hearts and shows us how conditional and selfish we are. *"But as we have been approved by God to be entrusted with the Gospel, even so we speak, not as pleasing men, but God who tests our hearts"* (1 Thess. 2:4). Our focus must be to please God; the test comes when we must choose to be selfless, or extend love. To love others (our children) is the overarching factor in obeying God's Word. The Bible says, *"For all the law is fulfilled in one word, even in this: 'You shall love your neighbor as yourself'"* (Gal. 5:14); and *"Owe no one anything except to love one another, for he who loves another has fulfilled the law"* (Rom 13:8). In order for this to happen, self has to be submitted to Christ, which is why He said, *"If anyone desires to come after Me, let him <u>deny himself</u>, and take up his cross daily, and follow Me"* (Luke 9:23). Denying self and taking up one's cross means putting our selfish expectations and ways to death for His ways—living for Christ. We are transformed through a purifying process as we are raising our children.

Selfishness is purged out of us like metal is purified. In order for metal to be purified, it must be placed in huge vats with extensive heat underneath. As the metal inside becomes red hot, all kinds of black stuff, called *dross,* begins coming to the surface. The dross is the impurity inside the metal, which is then scooped off the top to make it pure.

God clearly did this with His people Israel, He said, *"I will turn My hand against you, And thoroughly purge away your dross, And take away all your alloy"* (Isaiah 1:25); and *"He will sit as a refiner and a purifier of silver; He will purify the sons of Levi, and purge them as gold and silver, that they may offer to the Lord an offering in righteousness"* (Malachi 3:3). Notice that the end result of purging is *positive*, it gives us the ability to offer righteousness to the Lord.

God does the same thing to us. He brings about circumstances in our lives that "heat us up," and guess what comes to the surface? Our impurities. If we fail to remember that God is transforming us (Rom. 12:2), and using our children to reveal our selfish condition of heart, we will then blame our sinful actions on our children. God wants us to understand and embrace this truth, and deal with the dross properly. God wants to deal with your **heart**, because *"The heart is deceitful above all things, and desperately wicked; who can know it? I the Lord, search the heart, I test the mind"* (Jer. 17:9-10a). God wants to *change* us from the inside so we can apply it outwardly and reflect Him.

God knew every mistake we would ever make when He chose us as parents. It's good to know He is not going to apologize to our children for picking us. It is imperative every time we do fail as parents, when we get angry and *react* in the flesh, that we take full responsibility. We need to go to the Lord and say, "God, I'm sorry. I blew it," and then to that son or daughter and say, "Honey, what you did was wrong, but the way Mommy or Daddy reacted was wrong too. Please forgive me." We still discipline them, but we take responsibility for misrepresenting Jesus and ask for their forgiveness as well. That, my friend, is acting in love. That is how the dross is scraped off and we are transformed. If we do not do those two things, it is like taking a big spoon and stirring the dross back into us, which is guaranteed to resurface.

As I shared with you previously, my son Nicholas was sent by God to reveal what an evil, selfish, and angry person I was. It was the greatest miracle to me when I was able to look at Nick, when he made a mistake or challenged my authority, and calmly say, "Poor choice!" without any emotion. To not scream, yell, or want to take his head off. It was great - praise God! He had proved Himself true. I had prayed for it, desired it; once I began to take responsibility for my failures, I witnessed God's transformation *in* me. I had to learn NOT to put my selfish unrealistic expectations on Nick, except how God was using him to reveal my sin and obey God's discipline to me by asking for forgiveness.

My son witnessed his daddy change right before his eyes. Yes, it took a season for this to take place. It did not happen over night. Today, Nicholas has strong faith and a healthy fear of God because in part he witnessed his father's transformation right before his eyes. This is one of the greatest examples of discipleship that you and I can give our kids.

God is purging us. He is heating us up and revealing our ugly, selfish conditions. We cannot run away from this process; we must embrace it and take responsibility in order for our transformation to occur.

SELF-EXAMINATION

What are some of the "heated moments" with your children and what are they revealing about you? Write them down below and take them to the Lord in prayer.

_____

_____

_____

_____

_____

_____

If, after reading this material about properly loving your children, you have found that there is room for improvement, your first step must be admitting to the Lord, "I need help. I have failed. I need to change, God. I misrepresent You by _____, (you fill in the blank). I'm sorry."

Then, write out a commitment to change in the area of loving your children. What things did the Lord bring to your mind? In addition, I encourage you to pray about a time (soon) that you ask your children to forgive you. Loving our children is essential to successful parenting; we cannot allow anything else to take precedence.

_____

_____

_____

_____

_____

_____

_____

_____

_____

_____

Now please turn to **Appendix I** and fill out the "Effective Listening Self-Evaluation" worksheet along with the "Effective Listening Self Scoring Ides," if married do it separate and then compare notes.

Week 6: Training Up Your Children Part 1 - God's Management Style

WEEK 6: DAY 1

Introduction

As we enter the subject of training up children, we must keep in mind that discipline and training are most effective when there is a healthy relationship between parent and child. If this relationship is strained, or weak, the parent's role as teacher and trainer is hindered. In fact, without a positive relationship the exercise of authority actually creates hostility. Our modern penal system, primarily based on punishment, is a good example of this principle. Punishment alone does not produce reformed individuals; statistics reveal that most, after release, will commit a crime and return to prison.

Although discipline is a part of training, effective parenting depends more on love. The most powerful motivator for encouraging children to make right decisions is love. And remember, teens are children, too. Even though they are older and fighting for independence, they are equally in need of consistent parental love. When we do not use loving communication with our children, we are actually reducing their desire, or ability, to make good choices. The Bible has much to say about love, because God wants us to understand the importance of loving one another. He defines love very specifically, as we learned when studying 1 Corinthians 13. In those verses, God gave us guidelines so that we can evaluate ourselves, correct any mistakes, and properly communicate love to our children.

A discussion on love is not complete without mentioning the bond between husband and wife. This is a relationship where loving communication is absolutely necessary, it is the foundation and the source of a successful partnership. And this partnership is the starting point for administering discipline in the home. If agreement does not exist between husband and wife, it will confuse children and defeat discipline. Parents need to consistently use loving communication with each other, and also during the process of disciplining their children.

As you begin this next study, notice that it comes *after* the chapter on love. Training is essential, a mandate from God to parents, but remember that it is most effective when a child is first secure in your love. Loving communication and training work together, and build upon each other. Love without *training* produces a self-centered child with weak character, while discipline without *love* will provoke and embitter, foster rebellion, and may emotionally cripple them.

Training is Twofold
1. DISCIPLING A CHILD

The first essential of training up a child is *discipleship,* or teaching biblical morals and values. As we disciple our children, we instill God's Word into their hearts both by example and instruction. It is the parents' responsibility to teach a child how to identify right and wrong behavior, how to pray, how to study God's Word, and how to have an abiding relationship with God. A child is *not* born with biblical "morals and values," they have to be *learned*. Did you know that God not only *commands,* but considers it a *privilege* for parents to disciple their children? (Gen. 18:19; Deut. 6:7; 11:19; Pr. 22:6; Eph. 6:4)

> **Genesis 18:19** *"For I have known him, in order that he may command his children and his household after him, that they keep the way of the LORD, to do righteousness and justice, that the LORD may bring to Abraham what He has spoken to him."*

> **Deuteronomy 6:7** *"You shall teach them diligently to your children, and shall talk of them when you sit in your house, when you walk by the way, when you lie down, and when you rise up."*

> **Proverbs 22:6** *"Train up a child in the way he should go, And when he is old he will not depart from it."*

DIG DEEPER: *FURTHER STUDY*

Please read through the following scripture a few times. Take some time to write down what the Lord is saying to you. This is an exercise for both parents; even though it is specifically addressed to fathers, every wife is equally important in her God-given role as helpmate. As mentioned before, parents function as a team and both are responsible for discipling and disciplining their children.

> **Ephesians 6:4** *"And you, fathers, do not provoke your children to wrath, but bring them up in the training and admonition of the Lord."*

FACT FILE

Bring them up - *ektrepho (Greek), to nourish, rear, feed. To nurture, rear, to bring up to maturity such as children, in the sense of to train or educate.*[1]

FACT FILE

Training - *paideia (Greek), means chastening, because all effectual instruction for the sinful children of men includes and implies discipline, correction...as the Lord approves.*[2]

---

1   Zodhiates, 557.

2   Zodhiates, 1088.

FACT FILE

Admonition - *nouthesia (Greek), warning, exhortation, any word of encouragement or re-proof, which leads to correct behavior.*[3] *It is the idea of having a corrective influence on someone by imparting understanding.*

We will be referring to Ephesians 6:4 throughout the study of training up a child. As you can see, God has given clear and specific instruction. Remember, our children are His children, and His desire is that they are given every opportunity to become spiritually *mature* adults. It is our responsibility to learn His plan, and then adhere to it. The verb tense of *"bring them up"* indicates continuous action, to do and continue doing without stopping, and is also a *command*. We are to do this faithfully until a child is no longer our responsibility.

At this point, there is a misconception that must be addressed. God did *not* give the church primary responsibility for this task. I would dare say from my many years in family ministry, that more than 90% of children from Christian families are *not* being discipled at home. *Parents* have relinquished this responsibility to the church because most fathers never received any training in how to disciple their children, or have misplaced *priorities*. Praise God for fathers and mothers who are exhorting other parents to take responsibility for the spiritual training of their children - discipleship within their homes. The church is commissioned by God to support, come alongside, and encourage parents and families (Eph. 4:11-16), not to take away the responsibility of discipling the children.

2. BUILDING A CHILD'S CHARACTER

The second essential of training up a child is instilling the character traits of a mature adult, which are personal responsibility and self-control. No one is born with these traits, nor do we naturally acquire them. These qualities result from training. God's Word clearly teaches that this, as well as spiritual discipleship, is the role of the parent.

---

3   Zodhiates, 1017.

> **FACT FILE**
>
> **Disciple** - (verb) Instilling God's Word and morals and values into our children's hearts through example and instruction, teaching them to pray, and how to have a relationship with God (spiritual training).

> **FACT FILE**
>
> **Discipline** - Instilling the character traits of a mature adult, which are **personal responsibility** and **self-control**, into our children (training behavior).

⌕ SELF-EXAMINATION

Are you discipling your children in the Lord at home?   ❑ Yes ❑ No

Explain:

_____

_____

_____

_____

If not, are you willing to learn and start?   ❑ Yes ❑ No

Write out your prayer asking God for the faith and wisdom to apply the things you are about to learn.

_____

_____

_____

_____

_____

_____

_____

_____

We will be discussing these two subjects, *discipleship* and *disciplining,* in the coming chapters. But first, the issue of God's Management Style must be understood. As we construct our spiritual homes, if it is out of order, it will **not** create the strong, protective environment that we need to raise our children in.

Using God's Management Style

God has *not* given parents an impossible task, because He has given us His Word and His Spirit. In His Word, God gives us specific instructions regarding raising children and, with the Holy Spirit inside us, we have the power to do *all* things according to His will (Eph. 1:11, 19).

DIG DEEPER: *FURTHER STUDY*

Read the following verses and write out in your own words what they mean and how they can relate to our task in parenting.

Ephesians 1:11 *"In Him also we have obtained an inheritance, being predestined according to the purpose of Him who works all things according to the counsel of His will."*

_____

_____

_____

_____

Ephesians 1:19 *"and what is the exceeding greatness of His power toward us who believe, according to the working of His mighty power*

_____

_____

_____

_____

God has also outlined a management style in His Word, which we must follow if we desire His blessing on our endeavors. *Our* responsibility is simply to search His Word and obey what He tells us to do, in His power and might.

FOR SINGLE PARENTS

Again, I want to encourage any single parents at this point. All these instructions may not apply specifically to your situation, but you may be called upon to give advice to other parents and, to respond in a biblical fashion, you will need to know what God says about this subject. Additionally, you may marry again. So please, as you read this chapter, take it in as wisdom and understanding that God wants to teach you, to prepare you for what may be in the future. Besides God wants every believer to know the whole counsel of God (Acts 20:27). If you do not know, how can you counsel your own children correctly in this area? Turn to **Appendix F**, *Essentials for Single Parents*, where you will find helpful insight and encouragement for parents raising their children alone!

A BLENDED FAMILY

If you are in a blended-family marriage, please note that none of these instructions change; they apply to you the same as the traditional family. Nowhere in His Word did God say if you are a blended family, you are excused from this management style. God does not have a plan A, B, C, He has only one plan that we are all to follow. See **Appendix S** for more help and encouragement for Blended Families.

The Logic of a Management Style

If you have worked in a group setting, large or small, you know that there was a management style in place. Without this structure, there is no leadership, and disorder, division and chaos will bring devastating consequences. We can all agree that a home is a group, so it is important that our homes operate according to a management style - God's management style. Many families that I have counseled have suffered major problems due to the fact that their homes were out of order. The division present within the home is reflected outside the home as well. When Christian families are disobedient to God, even out of ignorance, they malign the Word of God and ultimately God Himself.

As a Christian couple, you must both agree to embrace what God's Word says. If you adopt any other standard for family management, you are not under His blessings. When we are disobedient to God's management style, there are consequences. God has pre-warned us for our protection and, as with any disobedience, He will administer discipline so that we repent and come into line with His Word (Heb. 12:3-11).

DIG DEEPER: *FURTHER STUDY*

Read the following Scripture and write out what God promises to do to ALL his children.

Hebrews 12:3–11 *"For consider Him who endured such hostility from sinners against Himself, lest you become weary and discouraged in your souls. You have not yet resisted to bloodshed, striving against sin. And you have forgotten the exhortation which speaks to you as to sons: "My son, do not despise the chastening of the LORD, Nor be discouraged when you are rebuked by Him;* <u>*For whom the LORD loves He chastens,*</u> *And scourges every son whom He receives." If you endure chastening, God deals with you as with sons; for what son is there whom a father does not chasten? But if you are without chastening, of which all have become partakers, then you are illegitimate and not sons. Furthermore, we have had human fathers who corrected us, and we paid them respect. Shall we not much more readily be in subjection to the Father of spirits and live? For they indeed for a few days chastened us as seemed best to them, but He for our profit, that we may be partakers of His holiness. Now no chastening seems to be joyful for the present, but painful; nevertheless, afterward it yields the peaceable fruit of righteousness to those who have been trained by it."*

_____

_____

_____

_____

_____

_____

Consequences can come in many forms: feeling separated from the Lord, lacking the strength to live for Him, no peace or contentment, confusion, turmoil, depression, and contention just to name a few. But the good news is when we line up with God's Word and repent, He will restore us and *keep us* on track. It is these negative consequences *God* uses to get our attention.

DIG DEEPER: *FURTHER STUDY*

Read the Scripture below and write down what the negative consequences are when we do things our own way.

> **Romans 2:8–9** *"but to those who are <u>self-seeking</u> and do not obey the truth, but obey unrighteousness—indignation and wrath, tribulation and anguish, on every soul of man who does evil, of the Jew first and also of the Greek."*

_____

_____

_____

_____

_____

_____

_____

FACT FILE

Self-seeking - means doing things in our own way, using ours, or this world's wisdom in making choices.

The Institution of Family

As we discussed previously, the family is an institution created by *God* and, as such, is subject to His design. In order for a family to operate correctly, God has ordained that there must be leadership and authority within it. Let us now look to the structure He established for this vitally important institution.

According to the account in Genesis, God, seeing that it was *not* good for the man to be alone, gave him a helper, or a helpmate, *"And the LORD God said, 'It is not good that man should be alone; I will make him a **helper** comparable to him'"* (Gen. 2:18). Notice the word He used here is *helper*, not *leader*. God formed the man out of the dust of the ground (Genesis 2:7), but He also formed or, literally, *built* the woman out of the rib of the man (Genesis 2:21-22). God was demonstrating the role that the husband and wife would have in one another's lives. They would be mutually dependent upon one another. The man needed companionship. The man needed help! God provided that help through the woman. A woman would *make up* for what was lacking in the man, and vice versa. The woman's life came from the man, and man's life would proceed from the woman.

⌕ SELF-EXAMINATION

- Wives, do you want to be a helper/helpmate to your husband?
  ❏ Yes ❏ No (Tell him now.)

- Husbands are you willing to admit to yourself and your wife that you need her?
  ❏ Yes ❏ No (Tell her now.)

- Are you both open to learn how to work together under God's management style?
  ❏ Yes ❏ No

On that day there was no power struggle, no conflict, no misunderstanding between them and no battle of the sexes! They were naked and not ashamed. They were oblivious to evil and absolutely innocent.

God made the man responsible for *tending* the things He created. Genesis 2:15 says, *"Then the LORD God took the man and put him in the garden of Eden to tend and keep it."*

Further, we read, *"Therefore a man shall leave his father and mother and be joined to his wife, and they shall become **one** flesh"* (Gen. 2:24). God instructs that we are to see the relationship between husband and wife as *one*, unified. Both need to be in agreement, thinking as one, or "unified" in following what the Bible says.

SIN ERODES GOD'S MANAGEMENT STYLE

Unfortunately, as we turn the page of our Bible to chapter three of Genesis, we learn that domestic tranquility was short-lived.

In Genesis 3:1, the serpent enters the scene with no introduction or explanation. We learn that, in contrast to man's innocence, the serpent was shrewd and *cunning*. Satan disguised himself as a shining serpent in order to converse with and ultimately *deceive* the woman.

Take note: where was Adam when this was happening? Why didn't he step up and *lead* here? Adam's *lack* of leadership and interceding makes him equal in blame.

- **Husbands do you want to do what Adam did in your family?** ❏ Yes ❏ No

In verses 1-8, the downfall of man unfolds:

Satan planted *doubt* in Eve's mind.
   "Indeed, has God said..." V. 1

Satan *lied* to the woman.
> *"You surely shall not die." V. 4*

Satan *enticed* Eve with an evil desire.
> *"For God knows that in the day you eat from it your eyes will be opened, and you will be like God, knowing good and evil." V. 5*

Satan *deceived* the woman and she sinned.
> *"...the woman saw...she took and ate..." V. 6*

FACT FILE

Deceived - *To cause to accept as true or valid what is false or invalid, to believe a lie, to be lead astray, or ensnared.*

When she took and ate, she was deceived, believing the lies of the enemy.

Satan used the woman's *influence* toward her husband to encouage him to sin.
> *"...she also gave to her husband, and he ate." V. 6*

God's order had been *violated*. The couple's relationship to God and to one another was marred. Stripped of their righteousness and innocence, they would suffer the *consequences* of their rebellion. The curses resulting from the fall are recorded In Genesis 3:16-19.

> *"To the woman He said, 'I will greatly multiply your sorrow and your conception; in pain you shall bring forth children; your **desire** shall be for your husband, and he shall **rule** over you.' "*
> *V. 16*

The word *desire* in Genesis 3:16, also in Genesis 4:7, means *a desire to dominate*. The man has been given authority over his wife, yet she would thereafter struggle to submit and, in fact, have a carnal *desire* to not yield to her husbands leadership.

Adam did not obey God's instructions when he failed to lead and protect his wife, but rather did as she requested, and he also was cursed (vs. 17-19).
> God said to Adam, *"Because you have heeded the voice of your wife." V. 17*

By failing to guard his wife from Satan's spiritual attack, and to lead, and then following her into sin, Adam **neglected** to carry out the *responsibility* that God had given him to oversee his family. He would forever be held responsible for sin entering the world. The *curse* of sin continues to take its toll. In countless homes, husbands struggle with insecurity in their leadership role, and just as many wives are resisting their husbands attempts to lead. Typically, men today follow the example of Adam by failing to exert their authority in the home, and women, like Eve, feel they do not need protection and demonstrate a desire to rule.

> **Romans 5:12** *"Therefore, just as through one man sin entered the world, and death through sin..."*

Concerning this subject, one author says,

> "God gave headship to man before sin entered. Paul argues this fact from the order of creation (man was created first) and the purpose of creation (woman was made for the man) (1 Cor. 11:8, 9). Also, although it was Eve who sinned first, it is by Adam, the head, that sin is said to have entered the world. He had the position of head and was thus responsible."[4]

- Husbands, are you willing to learn to protect and lead according to God's Word?
  ❏ Yes ❏ No

- Wives, are you willing to hear and yield to God's instruction in how to manage the home?
  ❏ Yes ❏ No

God never intended for a woman to be the authority figure in the home; instead, to be her husband's helpmate. The man, on the other hand, needs the help and support of his wife in order to fulfill his role as head of the family under the lordship of Jesus Christ. This is God's wonderful plan, the *management style* that we, as Christians, are to follow in order to be blessed.

WEEK 6: DAY 2

Looking to God's Word

Remember, it is *God's* will and purpose we seek and obey, *not* our own, or what we find in worldly philosophy. We discussed the following verse in week one.

DIG DEEPER: *FURTHER STUDY*

Read and write down how this may apply to following, or not following, God's management style for your home.

---

4   William MacDonald, *Believer's Bible Commentary: Old and New Testaments*, ed. Arthur Farstad (Nashville: Thomas Nelson, 1995), 35.

Colossians 2:8 *"**Beware** lest anyone **cheat** you through **philosophy** and empty deceit, according to the **tradition of men**, according to the basic **principles of the world**, and <u>not according to Christ</u>."*

_____

_____

_____

_____

_____

_____

_____

Paul was concerned that the Colossians would be *cheated* by following unbiblical philosophies. When it comes to marriage, parenting, and how the home should operate, there are plenty of worldly philosophies, traditions of men, and principles of the world that are NOT according to Christ. The word "beware" or I should say, "be aware," encourages us to watch for what is happening around us. In this case, it warns us to use Godly discernment for separating truth and error. We must have *discerning minds* that can identify and lay hold of the *truth* in order to fight off any lie. (<u>You see, many families have been cheated by believing lies, and therefore have forfeited the blessings and peace that comes from functioning according to the principles of God's Word</u>.) The conclusion is that the worldly philosophies, traditions of men and principles of the world rob us from what Christ wants to do in our families.

FACT FILE

Cheat (take you captive NASB) means to plunder or rob as when plunder is taken in war. In this case it is to rob believers of the complete riches that they have in Christ as revealed in the Word, plus His power and intervention.

The question you need to ask yourself is, "Have I been cheated by believing something that is not based on God's Word?" Many times we do not examine ourselves, but just go with the flow. We who are spiritual are to "judge all things" (1 Cor. 2:15), and operate according to the wisdom of God, not the wisdom of man, or of this age (1 Cor. 2:5, 6, 13). As we move through God's management style, "be aware" of the leadership structure within your home. We must willingly abandon the influence of all traditions, cultural norms, ethnic traits, or past personal experience if they are *contrary* to God's ways. I realize that this may be very hard because it requires breaking some generational sins and/or bad habits, and totally changing the way that you operate and think. But we serve a God of great compassion and He will empower you to change, so that you may *"be renewed in the spirit of your mind"* (Eph. 4:23).

We need to "be aware" of letting our thinking and behavior fall under the influence of the following philosophies.

CULTURE/ETHNIC

Many people I have counseled say, "Well, in my culture (meaning ethnic background), this is the way we do it." Or "As a _____ (you fill in your ethnic background) the woman has no say so in the home, or the woman does all the training of the children." I respond with, "Well, are you a Christian?" "Yes." "Well then, for this issue you must put your cultural beliefs aside, because they are in direct conflict with the Word of God." Many times, cultural beliefs are just preferences with no moral implications and it is totally fine to practice them, however, when a cultural belief is contrary to the Bible, it becomes a moral conflict, which is *sin*. We must "ALWAYS" check our beliefs about marriage and family with God's Word.

CULTURE

Our culture, or the "philosophies and principles of this world", is all around us. The wisdom of the world comes via the media (books, TV, movies, magazines, and internet, just to name a few), or often through education and peer pressure. Any of these can influence us to view marriage and family through the lens of the world. Beliefs and philosophies get so ingrained that we actually believe that "this is the truth, this is the way I am supposed to operate my family," until we compare it to the Word of God.

RELIGIOUS TRADITIONS

I would like to mention that there are many religious teachings about marriage and parenting that have become traditions. Something like, "In our religion we have always done it this way." My prayer is that everyone would be like the Christians in Berea, who after hearing the teaching of Paul, "searched the Scriptures daily to find out whether these things were so" (Acts 17:11). Do not blindly take anyone else's word on truth, not even mine, but open the Word and verify that it is true.

TRADITIONS OF MEN

Traditions are those beliefs and behaviors that are passed down from one person to another, one generation to another. This happens all the time with marriage and parenting styles. Too often, parents give their grown children bad parenting advice, such as, "When we raised you, we did it this way so you should, too!" As Christians, we all have to make tough decisions when it comes to following Christ; when the Word of God is your standard, you must *always* honor God and His Word above all others, including your parents. Again, not all traditions have moral implications, but when they do, they must be rejected.

Jesus' Perspective on Traditions

Dealing with the confusion of separating tradition from truth is not new. Jesus had to deal with certain religious leaders who preferred to live their lives according to the traditions which dominated the religious culture in which they were raised. We see now, by reading the scripture, that by stubbornly refusing to give up those ideas taught to them by men, they eventually rejected the Savior who came to save them.

Here is what Jesus said,

> **Mark 7:9, 13** *"All too well you reject the commandment of God, that you may keep your tradition…making the word of God of **no effect** through your tradition which you have handed down. And many such things you do."*

Jesus was telling men that God had given instructions (commandments) to live by, but they were following man-made rules, or principles, not truth. By doing this, they were making the Word of God of *no effect*. In this context, the Pharisees were saying that they could not take care of their parents financially because the money was "corban," a sacrificial gift to God. In reality, they were saving the money for their own purposes. They had devised a way of legally avoiding the fifth commandment to honor father and mother. The reason I bring this up is because we have a tendency to spiritualize, or put our own twist on the Scriptures to suit our own purposes. Jesus told them, *"in vain they worship Me teaching as doctrines the commandments of men"* (Mark 7:7). No word or deed goes unnoticed by the Lord.

Biblical Traditions

There are traditions to which we should hold tightly. Paul told the church at Thessalonica, *"Therefore, brethren, stand fast and hold the traditions which you were taught, whether by word or our epistle"* (2 Thess. 2:15). Paul was saying stand firm and hold onto the *biblical truths* that had been given to them by the apostles through their preaching and letters. We must all hold tightly to the *truth*.

Jesus' Perspective on Family

Jesus also gives an exhortation on whether to follow a family member's principles or His, He says, *"If anyone comes to Me and does not **hate** his father and mother, wife and children, brothers and sisters, yes, and his own life also, he cannot be My disciple"* (Luke 14:26).

Jesus is *not* saying that to love Him we must *hate* our families, spouse, or our children. Rather, if it comes to a choice of doing something God's way or our *parents'* way, or the *world's*, or our own way, we *must* choose God's way. Basically, the word translated in this verse as "hate" would be better translated "love less"; meaning that our love for God, His Word, and what He desires is so great that neither my desires nor my families' will keep me from obeying what He wants. That is the commitment of a true disciple. In Christ's day, Jews who became followers of Christ were shunned as those who had abandoned the faith, or Judaism. Many times a family would cast them out.

We cannot let any other relationship cause us to compromise the truth in Christ, no matter how it may look to others. And as Christians, we will sometimes be considered strange when we follow biblical principles that are contrary to the world's viewpoint.

1 Peter 4:4 *"In regard to these, they think it <u>strange</u> that you do not run with them in the same flood of dissipation, speaking evil of you."*

We should look strange, because we are strangers, aliens to the world, and God's Word now dictates and governs how we do all things.

Ephesians 2:12 *"that at that time you were without Christ, being <u>aliens</u> from the common-wealth of Israel and <u>strangers</u> from the covenants of promise, having no hope and without God in the world."*

DIG DEEPER: *FURTHER STUDY*

Read the following verse and write down, in your own words, *who* God says you are and what *He* has called you to *do*.

1 Peter 2:9 *"But you are a chosen generation, a royal priesthood, a holy nation, His own special people, that you may proclaim the praises of Him who called you out of darkness into His marvelous light."*

_____

_____

_____

_____

_____

I covered these controversial issues now because, as we discuss this next section, we need to put all other ideas aside and fully *embrace* what we find in God's Word.

Biblical Leadership in the Home

Remember, God created the institution of family and has established a line of authority, clearly appointing husbands, or fathers, to lead. In understanding this, our goal must be to fulfill God's will and purpose, and to glorify Him.

Read the following verses, and fill in the chart below.

1 Corinthians 11:3 *"But I want you to know that the **head** of every man is Christ, the **head** of woman is man, and the **head** of Christ is God."*

Colossians 3:18-21 *"Wives, submit to your own husbands, as is fitting in the Lord. Husbands, love your wives and do not be bitter toward them. Children, **obey** your parents in all things,* *for this is well pleasing to the Lord. Fathers, do not provoke your children, lest they become discouraged."*

_____ is the head of Christ

_____ is the head of the man

_____ is the head of the woman

Children are to submit to _____

It seems that these Scriptures would clear any debate over meaning, but there is division among certain circles of thought. The debate is raised over whether or not the man is the head over the wife. Is the husband really to be the leader of the home? This question must be answered by both the husband and wife; they must agree on *God's* perspective, and then *embrace* the roles God has designed for each of them. As we discussed above, the natural desire of the women will be to rule as it is part of the curse (Gen. 3:16). God did not put that in the Bible by accident, but for us to understand that a struggle will occur, and must become subject to His will.

The word head, *kephale* (Greek), is translated different ways in the New Testament. One Greek scholar explains the use of the word *head*, in the metaphorical sense, as it appears in the verse above.

FACT FILE
Head: means the chief or lead person to whom others are subordinate.

If you look up each of the passages below, you will understand the importance of the headship principle. For our purposes, it describes the relationship between husband and wife.

Metaphorically of persons, i.e., the head, chief, one to whom others are subordinate, e.g., the husband in relation to his wife (1 Cor. 11:3; Eph. 5:23) insofar as they are one body (Matt. 19:6; Mark 10:8), and one body can have only one head to direct it; of Christ in relation to His Church which is His body, and its members are His members (cf. 1 Cor. 12:27; Eph. 1:22; 4:15; 5:23; Col. 1:18; 2:10, 19); of God in relation to Christ (1 Cor. 11:3). In Col. 2:10 & Eph. 1:22, God the Father is designated as the head of Christ.[5]

Let me help you understand the train of thought that is being communicated. In 1 Corinthians 11:3 it says,

---

5   Zodhiates, 860.

"the head of Christ is God." I have never heard anyone debate that. Why? Because it is very clear from the gospel of John that Jesus fully submitted to the Father's will (Jn. 5:30). His food was to do the Father's will (4:34), planned before time began so that we would be saved (Eph 1:4). Jesus *willingly* submitted to the headship of the Father, all the way to the cross.

Jesus Christ was functioning in the *role* of son and redeemer, even though He was *equal* with God in every way. The issue is not who is better or more qualified, Jesus was just *fulfilling the role* that was given to Him. In the same way, the husband/father or the wife/mother has been given a *role* by God in which to function. It is not who is better or more qualified, we are all equal in God's sight, it is who God *designed* you to be: a man is a husband/father, a women is a wife/mother.

Next, I have also never had anyone debate whether Christ is the head of the Church. Ephesians 1:22 states that *"He put all things under His feet, and gave Him to be head over all things to the church."* God the Father gave Christ authority to function as the head of the church. What is our role, or how are we to relate to Christ as the head? We are to have an attitude of *willingly* submitting to the Father's plan of Christ being *head* of the church, and we are to recognize that Christ has all authority (*"all things under His feet"),* and we are to *willingly* submit to Christ. Obedient Christians acknowledge this and act accordingly.

I also have never heard a Christian debate that *"the head of every man is Christ"* (1 Cor. 11:3). Every Christian understands that mankind, and in this case the husband, is to submit to Christ. Again, as Christians we willingly *submit* to Christ because He is the head.

With that background in mind, when we read, *"the head of women is man"* (1 Cor. 11:3), and *"For the husband is head of the wife, as also Christ is head of the church; and He is the Savior of the body"* (Eph. 5:23), what conclusions should we come to?

1. Just as Christ *is* the head of the church, so *is* the husband the head of the wife. Husband, this **is** your calling, role, and/or how you are to function.

2. Just as the church is to submit itself to the headship of Christ, so the wife is to submit herself to the headship of her husband. Wife, this is your calling, role, and/or how you are to function.

3. Just as Christ has the responsibility of leading the church because of His *headship*, so the husband has the responsibility of leading his wife and his family because of his *headship*.

4. Just as God the Father had a *plan* in making Christ the head of the Church, so He has a *plan* in making the husband the head of the wife and family.

Isn't this outdated?

I have heard it said, "Hey, we are in the 21st century and things have changed, so we need to update the Bible to fit our times." The Bible has proven itself to be the source of truth in every *century* and *culture*, including ours. *It never becomes out dated.*

Just to illustrate that headship does not change over time, I would like to use Abraham and Sarah as an example, from 1 Peter. When Peter wrote this letter, it was about AD 64, and here we are about 2,000 years later. In chapter 3:1-7, he covers the subject of husbands and wives. Peter encourages wives to be submissive to their husbands (3:1-4), and then uses the story of Abraham and Sarah to illustrate his point. Peter said, *"For in this manner, in former times, the holy women who trusted in God also adorned themselves, being submissive to their own husbands, as Sarah obeyed Abraham, calling him lord, whose daughters you are if you do good and are not afraid with any terror"* (1 Pt. 3:5–6).

Something noteworthy is that Abraham and Sarah lived about 2,000 years before this was written, and Adam an Eve lived 2,000 years before that. So, following the timeline from creation: God designed the husband to lead and Eve to help, 2,000 years after that Abraham and Sarah are following the same pattern, then 2,000 years later Peter is directing the New Testament believers to follow the same pattern. We gather from this that time (4,000 years) did not change how God designed marriage to work at creation. If God was going to change the management style, He would have done it in the New Testament. And, since the Word of God is complete and we are not to add to it or take away from it (Deut. 4:2; 12:32; Prov. 30:6; Rev 22:18), then we need to embrace it.

> **Deuteronomy 4:2** *"You shall not add to the word which I command you, nor take from it, that you may keep the commandments of the LORD your God which I command you."*

> **Proverbs 30:6** *"Do not add to His words, Lest He rebuke you, and you be found a liar."*

DIG DEEPER: *FURTHER STUDY*

Warning: Read the following Scripture and write out what many people will be doing prior to Jesus' return.

> **2 Timothy 4:3–4** *" For the time will come when they will not endure sound doctrine, but according to their own desires, because they have itching ears, they will heap up for themselves teachers; and they will turn their ears away from the truth, and be turned aside to fables."*

_____

_____

_____

_____

_____

We must not forget that all are born with a sin nature that wants to follow Satan, the world, or the flesh. Therefore, if not watchful, we can wind up polluting God's Management Style with philosophies that are contrary to Scripture. That is why we must weigh every thought and action against His precious Word; ignorance will not stop the negative consequences from happening.

Note on a Successful Woman

If you remember the TV series *Full House,* DJ was played by Candace Cameron (now Bure) whose brother, Kirk Cameron, starred in *Growing Pains.* She is still acting and is also successful as a wife and mother. Candace met her husband, Val Bure (a Russian hockey player) at a charity hockey game, and not long after they were married and had children. After being married 10 years, here is what she had to say about marriage and God's Management Style.

> Like any marriage we've had our happy days and our growing pains (no pun intended), but it wasn't until nearly a decade into our marriage that I really began to understand the impact that my role as a wife could have in this union. With some changes of my own, I was excited to discover that an already good relationship could be transformed into a great one. The first step I took was understanding that although marriage is an equal partnership where husband and wife are equally important, we aren't *designed* to share the same *roles* [emphasis added]. Holding the Bible, I read, "For the man is not of the woman: but the woman of the man. Neither was the man created for the woman: but the woman for the man" (1 Cor. 11:8–9 KJV). Today's society had me believe that there should be no differences between a man and a woman. Society had it wrong. Val and I were created equally but differently, and so we have differing responsibilities in our marriage—mine being his helpmate. God created Adam, and when he saw that Adam was alone, he created Eve to be his helper. Was this an important lesson in reshaping me? Very much so...If we can learn to yield to the authority God has placed in our lives, in turn we learn that our flesh must yield to our Spirit.[6]

SELF-EXAMINATION

Write down what has the Lord been revealing to you about your disposition as a husband/father or wife/mother.

_____

_____

_____

_____

_____

---

6   Bure, Candace Cameron; Darlene Schacht (2010-12-20). *Reshaping It All* (pp. 108-109). B&H Publishing Group. Kindle Edition.

WEEK 6: DAY 3

The Power of a Father

Fathers, I want to say this to you before I move ahead. It is so important that you truly understand the power that God has given you. It is *supernatural*. God has given you *influential* power over your children that are absolutely beyond anyone else's influence.

For years, studies have proven the power of a father in the life of his kids. Many of these studies looked closely at the family dynamics in the lives of men like Sigmund Freud, Karl Marx, Adolph Hitler and many other hardened criminals. The one thing they all had in common was either *no* father or a very *bad relationship* with their father. On the other hand, when we study some of the most powerful people in the world, who have blessed our society, we see that most of them had healthy relationships with their fathers.

God has put it in the hearts of children to look instinctively to their daddies for affirmation, encouragement and value. But for some reason, as we grow up and raise our own kids, we forget how influential our dads were to us, not realizing how damaging our lack of proper leadership or our words and actions can be.

I have a huge sword in my office, a King Solomon sword; it is beautiful. I use it as an illustration when I am counseling. I say, "Dad, every time you get angry and yell at your child, it's just like using that sword to slice up the heart of your child."

When you act harshly toward your child, you are abusing that influential power God has given you. Your children know you are supposed to lead; they want you to lead in all areas of your home, especially in the area of training them. That is why it is so important that you lead as Christ did.

Step-Families

As I mentioned in the beginning of this chapter, a blended family does not qualify for a change in management style. As a step-in dad, you must still lead, and as a step in mom, you are still to do as the Bible instructs. Neither of you should demand that the children call you dad or mom, nor embrace you like a biological father or mother. But children must understand that biological parenting is not the issue; you are going to do what the *Bible says*, which includes participating in the training of all the children.

I would venture to say that this issue has played a major role in as many as 80% of the divorces among blended families. These couples felt that their particular circumstances exempted them from these biblical principles and failed to embrace them. In reality, the Word of God instructs us that all children belong to *Him*. They are merely loaned to us by God to love and train. *God's plan* does not change when the children live in a blended family.

See **Appendix S** for additional issues to consider.

Husband/Father is not a Dictator

Headship is *not* dictatorship or lordship, but loving leadership, with Jesus Christ as the *example*. When our house functions in any other way, we are in direct disobedience to God. More specifically, the husband, or father, is to lead, as God instructs, not as a dictator with a heavy hand. God's Word describes leadership in this way:

> **2 Timothy 2:24-26** *"And a servant of the Lord must not quarrel but be gentle to all, able to teach, patient, in humility correcting those who are in opposition, if God perhaps will grant them repentance, so that they may know the truth, and that they may come to their senses and escape the snare of the devil, having been taken captive by him to do his will."*

DIG DEEPER: *FURTHER STUDY*

After reading the above verse, what are some key characteristics that mark a servant of the Lord, and secondly what are the hopeful end results?

_____

_____

_____

_____

_____

_____

In reality, we are *all* servants of the Lord and the exhortation is to be *gentle* to all. Please notice that gentleness also needs to be expressed to those who are in *opposition* to us.

FACT FILE

> **Gentle:** "denotes seemly, fitting; hence, equitable, fair, moderate, forbearing, not insisting on the letter of the law; it expresses that considerateness that looks humanely and reasonably at the facts of a case."[7]

When someone insists on the letter of the law, "you will do it my way," they miss the whole point of Godly leadership, which ultimately leads people to *truth* and reconciliation. Dictatorship leads to quarrels and separation. Paul, a great leader, teacher and apostle of Christ is described in 1 Thessalonians 2:7 as being *"gentle among you, just as a nursing mother cherishes her own children."* His behavior toward the

---

7   W.E. Vine and F.F. Bruce, vol. 2, *Vine's Expository Dictionary of Old and New Testament Words* (Old Tappan NJ: Revell, 1981), 144-45.

Thessalonian church was similar to that of a concerned, loving mother. When we dads meet opposition, this *is* the disposition we need to use. I am not saying to ever compromise the truth or Word of God, but to be willing to adapt or adjust so to get a cooperating agreement from your spouse.

Christ showed that He was a servant-minister; as fathers and husbands, we must have that same understanding. It goes right back to our strong foundation. As we rely upon God's strength, He gives us the ability to serve as Christ did - gentle to all, patient and humble.

"In humility" means without pride, or arrogance. I know that many men resort to the dictator's style by saying, "I'm the **man**, do what **I** say. I'm supposed to lead." But that is *not* the way God wants us to lead; that is the way of the flesh.

On the other hand, a husband, or father, leading as Christ did is *not* passive, or uninvolved. He does not *relinquish* his God given-responsibility, or authority, to his wife in the area of training, as many men today are doing, saying to their wives, "I work; you take care of the kids." Meanwhile, their wives are thinking, "I wish this guy would step up to the plate! I've been hoping and praying that would happen."

To show how our culture has changed the husband's role, we just need to look at a dictionary. I have an old dictionary, which I refer to periodically, a big leather-bound *Webster International Dictionary* published in 1944. The word *husband* in that dictionary is defined as follows: "one who manages or directs his household, a married man, leadership and/or authority within a house, to manage prudently[1]." A 1996 version of the same dictionary, however, says: "a male head of household."[8] Period, that is it! The 2012 version says "The state of being united to a person of the opposite sex as husband and wife in a consensual and contractual relationship recognized by law, 2) the state of being united to a person of the same sex in a relationship like that of a traditional marriage."

What are the major points that have changed?

_____

_____

_____

The word *management* in the 1944 version is defined as: "to conduct or direct, to handle successfully or cope with, to conduct, guide, administer, to render and keep one submissive, to guide by careful and delicate treatment, to treat with care, to *husband*." Isn't that amazing? You will not find that in today's dictionary!

---

8   *Webster's II New Riverside Dictionary Revised Edition, Office Edition*; Houghton Mifflin Company, 1996

My Wife, My Helpmate

God has given me a wife to complete me. Since God says she is the one who completes me, I must look to her for input, especially on the emotional condition of the hearts of my kids, which many times I do not see. Truthfully, as a man and the way God has wired me, I am not tuned into my kid's emotional needs. I think most men can relate to this.

When my children were young, if I would come home and the chores were not done, I would be thinking one thing and one thing only, they need to be done now! Why did my wife not reinforce this? I was ready to call down the discipline. I saw things in black and white, and as a man, I wanted to fix it. Most men are wired like this because we are designed to be leaders. Gradually, I *learned* to do a little investigating, getting my wife's input, which clued me into some new information like, "Honey, he was up until 2:00 am because he's had finals this week. I told him he could do his chores tomorrow."

I am the leader of the family but my wife is a *gift* from God, she is my helpmate. It is my male nature to see this situation from a different perspective. Rule - lawn was to be mowed by 6 pm every Thursday. Consequence - if not, child would receive discipline, and it is mowed the following day. It is logical and clear. But my wife has helped me to be more *sensitive,* and to *consider* situations differently.

Note: It should be the exception, NOT the rule, for a wife to change the discipline plan laid out for the children. She is to submit to her husband's leadership, and discipline plan, but husbands also need to seek help from a wife's sensitive and nurturing nature to *help them* become better fathers and disciples for Christ.

Because of my wife's input, I understood the stress my son was under and why she made the decision she did. I would also like to mention that this did not mean that every time the children wanted out of doing a chore, or wanted to change a rule, that they could go to their mother and she had the OK to make changes on a whim. We need to work together, as a *team,* to *prevent* any type of manipulation or undermining of what *we* have established.

As men, we need to *embrace* how God made our wives—they complement us because they often see things that we miss. We would be foolish to say, "I'm the man, and it's going to happen *this* way." Yet some men do exactly that, which is not following what God says. Your wife *completes* you, as your helpmate. You must endeavor to work with her, to work in *unison*.

There were, of course, times when we did not agree and my wife had to choose to submit. By doing so, she *trusted God.* Even when I was wrong, God blessed us, not for any other reason then we desired to do things His way. When these situations happened, did she do it happily? Well, not always. But did she pout and frown, ignore me and do all the other things some women do? Praise God, no! She had *learned* to trust the Lord with my authority and, by doing so, she was blessed. When we had set a rule and the discipline, if she wanted to change it, she knew to first try and speak to me. Was I always right when I made a decision? No! I had been wrong many times, as the Lord has shown me. But, praise the Lord, we learn from our mistakes, too!

Women are commonly more *driven* by their emotions, and may *react* to situations based on their *feelings*. If they allow these feelings to rule in the area of training, many will not follow through *consistently* with enforcing rules, or issuing discipline. Men need to understand that most women have to fight harder than we do against the urge to "let it go", or not administer discipline.

This is where men need to gently say, "Honey, I understand they had a hard day, but discipline is what needs to happen at this time." Training is about working together, and it is also showing love to our children.

Note: There are a small percentage of men who seem to be driven by their emotions. The interesting reality they usually marry a women who is not (God's sense of humor.)

DIG DEEPER: *FURTHER STUDY*

Read the following verse and write down what God says He will do for those He loves?

> **Hebrews 12:5–6** *"And you have forgotten the exhortation which speaks to you as to sons: "My son, do not despise the chastening of the LORD, Nor be discouraged when you are rebuked by Him; For whom the LORD loves He chastens, And scourges every son whom He receives."*

_____

_____

_____

_____

✓ACTION PLAN

Husbands, take a moment and write out some of your wife's gifts, or strengths. (For example: "She is more discerning of the children's feelings." or "She helps me see the children's point of view.") Then, thank her for the gifts God has given her and let her know that you want her input.

_____

_____

_____

_____

_____

Next, discuss and agree to work through issues, write them down. To begin to work together as a team using God's Management Style, take a moment and pray together asking God for His help.

_____

_____

_____

_____

_____

Resistance Brings Consequences

Romans 13:1-2 *"Let every soul be subject to the governing authorities. For there is no authority except <u>from</u> God, and the authorities that exist are appointed by God. Therefore whoever resists the authority resists the ordinance of God, and those who resist will bring <u>judgment</u> on themselves."*

When Paul wrote this, the Roman government was ruling *over* the Jews with a heavy hand. The Jews wanted to be released from Roman *authority* because of the oppression and unfair treatment. That is the context of this passage.

It is also noteworthy that Paul was addressing Christians being persecuted for their faith, and the natural tendency was to *resist* the authorities. For this reason, Paul takes quite a bit of time explaining God's perspective on authority. The only time to resist is when authorities ask us to sin, or not share the gospel (Acts 4:18-20).

Here are some biblical principles we can draw from these passages:

Notice that the Scripture says, *"there is no authority except from God"* (v 1). That is pretty inclusive, no authority. In this case we have government over all citizens (Titus 3:1; 1 Pet. 2:13-17), but God also speaks of the church and pastors' authority over all believers (Heb. 13:7, 17); the headship of husband over wife (1 Cor. 11:3, 8-9; Eph. 5:22); the rule of parents over children (Ex. 20:12; Prov. 6:20-22; 23:22; Luke 2:51; Eph. 6:1); and the position of masters over all employees (Eph. 6:5-8; Col 3:22; 1 Pet. 2:18). I think you get the point.

Notice, *"the authorities that exist are appointed by God"* (v 1). This same word for appointed is used in Acts 13:48, *"as many as were appointed to eternal life."* In other words, God so orchestrates things, so that He controls who is in authority. That means good government officials and bad, good pastor and bad, good husbands and bad, good parents and bad, good employers and bad. We may not understand this, but that is what the Word of God says. Why do you think there were, and are, so many martyrs? Christians have been killed under the hand of the government (as well as many other authorities) because they would not deny their faith, even when threatened with death. The martyrs lived and died by the principle that "God appoints *all* authority."

Scripture also notes that those who *"resist authority, resist the ordinance of God"* (v 2), which is rebelling directly against the Lord. By resisting this order, you bring divine judgment on yourself. God spoke these spiritual laws into existence; they are very similar to physical laws as we discussed earlier, like gravity. Gravity is a good thing; it keeps us down here on the earth with our feet firmly on the ground. That is what God's truth does, keeps us firmly planted in His will so that we can receive His blessings for obedience.

Husbands, according to what has just been said, God has appointed you to lead, you are in authority, God calls you to this position. When the husband says, "I know I am supposed to lead but ____" you fill in the blank, you are *resisting* what God has ordained you to do, breaking a spiritual law, and bringing judgment upon yourself. This judgment can come in many forms: lack of power to live the Christian life, trouble understanding God due to your disobedience, diminishing intimacy with the Lord resulting in loss of peace, joy, confidence and/or contentment, and much more.

I have heard many *excuses* for not leading: "my wife is a better leader," "she is more educated," "she is better with the kids," "she has more patience," or "I am not a real leader," or "I just don't know how," just to name a few. But more than likely you are leading something at your job, and I bet you are pretty good at it.

When a wife says, "I know God says I need to submit to the authority of my husband, but _____," you fill in the blank. You may not have physical pain immediately as a consequence, but you will eventually experience pain. The consequences are painful in the same way a man will suffer, as mentioned above.

When we choose to walk in the light, we have peace, joy, and contentment. When we don't, these gifts from God will begin to fade. Depression, un-fulfillment, and unhappiness will soon follow, along with the many possible physical ailments.

When I started counseling one particular couple, the wife looked like she had five hundred pounds on her back. She was all hunched over and looked very depressed. She sat down and poured out her heart - how her house was a mess; she and her eighteen-year-old daughter were not speaking to each other; she and her fifteen-year-old son argued all the time; she was depressed, on medication, and seeing a psychiatrist. She went on and on. I looked at her husband, and said, "So, where are you in all this?" "She's right. Our kids argue with her all the time." I said, "What do you do about that?" "Well, when she wants me to help, I help her. When she comes and gets me, I go in there and yell and say, 'Alright, that's enough.'"

Then, this mom told me she knows that's not the right thing to do and explained why she was leading in the area of discipline rather than her husband, "My background is in psychology. I've been trained in this area." She said, "I can better deal with the children than my husband. I can communicate with them and talk things out."

I said to her, "So you are depressed, you feel like giving up and you're tired of the way you feel, right? Do you know why you are in this physical state? For sure one of the main reasons is because your home is out of order. You feel that way because you are *supposed* to. It's a *consequence* of disobedience to God's way. You're leading in the area of discipline, and your husband is supporting you. That's backwards. That's not the way it's supposed to be done."

From creation forward, the authority structure God has ordained for man is: God, man, woman, children. It does not have anything to do with inferiority. It simply means that the husband, not the wife, is head of the home, which includes the training of children. Think of it this way: dad—president, mom—vice-president. Does it hurt to think that way or to hear that? If it hurts, you need to take it up with the Lord. You need to ask God to help you trust Him in this area. Husbands need to protect their wives, and take the lead at home.

What If Parents Disagree?

Dads, remember you have to be stepping up to the plate in your leadership within the home; you are to *"bring them up in the training and admonition of the Lord"* (Eph. 6:4). I will be showing you how to set the rules and disciplines to train your children, but you have to be *motivated* to do this in unity with your wife in order to keep peace, at least as much as depends on you (Rom. 12:18). So, what if you and your wife disagree concerning an issue with the children?

"Wives, submit to your own husbands, as is fitting in the Lord" (Col. 3:18). In other words, a wife is to submit to her husband's leadership, *unless* his request is in direct conflict with *scriptural commands*. For example, if your husband, who is not saved, tells you, "Don't talk to our children about the Lord," that is directly against scriptural mandates to teach our children (Deut. 6:7).

But let's say you have an unsaved husband who does not go to church, and you have a fifteen-year-old son who says, "Dad, I don't want to go to church anymore." So Dad says, "Well, don't."

Should you as the wife try to discipline your son, or become angry with him because he is choosing Dad's side instead of yours? Do you hold back affection, or debate with your husband? No, none of these things are good. Just trust in the Lord, yield to the authority of your husband and pray. I know it is hard to do, but God's Word is clear. There is no exception. There are consequences when a wife tries to undermine that authority. You must always keep in mind that when you are a Christian, God *"works all things according to the counsel of His will."* (Eph. 1:11).

What if you are the step-dad in a blended family, and there are rules being set in the home that your wife does not want for her biological children? The moment the wife says, "I don't like that rule; I don't think my son should have to do that", she's then taking things out of God's hands and saying she can do this on her own, in her own strength. Later on, I will show you the importance of writing rules down together, but again, if the wife does not agree with a particular discipline then she must trust that the Lord will work it out. Obviously it will take patience and time to work through these issues.

Disagreements' regarding the training of the children is one of the main reasons so many blended families end in divorce. The attitude "I discipline my kids and you discipline yours," opens the door to a non-biblical management style. Actually, there are no biblical grounds for that whatsoever. When you together design your training process, it is for *all* the kids living in your home. Remember, *all* children are a *gift* to us from the Lord. (Ps. 127:3)

Let me give you an example: moms, when your non-biological child challenges your authority as a wife and step-in mother, tell them, "This is what Dad wants." When they respond with, "You're not my mom!" you reply: "That's right, I'm not your mother; you already have a mother. I'm not trying to tell you I'm your mother, but when I married your dad, I embraced the authority structure in God's Word. And God's Word says that he must lead. So I'm supporting him. If you don't like the rules and discipline, you can take it up with him. In the meantime, you need to accept the rules and discipline."

WEEK 6: DAY 4

Doubting Your Husband?

1 Peter 3:1-2 *"Wives, likewise, be submissive to your own husbands, that even if some do not obey the Word [even those who do not proclaim to be Christians, or say they are Christians but do not act as such], they, without a word, may be won by the conduct of their wives, when they observe your chaste conduct accompanied by fear" [emphasis added].*

FACT FILE

Submissive; *hopotasso* (Greek), means a voluntary attitude of giving in, cooperating, assuming responsibility, and carrying a burden.[9] "The New Testament usage of this word, meaning "to submit," "be subject to," or "rank under," is common (cf. 1 Peter 2:18; 3:5; 5:5; Luke 2:51; 10:17, 20; Rom. 8:7; 10:3; 13:1, 5; 1 Cor. 14:32, 34; 15:27; 16:16; Eph. 1:22; 5:21, 24; Phil. 3:21; Titus 2:9; 3:1; Heb. 2:5, 8; 12:9; James 4:7)."[10]

This verse speaks to a wife with a problem. She has a husband who is not obeying God's instructions – he may be ignorant, rebellious, or an unbeliever. There are no specifics about the area of disobedience, but

9   http://www.blueletterbible.org/cgi-bin/words.pl?book=1Pe&chapter=3&verse=1& strongs=5293&page=
10   John F. MacArthur, Jr., *1 Peter*, MacArthur New Testament Commentary (Chicago: Moody Publishers, 2004), 177-78.

the instruction to the wife is quite specific – continue to be submissive. The real focus of this verse is the potential to win a husband into fellowship with the Lord ("may be won"). The most powerful thing that a wife can do according to God's Word is let her conduct (not words v. 1) do the winning over of her husband. God tells a wife to put her trust in Him (God) and surrender to God's will, as a wife, and He will do the work.

I have counseled many couples who have an unbelieving spouse, and or ones that are disobedient to the Word, and it is not easy for them. God promises blessing, but does not promise an easy road. We sometimes fail to embrace the verses that speak of self-denial, the cross, and denying one's life in order to follow Jesus (Matt 16:24-25).

When husbands make foolish choices, or bad decisions, where the wife disagrees and knows that God does, too (*even if some do not obey the word* v. 1), the *natural* tendency is to debate and argue until she wins him to her perspective. I say *natural* because, after the curse, wives have been plagued with a desire to rule. The Bible says to win husband over *"without a word"* (v.1). It is one thing to say, "Honey here is another way to look at it, but I will follow your leadership and your decision," but totally different to debate and/or manipulate with bitter anger, defensive threats, and non-affirming behavior like sarcasm, criticism, pouting, and rejection, just to name a few. A Christian wife is to be praying for her husband to be a godly leader, or if he is unbelieving, for him to be saved.

Wives, do you realize it is God's goal that your husband *"may be won"*? In the context of 1 Peter 3:1-6, God is telling wives how *He* designed the relationship to operate, so that the husband *"may"* be won. Notice, this is not a promise, but a *pathway* on which God can work through you to bring your husband to Himself. Also, notice there is no time limit on following His plan. By remaining faithful to God's will for you, *Marriage is a Ministry*,[11] you are ministering to your husband and glorifying God through obedience. This process can *transform* both you and your husband by Him.

During my years as a counselor, I have seen countless marriages on the verge of divorce, papers already filed, which totally turn around when husband and wife follow *God's* plan. Husbands get saved, those already believers are inspired to learn and grow spiritually, and I see restoration for the entire family. God is so good!

Wives be encouraged; God's plan is that husbands *"may be won by the conduct of their wives, when they observe your chaste conduct"* (1 Pet 3:1c-2a). To *observe* means to look upon, to behold and contemplate.[12] Reviewing what we have learned, God created woman to be the helpmate, and a husband will know (by observing, contemplating, and looking upon his wife's conduct), whether she is supporting him. *Chaste conduct* means abstaining from all behaviors toward your husband that are contrary to God's will.

---

11 *Marriage is a Ministry* is another series that can be found on our website and is available at no cost.

12 Zohiates, 646.

One writer says that a wife may have "things in her conduct and temper which would mar the beauty of her piety, and prevent any happy influence on the mind of her husband."[13] In other words, a wife has *great influence* upon her husband, either leading him toward God, or away.

So, how does a wife accomplish this obedience? It starts in the *heart*; 1 Pt.3:3 speaks of a woman's natural concern for her hair, jewelry, and apparel (today we would add make-up), which is OK in the proper perspective. (The late J. Vernon McGee, noted pastor, said, "If the barn needs painting, paint it."), But God, in verse 4, defines real beauty and feminine character as, *"rather let it be the hidden person of the heart, with the incorruptible beauty of a gentle and quiet spirit, which is very precious in the sight of God."* God wants us to renew our minds (Eph. 4:23), and strengthen the inner person (Eph. 3:16), for out of our hearts spring the issues of life (Prov. 4:23,) and our actions (Matt. 15:18-19).

- **As a wife, what do you think "very precious in the sight of God" means in 1 Peter 3:4?**

_____

_____

_____

Please note that the one who ultimately watches is God. When a wife behaves properly, it is *"very precious"* in God's sight (1 Pet 3:4). God wants a woman to know that if her *heart* is *gentle* (meekness, mildness with forbearance), and she has a *quiet spirit* (tranquil, undisturbed), and is willing to submit, that this is of great value to Him. The reason this is precious in His sight can be found in verse 5, *"For in this manner, in former times, the <u>holy women who trusted in God</u> also adorned themselves, being submissive to their own husbands."*

God created woman for a specific relationship to man and when she takes the role of wife, or helpmate, obedience means submitting to the management system *He* has designed. To do this, a wife must willingly yield to the authority of a husband (unless it is sinful, as explained above).

The Downward Spiral to Disorder

A question for Dads: How do you act, or *react,* at home? For the first few years of my son Nicholas' life, he got me angrier than any human being on earth! I would overreact, yell, spank in anger, and generally do the opposite of love when he made mistakes. How do you think my wife reacted to my overreacting? *"Let just say she was not happy."* As a nurturer, she wanted to protect her little *chick* from his foolish father. Because I was out of control, she began defending him and correcting me in his presence. I was thinking, *"don't you undermine me, wife."* This conflict was the natural result of our handling of things in an unbiblical manner. Dissention set in, and our marriage relationship was affected. Unfortunately, this same scenario is all too common. I'm thankful that the Lord used the downward spiral in my home as a wake-up call for me.

---

13   Albert Barnes, *Notes on the New Testament: James to Jude*, ed. Robert Frew (London: Blackie & Son, 1884-885), 157.

There is an illustration of a high priest in the Old Testament, Eli that had two sons and they *"were corrupt, they did not know the Lord"* (1 Sam 2:12) but they served as priests within God's house. Eli heard everything his sons were doing, how they lay with women (1 Sam 2:22) and he finally said to them, *"No, my sons! For it is not a good report I hear. You make the Lord's people transgress"* (1 Sam 2:24) but then did *nothing* about it, he did not stop them. God had warned him many times and He finally said through the prophet Samuel,

> **1 Samuel 3:13** *"For I have told him that I will judge his house forever for the iniquity which he knows, because his sons made themselves vile, and he did not restrain them."*

This did not just happen overnight, it was a downward spiral. The very next chapter both him and his sons died as part of God's judgment. Dad's we need to act when our kids are disobedient but in a gentle and loving way. Eli showed poor leadership concerning his family, which gave a bad testimony, and set his family on a course of destruction.

The following verse explains what happens when there is foolish son and a wife who is not a team player.

> **Proverbs 19:13** *"A <u>foolish son</u> is the ruin of his father, and the contentions of a wife are a continual dripping."*

In this verse, a *"foolish son"* is one who will not *yield* to the authority and discipline of a father. That was not the case of my son; it was my sin to *react* in anger when he broke a rule. However, the second principle of this verse points out that being *contentious* is the wrong way for a wife to respond to her husband. It should be noted that a wife who argues constantly with her husband, over child-rearing or any other issue, is in disobedience (obviously, if violence is present, the issues change.)

One noted Christian author wrote about these Scriptures more than 100 years ago, showing that the issues have not changed.

> *"How unhappy the home where both a foolish son and a contentious wife are found! They are very likely to be found together; for where the wife disputes her husband's authority, siding with the children in opposition to his proper discipline, the effect on the home will be anything but good. It is a very common thing to see parents disputing and wrangling before their household. The deadly result is that the sons and daughters learn to despise the father's authority and to defy the mother's correction when she does attempt it. These children grow up with a lawless, disobedient spirit, bent on having their own way and persisting in their refusal to submit to proper discipline."* [14] *-H.A. Ironside, 1908*

---

14   H. A. Ironside, *Notes on the Book of Proverbs* (Neptune, NJ: Loizeaux Bros, 1908), 246-47.

- **Is there a similar scenario in your home?** ❏ Yes ❏ No

✓ACTION PLAN

If you responded *yes*, write down what the problems are and confess this to God, asking Him to forgive you. Then go to your family members and ask them to forgive you. As you walk in humility and obedience, God will both bless you and empower you to follow His ways in your home.

_____

_____

_____

_____

_____

Unless God is *allowed* to intervene and establish His order in the home, the *downward* spiral continues, eroding the foundation of the marriage relationship. Over a period of time, there is a loss of respect and trust, which adversely affects intimacy in the marriage. Most men will only hold out for so long when this happens, yielding in most areas to preserve some kind of sexual relationship. *"Alright, you can have authority over the children. Let me know if you need my help."* Dad steps back, and mom steps up to the plate, becoming the *main* disciplinarian and *authority* over the children, believing that she can do a better job than her husband. Dad only gets involved when things really get out of hand, or if mom asks for his input. This is "NOT" God's plan for you.

This system may work for a while in homes with complacent children. However, *if* you have a strong-willed child, or when adolescence hits, watch out! This system will crumble! When mothers abandon their God-ordained role of nurturer and cherisher and *become* leader, disciplinarian and coach rather than cheerleader, their children will eventually *resent* them, their husbands will *criticize* them and they will bear the guilt of being out of God's will.

Our main objective in life should be fulfilling *God's* will and purpose, and that includes *glorifying* Him within the walls of home. Along with King David, our attitude and purpose should be:

Psalm 101:2 *"...I will walk within my house in the integrity of my heart."* (NAU)

When *we design* substandard methods for managing our families, we are living in disobedience and dishonoring God within our homes. Some of you may have many years of unbiblical habits in your marriage. Change is always hard at first, but the rewards for obedience far exceed the work and sacrifices.

You begin with a willingness to embrace God's management style. *Dads*, for you this means that you must commit your laziness and fears to God and step forward as the leader. *Moms*, for you this means that you must put your trust in the Savior, support your husband's decisions and follow through by daily stepping back and allowing him to lead. Your children may be in a state of shock for a while, but you must proceed in obedience to the Lord, and watch Him work!

> **2 Thessalonians 1:12** *"...that the name of our Lord Jesus Christ may be glorified in you, and you in Him, according to the grace of our God and the Lord Jesus Christ."*

SELF-EXAMINATION
Management Style Evaluation

As a couple, read and ponder the following questions. Keep in mind that the purpose of this exercise is **not** to find fault in your spouse, but to allow God to speak to **you** about your own weaknesses! Be aware that if you respond with resentment, or pride, you will be hindered from yielding to the conviction of the Holy Spirit.

1. **Dad**, when your children are in your presence, do you discipline them (or do you leave it up to your wife)?
   ❏ Yes ❏ No ❏ Sometimes

2. **Mom**, do you consult your husband for input on all aspects of discipline with the children?
   ❏ Yes ❏ No ❏ Sometimes

3. **Dad**, do you listen to your wife's input on the emotional state of your children?
   ❏ Yes ❏ No ❏ Sometimes

4. **Mom**, do you keep information from your husband, not informing him on everything regarding the children?
   ❏ Yes ❏ No ❏ Sometimes

   For example: "We can't tell daddy about this because he will get really upset."

5. **Dad**, when mom says "no" and the kids come to you, do you always consult with your wife before responding?
   ❏ Yes ❏ No ❏ Sometimes

   That is, do you even think to ask your children, "Well, what did your mom say?"

6. **Mom**, do you find yourself arguing with your children, defending yourself and your rules, or disciplinary decisions?
   ❏ Yes ❏ No ❏ Sometimes

7. **Parents**, have you sat down together and agreed on the rules and disciplines you will use with your children?
❏ Yes   ❏ No   ❏ Sometimes

8. **Parents**, do you disagree in front of your children over rules, or discipline issues?
❏ Yes   ❏ No   ❏ Sometimes

(Correct answers: 1-Yes, 2-Yes, 3-Yes, 4-No, 5-Yes, 6-No, 7-Yes, 8-No).

If your answers did not match these, there's a good chance your management style is out of order. How did you do? Most couples agree there is room for improvement in their management style.

✔ACTION PLAN

If you have been convicted by this evaluation, take some time right now and write out a few specific issues. If married, discuss them as a couple, ask each other for forgiveness and make a commitment to change.

_____
_____
_____
_____
_____
_____
_____
_____
_____

WEEK 6: DAY 5

Biblical Roles of Mother and Father

Because God places such high value on the family, and He knows raising a child is challenging and often overwhelming, He has lovingly provided parenting principles in His Word. Never intending dads and moms to try and figure things out, He gives us clear direction for our responsibilities.

Note: The following is divided into the father and mother's role. But you must realize that when it comes to parenting your children, there is going to be some overlap. In other words, even though the father has the primary role of teaching and disciplining the children, there are times mom will have to do this, especially when he isn't there. And just as a mother has the primary responsibility to nurture her children, there will also be times when dad has to put on the hat of a nurturer. If a mother tends to have a disciplinary mindset, she will need to cultivate the tender side of love, nourishing and caring for her children. As you move through this section, you will notice that Paul took on all these characteristics with the people in Thessalonica, a church he dearly loved.

The Father's Role and Responsibility

Along with knowing that you are called to lead, there are other important biblical concepts for fathers that go hand in hand with leadership.

1. THE RESPONSIBLE FATHER IS A *SERVANT-PRIEST* OVER HIS FAMILY.

> **Ephesians 5:25-26** *"Husbands, love your wives, just as Christ also loved the church and gave Himself for her, that He might <u>sanctify</u> and <u>cleanse</u> her with the washing of water <u>by the word</u>."*

Paul makes it very clear that as Christ, our high priest, loves us and gave Himself for the church, so the husband is to do for his wife (which also implies his family). The goal is to *sanctify,* which is to make clean, render pure and holy, also known as sanctification. It is through the husband/father's leadership that this is to happen—he leads the way. The objective is to *cleanse,* which is to purify from the pollution of sin and selfishness. Our instruction manual is the *Word of God*. The priests in the Old Testament were stewards of the Word of God, and so it is with the husband/father.

In a sense, we fathers are to pastor our families. He has placed us as priests over our homes. A priest has the authority to perform the sacred duties of a religious institution, such as the family. The sacred rites of the family include spiritual *discipleship* of both wife and children, *overseeing* the discipline of the children, *keeping* fellowship in church a priority, *directing* the finances, and being a godly example. When fathers perform their *function* they are not only serving God, but their wives and children also.

In the Old Testament we read of Job who, acting as *priest* of his home, regularly rose early to make *"burnt offerings"* (animal sacrifices) for his children. Though we no longer offer sacrifices for sin, fathers fulfill this priesthood through *spiritual* leadership in their homes, by *discipling* and *disciplining* their children and praying with their families.

> **Job 1:4-5** *"Now his sons would go and feast in their houses, each on his appointed day, and would send and invite their three sisters to eat and drink with them. So it was, when the days of feasting had run their course, that Job would send and sanctify them, and he would rise early in the morning and offer burnt offerings according to the number of them all. For Job said, '<u>It may be</u> that my sons have <u>sinned</u> and <u>cursed</u> God in their hearts.' Thus Job did <u>regularly</u>."*

Please notice that Job did this regularly, which means he practiced this type of leadership. His concern was that his children might have sinned against, or cursed God. In other words, he cared about their relationship with God. What a godly example!

The father is not the sole disciplinarian, or discipler, of the children; however, he is to make sure that this is carried out. Sadly, in most homes today, mothers are the spiritual leaders and the main disciplinarians. We will cover more of this in detail in the next two chapters. Most men have not been taught to see themselves as priests.

Fathers, are you willing to accept this calling from God to be a priest? ❏ Yes ❏ No

As Christian parents, our primary goal should be raising children into godly, *mature* adults. We should diligently pray for our children as the apostle Paul prayed for the young Thessalonian believers to *"...walk in a manner worthy of the God who calls you into His own kingdom and glory."* (1Thess. 2:12). As a priest, the father should *lead* the way in this, making it a *priority*.

SELF-EXAMINATION

After reading the Scriptures below, Dads, please explain how these passages relate to your relationship with God. Second, if obeyed, how would it affect your relationship with your family?

> **1 Thessalonians 4:1** *"Finally then, brethren, we urge and exhort in the Lord Jesus that you should <u>abound</u> more and more, just as you received from us how you ought to <u>walk</u> and to <u>please God</u>."*

_____

_____

_____

_____

_____

_____

> **Ephesians 4:1** *"I, therefore, the prisoner of the Lord, beseech you to <u>walk</u> <u>worthy</u> of the <u>calling</u> with which you were called."*

_____

_____

_____

_____

_____

_____

Write out in your own words how this principle applies to you.

_____

_____

_____

_____

_____

_____

2. THE RESPONSIBLE FATHER *WORKS* TO SUPPORT HIS FAMILY.

> **1 Thessalonians 2:9** *"For you remember, brethren, our labor and toil; for laboring night and day, that we might not to be a burden to any of you."*

Paul was letting the church know that he worked hard to make money, to obey God and not be a financial burden to them. He knew that God had set a standard for man to work; in the Garden of Eden, God told Adam that he was to *tend* and *keep* it (Gen. 2:15). Paul's occupation outside of pastoring was tent making (Acts 18:3), and he worked diligently to support himself. Paul's concern was not just for his own needs; he said in Acts 20:34, that *"Yes, you yourselves know that these hands have provided for my necessities, and for those who were with me."* Yes, he wanted to take care of his own needs, but he was also concerned with the welfare of others.

This is a very serious subject when it comes to the family, since Paul also exhorted men that *"if anyone does not provide for **his** own, and especially for those of **his** household, **he** has denied the faith and is worse than an unbeliever."* (1 Tim. 5:8) [emphasis added]. When it says" denied the faith", it means that he is not living up to what God expects from those who have a relationship with Him. The personal pronouns are directed at the man, and this is a strong statement. One commentator says:

> To default on the basic care and support of a family member is the same as denying the faith, for no one can claim love and allegiance to God and at the same time neglect his or her family (see Matthew 5:46–47). To do so makes a person *worse than an unbeliever,* for even unbelieving idol-worshipers understood the responsibility of caring for family needs... Our families provide an arena in which we can demonstrate the quality of our love for God.[15]

This is not saying that women cannot work, but please notice where the leadership and responsibility lies. It is with the man.

---

15   Bruce B. Barton, David Veerman and Neil S. Wilson, *1 Timothy, 2 Timothy, Titus*, Life Application Bible Commentary (Wheaton, IL: Tyndale House Publishers, 1993), 101.

DIG DEEPER: *FURTHER STUDY*

Read the following verses and write down what the biblical principles are concerning work.

Colossians 3:17 *"And whatever you do in word or <u>deed</u>, do all in the name of the Lord Jesus, giving thanks to God the Father through Him."*

_____

_____

_____

_____

2 Thessalonians 3:7–10 *"For you yourselves know how you ought to follow us, for we were not disorderly among you; 8 nor did we eat anyone's bread free of charge, but <u>worked</u> with <u>labor</u> and <u>toil</u> night and day, that we might not be a burden to any of you, 9 not because we do not have authority, but to make ourselves an <u>example</u> of how you should follow us. 10 For even when we were with you, we commanded you this: If anyone will <u>not</u> work, neither shall he eat."*

_____

_____

_____

_____

2 Thessalonians 3:12 *"Now those who are such we command and exhort through our Lord Jesus Christ that they <u>work</u> in quietness and eat their own bread."*

_____

_____

_____

_____

Titus 3:14 *"And let our people also learn to <u>maintain</u> good works, to <u>meet urgent needs</u>, that they may not be unfruitful."*

_____

_____

_____

_____

God's Word is not suggesting that fathers work to the point of neglecting their families, but rather to *work responsibly*, that the family not be burdened financially. The responsible father is instructed to maintain a job in order to care for the needs of his family, while not *neglecting* the priorities of a husband and father. The Scripture below also shows the importance of taking care of one's family.

2 Corinthians 12:14 *"...for the children ought not to lay up for the parents, but the parents for the children."*

Write out in your own words how this principle applies to you.

_____

_____

_____

_____

3. THE RESPONSIBLE FATHER IS A *WITNESS* OF CHRISTIAN FAITH TO HIS FAMILY.

1 Thessalonians 2:10 *"You are witnesses, and God also, how devoutly and justly and blamelessly we behaved ourselves among you who believe."*

Paul points to the unblemished testimony that he had, not only before the church in Thessalonica, but also before God. This is not bragging, but simply pointing out that the church could follow his example. The same should be true concerning our leadership as husbands and fathers. God, our families, and other believers should be able to see that our behavior represents Christ. Paul draws out three distinct principles that characterized his behavior and made his faith authentic.

> **FACT FILE**
>
> **Devoutly** - *Holy, pious, sacred, dedicated to God.* This describes your abiding relationship with Christ. When you are devoted, or dedicated to God, that relationship is the source of a *sacred* life, and the following two behaviors normally follow.

> **FACT FILE**
>
> **Justly** – *means with integrity and honesty, just, uprightness of character and behavior, daily desiring to live life according to what pleases God.* When you know the Word of God, you are able to judge what is right and wrong. As a husband and father, is it your desire to be obedient, empowered to do what you never could do before. You can have His divine power working in you. (2 Pet. 1:3; Rom. 1:4; 2 Cor. 12:9).

> **FACT FILE**
>
> **Blamelessly** – *means faultless, able to stand a critics' scrutiny.* As you move along in obedience to God's will, you are *transformed* into the image of Christ, and your Godly behavior becomes evident to others.

This does not mean perfection, but direction; even Paul struggled at times (Rom. 7:18; 1 Tim. 1:15). But these were principles he practiced on a regular basis. Fathers are called by God to be spiritual leaders in the home and role models to their children. A responsible father does not compromise in his speech, nor does he find pleasure in things that might stumble, or offend his children.

SELF-EXAMINATION

Read the following Scriptures and write down how living these truths could affect the relationship with your children.

Colossians 1:10 *"...that you may walk worthy of the Lord, fully pleasing Him, being fruitful in every good work and increasing in the knowledge of God."*

_____

_____

_____

_____

2 Corinthians 4:2 *"But we have renounced the hidden things of shame, not walking in craftiness nor handling the word of God deceitfully, but by manifestation of the truth commending ourselves to every man's conscience in the sight of God."*

_____

_____

_____

_____

Write out in your own words how this principle applies to you.

_____

_____

_____

_____

4. THE RESPONSIBLE FATHER MAKES TIME TO *TRAIN/DISCIPLE* HIS CHILDREN IN THE FAITH, BY *EXHORTING* AND *COMFORTING* THEM.

1 Thessalonians 2:11 *"...as you know how we <u>exhorted</u>, and <u>comforted</u>, and <u>charged</u> <u>every</u> <u>one</u> of you, as a father does his own children."*

Paul's leadership style in the church is compared to a father training his children. In fact, there is the inference that this is how fathers are to treat their children. There also is a strong reference that obedience to God is the goal. This model falls right in line with *Loving Communication*; love is the driving motivation behind each one of the underlined words. When Paul says, *"as you know,"* he is calling them to remember that he did not *neglect* to train/disciple them; it was an undeniable fact that he inspired them to godliness through proper training.

FACT FILE

Exhort – *parakleo,* (Greek), *to call to one's side, to aid, to encourage, admonish or exhort someone to do something.* This verb is a present active participle, which means that Paul continued to do this so they could grow in their relationship to God. He had a *positive impact* on their lives, and that is the type of leadership we must have as dads. We are to come alongside our children and help them grow in the things of the Lord. The attitude has to be like Psalm 34:11, which says, *"Come, you children, listen to me; I will teach you the fear of the LORD."*

FACT FILE

Encourage, or Comfort – *means to inspire, support; console in time of trouble or worry, soothing encouragement designed to cheer up and to inspire correct behavior.* This type of fatherly *influence* cannot fail to inspire correct behavior in our children. Of course, many times it means we must die to ourselves and put on tender love.

FACT FILE

Charged, Implore, Urging - *martyromenoi* (Greek), implies the "delivery of truth" and was likely meant to convey the more directive functions of a father. A good father encourages and provides guidance. Paul did not claim ultimate authority over his spiritual children in the Lord, requiring of them what he willed. Rather, Paul's function, as their spiritual father, was to train believers to "live lives worthy of God." It was not Paul's own will, but the Heavenly Father's, that governed both his actions and the guidance he gave to the church."[16]

What a perfect picture for us as dads to follow. We are to train our children, to *raise them up to maturity through discipleship and proper discipline.* The responsible father does not *neglect* his God-given role, or delegate it to his wife, but assumes authority as the leader, shepherd, and servant in the home.

Write out in your own words how this principle applies to you.

_____

_____

_____

_____

---

16   D. Michael Martin, vol. 33, *1, 2 Thessalonians*, The New American Commentary (Nashville: Broadman & Holman Publishers, 1995), 84.

5. THE RESPONSIBLE FATHER IS A *TEACHER-MANAGER* IN HIS HOME.

Ephesians 6:4 *"And you, fathers, do not provoke your children to wrath, but bring them up in the training and admonition of the Lord."*

We used this Scripture earlier to show the direct relationship between a father managing his home and bringing his children to Godly *maturity*. This passage is meant to show a father two possible effects of his influence - and the vital importance of using that influence in love, to direct a child closer to the Lord. This is not to say that mothers are not to be part of the training. They are to be involved in all aspects of discipline and discipleship, but not the one ultimately responsible.

The husband's/father's leadership role in the home is so vital, Scripture requires any man up for leadership in the church be first and foremost committed to fulfilling his leadership role at home. Leaders are called by God to set an *example* for the people. This does not mean that there is one *standard* for leaders and another *standard* for the people. This is why Paul urged the Corinthians, *"Imitate Me as I imitate Christ."* (1 Cor. 11:1). The home life of a pastor/ministry leader is like a miniature church where he shepherds his family. Paul gives explicit instructions to Timothy on how God wants *His* church to function, by outlining the qualifications for pastors and deacons (1 Tim. 3:1-13). A pastor must be:

1 Timothy 3:4 *"one who **rules** his own house **well**, having his children in submission with all reverence."*

FACT FILE

Rule - *To rule, manage, lead, shepherd and guide.* "By implication this means to take care of something, to be diligent, to practice."[17]

As you can see, God is concerned that a pastor/ministry leader first carries out the leadership role of a good husband/father by managing his house well. This is so important that he says in verse 5, *"for if a man does not know how to rule his own household, how will he take care of the church of God?"* If the pastor/leader can lead his family, which is small compared to the church, then he meets the qualification. Scripture is clear that a man who is *not* the spiritual leader in his home is *disqualified* from church leadership. Again, this does not mean perfection but it does mean that he has a firm grasp on Godly leadership in his home. According to God's instructions, one author says,

Paul demanded that the church leader be exemplary in controlling his own family. He was to raise children known for their obedience and morally upright behavior. The verb for

---

17   Zodhiates, 1220.

"manage" carries the idea of governing, leading, and giving direction to the family. The same Greek word appears in 1 Thess. 5:12 ("are over you"), and 1 Tim. 5:17 ("direct"), and also in v. 5 ("manage"). The term demands an effective exercise of authority bolstered by a character of integrity and sensitive compassion. Its use in v. 5 with the verb "take care of" defines the quality of leadership as related more to showing mercy than to delivering ultimatums.[18]

But it is not just the pastor/elders that need to have their homes in order, so do the deacons. The leaders are to set an example that the congregation can follow, especially when it comes to families.

1 Timothy 3:12 *"Let deacons be the husbands of one wife, ruling their children and their own houses well."*

What a blessing to have strong, godly families. It is a self-evident truth that this occurs when men are guided by the Bible, a perfect resource that provides all the information we need for success. God is so good!

SELF-EXAMINATION

Fathers, what have you learned from the 5 principles?

1. _____

_____

2. _____

_____

3. _____

_____

4. _____

_____

5. _____

_____

---

18 Thomas D. Lea and Hayne P. Griffin, vol. 34, *1, 2 Timothy, Titus*, The New American Commentary (Nashville: Broadman & Holman Publishers, 1992), 112.

How does this Biblical role differ from your current parenting style and does there need to be any changes?

_____

_____

_____

_____

✓ACTION PLAN

Commit these to prayer each day asking God to work them out in your life.

Dads, you have been chosen, and ordained by God, to lead and serve as a priest over the institution He created - your family. Quit looking at your inabilities and weaknesses, and start looking to God's promises (2 Pet. 2:4), and His grace (2 Cor. 12:9-10), to enable and empower you to accomplish the tasks *He* has given.

Biblical Roles of the Responsible Mother

THE MOTHER'S ROLE AS A CARING INFLUENCE

Mothers, besides knowing the role as a *helpmate* to your husband, there are key biblical principles guiding the relationship with your children. As we turn to 1 Thessalonians 2:7-8, we see Paul using motherly terms to describe his behavior toward the believers at Thessalonica. Even though these Biblical principles can apply to all Christians, there are some solid truths here for mothers.

1. THE CARING MOTHER IS *GENTLE* WITH HER CHILDREN.

1 Thessalonians 1:7a *"But we were gentle among you..."*

FACT FILE

Gentle = *Mild, peaceable, quiet, composed*.

This was quite a statement about the apostle Paul and his fellow ministers, since they were leaders who regularly used their authority. But their purposes were not selfish, rather carried out for the good of others. The Bible says that they were *"among"* them, serving with a gentle and kind spirit. Noted Bible scholar and author, John MacArthur says,

> The term **gentle** is at the heart of this verse. It means to be kind to someone and encompasses a host of other virtues: acceptance, respect, compassion, tolerance of imperfections, patience, tenderheartedness, and loyalty.[19]

---

19   John F. MacArthur, Jr., *1 & 2 Thessalonians*, MacArthur New Testament Commentary (Chicago: Moody Press, 2002), 45.

What a picture of gentleness; Paul is focusing on how he acted among them. He behaved this way, not *"as pleasing men, but God who tests our hearts"* (1 Thess. 2:4). His whole motivation was that of *pleasing* God. I do understand that some women are gentle by nature, while others have a tougher demeanor. But, since God is going to test your heart to see if you are gentle toward your children, then you should be ready to confess any wrongs when they come up, repent, and be transformed. It goes without saying that a gentle mother *is not* out of control, angry, yelling, judging, or manipulating toward her children.

The word *"were"* in this verse, as "we were gentle," originated from a Hebrew word implying *a state of change, condition, or the passing from one state to another, to become.*[20] This is a perfecting process, and by determining to *yield* daily to the Holy Spirit, God will cause you to become all that He calls you to be!

DIG DEEPER: *FURTHER STUDY*

Read the following verses; write out what they say about gentleness, and how it could be applied to parenting.

Proverbs 15:1 *"A gentle answer turns away wrath, but a harsh word stirs up anger."* NAS

_____

_____

_____

_____

2 Timothy 2:24 *"And a servant of the Lord must not quarrel but be gentle to all, able to teach, patient."*

_____

_____

_____

_____

James 3:17 *"But the wisdom that is from above is first pure, then peaceable, gentle, willing to yield, full of mercy and good fruits, without partiality and without hypocrisy."*

_____

_____

_____

_____

20   Zodhiates, 367-368

2. THE CARING MOTHER *NURTURES* HER CHILDREN.

1 Thessalonians 2:7b *"...as a nursing mother..."*

FACT FILE

Nurse - *The act of nursing, suckle, nourish, train, something that nourishes, to supply with nourishment, to educate or foster, to further the development of someone or something.*

The obvious picture here is a mother breast-feeding her child. The mother and child both know that this is the place of nourishment, love and attention, which is the way God has designed the mother-child relationship. A loving and caring mother *wants* to give to the infant but, as a child grows, this *type of sacrifice* and intimacy can fade away, or become dulled.

Paul brings to remembrance his actions toward those God has placed under his care, reveals that his heart toward them is faithful and tender like a nursing mother. Paul uses many examples of motherly love: Galatians 4:19 says *"My little children, for whom I labor in birth again until Christ is formed in you,"* and *"I do not write these things to shame you, but as my beloved children I warn you"* (1 Cor. 4:14). He also directs believers to imitate him, as he imitates Christ.

From conception, and throughout the life of her child, a mother is called to nurture. Obviously methods change with the maturity of a child, but a mother's heart should always be to nourish and build up. The role of a mother is to show her children love and acceptance by *actions* and *words*. A nurturing mother *does not* use harsh words, ignore or push her children away, or withhold affection from them. She does not indulge in mind games, or sinful manipulation as discipline.

Remember, *love* is the most powerful motivator, not just a demonstration of feelings and emotions. And unselfish love is only possible through a relationship with Jesus Christ, by abiding in Him. This involves knowing God's word, and going to Him in prayer for wisdom and strength. He can enable you to *give* continuously, expecting nothing in return, just as a mother loves her nursing infant. Take heed to what one author says:

> If a nursing mother does not feed herself, she cannot feed her baby. If she eats certain foods, her baby will get sick. Similarly, the spiritual diet of a Christian parent is vitally important to the health of a newer Christian. The gentleness and unselfishness of Paul as a spiritual parent shines through in this illustration.[21]

---

21   John F. Walvoord, Roy B. Zuck and Dallas Theological Seminary, *The Bible Knowledge Commentary: An Exposition of the Scriptures* (Wheaton, IL: Victor Books, 1985), 1 Th 2:7.

⌕ SELF-EXAMINATION

How are you doing in your abiding relationship with Christ?

_____

_____

_____

_____

_____

_____

Write out in your own words how this principle applies to you.

_____

_____

_____

_____

_____

3. THE CARING MOTHER *CHERISHES*, OR *TENDERLY CARES* FOR HER CHILDREN.

1 Thessalonians 2:7c *"...cherishes her own children." V. 7*

Cherish (tender care, NAS) - *To give heed to, to pay attention to, to minister, to soften by heat, to keep warm as of birds covering their young with feathers (Deut. 22:6), to cherish with tender love, to foster with tender care."* <u>Vine's Expository Dictionary</u>

Paul uses the Greek word *thalop*, translated *cherishes* in the NKJ version of the Bible. Also take special note of the words *"her own children."* God had given Paul the responsibility of not only bringing believers into His kingdom, through preaching, but also treating them as his own spiritual children. For Paul, that meant responsibility, and concern so great that he compares it to motherhood. The term *"cherishes her own children"* evokes thoughts of protective, tender care toward children who cannot be considered so precious by any other. Another translation, (NAS) *"tenderly cares,"* indicates continuous action. Isn't that the truth - a mom's work is never done when it comes to cherishing and ministering to her children.

A Christian mother will keep her heart soft and tender, which is not always easy. Because such love brings vulnerability, mothers can be tempted to become hardened, or calloused from the disappointments of neglect, rejection, or rebellion of their children. Frustration, fatigue, and worry are other pressures that can affect a mother's mood. To remain strong, a mother must continually be *yielding,* asking the Holy Spirit to guard her heart (Eph. 4:30; 5:18). A tender mother *forgives* her children and *seeks* their forgiveness when she has been wrong (Matt. 6:12, 14-15).

Read the following verses and write out how they could help you be a better mom.

Ephesians 4:32 *"And be kind to one another, tenderhearted, forgiving one another, even as God in Christ forgave you."*

_____
_____
_____
_____

Philippians 2:3 *"Let nothing be done through selfish ambition or conceit, but in lowliness of mind let each esteem others better than himself."*

_____
_____
_____
_____

Write out in your own words how this principle applies to you.

_____
_____
_____
_____

4. THE CARING MOTHER *AFFECTIONATELY* LONGS FOR HER CHILDREN.

1 Thessalonians 2:8a *"So, affectionately longing for you..."*

FACT FILE

Affectionately longing – "The Greek word, translated **fond affection** (*homeiromai;* (used only here in the New Testament) means to long for someone passionately and earnestly, and, being linked to a mother's love, is intended here to express an affection so deep and compelling as to be unsurpassed. Ancient inscriptions on the tombs of dead babies sometimes contained this term when parents wanted to describe their sad longing for a too-soon-departed child."[22]

Affectionately longing can only mean a love that is expressed through physical contact, and acts of kindness. It cannot be overstated that a truly loving mother must affirm her children with hugs, kisses, encouraging

22   John F. MacArthur, Jr., *1 & 2 Thessalonians*, MacArthur New Testament Commentary (Chicago: Moody Press, 2002), 46.

words, and other appropriate displays of *affection*. An affectionate mother *knows* her children individually and *studies* how to make each child feel special. Longing indicates continuously keeping them in your thoughts, desiring their companionship, and being creative to remind them of your love by perhaps baking cookies, leaving notes in their lunches, or spending time on individual activities.

✓ACTION PLAN

Take a moment right now and pray, asking God to show you any hindrances that may be keeping you from being affectionate toward your children. Write down some ways you are, and or can be showing affection.

_____

_____

_____

_____

_____

DIG DEEPER: *FURTHER STUDY*

Read the following verse and write out how it inspires new attitudes or actions toward your children.

Romans 12:10 *"Be kindly affectionate to one another with brotherly love, in honor giving preference to one another."*

_____

_____

_____

_____

Write out in your own words how this principle applies to you.

_____

_____

_____

_____

5. THE CARING MOTHER *GIVES* OF HERSELF TO DO WHAT IS BEST FOR HER CHILDREN.

1 Thessalonians 2:8b *"...we were well pleased to impart to you not only the gospel of God but also our own life, because you had become dear to us."*

FACT FILE

Impart – this verb has the idea of sharing something, which one already retains in part.

Paul and his companions not only preached in Thessalonica, but they also imparted their lives for the sake of Christ. In this context, it literally means, "they gave up their souls," deepest inner being, for the sake of the Thessalonians. A woman who fulfills the biblical role for motherhood does the same thing when she, at great cost to herself, unselfishly and generously sets aside her life for the benefit of her beloved children."[23] A godly mother understands that her priority is to place the loving and training of her children before self-interest. She loves her children with God's *supernatural* love, despite their mistakes, failures, and sins.

SELF-EXAMINATION

Mothers, what have you learn from the 5 principles?

1. _____
_____

2. _____
_____

3. _____
_____

4. _____
_____

5. _____
_____

How does this Biblical role differ from your current parenting style and does there need to be any changes?

_____
_____
_____
_____
_____

Commit to pray for these changes each day.

---

23   John F. MacArthur, Jr., *1 & 2 Thessalonians*, MacArthur New Testament Commentary (Chicago: Moody Press, 2002), 47.

Week 7: Training Up Your Children Part 2 - Teaching Them Biblical Truth

WEEK 7: DAY 1

Introduction to Discipleship

Now that we are building a *strong foundation* in Christ, and have learned how to properly love our children while working within God's management style, we are prepared for *training* them. Many believe that raising good children primarily depends on *discipline*, but it is important to understand that there are two processes essential for bringing them to *maturity*. The *first* is **discipling** (spiritual instruction), and the *second* is **disciplining** (instilling character).

Providing spiritual instruction for our children is called *discipling*. Leading your child to Christ is a great blessing, but so is the responsibility of teaching them spiritual truth. It is never too early to begin lovingly introducing a child to the Lord, to talk about His desire to have a relationship with them. Parents can fall into error, believing a child is too young to learn, or that this training should be done in Sunday School. Praise God for His church, and all who contribute to the spiritual growth of our children, but the *main* responsibility for discipleship belongs to parents.

Note: Please turn to Appendix C, *How to Lead a Child to Christ*.

It is important for all Christians to understand that *discipling* others is *not* an optional responsibility, but a calling from God. After His resurrection, Jesus appeared to His followers for a time. As He prepared to ascend to the Father in Heaven, He delivered a command we call *The Great Commission*. Jesus' instruction was not only to the disciples of that day, but to be passed down to all believers. We know this because His <u>command</u> was to *"make disciples of <u>ALL</u>."* May the following scripture give you a *passion* for making disciples of all, especially your children.

> **Matthew 28:19-20** *"<u>Go</u> therefore and <u>make disciples</u> of all the nations, <u>baptizing</u> them in the name of the Father and of the Son and of the Holy Spirit, 20 <u>teaching</u> them to observe all things that I have commanded you; and lo, I am with you always, even to the end of the age."*

The original language of this scripture is Greek and it is very specific. *"Make disciples"* is the main verb, and the rest of the sentence supports the action of that verb. *Go*, *baptizing* and *teaching* are all participles that refer to *"make disciples."* The main emphasis of Jesus' command is to *"make disciples,"* which is an imperative verb that means, "to do and *continue* to do". This means that we must be *intentional* about discipleship. It should be an ongoing *discipline* for every believer, which includes making disciples of our children. In order to carry out this vision we must understand three things.

FIRST... WHAT IS A DISCIPLE?

In order to make a disciple, we need to understand the biblical definition.

> **FACT FILE**
>
> **Disciple** - *(noun), Greek, mathētḗs, is a student, learner, or pupil, but it means much more in the NT. It is a follower who <u>accepts</u> the instruction given to him and <u>makes it his rule of conduct</u>.[1] In Classic Greek, mathetes is what we would call "an <u>apprentice</u>," one who not only learns facts from the teacher, but other things such as his attitudes and philosophies. In this way the mathetes was what we might call a "student-companion," who doesn't just sit in class listening to lectures, but rather, who <u>follows the teacher</u> to learn <u>life</u> as well as facts[2] and progressively takes on the character of the teacher.*

I hope you can grasp the picture here; our homes, and anywhere we go with our children, can be a classroom for them to become a disciple of Christ. It is where they learn true Christian conduct, attitudes and philosophies. I am sure you have heard the saying "more things are caught than taught." In other words, your children are watching you and they catch, and/or mimic, your actions even more than what you say.

As we read the gospels, we can see how Christ discipled his chosen twelve men. They spent about three years learning, watching, asking questions, listening to His teaching, and even imitating His behavior. The disciples where followers of Christ and wherever He went, that was their classroom. Jesus taught them as they went from one life lesson to another and, when they did not understand, He stopped and *explained* (Mark 4:34). If they did not comprehend a statement, He *clarified* (Mark 8:15-21), and when they lacked faith, He *rebuked* them (Mark 9:19-29). During Jesus' public ministry, as he responded to all who came to Him, He continuously said, "follow My *example*, *learn* from Me, be My disciple".

Your children can learn to be a disciple of Christ through your words and actions. They also can learn to be a disciple of unrighteous, worldly desires and behaviors. They *will* follow your example, whether good or bad.

---

1   Spiros Zodhiates, 936.

2   J.D. Watson, *A Word for the Day: Key Words From the New Testament* (Chattanooga, TN: AMG Publishers, 2006), 321.

⚲ SELF-EXAMINATION

How would you view the classroom of your family as husband/father, wife/mother? Are there bad habits, behaviors that need to be stopped? If so, take a moment and write out a confession to the Lord, along with your commitment to change.

_____

_____

_____

_____

_____

_____

_____

SECOND...HOW DO WE "MAKE DISCIPLES"?

Now that we understand the meaning of discipleship, how do we follow through and make disciples? First, we need to follow Christ's example. And He has told us what is expected: Jesus' mandate to *"make disciples,"* and *"teach them diligently,"* (Deut. 6:7), is an exhortation to all but, for our purposes, we are concentrating on parenting. Keep in mind; parents have more influence over children than anyone. Thankfully, God has clearly supplied us with enough information to help us guide our children in the right direction. As you study the following definition, take special notice of underlined points related to making disciples.

> ### FACT FILE
>
> **Make Disciples** – *(verb) Greek, matheteuo, is to make a disciple (Matt 28:19; Acts 14:21); to instruct (Matt 13:52) with the <u>purpose</u> of making a disciple. It is not exactly the same as "make converts," though it is surely implied. The term "make disciples" <u>places somewhat more stress</u> on the fact that the <u>mind</u>, as well as the <u>heart</u> and the <u>will</u>, must be won for God[3] <u>by instructing</u> new believers on how to <u>follow</u> Jesus, to <u>submit</u> to Jesus' lordship, and to take up his mission of compassionate service.[4] It also involves bringing people into relationship with Jesus as pupils to teacher and getting them to <u>take His yoke of instruction</u> upon themselves as <u>authoritative</u> (Matt 11:29), <u>accepting His words as true</u>, and <u>submitting</u> to His will as what is right.[5]*

If you look closely, you will notice that this definition describes the *purpose* and *process* that Christ followed with His disciples. Please take some time to meditate on it, and then answer the next question. Most people I talk with have never really given this subject much thought; therefore it has not become a priority

---

3   William Hendriksen and Simon J. Kistemaker, vol. 9, *Exposition of the Gospel According to Matthew*, New Testament Commentary (Grand Rapids: Baker Book House, 1953-2001), 999.

4   Bruce B. Barton, *Matthew*, Life Application Bible Commentary (Wheaton, IL: Tyndale House Publishers, 1996), 577-78.

5   Tom Constable, *Tom Constable's Expository Notes on the Bible* (Galaxie Software, 2003), Mt 28:19.

within their parenting. The fact that most fathers or mothers were not discipled by their parents therefore leaves them with no example, even those who were raised in Christian homes.

⚲ SELF-EXAMINATION

In your own words, write down some of the essential points for making a disciple.

_____

_____

_____

_____

_____

DIG DEEPER: _FURTHER STUDY_

Read the following verse and notice what Paul was encouraging the believers to do in Philippi. What are the key principles in this verse in how to disciple our children?

> **Philippians 4:9** *"The things which you <u>learned</u> and <u>received</u> and heard and <u>saw</u> in me, these <u>do</u>, and the God of peace will be with you."*

_____

_____

_____

_____

_____

THIRD...WHAT IS DISCIPLING/DISCIPLESHIP?

To "make a disciple" is to help another become an imitator of Christ. When obeying Christ's command to do this, *discipling,* or *discipleship,* is the *process* that we follow. Even though these specific words are not used in the Bible, the concept is clearly portrayed by the way Jesus taught His followers, and also throughout the New Testament. Further study will show a connection between the definitions we just studied and the process of *discipling*, especially as it relates to our children. I believe this definition of discipling, from Greg Ogden, also describes the Biblical concepts we should be using when discipling our children.

FACT FILE

Discipling/Discipleship – *"Discipling is an <u>intentional relationship</u> in which we <u>walk along-side</u> other disciples in order to <u>encourage, equip and challenge one another in love to grow toward maturity in Christ</u>. This includes equipping the disciple to teach others as well."*[6]

---

6   Greg Ogden, *Discipleship Essentials: A Guide to Building Your Life in Christ* (Downers Grove, IL: InterVarsity Press, 1998), 17.

Although this definition relates to *all* discipleship, I would like to particularly relate it to the parent-child relationship. This picture of discipleship describes what we should want to do with our children, as it also defines what Christ did with His disciples.

Truly *discipling* our children means having *intentional relationships* with them. This is *our* responsibility. Jesus called His disciples to follow Him, or *walk alongside* Him, but He was *intentional* by taking the first step. We must realize that intentional relationships do NOT happen by accident; there needs to be a pre-determined *plan* that is *maintained,* or *consistent.* That is what this chapter is about; giving you a *plan* that will help you get started on the discipleship process.

Having the proper attitude when *discipling* our children requires a commitment to *lovingly* help them *grow toward maturity* in Christ. Remember, *love* is the most powerful motivator. An atmosphere of love prepares your child's heart to receive instruction, especially when you *challenge* them to do what is right. Jesus challenged His disciples in a direct and uncompromising way, but it was always done in love. When a child is secure in your love, they are more apt to listen and obey what you are saying. The Scripture says we are to be *"speaking the truth in love."* (Eph. 4:15).

Discipling Children to Be *Like* Christ

We must never lose track of the *goal*: to teach our children about Jesus Christ, so that they will experience His love and learn His ways. Too many parents try to make their children into copies of themselves, or what "they" want them to be. The apostle Paul revealed God's will when he wrote, *"Imitate me, just as I also imitate Christ"* (1Cor 11:1). This is the Biblical goal of discipleship: helping our children find out who they are in Christ. Jesus spoke of this principle in Matthew 10:25, when He said, *"It is enough for the disciple that he <u>be like</u> his teacher,",* and in Luke 6:40, *"everyone who is <u>perfectly trained</u> will be like his teacher."* The single, overriding truth is that the disciple will emulate the teacher.

To be *"perfectly trained"* is the Greek word, *katartizo,* and the meaning is "to put a thing in its appropriate condition, to establish, equip so it is deficient in no part."[7] As parent/teachers, the objective of discipleship is to share the gospel with our children, leading them to receive Jesus as Savior; show them how to abide in Christ each day; and teach them how to study the Bible, understanding the concept of being transformed into His image (Rom 8:29).

Since God has commissioned us to make disciples on a continuing basis, the privilege of discipling our children never ends, even when they leave home. We are to be available, always in prayer, ready to share Godly wisdom, instruction, and encouragement when they need us. Discipling becomes a *way of life*, where we

---

7   Zodhiates, 842-843.

are always following Christ ourselves, and talking regularly to others about God's goodness and our need to follow Him in all things.

DIG DEEPER: *FURTHER STUDY*

Write out in your own words how the following verse describes the process of discipleship.

>**2 Corinthians 3:18** *"But we all...are <u>being transformed</u> into the same image from glory to glory, just as by the Spirit of the Lord."*

_____

_____

_____

_____

SELF-EXAMINATION

Take a moment and examine yourself. Are you experiencing this transformation? If so, write out a praise report to God; if not, write out a prayer for God's help, asking Him to make this real in your life.

_____

_____

_____

_____

_____

_____

Discipleship and Your *Strong Foundation*

In our lesson titled *A Strong Foundation*, we saw the *necessity* of building life upon a foundation of intimacy with Christ. Through this relationship alone comes our stability and strength, and the power to accomplish God's will and purpose. We also studied Deuteronomy 6:1-6, where God told the children of Israel that they, and their sons and grandsons were to *carefully* observe His commandments, out of love for Him. The faith of the fathers was to extend to following generations. Spiritual training (discipleship) of the children was the God-given privilege and responsibility of the parents. The *biblical directives* have not changed; we are to *"make disciples"* (Matt 28:19), and *"bring them up in the training and admonition of the Lord"* (Eph. 6:4). It is direct disobedience when we neglect, or refuse, to *actively* disciple our children.

May I remind you, we disciple our children first by our *example* and then by our *instruction*. As we raise our children, they observe what we *say*, but *what* we *do is even more powerful*. Our example can influence them to *follow* after God, or *rebel*. When they see hypocrisy is us, it can breed rebellion in them.

⌕ SELF-EXAMINATION

In what ways has your *strong foundation* grown since starting this workbook? How have you set aside time for prayer and the Word? Is this your daily priority? If not, why? What choices need to be changed? Write it out.

_____

_____

_____

_____

_____

_____

_____

_____

Hypocrisy Breeds Rebellion!

If we want our children to walk with the Lord, we must be an *example*. Charles Stanley wrote, *"Nothing makes the kingdom of God more compelling to unbelievers [or Christians] than Christians who demonstrate the Spirit's life within them."*[8] And I will add that nothing makes the kingdom of God more unappealing and undesirable to our children than growing up in a home where Christianity is preached, but *not* practiced. When your children see a *double standard* - you say one thing but do another - they *learn* to do the same and, by your example, lose respect for you and the God you proclaim.

There is a saying, "Do as I say, but not as I do," which literally defines hypocrisy. Too many Christian parents are living by this philosophy. Jesus delivered harsh words to the scribes and Pharisees, who said the right things but behaved the opposite: *"Hypocrites! Well did Isaiah prophesy about you, saying; 'These people draw near to Me with their mouth, And honor Me with their lips, But their heart is far from Me."* (Matt. 15:8).

A *hypocrite* is someone who acts phony, or is a counterfeit; a man who assumes and speaks, or acts, under a pretend character.[9] Like an actor playing a role, part or character that is scripted for him, Jesus called these people hypocrites; they were acting the part, saying the right things, but He knew their hearts. We have to be very careful that we are not one person in public, or at church, and someone different at home. Let's be real, we are very motivated to act our best at church, putting on godly character, looking like a Christian, and then find it more difficult to act that way at home.

I am sure we all have looked at other Christians, seeing this hypocrisy, but how many of us have considered

---

8   http://www.intouch.org/you/article-archive/content?topic=fruitful_living_article [accessed 8-23-2012].

9   Zodhiates, 5274.

ourselves? You may have even felt the sting of such behavior in another, thinking "I can't believe a Christian would do that to me!"

SELF-EXAMINATION

Stop right now and write out what you felt in that situation?

_____

_____

_____

_____

Now, put yourself in your child's place. How do you think they feel when you behave as a hypocrite?

_____

_____

_____

_____

When kids grow up in homes where God's love and true Christianity are lived out, they will not as easily be drawn into the world, where truth is compromised and righteousness is mocked. Be careful, parents. The enemy will use anything to draw our children away from Christianity, including our bad behavior.

SELF-EXAMINATION

Stop now for *self-examination*. Are you telling your children one thing, and excusing the same behaviors in yourself? God tells us not to judge others, but to judge ourselves. Has God revealed any hypocrisy in you while reading this lesson, if so write them out? Now, ask God and your children to forgive you, and commit to change. Remember to ask for forgiveness each time you fail (1 Jn. 1:9).

_____

_____

_____

_____

_____

DIG DEEPER: *FURTHER STUDY*

Read this Scripture from the Amplified Bible translation. In your own words, write out what Paul was saying about having a good testimony toward others.

Acts 24:16, *"Therefore I always exercise and discipline myself [mortifying my body, deadening my carnal affections, bodily appetites, and worldly desires, endeavoring in all respects] to have a clear (unshaken, blameless) conscience, void of offense toward God and toward men."*

_____
_____
_____
_____
_____

Thomas Woodrow Wilson, 28th president of the United States (1913-1921), also served as president of Princeton University (1902-1910). While president of Princeton, he spoke these words to a parents' group:

> I get many letters from parents about your children. You want to know why we people up here in Princeton cannot make more of them and do more for them. Let me tell you the reason we cannot. It may shock you just a little, but I am not trying to be rude. The reason is that they are your sons, reared in your home, blood of your blood, bone of your bone. They have absorbed the ideals of your homes. You have formed and fashioned them. They are your sons. In these malleable, moldable years of their lives, you have forever left your imprint upon them.[10]

The parents' influence in the home cannot be *underestimated*.

WEEK 7: DAY 2

Introduction for Discipling Your Children

Deuteronomy 6:5-9, describes how parents are to disciple their children. Moses is talking with the Israelites, explaining how love of God and His Word begins within the parent's heart and then, parents are command-ed (*"you shall..."*) to diligently teach their children.

> **Deuteronomy 6:5-9** *You shall love the Lord your God with all your heart, with all your soul, and with all your strength. 6 And these words which I command you today shall be in your heart. 7 You shall teach them [God's Word] diligently to your children, and talk of them when you sit in your house, and when you walk by the way, when you lie down and when you rise up. 8 You shall bind them as a sign on your hand, and they shall be as a frontal between your eyes. 9 You shall write them on the doorposts of your house and on your gates. [emphasis added]*

10   Steven J. Lawson, *Holmen Old Testament Commentary: Psalms 76-150* (Nashville, TN: Broadman & Holman, 2006), 289.

These passages are relevant to us today, declaring that we are to teach God's precepts and commandments *diligently* to our children. This means not only through *instruction*, but also by consistently *living out* the gospel. In my experience, less than 10 percent of parents in the body of Christ today are discipling their children. Instead, they have left this *God-given responsibility* to school and/or church.

Did you realize that there is not one single youth group, or children's ministry worker, mentioned in the Bible? I was a youth pastor, and I praise the Lord for youth pastors and the work that they do for our kids. But somewhere along the line, we have determined that it is someone else's responsibility to instruct our children in spiritual things. So now, what do you think? Has God said to you and me, as parents, that it is *our* responsibility to disciple our children? Other Christians, and Christian organizations, will never have the depth of *influence* over them that we do. They are here to assist us—*not* take our place.

Have you ever talked with a teacher, or youth leader about your child's spiritual growth? It is important to know and work with the people instructing your children. For example, ask how you can reinforce the Sunday lesson at home during the week. If you have not been discipling your child, this can be a way to get started.

SELF-EXAMINATION

Take a moment and list the people, places and practices that are currently helping your children grow spiritually.

_____

_____

_____

_____

_____

_____

Discipling Starts within a Parent's *Heart*

We find an *essential* aspect of discipling in Deuteronomy 6:5: *"You shall love the LORD your God with all your heart"* (wholeheartedly), all your *soul* and *strength* (has to do with your whole being and life). This *command*, to love God is given often in Deuteronomy (v. 5; 7:9; 10:12; 11:1, 13, 22; 13:3; 19:9; 30:6, 16, 20). So we can easily conclude that this exhortation is foundational and essential to *successfully* discipling our children. When verse 6 says that God's words *"shall be in your heart,"* or upon your heart, it refers to having an intimate, loving relationship with Him.

A noted Christian author wrote:

"For the love of God to be of the right kind, the commandments of God must be laid to heart, and be the constant subject of thought and conversation. *"Upon thine heart:"* i.e., the commandments of God were to be an affair of the heart, and not merely of the memory."[11]

An *abiding* relationship is essential; our hearts need to change, and be constantly *changing, growing closer to God*. As we *learn* and *grow,* we can communicate what God is giving us. What an awesome privilege, such an awesome experience! As you and I share the Word with our children, we will see them falling in love with the same God that we love and serve.

DIG DEEPER: *FURTHER STUDY*

Read the following verses and describe how the Psalmist felt about God's Word. How did this affect his life?

Psalm 119:11 *"Your word I have hidden in my heart, That I might not sin against You."*

_____

_____

_____

Psalm 119:97 *"Oh, how I love Your law! It is my meditation all the day."*

_____

_____

_____

_____

Psalm 40:8 *"I delight to do Your will, O my God, And Your law is within my heart."*

_____

_____

_____

In the following verse, what is God asking us to do? What can we expect from Him?

Jeremiah 33:3 *'Call to Me, and I will answer you, and show you great and mighty things, which you do not know.'*

_____

_____

_____

_____

11   Carl Friedrich Keil and Franz Delitzsch, *Commentary on the Old Testament* (Peabody, MA: Hendrickson, 1996), Dt 6:6.

WE MUST DISCIPLE OUR CHILDREN DILIGENTLY (VERSE 7):

Deuteronomy 6:7 talks about the committed *attitude* we must have when discipling our children. Teaching them *diligently* indicates a *proactive* approach to communication through both our words and deeds.

FACT FILE

Diligently - Perseveringly attentive; steady and earnest in application to a subject or pursuit; prosecuted with careful attention and effort; not careless or negligent.

Deuteronomy contains information given to God's children, the Jews, yet is equally descriptive of His will for us today. The analogy indicates that just as words are cut into a stone tablet with a sharp object, so the Law should be impressed on the hearts of the children of every generation.[12] God's Word tells us that His law is to be written/hidden in our *hearts* (Ps 119:11). This is a learning process, it does not just happen overnight. We must be *diligent* in our own learning, then *diligently* teach our children. God's Word is what we are teaching, because it is truly living and powerful, and can reveal the thoughts and intents of the heart, both good and bad.

DIG DEEPER: *FURTHER STUDY*

From this verse, describe the power of God's Word. Apply it to everyday life.

> **Hebrew 4:12** *"For the word of God is <u>living</u> and <u>powerful</u>, and sharper than any two-edged sword, piercing even to the division of soul and spirit, and of joints and marrow, and is a discerner of the thoughts and intents of the heart."*

_____

_____

_____

_____

So we see that a diligent personal commitment to seeking God and following His Word is essential and must precede our efforts to disciple others. And remember, our children will know when our words and actions differ, which is defined as hypocrisy. Our goal as parents is to introduce our children to the love of God and His Word; our most powerful influences are love and truth. Hypocrisy breeds rebellion, but seeing the fruit of God's Spirit in our lives will lead them to put their faith and trust in Christ.

When our children were at home, my wife and I found that one of the best tools for influencing our children

12   Warren Baker and Eugene E. Carpenter, *The Complete Word Study Dictionary: Old Testament* (Chattanooga, TN: AMG Publishers, 2003), 1179.

and teaching them about Christ was the *life* we lived out day after day. We committed ourselves to being examples of Christ, acted the way God wants. No parent can be perfect, but we can commit to the process of being transformed by God's Holy Spirit and, as our children observe us, this becomes one of the greatest tools of discipleship.

DIG DEEPER: *FURTHER STUDY*

Read this Scripture and list the warnings and exhortations to parents. How many generations are included?

Deuteronomy 4:9 *"Only take heed to yourself, and diligently keep yourself, lest you forget the things your eyes have seen, and lest they depart from your heart all the days of your life. And teach them to your children and your grandchildren."*

_____

_____

_____

_____

_____

Discipling and *Equipping*

Discipling an individual involves more than good Biblical instruction; the goal is to help guide them to spiritual *maturity* so that they can go on and disciple others. The "each one teach one" is a *process* of multiplication, and can eventually impact the entire world. In essence, we are reproducing Christ in our children through our Christ-like attitudes and behavior. Just as Jesus did with His disciples, we are *equipping* them with weapons to fight spiritual battles they will encounter in the world. The following Scripture gives insight into this vision for our children.

Psalm 127:3-5 *"Behold, children are a heritage (gift NAS) from the Lord, the fruit of the womb is a reward. Like arrows in the hand of a warrior, so are the children of one's youth. Happy is the man who has his quiver full of them".*

First, our children are *gifts* <u>from</u> God, His blessing, which should bring great pleasure to our homes. God calls children a "reward", and we need to value them as precious gifts, not see them as a burden. We have a *responsibility* to bring them up as God has instructed, being good *stewards* of the time. Children are portrayed as *"arrows,"* not only in the quiver, but also *"in the hand of a warrior."* This refers primarily to the father, since God has assigned him *ultimate* responsibility over the home.

We currently live in a culture that utilizes guns, bombs, missiles, drones, etc., for war, rather than bows and arrows. Visualize yourself back in history, or think of a film where arrows were used to assault the enemy from a distance. A skilled warrior aimed his arrows and hit the target; therefore, the picture of *"arrows in the hand of a warrior"* describes a child, in the hand of a parent, skillfully pointed in the right direction. Here is what one author says concerning this verse:

> *Arrows must be shaped.* No arrow begins straight, ready for battle. The soldier who would shoot a straight arrow must spend time whittling and shaping the branch into a well-fashioned arrow. So it is in raising children. Sons and daughters must be trained at an early age to pursue righteousness...This involves biblical instruction, moral correction, firm discipline, and loving affirmation.[13]

It is important to perceive our children as *weapons for the cause of righteousness*. An arrow is something you shoot *out*, away from you. It is an offensive weapon, fashioned to assault the unrighteousness of the world in which we live. Arrows are also seen as a *defensive* weapon; children prepared to overcome worldly temptations and the ungodly influences of peer pressure.

Parents are to equip children to *influence* their world for God. "They are **arrows** shot with great energy, going beyond the family—to a place where the LORD calls them to serve. Their influence can be great, sometimes beyond the community, the city, state and even the nation. This is the correct purpose and prayer for our children, rather than selfishly holding them back for our own desires and comfort."[14] Wow, what a vision!

Most parents think, "If I can just get my kids through high school free from drugs and sex, I've won." But that is a passive posture. God wants you to perceive your children as offensive weapons that you are aggressively equipping to impact their world for righteousness. As the old adage says, "If you aim at nothing you will hit it every time".

Think of it this way: someone gives you a beautiful piece of land, completely clear of any plants, weeds or trash, with the richest soil ever found, and says, "Here, this is yours, do whatever you want with it." You decide to wait a year or so to develop it. How foolish to believe the land will be in exactly the same condition as you received it, instead it will be full of weeds from the dropping of seeds, reproducing over and over and over again.

And that is what the world is doing - dropping seeds of deception and corruption into the untended soil of our children's *hearts*. If you and I are not there, tilling that soil and instilling God's Word into their hearts, then who is? Remember, no one has greater power and influence over a child than a parent. God wants us to use that opportunity to plant His truth. It is our responsibility; we cannot be passive, or the enemy will

---

13   Lawson, 289.

14   Ivan Raskino, *A Pastor's Commentary on the Psalms* (New Delhi, India: Mountain Peak, 2011), 772.

invade. If we diligently plant the seed of the Word of God in our child's heart, God promises that it will bear good fruit (Matt. 13:23).

⌕ SELF-EXAMINATION

By comparing a child's heart to fertile soil, how have you been faithfully tending to it? How can you improve?

_____

_____

_____

_____

Can you identify any weeds, or corruption in that soil? Take a moment and make a list of invaders that may need to be "pulled" out, or removed?

_____

_____

_____

_____

When I was a youth pastor, parents would often call me, saying, "Hey, I don't know what you've been teaching my kid on Sunday nights, but he's been talking about God. I think you'd better sit down with him; I think he's ready to accept Jesus Christ."

My response was always, "Why are you calling me, telling me to do this? Why aren't you sitting down with him? Have you ever thought about leading your own kid to Christ?"

We already discussed the fact that parents should begin introducing their children to Christ at a very early age. But we also must realize that salvation is God's work; we are not responsible for making our kids accept Christ. Jesus taught in John 6:44, *"No one can come to Me unless the Father who sent Me draws him."* It is true that your child cannot be saved without hearing the gospel. It is our *responsibility* to be continuously teaching our children what is right and wrong, what the Bible has to say about all things (*"teaching them all things"* Matt 28:20). We must explain to them who Jesus is, how one has a relationship with Him, and how to abide in Him each day.

WEEK 7: DAY 3

Principles for *Discipling*

The following 5 principles outline God's plan for discipling your children found in Deuteronomy 6:7-9.

1. DISCIPLING *IN* OUR HOMES

Let's go back to Deuteronomy 6:7-9. The first instruction is *". . . talk of them when you sit in your house."* (v. 7). In order to talk to someone, what must we do? We must spend time with them. God first says that teaching should take place *in your house*, because this is where we spend the most time with our children. Parents should be in control of what happens at home. Remember, dads, you are to set the *example* and make sure this is happening. You have the *leadership* role in the home.

I find it very interesting that the Hebrew word for *sit*, (*yasab*) is a verb, an action word. Even though we think of sitting as inactivity, we can see from this context that God is telling us to be busy with Biblical instruction. Of course this does NOT mean you are to have a Bible discussion every time you sit down with your child, but it should make us stop and think about how we are using our time at home.

Warning! We live in a time where electronics and media activities have replaced relationship interaction. Many children check out by watching TV, playing video games, and texting, to name a few. They will do this for hours and many parents allow it because they can be busy doing their own things.

Again, watch how the time is being spent in our homes.

There are two ways to approach the practice of discipling at home: *directly* and *indirectly*. **Direct** instruction-discipleship is the time that you set aside to have devotionals with your children. It is a planned activity that involves the entire family.

If you have young children and teens, it is wise to separate for study time. It can be challenging to keep a five-year-old and a teenager focused on the same Bible study. I know in some homes the father and mother teach at the same time, dad in one room with the older kids, and mom in another with the younger ones.

The **indirect** instruction-discipleship occurs when God presents an opportunity for an informal, or un-planned discussion of spiritual things. This usually means that a parent must immediately set aside other personal activities. You have to make yourself *available*.

When my children were younger, I was not always available to communicate with them. I'm a fix-it kind of guy. In other words, I always have some kind of tinkering to do around the house. For the first four years of my marriage, on my way home from work, I would think, "Which project am I going to tackle tonight?" I would get home and immediately start on that; meanwhile, my little boys would follow me, wanting my attention. Within a few minutes, they would realize that I did not really want them around, so they would start playing by themselves, or bugging my wife, because I was wrapped up in "mySELF".

We all get into ruts like this until days turn into weeks, weeks into months, and so on. Then, one day our kids don't want to talk to us; so they turn to peers, or unhealthy relationships for comfort. All too often, when they become teenagers we become interested in being with them, but it's too late. Thankfully, I did not let my problem get that far. I *learned* that when I got home, my *most important* job was tending to my family.

By the time my oldest was 5 I leaned that my most important ministry was at home; every day I would pray, "OK, God, I'm coming home, help me to be a servant, help me to be available for my wife and kids." I would have no other agenda than my wife and children. I learned that home is my *first* priority, not my work or hobbies. Instead of jumping into a project, I would make myself available to talk. I learned that, in my home, the best place was in the kitchen. Both my boys would run in and jockey for my attention. They would sit there for thirty minutes to an hour, telling me about their day. They knew that Dad was *available* to listen. That is the first essential of communication—*availability*.

Note: This time is made NOT found.

After I made myself available, I learned to communicate better. One of the important lessons is DO NOT lecture during this time. This goes for both moms and dads - don't lecture. When my son, Nick, would launch into a story, I was quick to respond by lecturing him about what he should have done. My wife *helped* me to see that they just wanted to talk while I listened. They did not need a four-point sermon; they needed a dad who would *listen*.

On one occasion, Nick was telling me about a problem he was having with another student at school. When he finished, I merely said, "Nicholas, what would be the right thing to do here? Maybe we should talk to this kid's dad."

He replied, "Dad, I can work this out on my own." He was not open for any input at that moment. Three days later, Nick and that student ended up fighting, and both of them were suspended from school for two days. Instead of saying, "See, I told you so," I sat down calmly and said, "Nick, if we had sat down with this boy's dad, talked it out, do you think you would have gotten in a fight?" He said, "No." I continued, "OK, you've got two days detention from school. During those two days, I have some projects for you to complete for your discipline."

Kids do *not* always listen to our instructions. But those times are wonderful opportunities for a life training exercise. However, to accomplish this, you must be available, approachable, and communicating with them.

When your children become teenagers, you realize they are *not* pursuing you as often for discussion. They often do *not* want to talk when you want to talk. They start pulling away, and you have to *learn to adjust*.

When my boys were older teens, I counseled two nights a week and would get home late. I learned that, although I was tired, I still needed to be *available* for my kids. My *first ministry* is not the people that come in to see me, or the people that I go speak to, it is my family. Teaching them takes *sacrifice*; for many teens, their time for talking is close to our bedtime.

Remember: loving communication is the foundation for healthy communication (see week 3 & 4). This involves being willing to interrupt *our* own activities, with a positive attitude, and also finding out what makes these times easiest and most enjoyable for the kids. The best place may be sitting at the kitchen table, in the living room, or out in the back yard. Remember, every kid is different, and you need to take the time to get to know *each* one individually.

⚲ SELF-EXAMINATION

After learning the principle of indirect instruction and the importance of being available, are there any changes you need to make? If so, take a moment and write out a prayerful desire for change.

_____

_____

_____

_____

_____

_____

2. DISCIPLING *OUTSIDE* THE HOME

Applying Deut. 6:7 further, we are given another aspect of discipling children "*. . . When you walk by the way. . .*". Walking indicates activity; God gives us plenty of opportunities to instruct our kids while driving in the car, working outside in the yard, camping, surfing, or wherever you are.

God's instruction reminds us to be sensitive to His Spirit at all times and in all places. When we are seeking God, we will see that He opens "windows" of opportunity to share at the most unusual times. When we take advantage of these opportunities, we are being *diligent* in our training.

I have great memories of surfing with my son, Nick, when we talked for long periods of time. It was like we forgot about surfing as we shared ideas about God's creation and how wonderful He is. I remember camping with my son, Justin, and talking about the concept of dating for hours, and lying on the trampoline next to my daughter, Katie, after jumping so long that my knees were killing me. There are many great opportunities for us to share God's wonderful truths and promises with our children. Some of the greatest Bible studies with my kids were *not planned*; they just happened in the course of daily living. We truly have to be mindful of every opportunity.

DIG DEEPER: *FURTHER STUDY*

Read the following Scriptures and write down what Jesus was doing, how available He was, how He approached sharing the Word.

> **Matthew 13:1-3a** *"On the same day Jesus went out of the house and sat by the sea. 2 And great multitudes were gathered together to Him, so that He got into a boat and sat; and the whole multitude stood on the shore. Then He spoke many things to them in parables, saying..."*

_____

_____

_____

_____

☑ACTION PLAN

How many outside activities come to mind where you can share biblical principles with your children? Take a moment and write them down. Be in prayer, *ask* God to remind you of these opportunities when they come your way. *Ask* Him for the boldness and wisdom to bring Christ and/or His perspective into some activity you are doing with your child.

_____

_____

_____

_____

_____

_____

3. DISCIPLING IN THE *MORNING* AND *EVENING*

You should pursue discipling your children *". . . When you lie down, and when you rise up"* (Deut. 6:7).

"What is the last thing on your mind when you go to bed, and the first when you get up in the morning?" All too often the pressures of this world squeeze out thoughts of God, and He automatically *becomes* last on the priority list. Jews were instructed to, at least, recite Scriptures in the morning and evening as a continual reminder of God. In this context, the parent can lead both by example and leadership. The *goal* is to *grow* in our commitment to God, and help our children develop the same practices.

☑ACTION PLAN

Do you pray with your kids in the morning and evening? How often do you pray with them? If you feel you do not have time, consider praying with them while taking them to school. Decide when you can start praying with them, listing here the days and/or times.

_____

_____

_____

_____

_____

I prayed with my children on the way to school, and each evening before going to bed. They would come into our room, gather around the bed, and we would all pray together. When my boys became teenagers, often after our prayer time we would have great discussions until 10:30 or 11:00 pm. The kids often wanted to talk about their friends, struggles they were going through, or poor choices they were making. Let me tell you, it's a great thing to have your teenagers wanting to talk to you. By trusting the Lord and *applying* these principles, I witnessed God doing a work in my kids that was absolutely *glorious*. I am still reaping the benefits of these blessed times, and I know this is God's desire for you and your family, too!

Scripture says to *"Be ready in season and out of season."* (2 Tim. 4:2). In other words, you need to *look* for opportunities at all times, being *mindful* of God's command that we teach our children both diligently and continuously.

☑ ACTION PLAN

This week, be mindful of times with your children. For example, while driving them somewhere, or during an outing, and ask God for a teaching opportunity. Discuss as husband and wife how you can begin to use these times more affectively by instilling biblical principles and write them down.

_____

_____

_____

_____

_____

Colossians 1:10 says, *"That you may walk worthy of the Lord, fully pleasing Him, being fruitful in every good work and increasing in the knowledge of God."* For this to happen, we have to go back to our foundation; through our devotional time and obedience, we increase our knowledge of God, grow closer to Him, and are inspired to good works.

Personally, I am terrible at remembering Scriptures, can't usually quote one from memory, but I remember principles very well. I can easily remember throughout the day what I read in my devotional time that morning. Many times, issues with my children came up that were directly related to what I learned that morning! When opportunities presented themselves, I would remember what I had read and share it with my kids. Consequently, they are convinced I am an amazing theologian. The truth is, I am not! I merely have the right foundation.

DIG DEEPER: *FURTHER STUDY*

Read the following Scriptures, write down the psalmist' attitude in the morning and evening. What was he doing and how can that help your devotional time?

Psalm 5:3, *My voice You shall hear in the morning, O LORD; In the morning I will direct it to You, And I will look up.*

_____
_____
_____
_____
_____

Psalm 55:17, *Evening and morning and at noon I will pray, and cry aloud, And He shall hear my voice.*

_____
_____
_____
_____
_____

Psalm 92:2, *To declare Your lovingkindness in the morning, And Your faithfulness every night,...*

_____
_____
_____
_____
_____

Psalm 119:147, *I rise before the dawning of the morning, And cry for help; I hope in Your word.*

_____
_____
_____
_____
_____

4. DISCIPLING BY *PERSONAL* EXAMPLE

God wants us to be constantly in mind of His teachings. He says, *"You shall bind them as a sign on your hand, and they shall be as a frontlet between your eyes"* (Deut. 6:8). The Israelites not only memorized the Bible, word for word, and rehearsed it over and over to internalize it, but they were also to wear visible reminders. God knows our human tendency to *forget* and *neglect*.

As we use our hands for just about everything; binding something there would be a continual reminder of it throughout the day. The "frontlet" is a small leather pouch worn on the forehead, indicating constant meditation on the Scriptures. Not likely you could forget something dangling in front of your face. These constant reminders are an example of what God *desires* from us as parents, to be mindful at all times of our responsibility to *disciple* our kids, both by personal example and by looking for opportunities to share God's love and Word with them.

DIG DEEPER: *FURTHER STUDY*
Read the following Scripture and write out how it applies to what you are learning.

> **Psalm 1:1-3** *"Blessed is the man who walks not in the counsel of the ungodly, nor stands in the path of sinners, nor sits in the seat of the scornful; but his delight is in the law of the LORD, and in His law he meditates day and night. He shall be like a tree planted by the rivers of water, that brings forth its fruit in its season, whose leaf also shall not wither; and whatever he does shall prosper."*

_____

_____

_____

_____

If you are putting God first, He will bless you in times of difficulty and trial - your leaves will be green and you will be producing fruit, even in seasons of drought.

Read the following Scriptures, list the biblical principles that can help you be a godly example to your children.

> **Deuteronomy 11:8,** *"Therefore you shall <u>keep</u> every commandment which I command you today, that you may be <u>strong</u>, and go in and possess the land which you cross over to possess."*

_____

_____

_____

_____

Proverbs 3:3, *"Let not mercy and truth forsake you; Bind them around your neck, Write them on the tablet of your heart."*

_____

_____

_____

_____

WEEK 7: DAY 4

5. DISCIPLING BY *HAVING* A GODLY HOME

Deuteronomy 6:9 says of God's laws: *"You shall write them on the doorposts of your house and on your gates."* **Doorposts,** *Mezuah* is a Hebrew word that translates "the upright framework of a door, or side posts of a gate or window". Here is what should be noted about this command from Tyndale Bible Dictionary,

> In Deuteronomy 6:9 and 11:20, the Hebrews were instructed to write the commandments on the doors of the houses and on the city gates. This practice is still followed by the Jewish community. Every Jewish home has a small metal or wooden container mounted about shoulder-height on the doorpost of the house. This container, which itself became known as a mezuzah, has inside a small piece of parchment inscribed on one side with the words of Deuteronomy 6:4–9, and 11:13–21, and on the other side with the word *Shaddai*, the Hebrew name for God Almighty.[15]

These passages of Scripture, also known as part of the *Shema*, are fundamental truths, to be obeyed. We can conclude that God wanted these passages fixed to the doorposts so that everyone entering the house would be reminded that *submission* to God and His Word was the *commitment* of that home. *Everything* must meet *His* approval.

That means all who enter your home, your friends and your children's friends, your stuff and your children's stuff, must glorify the Lord. Part of discipling our kids is *monitoring* the things that *we* allow in our home. God wants our homes to be a righteous environment, glorifying to Him. About 40 years after Moses wrote Deuteronomy, the people of Israel were getting ready to enter into the Promised Land. Their leader, Joshua, set out a challenge in the form of a choice.

---

15 Walter A. Elwell and Philip Wesley Comfort, *Tyndale Bible Dictionary* (Wheaton, IL: Tyndale House Publishers, 2001), 889.

Joshua 24:15, *"And if it seems evil to you to serve the LORD, choose for yourselves this day whom you will serve, whether the gods which your fathers served that were on the other side of the River, or the gods of the Amorites, in whose land you dwell. But <u>as for me and my house</u>, we will <u>serve</u> the LORD."*

Joshua knew, as the leader of his own home, that choices would be ahead. Just as we live in the world today, there were people in the Promised Land who did NOT serve the Lord, or know Him, or have the morals and values He demanded.

DIG DEEPER: *FURTHER STUDY*

Read the following Scriptures, write down what choices were presented to the people. Why was making the right choice so important?

Deuteronomy 30:19, *"I call heaven and earth as witnesses today against you, that I have set before you life and death, blessing and cursing; therefore choose life, that both you and your descendants may live."*

_____

_____

_____

_____

1 Kings 18:21, *"And Elijah came to all the people, and said, "How long will you falter between two opinions? If the LORD is God, follow Him; but if Baal, follow him." But the people answered him not a word."* (Baal was a false god)

_____

_____

_____

_____

Matthew 6:24, *"No one can serve two masters; for either he will hate the one and love the other, or else he will be loyal to the one and despise the other. You cannot serve God and mammon."*

_____

_____

_____

_____

The Book of Romans, chapter 1, relates a long list of sinful behaviors that were going on at that time, and that are still going on today. The apostle Paul closes that chapter with a stern warning: *"...who, knowing the righteous judgment of God, that those who <u>practice</u> such things are deserving of death, not only do the same but also <u>**approve**</u> of those who practice them"* (Rom. 1:32). As parents, the responsibility is ours for what happens at home. According to this scripture, we are judged for both our own bad choices and also what we approve for our family. You are guilty not only if you *do* these sins, but also if you find pleasure in *approving* them. Think now about the entertainment that you not only allow, but enjoy, at home: television, movies, video games, music, magazines, etc.

Parents often say, "When you're eighteen, you can watch this type of movie." But we need to realize that age is no qualifier for sin. This sounds like a reference to something that is inappropriate at any age; true for us and true for our children. Immorality is inappropriate at any age and at any time, and should be stopped.

One father came up to me after I taught a parenting class, explaining that he and his teenage son had gotten into a big argument over music. His son said, "Well, Dad, what about your Pink Floyd albums? I've read the lyrics of those songs, Dad, and they are bad. They're no better than what I'm listening to." That father told me those Pink Floyd albums ended up in the trash, because he had learned that hypocrisy breeds rebellion.

Many Christians today pay more for cable TV entertainment, which is mostly garbage, than they give in tithes. Just imagine what God will say to us when we stand before Him: "You paid **$47.50** every month for cable that poisoned both yours and your kids' minds, and you gave how much to *My* church?" Ouch!

Amazingly, many Christian parents sit right next to their children, laughing at shows full of sexual innuendos and destructive worldly philosophies. It is no wonder we have an epidemic today of young women "rooming" with guys—a disaster waiting to happen. Meanwhile, our media keeps pumping this type of philosophy into our kids' minds, and we open the door and let it in. We have to take a stand!

My wife received a copy of one women's magazine and, as I casually glanced through it, I happened upon an article about how to please your "man"; not your *husband*, but your *man*. That article was pornography in print! Flat out pornography, in a standard women's magazine!

Ladies, you can read those types of articles and look at Victoria's Secret catalogs, and think they do not affect you, but they do. In truth, women check out women more than men do. Usually, when you look at a beautiful woman's body, you are not thinking the way men do, you are not lusting. You are thinking, "I hate her, just wait until she has three kids." When mature men, young men, and even boys see a woman dressed provocatively on TV, or in a magazine, their reaction is different. Even picking up a newspaper today provides pictures of women in their underwear, advertising undergarments.

Things have certainly changed. When I was young, the only thing we watched was Disney on Sunday nights. Can you imagine, back in 1966, sitting there watching Disney with your mom and dad, and a Victoria's Secret commercial comes on? My dad would have shot a hole through the TV, and someone at ABC would have heard from him for sure. That would have ended our Disney watching night. If you look *closely* at the *content* of movies, you will find that PG13 movies, or the video game ratings often have ten times the amount of sex, sexual innuendo, and cussing as an R-rated movie. *Satan* knows exactly what he is doing to our kids. You must be *aware* of these things, and you have to know whom you can trust.

My wife and I have certain Christian friends that we know we can trust with movie selection. Have I seen an R-rated movie? Absolutely. But I choose them carefully, based upon the content. Likewise, you need to decide, between you and your spouse and the Lord, what you will allow. Remember, hypocrisy breeds rebellion.

I walked into my son Justin's room when he was twelve, and he was playing a video game. Periodically, little captions would pop up when the characters walked up to each other. While I was watching over Justin's shoulder, all of a sudden a couple of cuss words popped up. I said, "Justin, what's that?"

"Oh, Dad, I don't read those."

"But wait a minute, how much of that language comes up?"

"Well, they use it throughout the whole game."

I said, "Turn it off. Whose game is this?"

"My friend at school loaned it to me."

"I don't want to see it in this house again."

One time when Nick was a teenager, I came home and there were five kids in his room, laughing their heads off. They were playing his friend's video game. Nick called me into his room to see what they thought was so funny. The game featured a well-endowed woman in a hot-pants outfit kicking, shooting, and beating up all kinds of bad guys. The funny part was that while she was doing this, her breasts were bouncing all over the place. The boys were dying laughing. Although it did look funny, I told him it was not appropriate.

He said, "Wait, Dad, wait." He immediately went into the programming mode and changed the setting so the woman's breasts were no longer bouncy. Then he did the same kick, showing me that her breasts did not move.

I said, "But Nick, why do you think they have that program? Because of the emphasis they're putting on it. Turn it off. Let's not have it in the house again."

I had to implement a new rule, no video games in this house without my approval.

The Internet is just as dangerous, if not more so, than video games. Make sure you have software to protect your kids (and dads) from pornography. From 1998 to 2003, more than 240 million pornographic web pages were added to the Internet, over 100,000 per day.[16] And every day the pornography industry is using the smartest people in the world to try to find ways around your protection.

Pornography is an epidemic amongst our teenage boys, and it can be just as addictive as heroin to some people. We need to be in tune and involved. We need to watch the chat rooms they visit and monitor their communication. The new smart phones have opened a door to many more temptations for our children; you need to investigate every control option of your provider and continually monitor efficiency. We need to get involved, be aware of these avenues of possible evil that can and will corrupt our children.

DIG DEEPER: *FURTHER STUDY*

Read the following Scripture and write out what Jacob did as the leader of his home. What was his concern, and why do you think it was so important?

> **Genesis 35:2–3,** *"And Jacob said to his household and to all who were with him, "Put away the foreign gods that are among you, purify yourselves, and change your garments. 3 Then let us arise and go up to Bethel; and I will make an altar there to God, who answered me in the day of my distress and has been with me in the way which I have gone."*

_____

_____

_____

_____

☑ACTION PLAN

Take some time together as husband and wife, discuss and write down the changes that you believe need to be made after reading this chapter. Think of TV shows, movies, games, posters, books, Internet or cell phone applications, or anything that God shows you that needs to be changed. Now, write out together your commitment to make things right.

---

16   Accessed 2006, http://www.family.org/socialissues/A000001155.cfm

_____

_____

_____

_____

_____

_____

_____

_____

_____

_____

_____

I suggest you go into our website at www.parentingministry.org to learn about protective software to help you monitor this.

I would like to close this study on verses from Deuteronomy with a quote from the Bible Knowledge Commentary:

> God's people were responsible to meditate on **these commandments,** to keep them in their **hearts.** This enabled them to understand the Law and to apply it correctly. Then the parents were in a position to **impress them on** their children's hearts also. The moral and biblical education of the **children** was accomplished best not in a formal teaching period each day but when the parents, out of concern for their own lives as well as their children's, made God and His Word the natural topic of a conversation which might occur anywhere and anytime during the day (v. 7).[17]

WEEK 7: DAY 5

What about Privacy?

How many parents have heard, "Get out of my room"?

Back when Nick was thirteen years old, I was in his room and we were discussing our rules on the type of music we allowed in our home. Finally he said, "OK, now will you get out of my room."

_____

17   John F. Walvoord, Roy B. Zuck and Dallas Theological Seminary, *The Bible Knowledge Commentary: An Exposition of the Scriptures* (Wheaton, IL: Victor Books, 1985), Dt 6:6–9.

I sat down in his chair, and said, "What? Who said this was *your* room?"

He did not answer me, so I continued, "Nick, let me tell you where that lie came from: the pit of hell. I don't have a lease with you and you're not paying me rent. Nicholas, I am responsible for everything in this house. When I stand before the Lord, when I die, you're not going to be standing next to me, saying, 'God, those were *my* CDs and *my* tapes, don't hold my dad responsible.' God's going to hold me *100* percent responsible for *everything* in this house. Yes, you have different interests, but if they don't meet the standard that I have set as a priest in my household, those things will not be allowed in my house. And this room will never be yours. This room is mine. Because I love you, and you're my child, I allow you to live here. It doesn't matter if you're thirteen, Nicholas, or thirty-five, if you come to live in my house, my standard will remain. So please, Nicholas, don't listen to that lie again."

Our Commission

In the year 2000, statistics showed that when a mother in an unsaved family is the first one to accept Jesus Christ, there is a 17 percent chance the rest of the family will come to know Christ as well. When a father is the first one to accept Jesus Christ as his Lord and Savior, however, there is a 93 percent chance that the rest of the family will come to know Christ.[18]

Dads, you have supernatural, *ordained* power from God; use it! Do not be tempted to *relinquish* your responsibility. As we study these next principles, do not think, "I can't do that. My wife is a better spiritual leader, she knows the Bible better than me, so I'll just let her do it." Forget your insecurities. This is what God has commissioned and ordained; He *will* empower you!

As parents, we must constantly evaluate ourselves *biblically,* be faithfully obedient to Scripture in order to avoid hypocrisy when training our children. Remember, God is not looking for perfection, but *cooperation,* and He wants *transformation.* If you are using screaming and yelling for discipline, misrepresenting Christ, and not leading by asking forgiveness of God and your family when you fail, this will definitely affect your ability to get your children's attention. God forgives our failures, but we still must consistently obey His principles to bring about the *transformation* of both ourselves and others.

SELF-EXAMINATION

Parents are to be *one* in mind and judgment, in *unity*. Read the following Scripture, and write out the biblical principles for unity. As a couple, write down where you need to be more united.

    1 Corinthians 1:10, *"Now I plead with you, brethren, by the name of our Lord Jesus Christ,*

---

18   Accessed 2006, http://www.navpress.com/EPubs/DisplayArticle/3/3.11.32.html

that you all speak the same thing, and that there be no divisions among you, but that you be perfectly joined together in the same mind and in the same judgment."

Philippians 2:2, *". . . Fulfill my joy by being like-minded, having the same love, being of one accord, of one mind".*

_____

_____

_____

_____

_____

_____

These principles apply to all two-parent families, including blended families.

Mom, if you have an unsaved husband, can you disciple your kids? Absolutely.

If you are a single mom, can you disciple your kids? Absolutely. What if you are a grandparent or foster parent? Absolutely.

The Powerful Tool of Prayer

God's Word tells us we must *"pray without ceasing"* (1 Thess. 5:17). Prayer should be a fundamental part of discipleship. God tells us to come boldly to Him (Heb. 4:16), to ask, seek and knock (Matt. 7:7), and to bring everything to Him in prayer (Phil. 4:6). As *leader* of the family, fathers should pray with their wives and children every single day. The father is to set his mind on *being* a godly example in everything. God has given us a powerful tool in prayer; therefore, we should incorporate it into our daily lives. Obviously, single moms must be all these things to their children, in lieu of a missing father.

In my family, I was the only one who got to hear my shy, little daughter pray. She would not pray in front of my wife, or her brothers. By her teenage years, she was praying with more intelligence and intent than most adults: for God's strength, for forgiveness of her sins, for her friends and family, for people's salvation. Her prayers often brought tears to my eyes. I have had the privilege of watching her grow into this young lady of prayer because we prayed together every night. After praying with my daughter, my teenage boys would join me and my wife in our room, and we would all pray together. It was powerful!

Instill God's Word

Instilling God's Word in our children is the *heart* of discipleship. God tells us to *"...giving all diligence, add to your faith virtue, to virtue knowledge"* (2 Pet. 1:5). We must be diligent to learn God's Word for ourselves, then we can pass the Word to our children. *"Giving all diligence"* suggests a consistent, uninterrupted pattern. To that end, family Bible studies should be done regularly, not when you happen to have time. You must make a *plan* and stick to it.

Couples can split the duties, if that works for you. I discipled my sons as they were growing up. Since my daughter was home schooled, my wife discipled her. When we had our weekly Bible study nights, all participated together. I also spent personal time with my daughter in the evenings when we prayed together. I would invite her to share by asking, "What did you learn today in your Bible study?" That opened the opportunity for me to expand on what she was learning, and to oversee her spiritual growth.

Seven Simple Steps for a Weekly Bible Study

Simplicity

Keep it simple! Remember, the objective is to put God's Word in your child's heart; not produce a Bible scholar. There are plenty of age-appropriate materials available to help you have a great little Bible study. We have included a short list in **Appendix E.**

Time Appropriate

Keep it short! Family members vary in attention span. Be sensitive to the fact that Bible study should be a fun, family time, rather than a lecture.

When I started doing Bible studies with my kids, I was a youth pastor and my kids were very young. The first few times I did it, Nick would come in and be upside down on the couch and twisting around and throwing the pillow up in the air. I would get frustrated, "Nicholas, sit up! Stop it! We're doing a Bible study now!"

Then I remember my wife telling me when we went to bed, "Honey, when you teach the high school, you have fun with them so why, with your own kids, do you get all uptight?" I did not have an answer. So I *learned* to make our time together fun, *not* a lecture. Yes, chocolate shakes and popcorn is OK. Plus, I learned that Nick listens better upside down.

Excitement

Make it exciting! Get in touch with your own love and excitement for the faith, and then transfer that to your children. Are you excited about being in the Word? Are you excited about what God told you today? Are you excited to see the work that God is doing in and around you? If you are not excited yourself, it will be a lecture every time.

When our boys were young, they watched hours of a Christian, animated video series about people in the Bible. My son, Nicholas, now a man, can still remember things he saw on those videos when he was a kid.

My daughter and I used to play Bible board games when she was young. Often we would play it three times in a row. We could spend more than an hour in Bible studies that way. She would pull a question-and-answer card; I was able to expound on the answers to the questions, and she just loved it.

Flexibility

Be flexible! All families experience unexpected circumstances. Your kids may start soccer or baseball, and you should **not** say, "No, you can't play baseball because Thursday night is our Bible study."

I think our family has had a Bible study on every night of the week at some point. Nick started a band; he had band practice, so we moved to Sunday nights. Then Justin got into volleyball, and he had practice; so we moved it to Tuesday nights.

You have to be flexible, but not so loose that any spontaneous event is a good *excuse* to postpone Bible study.

Consistency

Be consistent! While flexibility is sometimes necessary, you must be consistent in your Bible study, thereby maintaining your commitment.

For example, parents consistently gather the family for Bible study over several months, then summer comes and schedules change, or the family goes on vacation. The Bible study is put on hold, and they think, "Oh, we'll start back next week, or the week after, or maybe the one after that." Then suddenly there is a crisis going on in their house, and they realize that it has been *months* since the family gathered together for Bible study.

God blesses obedience. Be consistent.

Realism

Be realistic! Keep your standards high, but your *expectations* within reason; the process of teaching your child about God continues over a lifetime. Right now you are sowing valuable seeds that will take time to grow, mature and bear fruit. Remember that *love* is the most powerful motivator, so keep a *balance* between love and discipline as you teach and train up each child.

One father told me that he made his kids read a chapter from the Bible every day, and write one full page on what it said to them. He was convinced that he was teaching his kids the Bible, but I could tell by his wife's reaction that she did not agree with his method. So, I asked him what happened when they did not fill up the whole page, or if what they wrote was not acceptable. He told me very proudly, in those cases, I make them do it over. I asked, "Do you think they enjoy that and got a lot out of it?!!"

Parents, remember to use materials and a teaching style suited to the *age* and *abilities* of your pupils. For parents who struggle with what to do, or how to make Bible studies fun - ask a teacher from your Sunday school if you can sit in and observe how they interact with the children. Look for what sparks the children's interest and ask the teacher for a little help.

Get Started

Perhaps the most important step in starting your study is, **Do It!** *Change* is always a bit uncomfortable, and you may be nervous and afraid things will not go according to your plan. Review the points above, and pray to God for wisdom and strength to do His will for your family. Do not let fear, pride, your job, or *insecurity* about your inabilities get in your way. Remember, you have more influence over your children than anyone. Use it for them; they already love you and really desire and need your parental attention and care.

One summer, we simply used a devotional called *Daily Bread,* because things were so hectic. I had Justin read the Scripture verse, Nick read the story, we each gave our input, and we prayed. It was simple, but effective.

When my kids were teens, and I saw them with their Bibles open, it just blessed me. They were mature enough to search God's Word for themselves. When I was a teenager, the last thing I ever picked up was a Bible. It never crossed my mind. I would have never made the time to do something like that.

To this day, I exhort my children to be in the Word on a continuous basis. I taught them how to have a personal, daily devotional life, but we all need to be encouraged once in a while. I still ask them, "Are you guys in the Word? How's your prayer life?"

Parents, do not allow the world to dictate what your children believe. Make time to *disciple* your kids!

Week 8: Training Up Your Children Part 3 - Disciplining Our Children

WEEK 8: DAY 1

Introduction to Discipline

As we went through our study on *Training Up Your Children Part 1,* I had a very good reason for covering the topic of discipleship before discipline. Truly, discipleship is *foundational* to living the Christian life; everything is built upon discipleship. Jesus told His followers to, *"go make disciples of all nations"* (Matt. 28:19). We have learned that this mandate applies to ministry in our homes; as parents it is our responsibility to disciple our children. To do this, we need to be disciples of Christ ourselves, through personal Bible study and obedient living. The result is an abiding relationship with Christ, which enables us to properly tend to our families. I wanted to restate this because parents often put more importance on discipline than discipleship: "let's get to the discipline!" But discipleship is vital: Jesus to parent, and parent to child. Remember, our relationship with Christ *transforms* us, so that we can bring *glory* to His name.

During the next few weeks, I want to help you understand biblical discipline, what it is and is not. Without realizing it, much of what many parents are doing is counter- productive and will *not* bring their children to maturity. God has given us all the information we need for success; He has a plan and a design for parents to follow.

Permit me to offer an illustration that will give you some perspective on discipline. A nine-year-old boy was walking home from school one day and found a cocoon hanging from a branch. He had seen a video on how a butterfly emerges from a cocoon, so he broke the branch off, brought it home, and put it in a jar with holes in the lid. Every day, he would come home from school and stare at the cocoon—hoping he would be able to see this miracle take place.

One day there was a small tear in the cocoon, and the butterfly was trying to wiggle out. So he sat for several hours, watching, but a nine-year-old boy has a limited attention span. Finally, he could not stand it anymore. He opened the jar, pulled out the cocoon, and began to carefully cut along the tear with a small pair of scissors. Once the cocoon was open, he pulled out the butterfly, but it looked very funny. The body was fat and the wings were shriveled. It was so heavy, it could not even hold up its own weight.

He continued to watch, believing that he would see this strange-looking thing turn into a beautiful butterfly. He even picked it up, tried to help, but it would do nothing. Eventually, it died right before his eyes.

That butterfly died because God's perfect process - the struggle, the strain, and the difficulty of emerging from the cocoon - forces the fluid out of the body into the wings. Then, when it gets out into the atmosphere, the air touches its wings and dries them out, so it can then fly. By removing the struggle that God had designed, the boy killed the butterfly.

DIG DEEPER: *FURTHER STUDY*

Read the following verse and write in your own words what it is saying.

> **Hebrews 12:11** *"Now no chastening seems to be joyful for the present, but painful; nevertheless, afterward it yields the peaceable fruit of righteousness to those who have been trained by it."*

_____

_____

_____

_____

_____

By failing to *discipline* children as God has designed and commanded, many parents are actually preventing them from growing to maturity. When you do not follow through with appropriate discipline, you do not instill the character traits that God wants your kids to have. We have learned that children do not naturally grow into mature adults, but must be trained according to God's word and plan. If this is not done, many will suffer the result. Lack of training can lead to many types of failures in life; surprisingly, prisons are not only filled with "bad" people, but with many average individuals who never received the proper training to develop mature character.

DIG DEEPER: *FURTHER STUDY*

Read the following verses, list the process and result of good discipline, and/or poor discipline. What is the parental responsibility in each?

> **Proverbs 29:15,** *"The <u>rod</u> (authority) and <u>rebuke</u> (training) give wisdom, But a child left to himself brings shame to his mother."*

_____

_____

_____

_____

_____

Proverbs 13:24, *"He who spares his rod (authority) hates his son, But he who loves him disciplines him promptly."*

_____
_____
_____
_____
_____
_____

Proverbs 19:18, *"Chasten your son while there is hope, And do not set your heart on his destruction."*

_____
_____
_____
_____
_____
_____

Training up our children is something God has called us to do (Prov. 22:6; Eph. 6:4). It is not often fun, and often quite difficult. Just as butterflies must struggle out of their cocoons, our kids do not enjoy the struggle of being disciplined into God's proper design for maturity (Hebrew 12:11, above). But we parents must follow through!

The wise King Solomon, knowing our natural tendency to despise discipline, encourages his son to think otherwise, considering the good reason that fathers correct their children.

Proverbs 3:11–12, *"My son, do not despise the chastening (discipline NAS) of the LORD, nor detest His <u>correction</u>*; for whom the LORD loves He corrects, just as a father the son in whom he delights." *(equals <u>training</u>)*

If we have no clear goal, or vision, for discipline and training a child to maturity, then it will <u>NOT</u> happen.

OUR GOAL GRAPH IN PARENTING

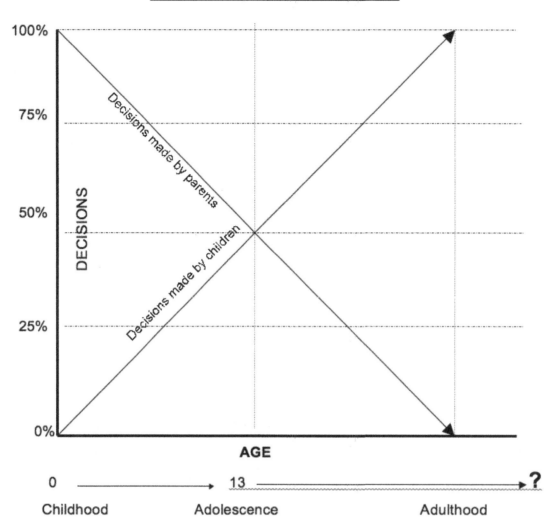

At the bottom of the graph, we have the age of our children, from birth to adulthood. On the left side is the number of decisions made by the children versus the number of decisions we, as their parents, make for them. In the beginning, all decisions are made by parents, which is logical. When our kids come home from the hospital, they are obviously not yet capable of choosing for themselves. But at some point on the graph, those lines cross and continue until our children are making all of their own decisions.

In other words, as our children get older, the goal is for them to make healthy, responsible, wise decisions without supervision. Now, you can look at this graph and think, "Of course, that is just common sense." But, if you do not have a plan in place, a method of training and instilling mature character, this will not happen. You must have a plan. I have met many young adults who do not know how to make wise decisions for themselves. We must move them into maturity by issuing proper discipline. Home is the primary training ground where children grow into adulthood. Or at least, it should be. Do not let your children be molded by outsiders into ideas and practices that are not under your guidance and authority.

Training Versus Controlling = Growth Versus No Growth

At this point, it is important to note that God has instructed us to *train up* our children, not *control* them. The difference between the two is mainly a mindset of how we perceive our job as parents.

FACT FILE

Controlling – To exercise power over, to dominate or rule, to restrain, a restraining force.[1]

Controlling parents are dictators, not trainers. A symptom of this is the inability to accept failure. From the controller's perspective, failure in a child is bad, wrong, and a direct threat to parental authority. They are motivated by self-fulfillment, not God's will. They take their children's failures personally, as deliberate, as if they were purposely trying to hurt them. These types of parents are often concerned about what others think, not about what is right.

Have you been told by your spouse that you are controlling? Have you been told that you are legalistic, or have _unrealistic_ expectations for your kids? Many times this behavior is a result of how you were raised; perhaps never feeling you lived up to your parents' expectations.

SELF-EXAMINATION

You may have control issues! Take time to pray and examine your response to failure in your children. Deeply consider what has been stated above. Write out what God shows you.

_____

_____

_____

_____

_____

_____

_____

If you are harsh and/or controlling, you must ask God, "Why do I perceive my kids' failures this way? Why am I *reacting* in this way? Is it because I have not forgiven my own parents?" Is it because you are letting your own carnal nature and selfish expectations govern your parenting instead of God's heart? It is essential that you deal with this issue.

Parents, our job is to *train*; it is part of our ministry. To do this properly, we need to understand "what is" childish behavior. A child can be foolish, disobedient, or defiant. A child's failure, even willful disobedience,

---

1   *Webster's New International Dictionary of the English Language; Second Edition Unabridged*; G & C Merriam Company, Publishers, Springfield, MA 1944

is *not* the same as defiant rebellion. If you believe it is, you will respond to your children in the wrong way, usually in anger.

FACT FILE

Defiance – is when a child rebels against the *discipline that follows* their foolish act of immaturity.

Understanding the difference between defiance and foolishness is crucial, as is your ability to adjust your response appropriately. And remember to handle all discipline with love, or your negative communication can actually make your child feel unloved.

Let's look at ourselves for a moment. We parents have studied the biblical principles of loving communication found in 1 Corinthians 13. And have we not all failed at some time to follow God's instructions? This is not because we defiantly said, "I don't care what the Bible says. I am going to do it my way!" Rather, it is because we lack the spiritual maturity and character to carry it out. However, I bet you have noticed some progress, and should realize that you are simply going through God's *training* process.

So, it is important to see that failure is not defiance. Even if your kids have been repeatedly told what not to do, their failures and mistakes are usually due to *immaturity*, foolishness. God clearly explains that children are foolish and that we parents are here to train them in Godly wisdom.

Proverbs 22:15 *"Foolishness is bound up in the heart of a child".*

The word "foolishness" means: "deficient in understanding, unwise, brainless, irrational, ludicrous, a lack of judgment."[2] Does that not perfectly describe our children? They are lacking character and maturity. So why do we get so angry when they act foolishly? God's Word declares they are born that way!

Proverbs 22:6, gives an exhortation to parents that *"the rod of correction will drive it (foolishness) far from him."* Discipline is viewed here as *positive*, as it will drive the foolishness out of a child. The rod represents parental authority and discipline. In essence, we are training them by using biblical discipline, not control. Note Christian author, H.A. Ironside says:

> To leave a child to itself is to ensure its ruin, for folly is bound up in its heart. Discipline, properly administered will correct the natural tendency to go astray. The rod is, of course, not necessarily strictly such. Corporal punishment is not always required, and might at times be

---

2   *Webster's New International Dictionary of the English Language; Second Edition Unabridged*; G & C Merriam Company, Publishers, Springfield, MA 1944

very unwise. But firm, yet kindly, discipline is what the passage declares the importance of. The rod, throughout Scripture, speaks of authority and power; in this case that parental restraint to which the child owes so much. It was the lack of this that was responsible in large measure for the evil ways of both Absalom and Adonijah (2 Sam. 14; 1 Kings 1:6).[3]

SELF-EXAMINATION

I would like you to take some time right now and read through the following paragraph and write out any of the characteristics of immaturity (foolishness) that you see in your children.

Proverbs gives us a picture of a child's lack of maturity and their need for training. They lack judgment (10:21), enjoy foolishness (10:23), gullible (14:15), avoid the wise (15:12), are proud and haughty (21:24), despise good advice (23:9), make truth useless (26:7), repeat their folly (26:11), trust in themselves (28:26), vent their anger (29:11), cause strife and quarrels (22:10), stir up anger (29:8), go their own way (15:21), lash out when they are discovered in folly (17:12), endangered by their words (18:6, 7), walk a troublesome path (22:5), must be guided by hardship at times (26:3), persist in foolishness (27:22) propensity for laziness (22:13), lustful (22:14) and greedy (22:16).

_____

_____

_____

_____

_____

_____

_____

_____

Training Means . . .

FACT FILE

Training – To cause to grow as desired; to make or become prepared or skilled.[4]

The proper trainer's goal is to fulfill God's will, not our own desires or expectations. Jesus carried out the Father's will (John 5:20, 30; 6:38) by training His disciples, and we are to do the same. Jesus' motivation was to glorify the Father (John 12:28), as we also should when training our children. If this is our motivation, then we will be able to carry out God's purposes in parenting with love and patience (especially with strong-willed children).

---

3   H. A. Ironside, *Notes on the Book of Proverbs* (Neptune, NJ: Loizeaux Bros, 1908), 309.

4   *Webster's New International Dictionary of the English Language; Second Edition Unabridged*; G & C Merriam Company, Publishers, Springfield, MA 1944

Let me give you an illustration. If you had a two-year-old tree in your backyard with a trunk about three inches in diameter that had a forty-five degree bend on it, wouldn't it be foolish for you to grab the tree and forcibly straighten it up in one try? What would happen to that tree? It would snap at the base, and you would destroy it.

A trainer, like a farmer (which means husbandman[5]), knows that when he finds a bent trunk, there is a proper way and an improper way to fix it. The proper way would be to train the tree by putting a light amount of consistent pressure in a pre-determined direction. As the tree conforms to the pressure, more can be gradually applied in the same direction until the tree is in a desired position, and no longer "bent". This is an example of proper training and perspective.

That is the way we need to perceive our kids; they come to us bent. Have you not noticed? We do not like them bent; we want them straight right now! Because they are "bent", acting their age, we say things like, "Don't act that way!" and send the wrong message to them.

God gives us the biblical instruction so we understand our job and what our mindset toward training should be. We can see that failure and foolishness in our children is to be *expected*, and is normal, merely a part of the whole journey.

> **Ephesians 6:4** *"And you, fathers, do not provoke your children to wrath, but bring them up in the training and admonition of the Lord."*

As previously discussed, the word translated *"bring them up,"* means to "bring up to maturity, to train or educate". This must be the goal for our kids in the area of discipline: to raise them to maturity.

The word "training" here means discipline, chastening, correction, and educative discipline, i.e., "discipline that regulates character."[6] Remember, we are instilling character in our children's lives. Proper training or discipline is the *means* by which we carry out the goal.

"To bring up" is the <u>goal</u>; "training" is the method by which we reach that goal.

The last part of this verse, *"admonition of the Lord,"* means "instructions, warning, exhortation, any words of encouragement or reproof that leads to correct behavior,"[7] as unto the Lord, or as the Lord instructs us to. The exhortation is to train our children His way, not our own way/

---

5   *Webster's New International Dictionary* 1994.

6   W.E. Vine and F.F. Bruce, vol. 2, *Vine's Expository Dictionary of Old and New Testament Words* (Old Tappan NJ: Revell, 1981), 183.

7   Zodhiates, 1017.

Instilling character is like training muscles.

Think of it this way: imagine you are a coach, your children are the members of your team, and the goal is to get them bench-pressing two hundred pounds. So, when your students show up on Monday, Wednesday, and Friday, your job is to train them to bench two hundred pounds. If they arrived ten minutes late the first day, and you spent half of your time *lecturing* them, what did you do toward training their muscles? What if you yelled and screamed and threatened to take away everything they had? Still nothing.

Until you lay them on the bench, doing bench presses with lighter weights, there will be no training-taking place. Discipline means training them, and every time they fail it is our opportunity to train them. How do they give us opportunities to train them? By their foolish choices and acts; we need to have a biblical perspective toward our children's foolish behavior, view it as our *opportunity* to discipline and train them to maturity. Not to get angry or frustrated.

Let me give you another illustration. If you laid two hundred pounds on your 10 year old child's chest, would you yell, "Pick it up, what's wrong with you? Come on, you should be able to do this?" Of course not! You know that a ten-year-old cannot bench press two hundred pounds! We need to view their failures or foolishness as a sign that training is not yet complete. If we become angry and aggravated, we are sending the message that we expect a child to accomplish the impossible. We also communicate that they are not valuable to us, we don't like them, and/or something is wrong with them. How do you think those types of hurtful expressions will affect your relationship with your child? And if things are not handled properly at a young age, it only gets worse.

We know that training begins with lighter weights; gradually increasing as the person demonstrates the capacity to lift more, until eventually they achieve the goal. In a similar way, a child's *character* grows slightly with each correction. When we parents shout, and act disappointed and upset, it is because of our own ignorance and sin nature. A child's failure merely *proves* to you that they cannot bench-press two hundred pounds at that moment. They do not have the character yet. Do you see the difference?

God wants us to have His viewpoint; it changes our concepts, methods, and our attitude about discipline. This can eliminate anger and the perception that a child's failure is unacceptable, or rebellion. *Foolishness* is bound up in the hearts of our children. Praise the Lord for telling us this truth, and showing us that our task is to instill mature character.

SELF-EXAMINATION

What has your attitude been when your children break a rule or disobey?

_____

_____

_____

_____

What is the attitude God wants you to have when your child disobeys?

_____

_____

_____

_____

Write out a prayer asking God to help you change your perspective to His.

_____

_____

_____

_____

_____

_____

_____

_____

WEEK 8: DAY 2

Mature Character

Of course, in order to instill mature character in our children, we must first formulate a definition of maturity. What is our goal? Most parents that I talk to do not truly understand the nature of a mature adult.

⚲ SELF-EXAMINATION

Take a moment right now and write out what you believe is the character of a mature adult.

_____

_____

_____

_____

_____

If married, did your spouse write the same description you did? ❏ Yes ❏ No

Can we agree that the ultimate mature adult, with perfect character, was Jesus Christ? As a general statement, all of us are to be seeking the maturity level of Christ. If fact, the church is called to equip the saints (Eph. 4:11-12), with this goal in mind: *"till we all come to the unity of the faith and of the knowledge of the Son of God, to a perfect (mature NAS) man, to the measure of the stature of the fullness of Christ"* (Eph. 4:13).

FACT FILE

Perfect/Mature – *teleios* (Greek), meaning goal, or purpose; finished, that which has reached its end, term, limit; hence, complete, full, wanting in nothing.[8]

We know that this is our goal, and when Christ returns we will be perfect and mature, *"...we know that when He is revealed, we shall be like Him..."* (1 John 3:2). Until then, we continue to grow into His image (Rom. 8:29). All of us have to go through the same process, from childhood to adulthood. Luke 2:52 states that *"Jesus increased in wisdom and stature, and in favor with God and men."* Note: Jesus increased in wisdom, or mental growth; in stature, or physical growth; grew in favor with God, or spiritual growth; and in favor with men, or social growth. We have limited influence in the physical growth of our children. But the other three – mental, spiritual and social - we have a big part in making this happen. It is not by accident that these characteristics are mentioned about Jesus, they are for our instruction. God wants our children to grow in these areas.

We want to be able to say of our children, as Paul said of himself, *"When I was a child, I spoke as a child, I understood as a child, I thought as a child; but when I became a man, I put away childish things"* (1 Cor. 13:11). He noticed in his own life that there was a progression. Through godly discipline and training, we will see our children gradually put away childish things and grow into mature adults.

Mature Character Defined

In order to succeed, certain character qualities and skills must be developed that will enable us to aim at and hit the bull's-eye of maturity.

They are:
1) **Morals and values**
2) **Personal responsibility**
3) **Self-control**

These all work in unison to produce **mature** character.

1. MORALS AND VALUES

First, we must instill biblical morals and values into our children, give them a foundation of knowing right from wrong. Every day they are bombarded with worldly morals and values through the media, public schools and their own peers.

---

8   Zodhiates, 1372.

FACT FILE

Morals and Values – for the Christian, *morals* are defined by what is right and wrong from God's perspective. *Values* are the principles, or actions you live by, meaning that your behavior shows what you value most.

Previously, we discussed the importance of *discipling* our children and instilling God's Word into their hearts. We are to follow Jesus' example, as He prayed to the Father for his own disciples: *"Sanctify them by Your truth. Your word is truth"* (John 17:17), and *"you shall know the truth, and the truth shall make you free."* (John 8:32). Once our children are discipled in the truths of Scripture, they will have that freedom of knowing what is contrary to the Word of God, and what results from disobedience. They will be able to discern truth from error and recognize temptations from the world, the flesh or Satan.

There are going to be times along the way when our children question biblical morals and values. When those times come, and they will, you must firmly stand for what God says is right and wrong, not offer your opinions, or worldly philosophies. When the Bible says something is right, or wrong, we should never compromise.

This is what God instructed our father of the faith, Abraham, to do with his children:

> **Genesis 18:19** *"For I have known him, in order that he may command his children and his household after him, that they <u>keep the way of the LORD</u>, to do <u>righteousness</u> and justice, that the LORD may bring to Abraham what He has spoken to him."*

As we have learned, God told Abraham to structure his house so that his children would be righteous and follow the way of the Lord. Righteousness means right standing with God; therefore, Abraham's *training* was to be directed in such a way that it drew his children into right thinking and right behavior in God's eyes. This describes the process of growing in wisdom and favor with God. We increasingly understand what is *pleasing* to Him (2 Cor. 5:9), and do it.

> **2 Corinthians 5:9** *"Therefore we make it our aim, whether present or absent, to be well pleasing to Him."*

Remember, we disciple our children by our example, instruction and Bible study.

2. PERSONAL RESPONSIBILITY

The quality of personal responsibility is instilled in a child by training and persistent biblical discipline. The graph we looked at previously shows the percentage and progression of choices we make for our children from birth. Everyone comes into this world completely dependent, but it is essential that we learn to make responsible choices for ourselves. It is sad, and difficult to watch a youth who has not learned personal responsibility. In my counseling, it does not take me long to realize that they are immature due to lack of training at home to develop this character trait.

FACT FILE

Personal Responsibility: the ability to take care of oneself; to follow through on things you have committed to do, or the things required, without anyone else having to prompt you; taking ownership, being accountable and accepting responsibility for your actions.

If you are *faithful* in training, your children will develop to a point where less discipline is needed and you will be rewarded by their growing maturity.

SELF-EXAMINATION

List two behaviors for each of your children that show personal responsibility (examples: I do not have to ask them to make the bed, clean room, take out trash or to do their homework...).

_____
_____
_____
_____
_____
_____
_____
_____
_____
_____

Now, write out two indications of irresponsibility (I have to keep asking them to...).

_____
_____
_____
_____
_____
_____
_____
_____
_____
_____

As we have learned, training a child is *progressive* and new challenges will appear with each new stage of their development. One of the major issues with youth is "not wanting to admit" to being wrong. When children become teenagers, they suddenly inherit some kind of superior wisdom, in their own mind, and now they know it all. When you confront them about something, they will blame someone else, come up with excuses and avoid being personally responsible. This is why the following chapters are **so** important. *We* have to structure our homes as a training ground, not as a debating or negotiating courtroom.

Most children are the same; blame shifting and avoiding responsibility was the first tactic used by Adam and Eve after they sinned by disobeying God. Back in the Garden of Eden, God stated that, *"of every tree of the garden you may freely eat, but of the tree of the knowledge of good and evil you <u>shall not eat</u>..."* (Gen. 2:16-17). Adam and Eve were personally responsible to obey this *one* command. Satan came to Eve, tempted her to eat the forbidden fruit (Gen. 3:1-5), she ate it, and then gave it to her husband and they both fell into sin (vs. 6) by disobeying God. When God confronted Adam and Eve about their sin, this is how they responded:

> **Genesis 3:12–13** *"Then the man said, "The woman whom You gave to be with me, she gave me of the tree, and I ate." And the LORD God said to the woman, "What is this you have done?" The woman said, "The serpent deceived me, and I ate.""*

Notice how Adam actually *blamed* God by saying, *"the woman You gave me,"* and the woman *blamed* the serpent with, *"the serpent deceived me."* They were avoiding personal responsibility for their sin. Instead of taking *ownership* of their actions and being accountable before God, they shifted blame.

If we are not mindful, our children can *develop a habit* of blaming circumstances, or others, to escape responsibility for their actions. Children will naturally want to blame a sibling – "he did it", or "she made me do this or that", or "it's his fault, not mine." Correct biblical discipline will help a child *learn* personal responsibility and take responsibility.

Instilling personal responsibility into a child takes *consistent* training, *time* and *patience*. Parents, this is something we must model before our children, showing them the way by example. Our personal life can display personal responsibility by the way we tend to our homes, jobs, possessions and our commitments.

⌕ SELF-EXAMINATION

Ponder this question for a moment, and write out your conclusion below.

How do you think it affects a 15-year-old child when their Christian parent gets angry, uses hurtful words, or ignores them as part of their discipline plan, and then never takes responsibility for the sinful actions?

_____

_____

_____

_____

_____

Parents can show irresponsibility in their jobs by being late often or by a house that is messy all the time because no one is keeping it clean. How have you been irresponsible in front of your children?

_____

_____

_____

_____

The principle of personal responsibility is that of *maintaining good works*. Parents have the awesome privilege of training their children to have a good work ethic. We asked you to write down some things that you do not have to remind your children to do, such as make the bed, clean room, take out trash and so on. For most children, doing chores and wanting to help around the house is NOT a priority. Without proper training, their childish character will continue into adulthood. Parents, our homes are the best training ground to prepare children for the work force and life. One of the main reasons so many young adults today make poor employees is because they were not trained in *personally responsibility* and to do a good job.

When Paul wrote Titus, a pastor he had trained on the island of Crete, he was concerned with the body of believers maintaining good works.

> **Titus 3:14,** *"And let our people also <u>learn</u> to <u>maintain good works</u>, to meet urgent needs, that they may <u>not</u> be unfruitful."*

Notice that he was writing Titus about a congregation, yet he called them *"our people."* Paul felt that he and Titus were personally responsible to train people to maintain good works and meet other's needs, and therefore be fruitful. To maintain good works means to be a responsible person, concerned for others, and able to do what is needed. Our children need a lot of help with this; they are born without the character of personal responsibility, are selfish, and do not care for others. One author says concerning this verse:

> *Titus was to teach the other Christians (**our people**) to show hospitality, to care for the sick and afflicted, and to be generous toward those who were in need. Instead of working merely to meet their own needs and wants, they should have the distinctly Christian vision*

of earning money in order to share with the less privileged (see Eph. 4:28b). This would save them from the misery of selfishness and the tragedy of a wasted, unfruitful life.[9]

An exhortation of what needs to be done within the church family, this also is what we should be striving for within our homes. We can teach our children to be personally responsible IF we know how. When doing this we are honoring God, exalting His name, and blessing our children.

DIG DEEPER: *FURTHER STUDY*

How can this verse apply to parenting?

Colossians 3:17 *"And whatever you do in word or deed, do all in the name of the Lord Jesus, giving thanks to God the Father through Him."*

_____

_____

_____

_____

Read each of the following Scriptures and comment how personal responsibility would be involved and the fruit from having it.

Proverbs 10:4 *" He who has a slack hand becomes poor, But the hand of the diligent makes rich."*

_____

_____

_____

_____

Proverbs 12:14 *" A man will be satisfied with good by the fruit of his mouth, And the recompense of a man's hands will be rendered to him."*

_____

_____

_____

_____

Proverbs 12:24 *" The hand of the diligent will rule, But the lazy man will be put to forced labor."*

---

9   William MacDonald, *Believer's*, 2146.

_____
_____
_____
_____

Proverbs 12:27 " *The lazy man does not roast what he took in hunting, But diligence is man's precious possession.*"

_____
_____
_____
_____

Proverbs 13:4 " *The soul of a lazy man desires, and has nothing; But the soul of the diligent shall be made rich.*"

_____
_____
_____
_____

Proverbs 14:23 " *In all labor there is profit, But idle chatter leads only to poverty.*"

_____
_____
_____
_____

Proverbs 15:19 " *The way of the lazy man is like a hedge of thorns, But the way of the upright is a highway.*"

_____
_____
_____
_____

Proverbs 21:5 " *The plans of the diligent lead surely to plenty, But those of everyone who is hasty, surely to poverty.*"

_____
_____
_____
_____

Proverbs 21:25 *" The desire of the lazy man kills him, For his hands refuse to labor."*

_____
_____
_____
_____

Proverbs 21:26 *"He covets greedily all day long, But the righteous gives and does not spare."*

_____
_____
_____
_____

Proverbs 22:29 *" Do you see a man who excels in his work? He will stand before kings; He will not stand before unknown men."*

_____
_____
_____
_____

Proverbs 28:19 *" He who tills his land will have plenty of bread, But he who follows frivolity will have poverty enough!"*

_____
_____
_____
_____

3. SELF-CONTROL

The third character quality that our children must develop is ***self-control***. This also can be considered the ability to self-discipline (to manage one's feelings and actions). As you will see, self-control is essential to living successfully according to godly morals and values.

FACT FILE

Self-control – the ability to govern oneself emotionally, physically, and spiritually; the ability to not always yield to the path of least resistance.

The vital importance of this area of character development is clear. When it comes to making moral, biblical choices, it requires self-control to stand firm and not take the path of least resistance, which means to *be lead by* the flesh. Being under the power of the Holy Spirit, emotionally, physically and spiritually, is God's will.

Self-control includes having the ability to **resist one's emotions.** As you well know, we sometimes *react* to people and/or circumstances with sinful behaviors. During week 3, we discussed the difference between *reacting* and *responding,* and came to the conclusion that a reaction indicates lack of self-control and is fleshly, and that a godly response is motivated by love, which is an aspect of the fruit of the Spirit. When we react to our emotional impulses, we often follow through with physical sinful actions.

DIG DEEPER: *FURTHER STUDY*

Read the following Scripture and relate it to the emotional aspect of self-control.

> **Proverbs 29:11** *"A fool vents all his feelings, but a wise man holds them back."*

_____
_____
_____
_____

SELF-EXAMINATION

Write out an incident when you let emotions get in the way, resulting in sinful behavior toward someone.

_____
_____
_____
_____
_____
_____
_____

Let's look further at the **physical aspect** of self-control.

> **2 Peter 3:17,** *"You therefore, beloved, since you know this beforehand, beware lest you also fall from your own steadfastness, being led away with the error of the wicked."*

What Peter is saying here is that there needs to be some self-restraint or self-control, when it comes to our choices.

DIG DEEPER: *FURTHER STUDY*

Read the following Scriptures and write out what the consequences are for the lack of self-control.

Proverbs 25:28, *"Whoever has no rule over his own spirit Is like a city broken down, without walls."*

_____

_____

_____

_____

We are commanded to exercise self-control.

1 Peter 1:13, *"So think clearly and exercise self-control…"* (NLT)

_____

_____

_____

Every Christian is to be self-controlled, but without proper training and or a desire to attain it, one will not acquire it.

Galatians 5:22–23 *"But the fruit of the Spirit is love, joy, peace, longsuffering, kindness, goodness, faithfulness, gentleness, **self-control**. Against such there is no law."*

What does this verse promise all of God's children?

Philippians 1:6 *"being confident of this very thing, that He who has begun a good work in you will complete it until the day of Jesus Christ."*

_____

_____

_____

In his book, *The Believer's Secret to Holiness,* Andrew Murray says:

Self-control in a Christian means that instead of insisting on having our own way, we choose God's way; we turn to Him for our marching orders and we obey His loving commands. We agree to allow God's Holy Spirit to live in us and work God's will through us. Then, when the Spirit has free reign, He is able to bring us closer to God's ideal of perfection, and holiness. [10]

---

10   Andrew Murray, *The Believer's Secret to Holiness* (Bethany House Publisher, 1984), quoted in God's Treasury of Virtues, (Tulsa: Honor Books, 1995), 422.

These three character qualities - **morals and values**, **personal responsibility**, and **self-control** - are our target, the *bull's-eye* we want to hit dead center. Do you know that every foolish act your son or daughter has done to date, and will do in the future, involves a violation of one or more of these? Why, because they were born without them. It is our job as parents to teach and instill them through training.

It is so important that you see and understand this, because having no clear bull's-eye means having no direction, and you will end up in a place you don't want to be. Having clarity also brings unity between husbands and wives, helping them work together toward a clear, common goal.

SELF-EXAMINATION

Answer this question. If we as parents do not have clear goals and a plan to reach it, how are we going to measure our success?

_____

_____

_____

_____

_____

_____

If a corporation wants to sell three million dollars worth of product in a 12 month period, it would be wise to have a clear plan and check quarterly, at least, asking, "Are we close to our mark?" It would be reckless and irresponsible to wait until the end of the year to measure success. Likewise, if you have clear goals and methods for training up your children, you will be able to measure your success. In a later chapter you will learn how to implement a procedure that can help you and your children see how close you are to your goals.

OUR KIDS NEED TO KNOW THE BULL'S-EYE

By the time I was fourteen years old, my distorted view of manhood included being a tough guy, using drugs, drinking, and having many girlfriends. I foolishly went after all that! I trusted no one who could tell me otherwise. No one ever gave me that *bull's-eye* of character, or encouraged me to shoot for it.

I have interviewed hundreds of teenagers over the years, and less than five percent even come close to giving the proper definition of a *mature* adult. When I ask them, "When do you think you should know?" most respond with, "I don't know." When I asked does it just happen or is it something you have to do? Their answer included "when you move out, I guess when you get a job, start taking care of yourself, or maybe when you get married and have kids. I don't know."

It is our responsibility as parents to make this clear. This generation of teenagers is so lost because a godless world is defining the wrong bull's-eye. Public schools, media, music, television shows, Internet, books, and magazines are forming the wrong bull's-eye. Satan is bombarding our children with lies, confusion, and misdirection. This is why it is so important for us to clearly define both our goals for *maturity* and the *method*s we are going to use to get them there.

More than likely, you were not fully taught the importance of instilling the three key characteristics we have discussed. The Bible says very clearly that God desires our children to acquire **morals and values**, **personal responsibility**, and **self-control**.

In closing this section I would like to restate something: it is going to take a combination of *discipleship* and *discipline* (training) for this all to take place. I would like to show you the importance of this from the following Scripture.

Proverbs 23:7 *says, "For as he thinks in his heart, so is he."*

"As he thinks in his heart" means what a person believes about right and wrong. *"So is he"* refers to a person's behavior, or what he does, which can be said to define who he is.

Most parents are more interested in changing the *"so is he,"* meaning their child's behavior, and less focused on training of the heart. You can see there are two principles at work in this verse, and *"as he thinks in his heart,"* comes before *"so is he."* So the priority must be to disciple our children, which will in turn affect their behavior. We must change the way our child thinks, as well as disciplining their behavior.

For example, your son calls his sister a hurtful name, so you need to follow through with a corrective consequence for his behavior, but you also need to teach his heart by discipling him in the knowledge of right and wrong.

The Word of God teaches us how to treat others, so we need to be faithfully discipling them.

Ephesians 4:29, *"Let no corrupt word proceed out of your mouth, but what is good for necessary edification, that it may impart grace to the hearers."*

By hearing the Word of God, a child becomes schooled, or discipled, in understanding right and wrong. Of course, this would not be complete after a one-time lesson. The principle of not letting corrupt communication proceed out of your mouth includes how to talk to each other. A combination of discipleship and discipline teaches personal responsibility and the knowledge that a *choice* to disobey always has a *corrective consequence*.

WEEK 8: DAY 3

Introduction: The Four Tools of Training

As we have learned, training children according to Biblical principles applies to various types of families, both two-parent and single parent. And, when married, a couple is to function as a team; both are responsible for discipling and training the children, although fathers have the primary leadership role. We also studied Ephesians 6:4, at the beginning of Week six, which presents the New Testament standard for training and disciplining children.

> **Ephesians 6:4,** *"And you, fathers, do not provoke your children to wrath, but <u>bring them up</u> in the <u>training</u> [**discipline** ESV] and <u>admonition</u> [**instruction** ESV] of the Lord."*

FACT FILE

The Goal – *"Bring them up,"* is *ektrepho* (Geek), and it means that we are to bring our children to maturity.

That is God's goal, and therefore should be ours as well. We learned that progress is measured by observing a child's improvement in the areas of *morals and values*, *personal responsibility* and *self-control*.

FACT FILE

The Method – The method that God uses to mature and train His children is discipline.

Discipline is a planned process covering all aspects of training a child, including discipling in righteousness and the instilling of mature character. In New Testament times, the Greek culture was attentive to the discipline of children. When writing Ephesians 6:4, Paul used the word *paideia* (Gk.), translated *training/discipline*, from the word *pais* (child), referring to the systematic training of children. This indicates correction for wrongdoing, further explained in a verse from Proverbs, *"He who spares his rod hates his son, but he who loves him disciplines him diligently."* (Prov. 13:24).[11] And, as *defined* in a theological dictionary, training "also denotes the upbringing and handling of the child which is growing up to maturity and needing direction, teaching, instruction and a certain measure of compulsion in the form of discipline or even chastisement." [12]

---

11   John F. MacArthur, Jr., *Ephesians*, MacArthur New Testament Commentary (Chicago: Moody Press, 1986), 319.

12   Vol. 5, *Theological Dictionary of the New Testament*, ed. Gerhard Kittel, Geoffrey W. Bromiley and Gerhard Friedrich, electronic ed. (Grand Rapids, MI: Eerdmans, 1964-), 596.

FACT FILE

Admonition or instruction – is the Greek word *nouthesia* in (Eph. 6:4), and translates as a "warning, exhortation, or any word of encouragement or reproof, which leads to correct behavior."[13]

This refers to having a corrective influence on someone through verbal instruction, leading to increased understanding of proper conduct. For our purposes, all instruction is to be ***"of the Lord."*** Our desire must be to instruct in God's way: We are doing God's will by instilling godly character in our children using God's method of discipline.

PARENTS MUST DISCIPLINE THEIR CHILDREN BECAUSE:

1. ***God commands us to discipline – Proverbs 19:18; 22:6; 23:13-14.***
Proverbs 19:18, *"Discipline your son while there is hope, and do not desire his death." (NAS)*

Discipline is the Hebrew word *yasar,* an imperative verb, which means that it is a command. God is exhorting us to discipline our children from the earliest possible age. This verse indicates that a child who is left undisciplined can reach a point beyond parental influence, and will not have the self-control to say no to sin, which could result in spiritual and even physical death.

Father's, did you hear the strong exhortation and consequences if this is not taking place in you home?

2. ***Discipline demonstrates God's Love – Hebrews 12:6.***
Hebrews 12:6, *"Because the Lord disciplines those he loves, and he punishes everyone he accepts as a son." (NIV)*

Just as God disciplines us because He loves us, so we should discipline our children because we love them. Discipline is a form of love.

Have you viewed discipline toward your children as love?   ❑ Yes ❑ No

If a parent is angry, agitated and/or threatening when disciplining, would a child perceive it as love?
❑ Yes ❑ No

I have worked with many kids in juvenile hall who have told me in anger, *"I know my parents don't love me!"*

---

13   Zodhiates, 1017.

This was not necessarily because their parents abandoned them, beat them, introduced them to drugs, or moved from place to place. These kids were convinced that their parents did not love them because they did not *discipline* them! A child realizes when a parent neglects them; won't take the time and effort to teach them right from wrong; fails to correct and train them; and does not enforce rules and discipline. This says loud and clear to a child that a parent does not care and does not love them.

3.   *Discipline produces mature, godly adults – Ephesians 6:4; Psalm 32:9.*

As we saw from Ephesians 6:4, *"bring them up"* means to raise our children to maturity, and *"training"* refers to discipline, which is the *means* by which maturity is developed.

By illustration, consider the horse, or mule, which is trained and guided with, a bit and bridle because they lack the ability to understand. In a similar way our children must be guided by discipline until they gain understanding. Thankfully, a child schooled with biblical discipline will someday not need that "bit and bridle" of parental discipline, but will be an independently responsible adult.

> **Psalm 32:9** *says, "Do not be like the horse or like the mule, which have no understanding, which must be harnessed with bit and bridle, else they will not come near you."*

They will reject authority and not take responsibility.

As parents, we sometimes discipline our children in reaction to their "foolish" behavior, forgetting that the goal of discipline is to raise mature adults. Mere age does not make an adult; rather, maturity is characterized by **morals and values, personal responsibility and self-control**. It is evident in our society that many individuals come of age and are not yet mature adults.

4.   *Discipline keeps peace in the home – Hebrews 12:11.*

Hebrews 12:11, *"For the moment all discipline seems painful rather than pleasant, but later it yields <u>the peaceful fruit</u> of righteousness to those who have been trained by it." (ESV)*

When proper discipline is consistently administered, it will yield peaceable fruit.

We would all agree that any home with children is a hotbed of excitement, noise, accidents, tears, hectic schedules, and countless unexpected events on a daily basis. But I also believe that, as Christians, our homes can be a place where God's peace reigns over all!

- Would you describe your home environment as peaceful, calm, harmonious and unified?
  ❑ Yes   ❑ No

THE "TOOLS" OF DISCIPLINE ELIMINATE CONFUSION:

I use the word "tools" because God has given us some practical principles, or tools, to help us carry out discipline. Many parents are confused, and have not considered biblical methods of discipline, as we often use the same processes that our parents used with us. A man and woman join in marriage, each with their own history, with "preconceived ideas" of discipline. Then, they each approach discipline with these ideas, as well as others from current trends, family members and friends. Eventually, the resulting confusion leads to division between husband and wife.

This is NOT the way God has designed the family to function. The Bible says that, *"God is not the author of confusion but of peace"* (1 Cor. 14:33). Sure, we may gain some "ideas" in how to discipline our children from other sources, but it always has to be in line with God's Word, because His Word is the truth that instructs us in the ways of righteousness (2 Tim. 3:16-17). God is the source of information, the provider of biblical principles for disciplining His children His way. And the Bible warns us that His ways are not our natural ways. God says, *"For as the heavens are higher than the earth, so are My ways higher than your ways, and My thoughts than your thoughts"* (Isaiah 55:9). That is why we must continually be in His Word, and following His instruction.

You may have noticed that I continually bring you back to the truth that *your* children are *His* children. Why am I doing that? Because it is so easy to lose that perspective and lapse into incorrect, self-motivated practices and attitudes with "our" children. This principle is so important; Proverbs shows us that even those ways that seem "right" to us can end in disaster.

DIG DEEPER: *FURTHER STUDY*

Read the following verses and in your own words, explain how parents can be deceived and the possible result.

Proverbs 14:12 *"There is a way that seems right to a man, But its end is the way of death."*

_____

_____

_____

_____

Proverbs 21:2 *"Every way of a man is right in his own eyes, But the LORD weighs the hearts."*

_____

_____

_____

_____

Before I explain how to use God's tools to build mature character, I would like to remind you again that the proper sequence for training our children is first discipling in righteousness, and then Biblical discipline.

Discipling **must** be the foundation for discipline. Remember, *"For as a man thinks in his heart, so is he"* (Prov. 23:7). In other words, until the heart is transformed, the behavior may be learned, but true righteousness cannot exist. As we discussed last week, many parents spend most of their time trying to change the *"so is he,"* or the behavior, rather than the heart. The *heart* is changed through love and discipleship. Remember, if you discipline without love, you will produce rebellion rather than obedience.

DIG DEEPER: *FURTHER STUDY*

Please read the following Scriptures and write out what they say about a man's heart and his actions.

Proverbs 27:19, *"As in water face reflects face, so a man's heart reveals the man."*

_____

_____

_____

Mark 7:21, *"For from within, out of the heart of men, proceed evil thoughts, adulteries, fornications, murders."*

_____

_____

_____

Proverbs 4:23, *"Keep your heart with all diligence, For out of it spring the issues of life."*

_____

_____

_____

Remember, Ephesians 6:4 ends with the phrase, *"admonition of the Lord"*, which is an exhortation for us to look to Him and His Word, and to follow the example of how He trains and disciplines us.

The following scripture shows us not only what our attitude and response should be to God's discipline, but primarily that He loves us and His motives are only for our good.

Hebrews 12:5-6, *"And you have forgotten the exhortation which speaks to you as to sons:* *"My son, do not despise the chastening [discipline] of the LORD, nor be discouraged when you are rebuked by Him; For whom the LORD loves He chastens, and scourges every son whom He receives.""*

There are important principles in these verses to help parents develop a clear plan for "chastening" and "scourging" a child.

> ## FACT FILE
>
> **Chastening or discipline** – is the same Greek word used in Ephesians 6:4 (*paideia),* and means correction or training. In other words, there is a consequence for every offense; some type of training/correction will follow.

> ## FACT FILE
>
> **Rebuke** – means to convict, to prove one in the wrong.[14]

In our context, God's Word is the standard for right and wrong behavior. Adults use the scriptures to guide and correct themselves. In the same way, parents need to define, develop and communicate biblical rules of conduct for the family, complete with a plan for corrective discipline when necessary.

> ## FACT FILE
>
> **Scourges** – entails all and any suffering, which God ordains for His children, which is always designed for their good. Also it includes the entire range of trials and tribulations, which He providentially ordains and which work to mortify sin and nurture faith. [15]

Another way to put it: God uses "a measured amount of pain to motivate us to accept His training," so that we may be conformed into the image of Christ. In a similar way, we are to do the same with our children in order to motivate them to accept our training.

Reviewing the principles just presented, our task as parents is to...

1) Define rules based on God's view of right and wrong behavior.

2) Have a plan for correction, or "consequence," when a rule is broken.

3) The use of punishment to help a child receive the corrective consequence, if they are refusing it. This would be used for rebellion.

DIG DEEPER: *FURTHER STUDY*

Read the following Scripture and explain what God's motive is for correcting His children.

---

14   Zodhiates, 562.

15   Zodhiates, 948.

Proverbs 3:12 *"For whom the LORD loves He corrects, Just as a father the son in whom he delights."*

_____
_____
_____
_____

SELF-EXAMINATION

How does this differ from your current motives?

_____
_____
_____
_____
_____

What are some of the unloving attitudes, facial expressions or words that are used during discipline that needs to be changed?

_____
_____
_____
_____
_____
_____

Remember the words of Jesus.

Revelation 3:19 *"As many as I love, I rebuke and chasten. Therefore be zealous and repent."*

It is in this spirit of love that I will elaborate further on these principles: I call this information the four tools of training.

WEEK 8: DAY 4

Four Tools of Training/Disciplining

The following categories include the "tools" you will need to build personal responsibility and self-control into your children.

1. **Rules/Boundaries**
2. **Corrective Consequences**
3. **Punishment/Motivator to Yield**
4. **Consistency**

TOOL # 1 – RULES/BOUNDARIES

Rules and boundaries must be clearly written.

First, we must establish boundaries, or rules, that are written. These give a child security and stability. Parents tell me, "My kids know what our rules are." But I have found that they are mistaken. I ask parents to tell me the rules, and then I bring the children into the room. They usually give me more rules than their parents did. This is due to a common style of parenting where mom or dad is upset, and shouting, "If you ever do that again, such and such will happen." After a while, parents forget what they say in the heat of anger; but the kids do not. Rules need to be clearly written out. God gives us a great example to follow.

> **Deuteronomy 4:13,** *"So He declared to you His covenant which He commanded you to perform, the Ten Commandments; and He wrote them on two tablets of stone."*

God wrote His commandments on stone! He knew we needed something written down. He governs the whole world with just these ten rules; in most homes you can get away with less than ten rules.

Rules must be written out for the following reasons:

1. **Written rules reduce confusion for both parents and children alike**. If anybody in leadership, whether in the work force, government, or church, does not articulate his expectations to those under his authority, he will surely fail. Clearly stated rules and boundaries define the behaviors desired, and indicate when a corrective consequence will be implemented. Example: You have a written rule, "clean up your own messes," and your child makes a peanut butter and jelly sandwich, leaving the jars out and a knife oozing with jelly stuck to the countertop. Clearly a violation of the rule. When children fail, it just means they need corrective consequences, which is the second tool of training.

2. **Written rules build and maintain unity between parents, promoting team spirit.** Unwritten rules are as confusing and divisive for husbands and wives as for the children. When parents agree on the rules, they are motivated to support one another when a

rule is broken. Children will try to manipulate one parent to not follow through on a rule; however, when you stay unified and stick to the plan, it promotes maturity in the child and blesses the marriage.

3. **Written rules eliminate double-mindedness and unfairness**. Parents frequently make the mistake of giving the youngest child, or "baby" of the family, unfair mercy compared to older children. Have you ever heard one of your children say, *"You love him more than me!"*? Also, without written rules and predetermined corrective consequences, there is the potential for parents to act differently toward a more challenging child than they do toward a compliant child. The challenging child will begin to perceive by your actions that you love their sibling more. When the rules are written, and the corrective consequence for breaking the rules is predetermined and equally enforced, most unfairness will be eliminated. This includes neglecting parental discipline due to physical and emotional factors such as illness, tiredness, or stress, which can and will be exploited by children, resulting in circumstances that are unclear and unfair.

4. **Written rules keep us from being inconsistent**. We are more inclined to follow through if a rule is written down. I have found this to be challenging for many parents because it requires persistence over the years. Many couples who started strong with this principle have revealed to me, *"Things were going great at home when we had our rules written down but, after a couple of months, we slowly slipped back into our old habits."* And the chaos is back.

Parents, this is so important. If we are not willing to make changes, be accountable, and remain consistent, how can we expect to train our kids to live responsible, self-controlled lives?

✓ACTION PLAN

Take a few moments to write out how your parents disciplined you. Next, write down the rules and consequences that you are currently enforcing in your home. If married, write your lists separately, then compare. If your children are over eight years old, ask them to give you their version of the rules.

_____

_____

_____

_____

_____

_____

_____

_____

TOOL # 2 – CORRECTIVE CONSEQUENCES

FACT FILE

Consequences – that which follows from breaking a rule. In other words, when you have a rule there *must* be a corrective consequence for breaking that rule.

Corrective consequences are like vegetables. Most kids don't like them, but they are vital to good health. Kids may tell you that they don't like rules and consequences, but they know in their hearts that they need them.

Throughout the Scriptures, God clearly communicates that there are conditions for blessing and consequences for disobedience. God gives man freedom to choose for himself. It is a simple principle. Even before sin entered the world, God established the principle of a rule and a consequence for breaking it.

> **Genesis 2:16–17,** *"And the LORD God commanded the man, saying, "Of every tree of the garden you may freely eat; but of the tree of the knowledge of good and evil you shall not eat, for in the day that you eat of it you shall surely die."*

The rule given to Adam was *"you shall not eat,"* of that one tree, and the *consequence* was that *"you shall die"* when you do. When Adam and Eve broke this rule, they both suffered consequences. And there are many more consequences resulting from breaking this rule listed in Genesis 3:16-19.

God continued this principle when He gave His "law":

> **Deuteronomy 11:26-28** *Behold, I set before you today <u>a blessing and a curse</u>: the blessing, <u>if you obey the commandments</u> of the LORD your God, which I command you today; and the curse [or a* **consequence***] <u>if you do not obey</u> the commandments of the LORD your God. —emphasis added.*

The law, or God's *rules,* where in the form of commandments given to Moses, and he wrote them down. We find them in the Old Testament books of Exodus through Deuteronomy, which also includes the 10 commandments. God always indicates that obedience brings blessing, disobedience results in judgment, or correction, sometimes called a curse. The blessings and curses are expounded upon in chapters 27 and 28, of Deuteronomy.

God provided written rules to help the children of Israel stay in proper relationship to Him, others, and the world, or cultures around them. He had their best interest in mind and Moses' writings made God's will quite clear. Unfortunately, most of the Israelites under Moses' leadership, headed through the desert to the Promised Land, rebelled repeatedly and suffered the consequence. God let them wander the desert for 40 years until they died and then their children were led into the land.

The principle is very clear: there is a boundary/rule; you break it, and there is a consequence.

Just as our discipline plan has predetermined rules, so we must have a predetermined consequence for correction when a rule is broken. We must give our children clear boundaries and, if they cross them, we must apply discipline in the form of a corrective consequence. When we do this, we can view their failures as an opportunity for training, a positive experience, as we remember that this is **love**.

This principle is well illustrated by sports. Consider football; if you step out of bounds, you have broken a *rule* and cannot go up to the referee and say, "Sorry, I didn't mean to do it," expecting him to excuse you from the *consequence*. Rather, the referee is going to proceed with the *corrective consequence* for that infraction by marking the ball down where you stepped out. It is not negotiable. Arguing, or claiming it was an accident will not matter and does not change the *predetermined consequence*. The consequences informs and motivates the players to discipline themselves to stay within the boundaries.

The *corrective consequence* should be predetermined and not thought up at the moment. Let me give you an analogy. Suppose one of your rules is "no jumping on the couch." One morning you walk past the living room and out of the corner of your eye you see your little seven-year-old, the compliant child, jumping on the couch. You think to yourself, "I don't want to deal with that right now, haven't had my coffee yet." In passing, you simply say, "Stop that right now."

Once you have had coffee, you are feeling much better. It is time to get ready for church and you are rushing everyone to get ready. You see your nine-year-old, the strong-willed child, doing the same thing - jumping on the couch. Instead of just saying "stop", you continue with "I have told you so many times not to jump on that couch!" and you spank, and/or impose even further punishment.

That was *not* a predetermined *consequence*; that was spontaneous, emotional parenting. The consequence was based on how you felt at the moment, not on a loving, *planned* process. This type of emotional parenting creates jealousy between siblings and can convince a strong-willed child, who will naturally receive more consequences, that parents love them less. It also exasperates them, and can push them toward a rebellious heart.

SELF-EXAMINATION

When disciplining your children have you noticed any inconsistencies? If so write them out.

_____

_____

_____

_____

_____

TOOL # 3 – PUNISHMENT = THE MOTIVATOR

FACT FILE

Punishment – A measured amount of pain to motivate, or the infliction of a penalty.

Punishment is part of the overall discipline plan, but it is different from a corrective consequence. Punishment motivates a child to yield to parental authority and accept the corrective consequence.

Read that description of punishment again. Do you see any reference to anger, yelling, cussing, disgust, judging, comparing, ignoring, or pouting in that description? No, you do not. Many of us have found ourselves believing that discipline will not work unless we are angry and raising our voices. That is a worldly philosophy and has no place in Christian homes. Every aspect of discipline must be done in *love*, because **love** is the most powerful motivator, not anger. We must always remember this scripture:

James 1:20, *"for the wrath of man does not produce the righteousness of God."*

Many parents have difficulty administering punishment; so we need to further consider what God tells us to do.

Proverbs 23:13-14, *"Do not withhold correction from a child, for if you beat him with a rod, he will not die. You shall beat him with a rod, and deliver his soul from hell."*

This verse often generates confusion; God is not telling parents to begin beating a child with an implement. Rather, it is an idiom in which the *rod* represents two things: a measuring tool, and authority.

God is telling us that sometimes people need to experience pain in order to mature, or learn to yield to authority. He is not telling you to grab a stick and beat your child into submission. You must take the whole Word of God as His counsel; God's Word is not contrary to itself.

I must admit, there were times I enjoyed spanking strong-willed Nicholas. But when it came to Justin (who I spanked less than five times in his entire life), and Katie (who I spanked only once), it broke my heart and was one of the most difficult things I ever had to do as a daddy. It was hard for me to follow through with Katie, but I had to do it, because she was testing my authority by refusing to do the corrective consequence.

DIG DEEPER: *FURTHER STUDY*

Read the following verse and write out what it means to you as a parent.

Hebrews 12:11 *"No chastening seems to be joyful for the present, but painful; nevertheless,* *afterward it yields the peaceable fruit of righteousness <u>to those who have been trained by it</u>."* (emphasis added).

_____

_____

_____

The word *chastening* is *paideia*, the same Greek word used in Ephesians 6:4, to indicate training/discipline. When you read this passage in context, Hebrews 12:3-11, you will notice that there is a comparison between how a father administers pain in the discipline process and God. In fact, God says that if you are without chastening, you are not His son. I do pray that you have felt the loving hand of God's correction when you sinned.

When it comes to carrying out discipline in the form of punishment/pain, I am sure you have heard the saying, "This is going to hurt me more than it's going to hurt you." Perhaps your parents said it. Punishment is given to a child only if they refuse the corrective consequence that follows the breaking of a rule.

There is much confusion about spanking, which is the most common form of punishment for children under the age of eight years. Some parents have told me, "I don't believe in spanking." But as Christians, God's Word tells us that if a child will not yield to our authority and training, we need to find a way to motivate them. You may have had parents who beat you within an inch of your life, or they never spanked you at all. What they did wrong should not dictate your obedience to God's Word. If you do not find a way to motivate your child to receive the corrective consequence, you will pay dearly later. That is not my opinion; that is what Scripture says.

I have been working with parents long enough to see the same strong-willed, three-year-old whose parents said, "We don't believe in spanking," turn into a fourteen-year-old engaging his father in a fistfight, along with many other irresponsible and rebellious behaviors. I am telling you, if a child is unwilling to accept the consequence, then we must find a way to get them to yield and accept it. When you have been blessed with a strong-willed mule, they have to be motivated often.

Some parents do not want to punish, fearing it will affect the child's psyche when pain is administered. Any form of punishment done wrong is "WRONG", and can cause emotional scars to a child. But pain is part of God's overall plan in life. For example, when I was about 11 years old, I was a daredevil. Down at the high school, my friends and I used to jump flights of stairs on our bikes. When we finally mastered one flight, of course, I had to try two flights. I crashed, tearing up my knees and bending both wheels. I was in serious pain, but I rode home, fixed the tires, and was on my bike again the next day. I did not go back and try to jump both sets of stairs again! I did not want to repeat that pain.

Today, when I drive down the road and see someone on a bicycle, I do not have a flashback of when I hurt myself; I have not developed emotional trauma. This is what worldly wisdom has led us to believe will happen if we use spanking as a motivation. Pain is a good thing, a part of life that teaches us. It taught me to never jump two flights of stairs on my bicycle again. Over the years, pain has taught me in many ways what I can and cannot do.

Certain strong-willed kids need to be *motivated*. They do not like the idea that you are the authority. Remember, God made them strong-willed and they often want to rule and run the household. Sometimes they need those motivators to get them to yield to your authority and accept the predetermined corrective consequence.

This is how a predetermined punishment is used in the overall discipline process. Let's say your rule is "no jumping on the couch", and the predetermined corrective consequence for your five-year-old is a five-minute time out in a chair. By refusing to sit in the chair until the five-minute timer goes off, your child is asking for the punishment/motivator. After a spanking (Principles of Spanking will be covered soon), put them back in the chair and restart the timer at five minutes. No anger, no yelling, no threatening, but a simple process. When your child accepts the corrective consequence by sitting for the five minutes, they are accepting personal responsibility for breaking the rule and also growing in self-control. When they rebel by not wanting to accept the corrective consequence, they simply are asking for the motivator/punishment.

Understand: punishment alone does **not** train. Many parents do not understand the correct sequence of corrective consequences and punishment. Remember, all correction is to be administered with *love*. Why is it that over 80 percent of people who are released from prison ends up back in prison?[16] Because the system is designed on punishment, not training. The moment they are out and "Big Brother" is off their back, they go right back to their former behavior. Learn the process; punishment is the motivator used to help your child accept corrective consequences. You must not lose sight of this truth.

WEEK 8: DAY 5

TOOL # 4 – CONSISTENCY

We must be consistent if we want to see growth in our children. As an example; if I took a survey of how many people drive above the speed limit, if people were honest, the results would show that virtually everyone speeds at one time or another. If I asked each person why he/she speeds, they might say, "Because everyone else does," or "I was late," and so on. But the reason people speed is not just lack of self-control, but the inability of the police department to enforce the rule in every location.

---

16   Survey of State Prison Inmates, 1991, U.S. Department of Justice, Bureau of Justice Statistics Special Report, August 1995

What if they put a computer chip in your car and no matter where you were, if you went one mile-an-hour over the speed limit, it would send a signal to the police department and three days later you received a ticket in the mail? What would happen to your bad habit of speeding? You would suddenly develop self-control because of the consistent corrective consequences.

Kids are no different. *Consistency* is important. ***If there is no consistency, it is as if there are no rules and no training, and it equals no peace.*** Being consistent will not make our children stop being foolish overnight. Remember, we are instilling character each time we give them a consequence for crossing a boundary (breaking a rule). It is like a muscle that is exercised; every time you discipline (train) your muscle, it grows a little stronger.

DIG DEEPER: *FURTHER STUDY*

Read the following verse and write out what it means to you as a parent.

> **Philippians 1:6,** *"being confident of this very thing, that He who has begun a good work in you will complete it until the day of Jesus Christ."*

_____

_____

_____

Consistency can be hard for moms because they are emotional beings. Moms, do not apologize for your emotions, just do not compromise God's will because of them. God did not give you that gift for you to use it wrongly. He gave you a nurturing heart, which is good, but you cannot allow emotions to block your obedience to Christ in regard to training your children.

Sometimes dads want to let offenses slide because discipline is too much trouble, or they avoid confrontation, or want to look like the good guy. Do not grow weary, but follow through. Your children need you.

Discipline that is not consistent can teach a child that manipulation is possible, and that everything is negotiable. Worse than producing manipulative kids is the fact that they are going to become adults and go into society, including marriage and the work force, repeating that behavior. Remember, God's view is that discipline is love in action. Learn to be supportive of one another as husband and wife, and pray for each other. Ask God to help both of you to be consistently obedient to Him in this area.

What About Counting?

Many parents, especially moms, use counting as part of the consequence process. "Stop doing that! I'm going to count to three, and you'd better stop!" But counting is a destructive component of the training process. Have you noticed that strong-willed kids cannot stand the idea that you are the boss? When you tell a strong-willed child not to do something, the first thing in his mind is, "I've got to win here. I've got to prove to myself and my parents that I'm in control."

For example, that child will approach a forbidden object, make sure you are watching, then reach out and come ever so close to touching it. Once you start with, "Don't you dare, don't you touch that," they have your full attention. Then you continue with, "I'm going to start counting. One . . . you'd better get . . . two . . . two and a half . . . I'm telling you!" By this time your veins are popping out and you are ready to explode. Then he walks away and your little mule merely says to himself, "See, I really am in control, I just consumed three minutes of her time, and look how angry I got her. I'm in control!" Counting can become a very destructive tool if used as part of your training method, and can provoke strong-willed children to continue to try and rule over you.

Instead, you merely say, "Get away from that, now." If they do not immediately move away, give them a corrective consequence. Follow through. Do not let yourself be sucked into these emotional debates that will get out of hand when they become teenagers, if you don't stop it now.

When Adam and Eve sinned, you do not read of God counting to them as they stood next to the tree of knowledge of good and evil. He issued the rule with a predetermined corrective consequence (Gen. 2:17), and then followed through with the corrective consequence when they disobeyed (Gen. 3). Even though Adam and Eve both made excuses (Gen. 3:9-13), even blaming God (vs. 12), He just followed through. He did not allow for manipulation.

Rules, Children and Choices

When I was growing up, there was a popular game show on television called "Let's Make A Deal." Many of you who are old enough probably remember the program. The studio audience dressed in wild costumes, hoping to attract the attention of the host and be selected to choose one of three doors on stage. Behind each door was either a great prize, or a *booby* prize. The contestants could go home with a car, a boat, or a can of tuna! When someone picked a door and won a motorcycle, I thought, "How cool, I want to be on that show!"

Many kids want to play "Let's Make A Deal" when it comes to rules and corrective consequences.

"Let's Make a Deal"

Door #1
Follow Rules

Door #2
Break Rule and
Accept Consequence

Door #3
No Rules,
No Consequence

The three doors represent a typical child's response to training. We want them to choose the first door and follow our rules. Choosing the second door represents breaking the rules and accepting the corrective consequence for the disobedience. Most kids, especially the strong-willed, want Door #3: *"I don't have to accept the rule, and I should not have a corrective consequence!"* This is like a driver getting pulled over for speeding, issued a citation, then going to court and fighting the fine. He chose to speed, knows that he is guilty, but doesn't want to accept the corrective consequence. This is childish behavior. A child learns to accept consequences as parents follow through with proper consistent training, which builds mature character.

Knowing that children are not yet mature, and do not naturally take responsibility for their actions, how should we respond when they choose Door #3? Shock, anger, screaming, yelling, judging, or becoming frustrated and bitter toward them? Unfortunately, this is the way many parents behave! Instead, we must remove Door # 3 as an option. We need to calmly and consistently enforce the written rules, and clearly communicate to them that they only have two choices, either accept the rule, or break the rule and accept the corrective consequence. Period! **Children who are raised *without consistent corrective consequences* for their actions become adults who do not take responsibility for their actions!** Many parents have unknowingly allowed their children the third option for years and so it is a challenge to re-train themselves and their children to break this ineffective parenting style.

Parents, do yourselves a favor and use a pen or pencil to put a big "X" over Door # 3. If your kids have been choosing number three on a continuous basis and you have been allowing it, do not be surprised that they are going to continue to ask for it. Explain to them, and show them by day-to-day discipline that things have changed.

✅ACTION PLAN

Here is an exercise you are to do with your children over the next two days. Sit down and explain to them about these three doors, and their choices. Then, when they start the behavior, you simply remind them, "I know you want door number 3, don't you? Remember our meeting? But it's not happening. Accept your consequence or you are asking for a motivator."

Most strong-willed children will try and pick door number three whenever possible. Your compliant children, like my son Justin and daughter Katie, will more often than not choose between doors one and two. Compliant kids have an inner desire that motivates them to cooperate. You see, for most compliant children it is very important that they please you and that you are pleased with them. Strong-willed children, on the other hand, often seem like they could care less whether a parent is happy or not; they just want to be in control.

Adapting Our Training without Compromise

> **Proverbs 22:6,** *"Train up a child in the way he should go, and when he is old he will not depart from it."*

Remember: This is NOT a guarantee but a probability.

"The way he should go" means every child is unique in their personality, and some may need more corrective consequences, tighter boundaries, and tougher consequences than others. This verse also means that we parents must be willing to adapt to each child's personality, or bent.

When Nick was in school, it was very typical for us to have two, maybe three teacher conferences a year due to him wanting to do his own thing. We were not that surprised to get a call: "Mr. and Mrs. Caster, can you come down to the school? We need to have a little meeting with you about your son, Nick."

I remember, when Nick was in the third grade, we received one of those calls from his teacher—who was newly married with no children—and she began telling us about Nick's behavior in class. When she was finished, she asked us, "Do you guys discipline?" We responded, "Well, sure we do."

But we could tell by her expression she thought we were lying, or that we did not know what we were doing. She ignored what we had said and continued, "It's really important for parents to set boundaries," then proceeded to give us advice.

I could tell my wife was getting upset, so I jumped in and said, "Look. I know Nick likes to run everything; it's his personality. Nick is strong-willed. Yes, we have rules at home. But you just told me this has been going on for several months, and we're just hearing about it now? Let's bring Nick in, let's go over what he's doing, and let's agree on a corrective consequence that you can give him here—like picking up trash during lunch or PE. And also, let's establish a way that you can communicate to us when we pick him up, and then we will follow through with additional corrective consequences at home."

That is my son. If he did not feel like doing math, he would simply interrupt the whole class, shouting out, "Who wants to go out and play?" That was just Nick. It was a blessing and relief when he began to redirect that strong will in the right direction during his teen years. But believe me, raising him was not always fun.

Two years after Nick, the same teachers got my second son, Justin, the straight-A-people-pleaser, who often wrote little notes on the bottom of his papers like, "I love you; you're the best teacher."

At Justin's sixth grade graduation, the teacher brought each child up and said something nice. When she got to him, this woman began to cry tears of joy, then other women began crying as the men were looking at each other with this puzzled, "What's up?" expression. She gave a five-minute speech about the wonderfulness of my son. Justin's teachers would always ask me, "Where did you get this kid? He's so good and sweet." I replied, "Don't you remember two years earlier when you had my other son Nick?"

Same house, same rules, same parents, different children. God is just so wonderful, He has a sense of humor. Remember He gave our children their personalities.

The Black Stallion

When Nick was around ten or eleven years old, I remember a day when I came home from work and he was in his room, having a rough day. He had been getting corrective consequences from the time he woke up 'til the time I came home. He was crying one of those deep, deep cries. I sat down next to him, and said, "What's wrong?" He replied, "Dad, I'm so bad."

At this point, I'm starting to get emotional, "What do you mean, you're so bad?" He answered, "I get so many consequences compared to Justin. I'm so bad." I just sat there, thinking, "God, help me out here." I wanted to say, "You're right." But God quickened my mind and rescued me.

Just a few nights earlier, we had watched a movie, *The Black Stallion.* I said, "Nicholas, remember that horse in the movie? They couldn't put that horse behind a normal fence, could they? A four-foot fence was nothing; he'd just jump it. That horse was a black stallion and he was strong-willed; God made it that way. Nick, you're just like the Black Stallion. Yes, you're harder to train, Son. Yes, you need more consequences, but think of it as just needing taller fences. I know it's hard on both you and us sometimes, but you are worth it, and God gave you this strong will. Your strength and your strong will are a gift from God, and someday you are going to use that strong will to do great things for God."

After we had already named Nicholas, we found out that the name means "a leader of people." These strong-willed kids are the Peters and Pauls. I praise the Lord for Nick's strong will. Parents ask me all the time, "Does Nick let you say, or write these things about him?"

My response is, "Are you kidding, Nick's a star! He'll even ask you, 'Want me to sign your book?'" Nick is so confident in who he is in Christ. He also knows he was a tool for the Lord, that God used him to help transform me into the image of Christ.

I never had to meet with Justin's teachers to set up a consequence for bad behavior, to be enforced at home. I never had to set a homework time for Justin. But with Nick, I had to do those things. He was different. He needed the structure because, without it, he ran amuck. He needed us to come alongside him to help him in these areas.

Be willing to come alongside your children, without comparing them to sisters or brothers. Each is unique, and if God has blessed you with a strong-willed child, do not look upon it as a genetic dysfunction. Praise God for that child.

✓ACTION PLAN

Stop right now and use the space below to write a prayer to the Lord, thanking Him for the personality of each child. If needed, write an apology for your critical heart.

_____
_____
_____
_____
_____
_____
_____
_____
_____

Use these tools and you will see God bring about transformation. Failures and mistakes are common; they are our opportunity to train them. Do not take their mistakes personally or forget that it is your job to train your children. The hard part is just our lazy flesh, but God will give us the grace to do it correctly "if" we desire to.

Would you intentionally rebel against God? Would you tell Him, "I don't accept Your plan"? You may not tell Him verbally, but you tell Him by your actions. If God has blessed you with a strong-willed child, be willing to engage and stay _consistent_ and give the extra _time_ and _energy_ it takes. When you get angry and yell, or give up and relinquish your responsibility, you are telling God, "I don't trust You; You made a mistake; You gave me a task that is beyond Your ability to help me do it correctly," and that is a very serious accusation.

⚲ SELF-EXAMINATION

Have any of your actions been saying this to the Lord? If so, write out a confession of what those actions are, and ask His forgiveness.

_____
_____
_____
_____
_____
_____
_____
_____

Train Behaviors—Not Attitudes

As parents, we have probably all experienced the "attitudes" and our response is, "Don't you give me that attitude, young lady!" Unfortunately, it is very easy to confuse bad attitudes with wrong behaviors; but they are not the same, and they must be dealt with differently.

This is a big issue, more for women than men, because God created women to be nurturers. When negative attitudes arise, the temptation for Mom is to follow the child around the house, pleading, "What's wrong with you?" When the child does not respond with the appropriate change in attitude, the situation can escalate to an argument.

FACT FILE

Attitude – is "a posture or position; a feeling, opinion or mood."[17]

Behavior – on the other hand, is "the act or manner of behaving."[18]

In other words, behavior is something that is done or not done, breaking a rule or not doing what is expected.

God gives each of us emotions, from joy to anger, excitement to boredom. And each of us experiences different emotions in response to the situations around us. Although our behavior is often tied to our emotional state, or attitude, there is a distinct difference. We cannot choose our emotions, but we can adjust our behavior. Children learn to adjust their behavior through *loving proper consistent discipline*.

Let me explain the difference between attitude and behavior. Psalm 4:4 tells us, "Be angry, and do not sin." Anger is the attitude; the bad behavior is an action. Parents, your response to a bad attitude is simply to tell your child, "You can be sad, or mad, but if that emotion leads you to kick the wall, that is a behavior that will get you a corrective consequence. You can be very angry because I'm the authority, and this is the rule of the house, but nothing disrespectful should come out of your mouth. You are allowing your negative attitude to manifest into a wrong action that will result in you receiving the *predetermined corrective consequence*."

Remember, attitudes are a matter of the heart, and the heart is *not* chiefly changed through the disciplining process. The heart of a child is primarily changed through Biblical discipling, training in righteousness, and their willingness to accept parental love, authority and instruction.

---

17   *Webster's New International Dictionary of the English Language; Second Edition Unabridged*; G & C Merriam Company, Publishers, Springfield, MA 1944

18   Ibid.

It is important to understand that a *rebellious heart* is a *miserable heart*. A child with a rebellious heart has no peace, no joy, no contentment, and no lasting pleasure—all by God's perfect design. What more correction can a parent add to that?

DIG DEEPER: *FURTHER STUDY*

Read the following Scripture and write out what Jesus says about 1) how you can acquire joy; 2) how would that joy be lost?

> **John 15:10–11,** *"If you keep My commandments, you will abide in My love, just as I have kept My Father's commandments and abide in His love. "These things I have spoken to you, that My joy may remain in you, and that your joy may be full."*

_____

_____

_____

_____

_____

_____

We must learn that we cannot *control* our children's attitudes and emotions, any more than we can control our own. Attempting to discipline a child for a bad attitude is a losing battle, it's controlling and can *provoke* them to wrath. Instead, we must allow them to feel the way they feel without getting drawn into something we will regret later.

As a parent, if you know that your child is harboring bitterness toward you, or is rebelling against God's plan for their life, your *response* must be prayer (1 Thess. 5:16), and patience (1 Cor. 13:4) without compromise. Do not compromise by allowing your child's bad attitude to make you angry, or resentful, or to misrepresent God in the way you treat him or her. Do not allow their bad attitude to rob you of your inner peace, or to dictate how you follow through with your planned method of training.

SELF-EXAMINATION

Take some time right now and write out any attitudes your children have that cause you to *react* toward them in *anger*.

_____

_____

_____

_____

_____

_____

✓ACTION PLAN

Question: have you asked God to forgive you for this? Now is a good time. Begin to pray each day for God's grace to help you stop, and to start taking responsibility by asking forgiveness of your child every time you lose control.

Week 9: Training Up Your Children Part 4 - Disciplining Our Children (Continued)

WEEK 9: DAY 1

Do Not Be Manipulated

All children, especially teens, will experiment with using attitude as a form of manipulation and/or revenge.

> **FACT FILE**
>
> **Manipulation-** means "to control or play upon by artful, unfair and insidious means, especially to one's own advantage."[1]

Manipulation is an attempt to avoid a corrective consequence, or to change the rules. For *example*, when a child frequently exhibits a poor attitude after a consequence is received, parents will sometimes refrain from giving one in the future because they are avoiding the misery. But the right response should be, "Let them be miserable and pray for them." Always follow through with the corrective consequence if they break a rule, and the motivator if they refuse the corrective consequence.

Children also use manipulation to pressure or guilt their parents into allowing them to do something not normally permitted. For example, one sixteen-year-old girl manipulated her mom into letting her go to a concert she knew was not allowed. The daughter acted sad and depressed every day for a week. As a typical nurturer, her mom asked daily, "What's wrong?"

All week long, the teen merely sighed, "Oh, Mom. I don't know. I'm just not happy. I don't know why." Finally, on Thursday, she said, "Mom, I'm just sad; I don't have any friends." At this point, her mom had been manipulated to the point where she just wanted her poor daughter to be happy.

So the young girl said, "If I could just go to this concert tomorrow night with my friends, I would feel better." "Well, what concert is that?" When the daughter told her mom which concert, she replied, "Oh, that's not a good concert." Once again, the young girl sighed, "Oh, Mom . . ." Her mom replied, "OK, I'll let you go, and

---

1   *Webster's New International Dictionary.*

I'll tell Dad . . . Oh, never mind; let's not tell him after all. I know he'll get mad. So let's keep this between us." The girl's manipulation had sucked her mom right in!

Do not let manipulative attitudes wear you down. This is not to say that every time a child is sad it is a form of manipulation, but when things like this happen you should always discuss it as a couple, if married. Remember, you are a team.

Warning: This starts at a young age with children wanting their own way, such as a two-year-old crying until you give in, which is a form of manipulation. This should not surprise us, since we are born prideful (wanting to have our own way), and with foolishness in our hearts (Prov. 22:15). I will give you an effective, age appropriate corrective consequence plan in the next chapter.

Do Not Seek Revenge

FACT FILE

Revenge- means "to inflict injury in return for an insult."

Some children know that a bad attitude will make their parents angry. When you bite the hook, it gives a child satisfaction, which feeds their flesh as well as erodes your foundation and authority. It takes two to play that game. Don't allow a child to entice you into revenge; don't let their attitude or behavior affect your inner peace. Watch your emotions; stick with your discipline plan. If you don't play, they will eventually quit this unhealthy, childish game. They will soon discover the attitude-revenge game is no fun when played alone. Yes, God has given us emotions, but we are to exhibit the character quality of a mature adult by exercising self-control, which comes from our strong foundation in Christ.

If you are allowing your child's manipulation to make you angry, you are showing them you are not on solid ground, and that your God is weak. They can simply cop an attitude and you flip out. Believe it, they feel superior when you exemplify sinful and weak character, when they can pull your emotional "strings" and get you to start *reacting* to them with anger, or revenge.

Reacting in the flesh to a child's attitude erodes your authority. No one wants to follow a weak leader that has a weak god. Anyone who has been in the armed forces understands that if you have a weak, "wimp" of a captain, you have no desire to follow him. Children are no different. If a child can control your inner peace and get you angry by having an attitude, they will not want to trust the God you serve and trust.

Revenge Versus Training

When giving a consequence to your child, if you are motivated by a revengeful heart, your children will know it. This is sinful, selfish and immature. When we say things like, "Hey, you do that again, Buster, I'll ruin your life," is that training? No. "You won't go anywhere for a month if you try to pull that again." Is that love? No, that is revenge. *Reacting* with revenge distorts the whole plan that you are trying to put into place. Revenge does not train, but *causes* children to become defiant, and *causes* division between parents and children, along with eroding your influence.

If you and your children have been playing this sinful game for a while, it may take some time to break the *bad habit*, for both of you. Be patient (1 Cor. 13:4), stay the course, and the Lord will bring victory. Remember, if your child's bad attitude turns into a poor behavior choice, such as yelling at you, using a bad word, kicking the wall, slamming the door, etc., simply follow through with the *predetermined consequence* for that behavior, but do not *react* to the attitude.

The Lord has instructed us to *train up our children*, not to inflict injury in reaction to their childish and foolish choices. If our thoughts are to get even with them and/or hurt them in some way because they will not do what we ask, then this is *our* problem. The Lord gave us these children and expects us to raise them in the way *He* desires, even though sometimes it is hard to do.

✅ACTION PLAN

If you have had the wrong *motive* when giving a consequence to your children, repent and ask forgiveness from both your child and the Lord.

Training our children as the Lord requires means following *His* plan. We must provide a loving environment, proper rules and predetermined corrective consequences, motivation (punishment) if they rebel, and consistency. This process is fair, not motivated by anger or revenge, and will transform and shape a child's character into maturity. Children must be *motivated* by love, "*Let all that you do be done with love*" (1 Cor. 16:14), and our obedience to God – not by selfishness, anger, or the desire to get revenge.

Giving children things that they hate to do is revenge, not training. For example, forcing your son to write "I will not argue," 500 times, because he dislikes doing it, is not training. It is revenge. Similarly, many parents say, "My daughter's phone is her lifeline, so if I threaten to take it away every time she does something wrong, she will behave." That is revenge, not training. I'll bring more clarity to this shortly. Hang in there.

Stay the Course

When parents see children rolling their eyes, pouting, refusing to talk, wanting to stay in their room, doing all their artful, insidious, selfish, childish tricks, they must not flip out and stick to the training plan.

When I was a child, I used to hold my breath when I did not get my way. Eventually I would turn purple, and my mother would finally give in to my demands. At some point, my mother consulted a pediatrician. He told her, "Don't do anything" in response to my manipulating game. My mom worried, "What if he passes out?" The doctor said, "Let him."

A couple of days later, we came home from church with our good Sunday school clothes on. My brothers went running down the street, and I wanted to run, too. But my mother said, "No, Craig, go change your clothes." Of course, I started to hold my breath. My mother just stood there by the car, watching me. Pretty soon I started turning purple and wobbling. I looked down, and one foot was on the concrete, and one foot was on the grass. My mother could see that my brain was processing - which way should I fall? But before my brain could figure it, I passed out. And guess which way I fell? Yep on the concrete. I never held my breath again.

When your two-year-old child is throwing a fit and flip-flopping on the floor, casually ask him, "Does that make you feel better?" If he kicks the walls, remind him, "Don't kick my walls, don't scream, and don't say something mean."

If he does, just say, "Oh, poor choice. I understand you're upset, honey. Remember, that's disrespect. Here is your corrective predetermined consequence." Let your children go through their motions. When they know that you are not bothered by them, guess what? When you are not serving the ball back, they will eventually quit.

I once had a thirteen-year-old girl in my office throwing fits like a three-year-old, and her parents just said, "You don't understand how hard she is, she throws fits all the time when she does not get her way."

The girl obviously knew this behavior greatly bothered her mother. The mind games and manipulation had gone on for years, and her mom's reaction had trained her to continue to act like a baby, even as a teenager. Her father had never stepped up to make her stop, either. He should have told his wife long ago, "Honey, please don't argue with her and let me handle it from here." The girl had been able to continue this *childish behavior* due to her parents' reluctance to work at training her. They gave in to her demands and she escaped the corrective consequence necessary for change.

If a wife is unwilling to listen to her husband and yield to his authority when it's time to disengage from a child acting out in this way, it will *hinder* the relationship both with her child and her husband. A child will develop disrespect toward authority when parents are willing to argue and debate with them and each other.

There were times that I walked in on a conversation between my wife and son; it was escalating but she did not recognize it. I said to my oldest son, "Remember who you're talking to. She's my wife. She's my queen. You don't use that tone of voice, ever." My wife did not even see it; she was too engaged in the conversation. I would tell Nick to go do a consequence, *now!*

Later, my wife and I would discuss how they got to that point. She would say, "Well, he said this, then I said this, and it just seemed to escalate." My reply was, "Honey, OK, back here in the conversation you could have said, 'That's the end of this discussion. Nick, I heard your side of it, that's enough. I don't want to discuss it anymore. If you open your mouth one more time in regards to this discussion, you will get a consequence'." We need to support each other in this area.

Parents, work together as a team to train up your children. Pray, do not compromise, do not engage in foolishness, and you will have success.

A Day of Remembrance

I would like to remind you of five things that we have already covered, as a good review. Spend a full day examining how well you are doing. If you have been negligent in any of the following areas, please take some time right now, go before the Lord, confess where you have been failing and then ask Him for the wisdom and grace to change. If you have forgotten some of these principles, go back through the lessons prayerfully and identify those areas where the Lord has spoken to you—especially your personal notes. As you are doing this, use the space below to write down the page number(s), and what God is saying to you.

1. Remember we are **Ministers.** We are to represent Christ and carry out His will and goals with a servant's attitude. (Week 1) **Page ___**

2. Remember **Our Transformation**. God is going to transform us through these trials and difficulties; we must go through the process. (Week 1) **Page __**

3. Remember **His glorification**. We are to reflect Him to our children. Getting angry and upset does not reflect Him. (Week 1) **Page ___**

4. Remember **Our Strong Foundation**. This is where we get the strength and understanding to carry out the above, as well as what follows. (Week 2) **Page ___**

5. Remember the **Greatest Motivator is Love**. During the discipline process, it is love that motivates a child, not anger and harsh words. (Weeks 3, 4, 5) Also, remember the following:
    a. **Love** is responding, NOT reacting. (Week 3) **Page ___**
    b. **Love** is a choice, NOT necessarily a feeling. (Week 3) **Page ___**
    c. **Love** is practicing **1 Corinthians 13**. (Week 4) We discussed the character qualities of **Love** in depth. The first two are patience and kindness. Both of these take into account that home is a training ground where we correct our children's mistakes, understanding they are born foolish—without character. Our love walks them through this process, helping them grow to maturity. Our love is patient and kind, is not upset and angry with their foolishness.

    d. We need to **Love** them through the different seasons of life, including the teenage years. (Week 5) **Page _____**

_____

_____

_____

_____

_____

_____

_____

_____

_____

WEEK 9: DAY 2

Introduction: Implementing the Tools of Training For Ages Two and Three

Note: I encourage you to read this chapter, even if your children are now older. You may discover that some root problems, behaviors and/or resentments from these earlier days are currently affecting your relationship with a particular child, or with your spouse.

Before we begin practical implementation of the four tools of training, I want to explain the 10 "Toddler Property Laws" for those of you who are blessed with children ages eighteen months to five years:

1. If I like it, it is mine.
2. If it is in my hands, it is mine.
3. If I can take it from you, it is mine.
4. If I had it a week ago, it is mine.
5. If it is mine, it must never appear to be yours in any way.
6. If I am doing or building something, all the pieces are mine.
7. If it looks just like mine, it is mine.
8. If I think it is mine, it is mine.
9. If it is near me, it is mine.
10. If it is broccoli, it is yours.

When our little beauties come home from the hospital, they are absolutely self-consumed, lacking any mature or moral character. So, let's look at some things we can do during the toddler years, somewhat characterized by the term "terrible twos." These are the ages when your kids are spilling things, throwing things, hurting themselves, and often embarrassing you. Testing your authority in every area is also very common. Trying to keep a sense of humor during this time, in order to keep from losing your mind, is very important.

During the first five years, establishing authority and instilling boundaries are critical. Most children will challenge you daily. Do not panic.

When my son Nicholas was about two years old, I came home one day and found my wife very upset. I asked, "What's wrong?" She said, "He won't eat." I said, "What? Give me that bowl." He was in his highchair and I sat down in front of him saying, "Hey, you eat." He looked at me, shoved the bowel toward me and dumped it. In the beginning this got me angry. With Nick, you push his button and something in him wanted to push back. Do you think he understood why he did this? He also did not understand why my anger exasperated him. Something like throwing gasoline on fire! When you are trying to put it out, not a smart thing to do.

When Nick was between three and four years old, I got a phone call at work from my wife. She was crying and very upset. Finally, she was calm enough to tell the story. On a grocery store trip, she had Justin in the cart and Nick walking beside her, when he spotted the toy section. He ran over, picked out a toy and said, "Mommy, I want this." My wife said, "No, put it back." She continued to the end of the aisle, turned around, and saw that Nick was not following. So she said, "Nick, come on." He started walking the other way, so she left Justin and the basket to go after Nick.

She got halfway down the aisle, and Nick started running. Now she had a crisis, a two-year-old in the cart at one end of the aisle, and a four-year-old running the other way. She rushed back to Justin, but was really starting to panic. She began chasing Nick around the store while pushing this cart full of groceries. He stayed just out of her reach. Finally, she made a mad dash and caught Nick, went back to the cart and grabbed Justin, then exited the store in tears leaving all the groceries behind.

When I heard the story, I got in the car and drove home, spanked Nick and threatened his life (this was before I understood these principles I am sharing with you). I said, "Don't you ever do this again!" and returned to work.

Less than a week later, the phone rang at work again, and it was my wife, sobbing so hard that I thought someone had died.

"What, Honey, what?"

"He did it again."

"Did what again?"

She said, "In the store!"

I came home immediately, went into his room and gave him a licking you would think he would never forget. I came out, and my wife was still crying, still upset, sobbing, "I can't do this anymore."

I said, "Honey, look, you'll never shop with him again, I promise. You'll wait until I come home, or I'll go to the grocery store. You won't have to do it, I promise you. I won't put you through this again."

I went in and told him, "Nick, you're not going with Mom anymore to the grocery store. Either I'm going to do it, or you're going to stay home."

A couple of weeks went by, and my wife needed some milk and bread. I happened to be home. She said, "Would you go down and get some?" Nick piped up, "Can I go?" "Sure," I replied.

In my wildest dreams, I did not imagine that this little four-year-old, who was all of forty pounds, would challenge *my* authority in the store. On the way to the store, I looked at Nick and said, "Nick, you know the rules?" "Yes, Dad."

Once in the store, I got the milk and bread, and went to the express line to check out. As I looked around, Nick was not behind me. He was standing about 30 feet away with a toy in his hands. I said, "Nick, put it back." But he did not move. He just put his head down.

What started coming over me at that point was definitely demonic! The milk carton was ready to pop in my hands. The guy behind me started backing up and everyone began to notice what was going down, but I did not care. I was oblivious to the people around me; I was looking at Nick, thinking, "How dare you?" "Nick, do it NOW!"

Still, he did not listen. Then I said something that I pray none of you will ever say. I said, "Nick, if you don't do it now, I'm going to drop-kick you across the store. I don't care who's here." Finally he darted off and put the toy away. We got into the car, and I spanked him. We got home and I spanked him again. That was my little jewel, Nick.

Many situations like this led my wife and me to pray and look for help in dealing with Nick. I knew what I was doing was not right, and the spankings did not seem to help. I had to *learn* how to change, and learn how to discipline properly.

You parents, who are blessed with a strong-willed child like this, hang in there. The tools you are going to learn really do work.

Dads - Get Involved

It is important for Dads to get involved with the disciplining, but also helping in all aspects. We need to work together when our children are small. When I first got involved in lay ministry at our church, it was important to me that we arrived at church on time. It was very embarrassing for me to walk in late.

We lived about a twenty-minute drive from church. One Sunday morning, I was driving about eighty-five miles an hour down the freeway, and my wife looked over at me and said, "Why are you speeding? You should slow down!" I said, "If you wouldn't make us so late, I wouldn't have to speed!"

She could tell I was a little agitated. There was silence for a few moments; then she calmly said, "Why don't you help me in the morning?" That had never crossed my mind. I looked at her and said, "What do you mean, help? I get up; I get the cereal bowls out. Once in a while I even put the cereal in the bowls before the kids come to breakfast. I even make the coffee. What else do you want me to do?" I was completely oblivious. She said, "Why don't you help get the kids dressed?"

At this point, I had a crisis going on in my head. "Do I take this on or what?" I said, "OK, starting next week, it's mine."

The next week rolled around, and I got up Sunday morning knowing I could prove my efficiency. The kids were going to be dressed and we were going to be *on time*. I walked into the boys' room, "Hey, come on boys, let's get going; time to get up and get ready for church." I went downstairs, got everything all ready, but heard nothing from upstairs; it was silent.

So I went back to their room, and these two little boys were still in bed! So I yelled, "Get up, right now!" and pulled down the sheets. "Get out or I'm going to spank you!" Pretty soon they were upset and crying, and I was shoving their clothes on.

A *side note* about strong-willed kids: when possible, give them a *choice*. Nicholas always thought he had to be in control. I eventually learned to pull two pairs of Levis out for him to choose from. I could not even tell the difference between the two pairs, but that made him feel like he had a little bit of control. Sometimes you can just give them a choice in a small area, and it makes things work smoother. Justin did not care if you put a pink shirt on him with green pants.

Back to the first Sunday morning "dress rehearsal." I thought I had won, but I was wrong. We got into the car on time, and as we drove down the road I was feeling pretty accomplished. I looked over at my wife, and her expression said it all. She was looking at me with that face that said, "You big idiot." I said, "Hey, we're on time." She replied, "Yeah, but look in the back seat." Both of the boys were red-eyed, tears streaming. They did not look like they were ready to go to church and praise God!

As my wife and I discussed how I could do better, I learned how to put a sock on my hand and make a little puppet to sneak under the sheets saying, "Hello! Good morning!" Or I would do the old "wet Willy" in the ear. I would lie next to them and tell a story (I used to tell these dumb stories about a dog that would chase cats up a tree and not know how to get down, putting his head in a bottle, etc. I would make them up as I went along). I made wake-up time a fun time.

I *learned* that if I just got their minds running in the morning and thinking for 10 or 15 minutes, then, when I said, "OK, come on, let's get ready to go," they were much better about cooperating. I learned to *adapt* without *compromise*. Did it take time? Yes. But this was *my* job until my children were able to do it on their own. Dads, you can engage here and help. It is not "your part and my part"; it is "*our* part."

Points for Practice

Some practices are especially important when you have small children.

1. LOVE THEM, DO NOT YELL OR GET ANGRY.

Remember that love is patient, and you are to expect them to fail and act their age. Do not break a child's spirit by getting angry. Imagine someone 10 times your size coming at you in anger with a booming voice, neck veins popping and eyes bulging! Not fair! Think of it this way - would you use gasoline to put out a fire? My Nicholas did not understand why he was stubborn, or why he would struggle and want to debate over most rules. He didn't know why he was wired this way, not able to articulate and understand this. God gave him a strong personality, which I needed to train. When I yelled and got bent out of shape, I was exasperating him to further bad behavior. So, I encourage you to study how to answer.

Proverbs 15:28, *"The heart of the righteous studies how to answer, But the mouth of the wicked pours forth evil."*

Is this still a struggle for you? If so write out your prayer asking God to change you.

_____

_____

_____

_____

_____

_____

_____

_____

_____

_____

2. STAY CALM: LOSE CONTROL = LOSE CREDIBILITY.

When your kids see you *freaking* out, they learn to take advantage and manipulate you to get revenge. When you are out of control, they get out of control. When you disrespect them, they will disrespect you in return. If you have developed a habit of *reacting*, I suggest that you break it by first asking the Lord to forgive you (repent), then go to your children and ask them to forgive you (confess). Do not let another day go by! This is a very important principle: holding yourself accountable to God and your children.

☑ACTION PLAN

Make a commitment to ask your child's forgiveness each time you fail in this area. I cannot tell you how many times I have gone to bed, settling in for a good night's sleep, only to have the Holy Spirit nudge my heart about the way I *reacted* to one of my children. Many times, I left my bed and went to Nick's room, and humbled myself in this way:

"Hey, Nick, how I dealt with you today was wrong. Would you forgive me?"

Whether your child is five or fifteen, you owe them an apology if you have responded to them with ungodly behavior! "If" you are honest before God, truly want to be transformed and stop this ungodly, sinful habit, then you "<u>will</u>" faithfully take responsibility.

DIG DEEPER: *FURTHER STUDY*

Read the following Scripture, write down what it says will happen when we do not stay calm. What practice is needed to stay calm?

Proverbs 15:18, *"A wrathful man stirs up strife, but he who is slow to anger allays contention."*

_____

_____

_____

_____

Matthew 5:23–24, *"Therefore if you bring your gift to the altar, and there remember that your brother has something against you, leave your gift there before the altar, and go your way. First be reconciled to your brother, and then come and offer your gift."*

After reviewing Matthew 5:23-24, if you have failed in this area, how will you obey God's instruction?

_____

_____

_____

3. TEACH THEM TO OBEY AND RESPECT YOUR AUTHORITY.

Your kids must be taught that you are the God-given authority in their lives. They need to know that you are giving them rules, consequences, and punishing them when necessary, because this is what God has commanded you to do. This is why it is so important that you walk in intimate fellowship with God every day! If you expect your children to submit to your authority, you must show them that you are in submission to God's authority. Here is a Scripture you can share with them concerning God's instruction in this matter.

Ephesians 6:1, *"Children, obey your parents in the Lord, for this is right."*

4. BE CONSISTENT.

If you say you are going to do something, then follow through. Lack of consistency can hinder the whole discipline process, which is designed to lead a child to maturity. Follow your discipline plan; if you don't, children will figure ways to manipulate their way out of following any discipline plan.

5. IF POSSIBLE, TRY TO KID-PROOF YOUR HOME.

You may have a strong-willed child who keeps getting into the other kid's toys. For example, every day it is a big fight because your three-year old just cannot wait to go in there and play with those toys, and never puts them away, or breaks them, so you might want to build a high shelf. We do not think twice about locking up the poison, but it can be just as important to put out of reach those things that cause contention between siblings.

✅ACTION PLAN

List anything you need to change, or items you need to re-locate in your home, to minimize the amount of strife and/or corrections through a day.

_____

_____

_____

_____

_____

_____

_____

A young child's cognitive skills and understanding of life, their ability to process information and experiences, and their ability to make judgments and understand concepts are limited. They do not yet comprehend the difference between corrective consequence and punishment. They will understand eventually as you remain consistent, calm, and patiently work with them. When small children are corrected, or receive a consequence, they may respond with, *"You don't love me."* Maybe you have heard this from your child. If your habit has been screaming and yelling when correcting them, you may have a difficult time convincing them that this is what love looks like! *Learning* how to give a consequence correctly, and to train without showing anger and frustration is so *important*!

Sample Rules

You need to establish some real boundaries by the time your children reach fifteen to eighteen months of age. Here are some suggestions.

SAMPLE FAMILY RULES AND CORECTIVE CONSEQUENCES
Examples for 18 months to 5 years old

Rule 1:	**Respect one another at all times**
	- Parents and siblings.
Consequence:	Time out (3 to 5 minutes – use timer)
Rule 2:	**No physical fighting or verbal arguing.**
Consequence:	Time out 3 to 5 minutes.
Rule 3:	**Help clean up your own messes, toys, etc.**
Consequence:	Time out and (if a toy) toy gets put away for two days.

Parents Deserve Respect and Obedience

The number one rule must be that your children *respect* you. Remember, during the first five years, when you are teaching them this rule, you are also defining their concept of respect. Obviously, a three-year-old does not know what the word "respect" means. When they get mad and say, "I hate you," the first time, they do not understand that was disrespectful. When things come up and they respond in the wrong way, you need to say, "Now look, I understand you're upset, but what you just said was disrespectful. So the next time you say that, you will have a consequence for disrespect."

By doing this, you are also beginning the work of defining and instilling morals and values. Respect means that they are honoring you; Ephesians 6:2 says, ""*Honor your father and mother," which is the first commandment with promise:*" In essence, you are also helping them to understand God's will, which honors God as well.

Not obeying your command is a form of disrespect. If you ask your child to come here, stop doing that, get away from that, etc..., and they do not comply, you need to give them a corrective consequence. Do not get into the habit of raising your voice, or using their middle name to get their attention. If they do not comply, just *follow through* and give them the *predetermined* corrective consequence. As part of your follow-up, they need to be reminded that obeying parents also pleases God.

Colossians 3:20, *"Children, <u>obey</u> your parents in <u>all</u> things, for this is <u>well pleasing to the Lord</u>."*

A typical corrective consequence for disrespect would be *Time Out*. Many parents use a child's bedroom, or a certain chair. I recommend you purchase an inexpensive kitchen timer. Set the timer according to the child's age; if they are three, they sit for three minutes, etc. You can use a playpen for little kids, so they are not able to crawl out. They will understand the concept: when you say, "No," and they continue a behavior, you pick them up and put them in the playpen, then set the timer.

I also suggest that with children age two to five; you choose a chair conveniently within your view. I do not suggest that you stick them in a corner to stare at a blank wall; that is demeaning and does not teach or train them. The principle of giving a corrective consequence is not for parents to choose methods that kids hate, but methods that make them willing to yield to authority and receive training.

When was the last time God made you stand in the corner with your nose against the wall for your disobedience? God does not do that to us and we should not do it to our children. Remember that foolishness is normal, not bad; children just need to be *trained*.

Now, with a strong-willed child, you need to define what "sit in the chair" means. If you do not define it, they will soon be standing on the chair, scooting it across the floor, etc. What they are thinking, "I've got to win here. I'm not in control right now and I don't like this." So you have to define it for them, "Butt on the chair, chair in the same spot." Your more compliant children will just sit there.

If they get out of the chair before the timer is done, they are asking for the motivator/punishment. If you use spanking as your punishment, just spank and put them back in the chair, and start the timer again.

NOTE: PRINCIPLES OF SPANKING TO FOLLOW.

Bedtime (in their own bed)

There is no biblical instruction for when a child should stop falling asleep in your bed, if you have chosen to allow this. Some people use scripture to indicate that this will cause emotional damage. Now *that* is foolish. There is nothing wrong with allowing your kids to fall asleep in your bed, but there may be some difficulty when you want to break this habit.

With my boys, I shared with my wife that I did not want this to happen. There were isolated times, when they were scared or sick, that we would allow it. But it was different with our daughter. She was our little princess: both my wife and I let it happen often. After she would fall asleep, we would carry her to bed. My wife finally said, "Honey, I think it's time for her to learn to fall asleep in her own bed." I do suggest that by three years old, children should be trained to fall asleep in their own bed.

A couple came to me for counseling who had a thirteen-year-old child still sleeping in their bed. The husband was very unhappy about this. As a child, the wife had been physically abused by her stepdad when she was in bed; hurt, fear, and unforgiveness led her to allow their son to fall asleep with them since birth. That is wrong, and very unhealthy for the marriage and the child. It was very difficult breaking both the son's bad habit and this mother's emotional fears, but they found victory through forgiveness and a good plan.

If dad is home at bedtime, it is good for mom to let him lead in putting the children to bed. Wives often end up lying down and falling asleep with the kids, leaving the husband to go to sleep by himself. Men, you need to step up and participate in this area, if needed.

It is helpful to tie the *transition* to a birthday. Dad could handle it something like this, "OK, you're three, you know what that means? It is time for you to start sleeping in your own bed." The child will reply, "I don't want to, I like falling asleep in your bed." You answer, "I understand that, Honey, but it's now time; 8:30 is your bedtime. Here's your water. Here's a nightlight. I'll pray with you and leave the door open." Child replies, "I want Mommy." Your final word is, "No, you already said goodnight to Mommy."

For the next five days, you may want to lie down with them or kneel next to their beds for a few minutes to help the transition, but you need to work toward training them in this. You explain to them, "If you get out of your bed, it will be a swat on your butt (a rare exception to the rule) and back to bed." If it happens, you comfort them for just a few moments and then walk out of the room.

When you walk out, they will usually begin to cry. Set a timer for five minutes. The timer is for you because 5 minutes with a child crying is a long time. After five minutes, go back and comfort them (just for a few moments), saying,

"I'm here, we didn't leave you."

"Where's Mom, did she leave?"

"No, she's here, but it is time for bed now."

"I want to see her."

"No."

"I want Mom."

"No, Dad's here."

You explain that you know this is hard, but it is part of growing up. After you leave the room a second time, you set the timer for ten minutes and do not go back until that time is up, unless they get out of bed. If they do, you follow through with one swat, put them in bed, and walk out again. Stay *consistent* with this. Every time you do it, add another five minutes to the timer. Usually, the transition is complete in three to four days.

Bedtime was difficult for my son, Nicholas. He didn't want to fall asleep because he would be missing something. One of those special, strong-willed children, he would purposely wedge himself in the corner of his bed so he could not get comfortable. He knew if he would lay flat, he would fall asleep. There were nights when he would cry for over two hours before falling asleep.

He would cry until his little eyes would swell into slits. My wife and I would lie in bed thinking, "We should invent some kind of smelling stuff to knock him out; we would be millionaires—because there *has* to be other kids like Nick!"

It was very hard on both of us! A few times when I went out of town, my wife got suckered into letting him fall asleep in our bed. We had at least two more nights of struggle to get it back in order after I came home. With our other son, Justin, we said, "Hey, Justin, this is the bedtime." He said, "OK." And that was it.

I come from a large family, and between my brothers and sisters, we have lots of kids running around. My parents have a total of 41 grandchildren, 34 in San Diego. We have a great time together! When my kids were young, we would all go camping together. The sun would rise at six o'clock, and there was five-year-old Nick wide-awake. Everyone else was asleep, but he would be demanding, "Get me dressed." He would go out walking around, knocking on everyone's camper doors. Ten o'clock at night, he would still be out there by the fire when all the other kids were asleep, saying, "What's next?" He was a special boy (*and you thought you had the only strong-willed, hyper child*).

Pick up your Own Messes

Another rule should be: "Pick up your own messes." Moms, you are not maids. You can start this at a young age with their toys. Obviously, most three-year-olds are not going to independently pick up toys; it is OK to sit down and help them. If they do not help you, the consequence is that you confiscate the toy (make sure they see you), put it in a brown bag, and stash it in the closet. Say, "The corrective consequence for not helping Mommy is that your toy stays there for one day."

My son, Justin, would usually forget about that toy. But guess which toy Nick wanted most for the next two days? That one. This is an example of a sensible consequence, one that directly relates to the violation.

"No" Means "No"

"No" can be a rule. Give them a consequence for asking over and over after you have already said "No." Another typical rule for small kids is "**no whining**." Whining is simply a form of manipulation. Give them a Time Out when they indulge themselves in whining to get their way.

Other rules could be no biting (if it is a problem), no hitting, or both if needed, which could be handled with a Time Out.

Exceptions to the Time-Out and Spanking Rules

In some cases, such as bedtime, Sunday morning church, or any time when you are pressed for time to get out the door, you cannot give a time out for not getting out of the bath, or not getting dressed, etc. Instead, you can say, "Listen, I want you out of the tub now. If you do not get out of the tub now, you're going to get a spanking." That is the exception, not the rule. There are times when you do not have a choice in the matter; you have to say, "Here's the rule, here's the punishment/motivator. Respond correctly, or I will follow through." Going directly to spanking is used only in time-constraint situations.

SELF-EXAMINATION

(This is an exercise only)

1. Take some time as a couple (if married) and write out your current rules and your corrective consequences (all ages). If you need more space use a separate sheet of paper. If there are any rules or corrective consequences that you do not 100% agree on together, put an asterisk beside them.

Rule 1: _____
Consequence _____

Rule 2: _____
Consequence _____

Rule 3: _____
Consequence _____

Rule 4: _____
Consequence _____

2. What has been the punishment you are using in the event that your child refuses to accept the corrective consequence?

_____

_____

_____

_____

_____

✓ACTION PLAN

Take some time right now to fill out your own rules and corrective consequences for this age group, 18 months to 5 years, if married do it as a couple. You will find a **blank worksheet in the appendix**, please feel free to make copies. *I strongly suggest you not implement these rules until you have completed the chapter titled "Starting Over."*

WEEK 9: DAY 3

Principles of Spanking

#1—Plan Ahead

Choose ahead of time what will be corrected with spanking (Prov. 6:16-19). Most parents go directly to the punishment rather than the corrective consequence. That does not work. You must go to the *predetermined corrective consequence* first, and if they refuse the *consequence*, "rebel", then you go to the punishment. It is very important that you establish how, when, and for what you are going to issue this type of punishment, so you are not ruled by your *emotions*.

#2—Use Love

Spank in love. For a punishment to be effective, it must be done in the context of a loving relationship. That means being in control of your own emotions - no angry yelling and screaming. It is okay to spank your child without smiling; but you can also be firm without twisting your face in anger.

#3—Find Privacy

Spank your child in private, away from brothers and sisters, or other adults.

Think about this: let's say you are on your way to church, and almost there you get pulled over by the police for speeding. You are on the roadside, and everyone you know is passing on the way to church. Would you get out of your car and call out, "Hey, I'll be there in a minute. Save a place for me!" No, of course not. You would be saying, "Come on officer; please hurry. Everyone's going by, somebody might see me," and all the while wanting to hide your face. It is embarrassing to us as adults. Do you think it is any less embarrassing to our children? No, it is not.

When you are at home, visiting friends, or in a public setting, find somewhere private for this type of discipline. Many people in our society believe that spanking is illegal. Note: you may live in a country where spanking **is** illegal. If so, you need to decide for yourself how you are going to motivate them to yield. See below for alternative punishments. Spanking your children **correctly** is still legal in most countries, but spanking in public could bring social services to your home for an interview. They may even try to remove your children from your home. I have worked with cases like this when they did remove one of the children for this reason. In some cases, it went on for several months in court. If the spanking was done correctly, the judge would merely assign counseling and return the child home because there is no law against spanking in the US. You **must** be wise when using this form of punishment.

ALTERNATIVE PUNISHMENTS
For Children 18 months to 5 years

1. Child is put into play pen or bedroom for a period of time or until they are willing to accept the time out (corrective consequence).

2. Physically hold the child in your lap until they are will to quit defying you and accept the corrective consequence. The timer will start again only after the child sits on their own without any physical constraints by you.

#4—Be Consistent
Be consistent. If you say you are going to spank, then make sure to follow through. Equally important is them understanding why they are receiving the punishment.

#5—Explain
Talk with your child in a firm but loving voice, and explain why the punishment is taking place. "I'm spanking you, Honey, because you're refusing to sit in the chair. If you would sit in the chair and accept the corrective consequence, then you would not have to receive the punishment."

#6—Affirm Your Love
Affirm your love after punishing. For example, hugs are good, but *only* if they want to be hugged. Be *open* and willing to show loving affection in a way that is comfortable for your child and remember that every child is different.

The last thing Nick wanted after he was punished, or even given a corrective consequence, was to be hugged. He would wait about 30 minutes, and then he would just come and jump on my back and want to wrestle. Justin, on the other hand, immediately wanted someone to hug him. He wanted to be reassured right away, and he is a hugger. So was Katie.

Each child is different. If one does not want affection, then do not push it on them. Study each child to learn what makes them feel loved and what strengthens the parent-child relationship.

#7—Make It Immediate
Spank your child as soon as possible after the act of defiance, as this is an *opportunity* to motivate your child to accept training. Remember that sometimes this is not possible; you may be in public or at someone's house where there is no private place. In those situations, you may have to say, "Honey, sit right here next to me for a while." If they still remain defiant, in some cases you may have to leave and handle it immediately upon arriving home.

#8—Never in Anger
Never spank in anger or when you are not in control of your own emotions.

#9—Show Respect
Never spank a child in a way that shows disrespect. This includes verbally lashing them during your emotional meltdown over their behavior. Some parents make their children pull their pants down. Obviously, most kids are not going to turn around and say, "OK, spank me." Nick was like a rabbit. I had to hook my hand right up underneath his armpit and back him up against the bed so that he would not spin around me.

The right place to spank is on the buttocks, in the fatty area. If you stay within that butt area, you are also on safe ground with most legal authorities. When you move out of that area, you are crossing some lines.

#10—Use the Right Amount
Never spank more than necessary; use a *measured amount of pain*. Determine ahead of time how many swats they are going to get. Do not become agitated or surprised if they say, "That didn't hurt." The goal is not to make them cry, but to establish a way to motivate them when they rebel and refuse the corrective consequence.

As a suggestion, if your child responds to your swats with, "That didn't hurt," you say, "OK, I'm going to ask you a question, and you're going to have five seconds to answer. Now, five seconds is: one, two, three, four, five. That's how long you have to answer this question. If you don't answer, you're going to get another two swats. Here is the question: Do you want another spanking?" Now, that strong-willed child has to make a choice.

If they say, "No," that means the spanking worked. If they say, "Yes," they are still acting foolish and need another spanking. Most of the time they say nothing at all the first time you ask this question, until you follow through with another spanking, and that usually ends the problem of them responding with, "that didn't hurt."

#11—Spank for the Right Reason

Never spank a child for childishness, or messiness. Spank them for willful *defiance*, when he or she is unwilling to accept the corrective consequence.

When I was about eight or nine years old, I loved chocolate milk. We had eight kids in our family; you can imagine there were not many desserts around, so chocolate milk was a big thing for us. We must have gone through five gallons of milk a day in our house.

I remember one time, after my parents had just laid new carpet, I was making chocolate milk. Half of the kitchen was carpet, and half linoleum. I was, of course, on the carpet side, and I spilled the chocolate powder all over the brand new carpet. Being a child, I did not know I should get the vacuum and I used a wet rag instead. No matter how much I rubbed and scraped, the stain just kept getting bigger and blacker. That is an example of childishness, an accident.

When you discover your ten-year-old got into your tools, left them outside during the rain and they rusted, remember: What do you value more, your kid or the tools? This is when you say to him, "Poor choice, here's your corrective consequence." God knows how to bring around these tests that reveal our hearts, what we really value. Remember, when you blow it, ask your child to forgive you.

#12—Deal With Manipulation

Do not allow your child to manipulate. Many times a child will try to divert the deserved spanking by accusing you of not loving them, or by apologizing profusely. The reality is, if they did not respond properly to corrective consequence, you must *follow through immediately with the punishment/motivator.* Do not let them turn this into a temporary power struggle.

#13—Deal With Excessive Crying

Excessive crying, screaming, or yelling during and or after spanking must be handled. What can you do when your child is screaming like you are killing them? Here is a way you can break the cycle: let them know if they act this way, they will also be put into their room for a period of time after the spanking. You may use a timer for this, if you desire. Let them know that when they have stopped screaming or yelling then the timer will begin. Also add, "If you come out of the room before that timer goes off, you will get another spanking, and go back in your room." Once they figure out that you are going to stay *calm* and *consistent,* they will begin to break this childish behavior.

The Paddle or the Hand?

Worldly psychology has taught for many years "don't use your hand—you need to separate yourself from the spanking." But do you really think when you are spanking your child with an object that they do not know who is swinging it?

Personally, I am a firm believer in using your hand. When God speaks of "the rod of correction (Prov 22:15)," He is speaking of the tool of measurement and the authority. I encourage using a hand, which gives full control of how hard you spank. With your hand, you can also more effectively control the area of the spanking. The same hand that rubs their face that holds them, wipes their tears, feeds them and loves them is the same hand that corrects them if they need it.

I suggest that if you are going to use an object, throw the spoon away and get a flat paddle. If you use a spoon, and you hit too far down, leaving a bruise, you are opening the door for accusations of abuse.

I counsel many kids and hear the responses to what they felt when a parent used an object for spanking. It was not so much the spanking that bothered them, but the *object* their parents used. My experience is that your hand is the *best* tool for spanking. God set the example for us (1 Sam. 5:6, 9, 11; 7:13; 12:15; 2 Chron. 30:12; Job 19:21).

> **1 Samuel 12:15** *"However, if you do not obey the voice of the LORD, but rebel against the commandment of the LORD, then the hand of the LORD will be against you, as it was against your fathers."*

> **2 Chronicles 30:12** *"Also the hand of God was on Judah to give them singleness of heart to obey the command of the king and the leaders, at the word of the LORD."*

> **Job 19:21** *"Have pity on me, have pity on me, O you my friends, for the hand of God has struck me!"*

The same hand that blesses us also motivates us if we need it. God is always there with His tender love, to discipline us when needed. He handles all the training Himself, but that is not the case within our homes. Dad, you should be the primary one responsible for establishing the training and issuing the corrective consequences and punishment in the home. But remember that both dad and mom are a team, and are to work together.

When Dad is not Home

What happens during a typical day, when Dad is not home and the kids need discipline? Example: Mom says,

"Help me pick up these toys."

"No, I don't want to."

"Well, this is one of the rules Dad has established. If you don't help me, the toy gets picked up and put away for two days."

Married moms, lean on Dad; we are following Dad's rules, lean upon his protective authority. Your greatest companionship need as a wife is loving security, so let your husband protect you here. Don't argue with your kids over why a rule exists, or why a corrective consequence is being given. Just say, "This is what Dad and I decided to do, but these are **his** wishes."

While There Is Still Hope . . .

Proverbs 19:18, *"Chasten your son while there is hope, and do not set your heart on his destruction."*

The command here is to discipline your children; it is also a warning against parental passivity. A child guilty of wrongdoing should be chastened (disciplined) with a corrective consequence and punishment when needed in the early years while there is still hope. To neglect needed discipline may contribute to even capital punishment under the law later in life.

WEEK 9: DAY 4

The Myth of Positive Reinforcement

Our society has embraced the "positive reinforcement" concept of parenting; sadly, most of it is just so wrong and distorted. Using charts and rewards seems to work well with compliant children, but has some serious side effects. Have you noticed how many teens and young adults today have this entitlement mentality? Someone owes them, and, if the reward does not seem good enough, they will just quit and/or blame someone else for not getting what they feel they deserve! Our culture is infected by this today. This type of parenting does not work, especially with strong-willed kids.

Love is the most powerful motivator, and the most effective way to build self-worth in a child, not gifts and gimmicks. As we learned previously, we are to praise our children and practice our love toward them daily, because they are a gift from God. Good behavior is expected, not rewarded. When the apostles were asking Jesus to increase their faith and duty (Luke 17:5-10) He gave them a humble perspective of the type of attitude they needed after they had done what God asked of them, He said,

Luke 17:10 *"...when you have done all those things which you are commanded, say, 'We are unprofitable servants. We have done what was our duty to do.' ""*

We are carrying out a humble service for God in loving our children, and likewise our children are obeying us because that is what He asks of them (Eph 6:1).

Have the Right Attitude

Remember when your children were beginning to walk? You helped them and encouraged them as they took their first steps. You did not say, "You're embarrassing me! Get up! I was running by the time I was your age." When they fell, you picked them back up again and continued to help them. God says we must maintain that same type of attitude toward training our children.

That is not to say that it is never OK for you to put a carrot out there to encourage a particular behavior. For example, my son Nicholas struggled with reading retention; he could read a paragraph several times and still not understand it. This affected his academic progress and feeling of self-worth. Both my dad and I struggled with this, as have seven other family members that we know of so far.

Nick would spend hours on his spelling words during a week and get a C on his test, while Justin would look them over for fifteen minutes and get an A. It seemed really unfair for Nick, so I would say, "Nicholas, I know this is hard for you, but if you do well, if you work hard on this thing, we're going to do this for you." If I did something like that, I would make sure I took Justin aside, and say, "Look, Justin, I'm going to do this for Nick, because you know how he struggles academically." Then I would make sure I did something for Justin also. In those cases, positive reinforcement is OK.

SELF-EXAMINATION

Are you using any charts, graphs, or some other system to record a child's good or bad behaviors accompanied with rewards or demerits? If so, share with your spouse how it is working for you as a father or mother.

Write out how you believe this system is or is not working with your strong-willed child.

_____

_____

_____

_____

_____

Have either of you noticed that your more "compliant child" acts like and or makes comments that there perspective of themselves is being "better than" there strong willed sibling? If so, write out what they are.

_____
_____
_____
_____

Gifts or merits can motivate children to work hard or to try harder at certain things but they will not build self-worth in them.

As parents, how often are you complimenting and praising your children because they are a gift from God and wonderfully made?

_____
_____
_____

Is most of your praises tied only or mostly to there performance? Explain;

_____
_____
_____
_____

Is good behavior expected in your home because this is right or is rewarded as a way to get something? Explain:

_____
_____
_____

Does your love toward them and how you show it change because of their failures?

Do you have a compliant child whose natural bent is to please mom and dad?

Do you have a strong-willed child that resents their compliant sibling and struggle with their own self-worth?

They can become discouraged because their compliant sibling receives more gifts and/or affirmation than they receive from what they perceive comes more natural to the compliant sibling.

A perpetual system of rewards for good behavior for compliant child can set the stage for an entitlement mentality, as he or she grows older. This is teaching the child to serve, to do or to sacrifice only when it has a personal benefit for them that they believe is worth it.

How do you think this can negatively affect your child as an adult?

_____

_____

_____

_____

_____

Is your attitude toward all your child's failures similar to when they first began to walk; proud and excited when they first stood on their own and took their first steps? When they fell, you lovingly picked them up and encouraged them to try again, confident that in time they would develop, mature, and learn to walk on their own.

If not, explain your attitude toward your child's failures?

_____

_____

_____

_____

A Great Idea for Corrective Consequence
The Corrective Consequence Box

I want to share with you a wonderful little tool called the "consequence box", which can be used in place of time outs. This should be introduced when your children are around six and older. It can be a jar, shoebox, or any container that you can get into easily. In the box, you place little pieces of paper on which are written chores that are age-*appropriate*; if you have a six- and an eight-year-old, they could use the same box. Chores like dust a certain room, vacuum the living room, sweep the back patio, pick up toys in playroom are acceptable. You fold the papers up and put them in the box.

Have your kids help put it together. It is so fun when they sit down and help you think up the corrective consequences to put on those pieces of paper. They are not thinking about themselves getting the consequence; they are thinking about brother or sister getting it and they can be pretty creative.

When it is time for a corrective consequence, you grab the box; they reach in and randomly pull out a piece of paper, then do whatever it says. If the task has recently been completed, just have them pull another one.

What happens if they say, "I'm not going to do the consequence"? You *motivate* (spank) them for rebellion. If, after you spank, they still do not accept the corrective consequence, they go in their room until willing to come out and do the discipline. Do not let them out of that consequence. Remember, punishment is *not* the trainer; it does *not* educate or build character—corrective consequence *does*. Follow through with the punishment, but they must finish the consequence also.

Once, when Nick was around eleven-years-old, he pulled from the corrective consequence box, which he did often, and the consequence he got said, "Clean all the toilets." The house we had at the time had four bathrooms. My wife and I looked at each other, and said, "Clean the toilets? We don't remember putting that in there." My wife grabbed her rubber gloves and the toilet brush, marched him into the bathroom, started showing him how to do the first one, and he was off and running.

While she was gone, I looked in the box. When she came back into the kitchen, I said, "Look, there are twice as many papers." So we dumped them out and started reading. Eventually, we came across one that read "Do all of Justin's chores." You see, two days earlier, Nick had been bothering Justin, and Justin wanted to get back at him so he spiced up the consequence box. Justin would get a consequence, on average, every fourth day. Nick, on the other hand, would sometimes get five plus a day. He thought is was the best way to get back at Nick.

We all thought it was quite funny, what Justin did. As a matter of fact, we left in at least half the ones he added. He was very creative. But I encourage you, put the box up high because things may happen to that box. If it does not disappear altogether, all the hard things that were written on those sheets of paper will disappear.

Using Related Corrective Consequences

As a child matures, at about the age of eight, it is important to introduce *related* consequence when appropriate. For example, you live on a dead-end street, which is a safe place to ride a bicycle. You feel that it is dangerous beyond that, so you tell your child, "OK, you can ride your bike up to this point, but if you cross that line, past that telephone pole, without getting permission from Dad or Mom, you will lose the privilege of that bike for a two-day period. So choose wisely."

You can be creative, but make sure it is related to the bicycle. Do not say, "I'm going to take away your game boy." What does that have to do with riding your bike down the street?

Sibling Rivalry
No Fighting

One of the rules I want to cover here is "no fighting and/or verbal arguing" between siblings. When your children are in a mutual conflict that spills over into your attempt to discipline them, you are battered with information on who started it, who did what first and so on and pretty soon you are frustrated. If you have a written rule like no fighting or arguing, you merely walk into the room and say, "Alright, the next one that speaks to the other in the next fifteen minutes will get a corrective consequence." You set the timer, and separate them into different areas of the house and go about your business.

When one of them runs in and says, "He stuck his tongue out at me," you say, "You go do a corrective consequence, because you shouldn't have been looking at him." Then you go get the other one and give him a corrective consequence too. Don't let their childish foolishness control you.

No Lying

A "no lying" rule is a good one. Tell them if they get caught lying, they have double consequence. Simply give them two consequences from the list or box, if you catch them lying about anything.

Clean Your Own Mess

The rule is clean up your own messes. You walk into the house, see a mess, and tell your child, "Clean that up. And when you're done, go do a corrective consequence. Remember, I'm not your maid."

I believe a good rule is to "keep your own bedroom clean." My children were expected to make the bed and straighten the bedroom before they went to school. Note: if your own room is not cleaned up, then do not expect your kids to do it.

When we presented this rule, my kids said, "We're not going to have time to pick everything up and make the bed." My response was, "That's right, if you have your bedroom picked up before you go to sleep, the only thing you have to do in the morning is pull up your sheets." The bedroom is a wonderful training tool.

SAMPLE FAMILY RULES AND CORECTIVE CONSEQUENCES
Examples for 6 to 12 years old

Rule 1:	**Respect one another at all times**
	- Parents and siblings.
Consequence:	Draw one item from the consequence box or list.
Rule 2:	**No physical fighting or verbal arguing.**
Consequence:	Draw one item from the consequence box or list, if physical add ½ day room restriction.
Rule 3:	**Be ready for school by 7:15 a.m.**
Consequence:	Be awakened at 5:00 a.m. the following morning or go to bed ½ hour early.
Rule 4:	**Clean up your own messes expediently.**
Consequence:	Draw one item from the consequence box or list and clean up mess.

Rule 5:   **Return home by the specified time from an approved outing.**

Consequence: Home restriction for two days.

Rule 6:   **Telephone privileges until 9:00 p.m. (with approval).**

Consequence: No telephone privileges for two days.

SAMPLE FAMILY RULES AND CORECTIVE CONSEQUENCES
Examples for 13 to 18 years old

Rule 1:   **Respect one another at all times**
                                   - Parents and siblings.

Consequence: Draw one item from the consequence box or list.

Rule 2:   **No physical fighting or verbal arguing.**

Consequence: Draw one item from the consequence box or list, if physical add ½ day room restriction.

Rule 3:   **Be ready for school by 7:15 a.m.**

Consequence: Be awakened at 5:00 a.m. the following morning or go to bed ½ hour early.

Rule 4:   **Clean up your own messes expediently.**

Consequence: Draw one item from the consequence box or list and clean up mess.

Rule 5:   **Return home by the specified time from an approved outing.**

Consequence: Home restriction for two days.

Rule 6:   **Cell phone to be off when in school, driving a car, when doing homework and between 9 p.m. and 6 a.m.**

Consequence: No telephone privileges for three days. [2]

Rule 7:   **Cell phone: any inappropriate use of texting or pictures will result in a consequence.**

Consequence: Loss of both text and picture capability on your phone for a predetermined amount of time.

---

2   * One way to check and make sure this rule is followed is be checking the cell phone bill, it will have the times the phone was being used.

Rule 8:	**Room to be cleaned before leaving for school and or by 11 a.am on weekends "bed's made, cloths off floor and put away."**
Consequence:	Draw one item from consequence box and clean room.

Examples of Alternative Punishments For Ages 7 To 18

SHUT DOWN

If your child refuses the corrective consequence, an effective punishment is *Shut Down*. *Shut Down* means that your child has no privileges; no television, telephone, music, or friends over, and may include being confined to their bedroom. Their only freedoms will be to go to school, church, eat meals, use the restroom, and do their chores and homework. This continues until they are willing to accept the corrective consequence. *Shut Down* can last for five minutes or five days (or longer). It is up to them.

SATURDAY WORK DAY

An effective punishment for a teenager who refuses to accept the authority left in charge in the absence of the father (i.e. mother, stepparent, grandparent, babysitter, or guardian).

- Have your child work on Saturday morning to complete tasks given. For example, give them a "TO DO" list to begin at 8 AM and they will be done when everything on the list is finished correctly. This is a great time to get those things done around the house you can't seem to get to. If they choose to drag the work out longer than it should take, let them, but until all the work is done correctly, they are in that *Shut Down* mode.

DRIVER'S LICENSE

Rescind license or permit (this can be done with written request from parent to the DMV). This should only be used if a child is rebelling against the rules and corrective consequences and is leaving in their car or your car. If used as a discipline – you must have a designated time period that it is taken away for and returned after that set time, not when their attitude is better.

✓ACTION PLAN

Take these rules and corrective consequences to prayer, ask God to help you and to give you wisdom in writing out your rules. You will find a **blank worksheet in the appendix**, please feel free to make copies. *Ask Him to help you be unified (if married) as husband and wife. I strongly suggest you not implement these rules until you have completed the chapter titled "Starting Over."*

Tools for Training Older Children

If parents have trained with well-defined rules/boundaries, and consistently used corrective consequences during a child's first nine years, the transition into adolescence will be relatively smooth. Many changes occur between ages 13 and 15; this season of life is called *puberty*. Puberty is a period of two to four years when a child's body is undergoing changes leading to what we call adulthood. This wonderful transformation can be frightening for them and frustrating for us! It could be, probably will be, a bumpy ride; we must remember that this season is God-ordained, a prescribed process fully known to Him, as He designed it.

Ecclesiastes 3:1, *"To everything there is a season, a time for every purpose under heaven..."*

Puberty is a time when kids experience a real growth spurt. As size and physical strength increase, the body shape begins to look more like an adult. Your son's voice will begin to change. Ironically, before they acquire a deep *manly* voice, like dad, they can go through a *squeaky* period where they sound more like mom, especially over the telephone! Your daughter will experience the embarrassment and excitement of getting her first bra. Parents must remember that they are the adults and need to have *patience* and *compassion* with their maturing child!

Emotional changes also occur during this period as a child begins to think more independently, and will seek distance from parents. They have a strong desire to be accepted by their peers and begin to pursue close friendships. Heightened awareness of the opposite sex, with feelings of attraction, is part of maturing sexuality. In our sex-obsessed society, teens are exposed to many temptations, pressures and mixed messages about sex. During this time, it is vitally important that home is where sexual purity and godly morality is taught and expected as the behavioral standard. It is also very important that parents openly discuss sex; a child must hear the truth and develop healthy attitudes, which should come from you. If you don't answer questions and satisfy their curiosity, they will get information, or *misinformation,* from their friends!

Note: To help you better understand adolescents, check our website for material on *"Understanding Teens,"* and to assist you in setting healthy boundaries for your child with opposite sex friends, refer to, *"What Is Teen Dating Anyway? Biblical Principles for Opposite Sex Friends."*

The teen years are a period when your developing child will begin to think abstractly and symbolically, which means, in a nutshell, that they are thinking a lot like you think! When they perceive that something is not right, they have the ability to look at the situation with understanding and are better able to see another person's point of view.

Teens will usually, to varying degrees, test the structure and values that you have taught them at home. Your children have been observing and absorbing your words and actions for their entire lives. They know you very well. Be warned that when a pubescent teen senses division between Mom and Dad in management style, contradictions in rules, or any hypocrisy, they will surely point it out!

As a child progresses toward adolescence (girls at ages 11 to 13, and boys at ages 12 to 15), we should move from spanking into different methods of punishment. I have found that spanking older children usually does more harm than good, by provoking and humiliating them. Using total restriction is a great motivator/punishment to convince an adolescent to accept the corrective consequence.

As a child matures, if they received this type of training, they most often will become goal-oriented and have a desire to get on with life. While feeling this unstoppable need for more independence, they can become antsy, impatient, anxious, and even seem rebellious. Remember, they do not have the answers to important questions about what is happening to them. Such questions as: What is the source of all these changes that come with adolescence? What is a mature adult and how do I become one? This is why parents need to *define* these questions and be guiding an adolescent in positive directions, keeping them focused on the goals of maturity.

The changes that teens experience are unavoidable, healthy, and part of God's perfect design. Our children did not ask for puberty; many have a difficult time adjusting to these changes, which is why parents need to educate themselves. Every child needs parental wisdom and help getting through this period, some much more than others. Think of it this way, each one of these changes (physical, emotional and cognitive) are tools that God has provided for them on the path of becoming mature adults.

Begin to give your teen more freedom and independence; respect their privacy, but do not compromise standards. Don't snoop in their room just for the sake of snooping! Your sons and daughters need to know that you see them as *young adults*, not children! One of the ways to do this is by making their thirteenth birthday a very special event. Spend time with your child, discussing the changes they are facing. Take every opportunity to reaffirm your love for them and their value to you. Let them know that you are on their team, and that you will be there to support and help them through this time.

✅ACTION PLAN

After reading the characteristics above, list some of the changes you see in your adolescent child/children. If you have not been sensitive during this time of change (all ordained by God), ask God to forgive you for your negative actions, then write out a prayer for help. Go to your teen and ask forgiveness if needed.

_____

_____

_____

_____

_____

_____

_____

_____

_____

_____

_____

_____

_____

Our adolescent kids may be _looking_ like adults, but they are not yet mature. Many parents make the mistake of pulling back from the training process with teenagers. You can stop training when they become responsible, mature adults, or when they leave your home, whichever comes first. You need to make this clear to them. And remember that you are _training_ them, not _controlling_ them.

WEEK 9:DAY 5

Adolescents will naturally begin to test your authority; it feels like the "terrible twos" are back, but this child has gained a hundred pounds! Here are some areas where you should not compromise during this season.

Respect-Obey Parents

Number one, no exceptions: **_show respect to both parents_**. This means obeying and speaking respectfully, and no mouthing off. This also can include them trying to help you in parenting the other siblings. It is common for teens to act like you need help in parenting their younger siblings, so make it clear that, "We've got two parents in this house; we don't need another one!"

Also, be on the lookout for them to start telling you what they are going to do, rather than asking for permission. Example: "I am going to Kathy's house and I'll be home by 7:00." To which you reply, "Whoa, are you asking me, or telling me?" Your teen may then say, "What's the big deal?" So you clear it up by telling them, "Well, let me explain. If you're telling me, then no, you're not going any place. If you're asking me, I'll think about it."

This is a typical power struggle during these years, but it can sneak up and leave you wondering when they seized control. Although this behavior needs to be identified and checked, consider it normal. Do not get upset and react in anger, just correct it lovingly and consistently.

Morals and Values

Number two: do not compromise the *morals and values* that you have established within your home. This includes personal interests and pleasures—music, TV, games, etc. My son, Nick, was really into music, so we made a **rule**: you can have any music you want but, if it is not Christian, I had to read and approve the *lyrics* first. Did we ever catch Nick with inappropriate music? Yes, we did. One time, my wife found some CDs at the bottom of a drawer in his room. We got on the Internet, looked up the bands, and could see by the first picture that popped up what they were about. Most of the lyrics were on the Internet as well. So, the consequence was the CDs got destroyed, and he had a consequence from the corrective consequence box—one for each CD.

On one occasion, seven of the CDs we destroyed were not his; they belonged to his Christian friend. When it got back to the parents that we had destroyed their son's CDs, and my son had to do corrective consequences, they called us, "Oh, we're so sorry. Tell your son he doesn't have to pay him back, because we don't want that in our house either." Then, they asked me for advice on how to deal with this out-of-control problem with their son.

Training is Mandatory

Number three: explain that *training can stop when they become responsible adults, or when they leave your home*, whichever comes first. Often an adolescent will say, "Well, I think I don't need to receive training anymore." You just say, "OK, I'll make you a deal. If you stay within the rules, I'll never give you a corrective consequence again. But, if you break a rule in my house, you are demonstrating both to you and me that you need to receive further training."

Sample Rules for Adolescents

Wake-Up Time

We had a rule about waking up in the morning. If you have a teenager, and you find yourself going in two or three times every morning to wake them up, you are not helping that child. Get them an alarm clock. When my boys turned nine years old, I gave them an alarm clock and said, "Wake yourselves up. Get up on your own, get yourselves dressed, and get ready for school."

The longer you put off, the harder it is to implement. If your teenager runs late, is not ready by a certain time, give them a corrective consequence. It could be going to bed a half hour, or an hour early that night, plus a consequence upon arriving home that day.

Bathroom Schedules

Sharing bathrooms in the morning can be hectic. Give your teens a schedule: "You have from 6:00 to 6:15 AM. At 6:16, you'd better be out of that bathroom. If you're not, you get a corrective consequence." You will find that this will help in keeping peace in your home. Fix any areas that may be creating havoc for the family.

Curfew

I want to say this about curfew: one of the worst things you can say is, "Curfew is 10 PM." When you tell them that, they want to be out every night until that time. Instead, make curfew situation specific. Every time they leave your presence, they need to let you know *where* they are going, *who* they are going with, which *parent* is going to be there, *who is driving*, and *when* they will be home. If the plans change, they had better call you *first* and get permission. Be careful here: don't let them begin to *pull away* too soon by being out three or four times each week.

Telephone Privileges

Usually, by the time your child reaches 13 years old, the phone is ringing off the hook with friends calling, and or you may rarely see them anymore because they stay their room. The answer to that problem can be no phone in the bedroom, or no cell phone. This is not the only answer, because a very strict policy can cause them to pull away from the family prematurely. The rule must make sense, as perhaps the phone is interrupting homework, or other responsibilities. Encourage your teen to participate with the family, making together time appealing.

I will give you a couple phone rule examples at the end.

Of course, most kids now have their "own phone" at a very young age. Be careful, cell phones provide advantages but can become distractions from spending time with family. If you see this is a problem, I suggest you make rules for the phone. As long as they live under your roof, you have the say so.

Let me encourage you: having cell phone and computer rules are important, especially concerning your child's communication with the opposite sex. Set a schedule for days and times that they can communicate with their friends on the phone, or via computer. Also, *know* the friends they are talking to. **Example:** phone or computer chat time is 7:30 to 8:00 PM; the corrective consequence, if the rule is broken, is two days no phone or computer.

On our website at www.parentingministry.org we have more suggestions for computer parental controls.

Creative Punishments for Teens

As I stated before, it is a good idea to wean yourself and your children off spanking by the time they are eight to ten years old. One alternative is what I call

"Shut Down," meaning room restriction with no friends, phone, radio, computer, games, or iPods.

Teens Challenging Mom's Authority

This can become a problem, as moms often are not as intimidating as dads when it comes to dealing out corrective training. Mom, what will you do when Dad is not home and your eleven-year-old son will not perform the corrective consequence you have just given him? At that point, he goes into "Shut Down," until Dad gets home, or he accepts the corrective consequence. If he has not cooperated by the time Dad arrives, I suggest you implement a double corrective consequence. No freedom is given until your son performs his consequences.

When my son, Nick, would begin to challenge my wife and not accept the corrective consequence, she would then send him to his room. When I would come home, my wife would tell me what had happened, and I would go in, sit down, and say, "Nick, what happened?" He'd give me his side of the story. "OK, the reality is, <u>you wanted door number three</u>. (See Week 8:Day 5 for review) We told you door number three does not exist anymore. Go do two consequences for not doing it when Mom asked you to."

What if a Teen Refuses Punishment?

Say a teen will not receive Shut Down when mom deals it out, refuses to take the time in isolation. It's time to call Dad and describe the problem so that he is prepared to resolve the situation when arriving home. Dad begins, "What was the problem today?" "Well, I don't think this is fair." "Really? Go do that corrective consequence now, and for not submitting to your mom's authority by refusing to go to your room, your additional **punishment** is Saturday work. You will receive one hour's worth of work every time you don't listen to Mom when she tells you to go to your room for not doing the predetermined consequence. Saturday work is punishment to remind you that you are required to submit to mom's authority. When I'm not here, Mom is the authority. I have delegated my responsibility to her when I'm gone; she is doing what I have asked her to do."

Put Them to Work

I have found that assigning work, beyond normal chores, is an effective punishment/motivator. When Nick hit 12 to 13 years old, he began to really challenge my wife's authority. She would give him a corrective consequence, and sometimes he would argue. By that point, he was too big to spank.

DIG DEEPER: *FURTHER STUDY*

Read the following scriptures and list the pro's and con's concerning work.

Proverbs 14:23, *"In all labor there is profit, but idle chatter leads only to poverty."*

_____

_____

_____

_____

_____

_____

Proverbs 10:5, *"He who gathers in summer is a wise son; He who sleeps in harvest is a son who causes shame."*

_____

_____

_____

1 Thessalonians 4:11–12, *"that you also aspire to lead a quiet life, to mind your own business, and to work with your own hands, as we commanded you, that you may walk properly toward those who are outside, and that you may lack nothing."*

_____

_____

_____

_____

_____

_____

I always assigned one hour of work for challenging my wife's authority. I did not say, "Go work for an hour," or I would have gotten one weed pulled. I would say, "You weed from here to here, and if you're done early for working fast, great. If it takes four hours, or if you take all day, I don't care—your choice, but you will have no freedom until that work is complete." Nick became a machine, realizing that if he worked fast and hard, he could finish in less than an hour.

"Shut Down" Defined as Punishment

On "Shut Down," there is no TV, radio, iPod, no friends, no computer, and no cash flow. Their life consists of school, schoolwork, chores, dinner table, and bathroom. It is used as a punishment if a teen does not accept and do the corrective consequence. At any point, if they do the consequence correctly, freedom starts again.

Note: Restriction and shut down are *not* the same thing. **Example**: you have a rule to be home by a certain time; miss it and the corrective consequence is 2 days restriction. Notice that the restriction is a corrective consequence that is tied to the privilege of being away from home and the responsibility of obeying the rule. If your child violates the restriction, they are refusing to accept the corrective consequences, and the result is Shut Down. When the attitude is right, then the two-day restriction begins again. Freedom is gained when the restriction is successfully completed.

Many parents use restriction for everything, but it really should only be used in specific instances. For example, as a related consequence for missing curfew. You told them to be home at 6:00, and they came home at 6:30. Your response is, "Poor choice, you are on restriction for the next three days, since you don't have the self-control to choose wisely and be home on time." The restriction is a corrective consequence related to the offense.

Restriction Defined

Restriction should consist of staying home for a designated time, with no friends allowed over, this is not to be confused with "Shut Down." Remember "Shut Down" is appropriate when a child refuses the corrective consequence. At that moment they lose all privileges—they remain in "Shut Down" until they accept the consequence. If it takes five minutes or five days, what do you care? Act like you have all the time in the world.

They may say to you, "This is ridiculous!" So you say, "I know; I can't believe it either. For something that's going to take you a few minutes, you have chosen to be in your room for three days. I can't figure it out, but if that's what you want, that's OK with me."

God wants us to use these incidents of disobedience for training our kids and, of course, we are motivated to be consistent because our goal is to form in them the character of a mature adult.

Corrective Consequences for Teens
Consequence List

My kids grew up with a consequence box, so they were still pulling papers from the box up to their teen years. But when introducing such a box to your thirteen-year-old for the first time, they might think, "What is this baby stuff?"

So, for kids 13 years and older, I recommend using a consequence list, it is the same exact concept, but on a list instead of in a box. See bellow.

Remember, make the corrective consequences age-appropriate. If you have several teenagers, they can all use the same list. For example: wash mom's car, wash dad's car, vacuum the inside of mom's car, wash five windows inside and out, etc.

These are corrective consequences that are over and above their normal chores, to be given when they break a rule. Mom, think of all the spring cleaning that you do and put those things on the list—tasks that take between five and fifteen minutes.

When your child breaks a rule, and using the corrective consequence list makes more sense than a re-lated consequence (i.e. restriction for missing curfew), then you go to that list. The list is assigned from the first task to the last, and when they get to the bottom, it starts over. Obviously, if the consequence is to go out and sweep the back patio and it is 9:00 at night, you have the option to assign that task for the first opportunity the next day, or to choose the next task from the list that can be done immediately. Parents, do not assign tasks out of order because you know it is the one your child hates most.

ACTION PLAN

Please follow the instructions below to create a list. We have also included this in the **appendix**.

THE CORRECTIVE CONSEQUENCE LIST

(Review and discuss as a couple, if married)

- Make a list of work projects that are not already part of your children's weekly or regularly assigned chores. These short work projects should be those that are not normally completed on a weekly basis, like spring or fall cleaning projects, or they can be those work projects that the parents do themselves on a regularly scheduled basis.

- Keep in mind the consequence work should take between 10 to 20 minutes.

- For a consequence, they do whatever is next on the list.

- Avoid making the list too difficult. Remember this is a training tool for teaching them the personal characteristics of a mature adult. This is <u>not</u> the parent getting revenge on their children.

- This list can be used when a related consequence is not applicable. For example: if your child is disrespectful, use the list. If your child comes home late, a related consequence of in-home restriction for 3 days can be used instead of the list.

- If you have a strong-willed child, you may need to consider having a large number of work projects on the list so that your child is not doing a corrective consequence he/she has recently done.

- If the child does not perform the corrective consequence satisfactorily, as you have previously trained your child, then inform your child that he/she is to complete the original consequence and be in *Shut Down* until it is done correctly.

- We recommend that the parent put their initial in the box after he/she has inspected the work performed by their child versus putting a check mark that any child can write.

- When your children have completed the list, start again at the beginning of the list.

THE CORRECTIVE CONSEQUENCE LIST

1. Vacuum a particular room										
2. Clean all mirrors in bathroom										
3. Clean sink and bathtub in bathroom										
4. Clean toilet										
5. Clean behind couch, silk flower in basket, & TV										
6. Clean up backyard – dog										
7. Sweep back Patio										
8. Pull weeds in front yard for 10'x20' area or 15 min.										
9. Water back yard – 20 minutes										
10. Water front yard – 15 minutes										
11. Wash four windows inside and out										
12. Wash car										
13. Vacuum inside of car										
14. Sweep garage										
15. Clean out refrigerator										

Giving Our Children Chores

Chores are a powerful training tool and can instill a great work ethic in your child, as well as help build character, personal responsibility and self-control.

Five guidelines for using chores correctly:

1. **Make them fair**. Let me give you an example. You have an eleven-year-old girl who washes dishes five nights a week, and you have a ten-year-old boy that his only chore is mowing a 20' x 20' piece of grass once a week. Is that fair? No, it is not. A ten-year-old boy can learn how to do dishes, cook, and fend for himself in the kitchen.

2. **Make them age-appropriate**. Be sensitive about what a child can handle. Example: asking

an eight-year-old to wash your car may be beyond their ability. But, they can vacuum a room.

3. **Write them out**. Just like the rules, chores need to be written down.

4. **Put in writing the day and time for completion.** For example, the trash needs to be out Wednesday night because collection is on Thursday morning. You do not want this scenario: Son arrives home, "Hey, today's Wednesday, you've got to take the trash out." "OK." At dinner time: "Did you take the trash out?" "No, I will after dinner." After dinner, he sits down in front of TV and an hour later you say, "Turn that TV off, go take the trash out." "I'll do it after this show." Bedtime: "You didn't do the trash! Now you have to get up early tomorrow morning and do it." Next morning: Guess what you are doing at 5:45 AM?

Instead, you write on his chore list: The trash must be out by 6:00 pm on Wednesday. This means that at 6:01, if that trash is not out, no matter what he is doing, short of something that has been approved by you, he is taking that trash out *right then*. And on top of that, because he waited until 6:01, he also does a corrective consequence. Use the consequence box or the list for your consequence. In other words, they have to actually think for themselves, keep track of time, and say no to some other things in order to take care of the chore. All of this is instilling the character of a mature adult.

5. **Train, do not nag.** Stop the arguing, nagging and threatening—just set up your plan and *consistently* follow through.

✓ACTION PLAN

Take some time to write out your chores and the corrective consequences they will receive when they are not doing it right, or on time. There are **blanks in the appendix**. A note to the perfectionist: remember, no kid is going to do it perfect, so be reasonable. You will find **blank chore sheets in the appendix.**

SAMPLE CHORE LIST WITH CORRECTIVE CONSEQUENCES

Chore: **Feed the Dog**
Day: Everyday   **Time** by: 5 p.m.
Consequence: Consequence box or list.

Chore: **Take the Trash Out**
Day: Wednesdays **Time** by: 6 p.m.
Consequence: Consequence box or list.

Chore: **Clean the Bathroom**
Day: Saturdays   **Time** by: 8 p.m.
Consequence: Consequence box or list.

Chore: **Mow the Grass**
Day: Saturdays   **Time** by: 5 p.m.
Consequence: Consequence box or list.

Chore: **Vacuum Living Room and Dust**
Day: Saturdays   **Time** by: 8 p.m.
Consequence: Consequence box or list.

What About Allowance?

I am a firm believer that allowance should *not* be tied to individual tasks. Otherwise, when you ask for help bringing in the groceries, you may hear the kids saying, "How much money do I get?"

So I say, especially when your children are younger, if you plan on giving them an allowance, think about how many hours of chores you give them in a week's period, and come up with a dollar amount that you agree to as a couple. Then you simply say, "OK, I'm going to give you $5 a week for helping, and *because* I *love you*. It's your spending money."

Nick always wanted to earn extra money; he always had something he wanted to buy. So I would assign dollar amounts to certain projects, not related to his regular chores, as a way for him to earn money over and above his allowance.

Kids need to *learn* how to work, but don't treat them like slaves.

When I need help with a special project, beyond their normal chores, I tell my kids, "Hey, next Saturday, guys, I'll need your help in the morning. We're going to spend from 9:00 to 10:30 AM on this project." Sometimes I pay them for that, but I also believe it is good to teach children to participate in keeping up the house without expecting to be paid.

> **Proverbs 13:4,** *"The soul of a lazy man desires, and has nothing; but the soul of the diligent shall be made rich."*

God tells us to train up our children with a gentle reproof (Eph. 6:4). By formulating plans to be followed both by parent and child, real progress can be made in training them, with a minimum of drama and emotion. Failures along the way can be cleared up quickly through communication, confession, and asking forgiveness. Remember, we are adults – they are children.

A plan for training includes, in writing, clearly defined rules, a source of corrective consequences (box, list, restriction), and a way to motivate them when rebelling (spanking, Shut down). Consistency is essential.

Final Exhortation
In the next chapter, we will discuss how to take the information you have acquired and begin to implement it in your home.

Week 10: Starting Over

WEEK 10: Day 1

Introduction

Starting over is just that. You take the new truths, tools and principles of parenting that you have learned and use them to formulate your new family discipline plan. Throughout this study, God has revealed the need for change in your current parenting methods, and management style in your marriage, by showing you where you are failing to live up to His standard.

Whenever we read God's Word, His Word also reads us! It reveals our wrong ways and our motives for practicing them.

> **Hebrews 4:12,** *"For the word of God is living and powerful, and sharper than any two-edged sword, piercing even to the division of soul and spirit, and of joints and marrow, and is a discerner of the thoughts and intents of the heart."*

As we obey God by applying biblical truth to our life, His Word washes us like water, cleaning away all impurities. Like the refiner's fire, God's Word exposes the dross, or things in our lives that do not glorify Him, which He wants to remove. Like a sword, the Word penetrates the hardness of our hearts. Finally, the Word is like good seed planted in our hearts and, when humbly received, grows deep roots and bears fruit for God's glory and the building up of others.

> **Psalm 1:1–3,** *"Blessed is the man who walks not in the counsel of the ungodly, nor stands in the path of sinners, nor sits in the seat of the scornful; But his delight is in the law of the LORD, and in His law he meditates day and night. He shall be like a tree planted by the rivers of water that brings forth its fruit in its season, whose leaf also shall not wither; and whatever he does shall <u>prosper</u>."*

Because our homes and families are so important to us, it can be very discouraging to face the fact that we have failed in any way. I want to encourage you that God's mercies are new every morning!

DIG DEEPER: *FURTHER STUDY*

Read the following Scriptures, list God's promises and what they mean to you.

Lamentations 3:22–23, *"Through the LORD's mercies we are not consumed, because His compassions fail not. They are new every morning; great is your faithfulness."*

_____

_____

_____

_____

Psalm 86:15, *"But You, O Lord, are a God full of compassion, and gracious, longsuffering and abundant in mercy and truth."*

_____

_____

_____

_____

Because we have a great, *compassionate* God, who *faithfully* loves us, we can hope in His promise to be by our side with His great strength, wisdom, love, and healing. God is able and ready to bless our homes, but we must desire it and strive to do all that He requires of us.

As an encouragement, I would like you to know that I speak to many parents around the United States, and abroad, and the most common response to this material is, "Why haven't I ever heard these things before? I've been a Christian for 20 years. Why haven't I ever understood these Scripture verses in application to the relationship I have with my children?"

I am well aware that a large percentage of you will be saying to your children: "We need to start over."

This can be daunting for parents raising young children, but some of you have older children, or are concerned about those who have already left home. After reading and studying this workbook, you may be thinking, "Oh, no wonder they're so angry with me. No wonder our relationship is so bad. I can see now how my parenting style affected them."

If you are feeling discouraged because your kids are teenagers, or you even have adult children at home, your big question is probably "How can I possibly *effectively* implement the strategies and tools from the preceding chapters this late in the game?

First, please stop and consider this: *God* waited until now to expose you to this material. He does not operate in the same time frame we do. So the next question is: Why did God wait until now? Be assured that it is not so that you would feel defeated and condemned. In God's eyes, according to His foreknowledge, this is the right time, the time when He knew that you would be ready and able to change your relationship with your children.

DIG DEEPER: *FURTHER STUDY*

Read the following Scriptures and write down what they say about God's involvement in our lives.

Ephesians 1:11, *"In Him also we have obtained an inheritance, being predestined according to the purpose of Him who <u>works all things according to the counsel of His will</u>."*

_____

_____

_____

_____

Romans 8:28, *"And we know that all things work together for good to those who love God, to those who are the called according to His purpose."*

_____

_____

_____

_____

So what can you do about strained relationships? *Everything*!. Even if your children are out of your house, there are some important steps you can take. Obviously, you can't bring them back home and start over with discipline; however, when it comes to relationships, every day is a new day, a fresh start.

You should be the one to reach out. And remember, the relationship you had with your own parents will affect the way you relate to your children. When I first came to Christ, one of the most difficult things God asked me to do was to forgive my father. It was hard, believe me, but it was worth it.

In this final lesson, I want to present the steps that I believe you must follow in order to move away from negative, ineffective, and perhaps destructive parenting - and start over.

Biblical Steps for Starting Over
STEP ONE: *Confess Your Sins to the Lord.*
The first step in restoring a right relationship with your children is to confess your own sins to the Lord.

Confess: is to agree with God that what you did ignorantly or deliberately was "wrong" and a sin.

Starting over is to be honest before God by *humbly* confessing, or admitting, our failures, mistakes and sins against Him and or others. God knows that we are sinners. Jesus shed His innocent blood on the cross because all mankind is guilty before God and incapable of saving themselves. When we accept Christ as Savior and Lord, we do not immediately stop sinning. The process of sanctification (separating from sin), whereby we become conformed to the image of Christ, takes place over our entire lifetime!

When we confess to God, we are not telling Him something that He does not already know. He has known *every* thought, known *every* motive, heard *every* word spoken and witnessed *every* action taken in our homes. Prayer is acknowledging to God that we are dependent on Him and are placing our trust in Him. Confession is not simply telling God what we have done, or failed to do, but *it is also agreeing* with Him that we have been wrong.

> **1 John 1:9,** *"If we confess our sins, He is faithful and just to forgive us our sins and to cleanse us from all unrighteousness."*

God cleans the slate, making it possible for us to start over, but notice that there is an "if" clause. We have to be *willing* to come to Him with all our garbage.

Read the following Scriptures, write down what happens when we do confess our sin(s), and what happens when we do not.

> **Proverbs 28:13,** *"He who covers his sins will not prosper, But whoever confesses and forsakes them will have mercy."*

_____

_____

_____

_____

> **Psalm 66:18,** *"If I regard iniquity in my heart, The Lord will not hear."*

_____

_____

_____

_____

> **Psalm 32:5,** *"I acknowledged my sin to You, and my iniquity I have not hidden. I said, "I will confess my transgressions to the LORD," and You forgave the iniquity of my sin. Selah."*

_____

_____

_____

_____

While reading this material, God has likely been bringing to your mind behaviors in your discipline routine that you now realize are sin. Remember, God is not angry with you; He is simply bringing the truth to light at this point so that you can change.

You must acknowledge to Him, "I see that it is sin, God. Please forgive me." Every sinful word and activity God has revealed to you (even things you did not do that you should have done), confess them to the Lord. Don't be vague—try and be *very specific* with the Lord. Remember, the things we did not do, like not leading properly, not discipling our children, or not being consistent with our discipline, all need to be confessed also.

DIG DEEPER: *FURTHER STUDY*

Read the following Scripture and briefly describe the result of unconfessed sin. How did the Psalmist respond? What was God's response?

> **Psalm 32:3–5,** *"When I kept silent, my bones grew old through my groaning all the day long. For day and night Your hand was heavy upon me; My vitality was turned into the drought of summer. Selah I acknowledged my sin to You, and my iniquity I have not hidden. I said, "I will confess my transgressions to the LORD," And You forgave the iniquity of my sin. Selah"*

_____

_____

_____

_____

_____

✓ACTION PLAN

Take the time right now to write down those failures and confess them to the Lord. Next, write out a prayer of commitment on how you are going to change.

_____

_____

_____

_____

_____

_____

_____

_____

WEEK 10: DAY 2

Essentials of confession:

A. BY FAITH, RECEIVE FORGIVENESS FOR YOUR SIN, TRUST THAT GOD HAS MADE YOU HIS CHILD.

FACT FILE

Faith – *pisteuo (Gk)*, means to have faith in, trust; particularly, to be firmly persuaded as to something.[1] This is more than just giving a mental assent, it means to act on what is believed.

DIG DEEPER: *FURTHER STUDY*

Read the following Scriptures, write out what it tells you about faith.

Hebrews 11:6, *"But without faith it is impossible to please Him, for he who comes to God must believe that He is, and that He is a rewarder of those who diligently seek Him."*

_____

_____

_____

_____

_____

John 6:37, *"All that the Father gives Me will come to Me, and the one who comes to Me I will by no means cast out."*

_____

_____

_____

_____

B. REPENT, OR TURN FROM SIN, AND DAILY TO WALK IN OBEDIENCE TO CHRIST.

FACT FILE

Repent – *To resolve; to amend one's life as a result of contrition for one's sins; to feel regret for one has done or omitted to do before God. To turn around and go another direction; to change one's mind, will and life, resulting in a change of behavior; to do things another way.*

---

1   Zodhiates, 160.

DIG DEEPER: *FURTHER STUDY*

Read the following Scriptures and briefly write out what is being presented concerning repentance.

Acts 26:20, *"but declared first to those in Damascus and in Jerusalem, and throughout all the region of Judea, and then to the Gentiles, that they should repent, turn to God, and do works befitting repentance."*

_____

_____

_____

_____

_____

Romans 2:4, *"Or do you despise the riches of His goodness, forbearance, and longsuffering, not knowing that the goodness of God leads you to repentance?"*

_____

_____

_____

_____

_____

Luke 15:7, *"I say to you that likewise there will be more joy in heaven over one sinner who repents than over ninety-nine just persons who need no repentance."*

_____

_____

_____

_____

_____

Isaiah 55:6–7, *"Seek the LORD while He may be found, Call upon Him while He is near. Let the wicked forsake his way, And the unrighteous man his thoughts; Let him return to the LORD, And He will have mercy on him; And to our God, For He will abundantly pardon."*

_____

_____

_____

_____

_____

_____

C. AFTER YOU CONFESS AND REPENT, BE ACCOUNTABLE TO YOUR SPOUSE, PASTOR, OR A GODLY FRIEND.

FACT FILE

Accountability – means subject to giving an account, answerable, a statement explaining one's conduct.

As members of the body of Christ, we are told to make ourselves accountable to God and to one another for the purpose of encouragement, protection, exhortation and correction. By sharing your commitment to change a sinful behavior with another, you bring yourself out of secrecy and open up to the support and prayer of someone you can trust. It helps to bring sin into the light.

DIG DEEPER: *FURTHER STUDY*

Read the following Scriptures and briefly write out what is being presented concerning accountability.

Romans 14:12, *"So then each of us shall give account of himself to God."*

_____

_____

_____

_____

_____

James 5:16, *"Confess your trespasses to one another, and pray for one another, that you may be healed. The effective, fervent prayer of a righteous man avails much."*

_____

_____

_____

_____

_____

Galatians 6:1 *"Brethren, if a man is overtaken in any trespass, you who are spiritual restore such a one in a spirit of gentleness, considering yourself lest you also be tempted."*

_____

_____

_____

_____

_____

Pray the following suggested prayer:

Lord Jesus, thank you for dying on the cross for all of my sins. Thank you for Your promise to complete the work you began in my life. Thank you for blessing me with my children. I now understand that they are gifts from You. Forgive me for not treating these children as gifts, and for the mistakes that I have made in raising them. Help me to put You first in my life, then to love and train Your children according to Your will and ways. In Your name I pray. Amen.

STEP TWO: Ask for Forgiveness

When starting over, you first confess and seek forgiveness from God, then ask forgiveness from others affected by your words, deeds, or lack of deeds (this applies to your parenting style).

God has given spiritual principles to govern us. Whether we are Christians, or non-Christians, believe God's principles or reject them, nevertheless, these spiritual principles govern our lives. One such principle is that of forgiveness and reconciliation. God commands us to go to those we have offended, when possible, and be reconciled by humbly asking their forgiveness.

Sadly, parents seldom admit to offenses against their children. The words "I was wrong by _____, I am sorry and will you please forgive me," are rarely spoken. But they are the most powerful words to bring healing and reconciliation between parent and child.

In the following verse, Jesus explains that when you are bringing your gift to the altar (today, this would mean coming to God to praise, serve, and/or ask for His blessing) and the Holy Spirit brings an issue or offence to your mind concerning another individual, (in this case, family) you are first to restore that relationship. This shows just how important it is to God that we be reconciled to one another. He is saying that good favor with Him is related directly to our relationship to others. Knowing this, we need to clear offenses quickly. With practice, you will find that this lifestyle brings blessing and peace.

> **Matthew 5:23-24,** *"Therefore if you bring your gift to the altar, and there remember that your brother has something <u>against you</u>, leave your gift there before the altar, and <u>**go**</u> your way. <u>First</u> be reconciled to your brother, and then come and offer your gift."*

The word *go,* is an imperative verb, a command. When we know we have sinned against our children, we must go to them and seek forgiveness. Notice that going is not conditional. There is NO "IF" clause, I will go if _____, (you fill in the blank). The Enemy and our own flesh will fight us, and provide many *excuses* for not following God's plan.

In this verse, we see that God has four requirements: 1) To properly worship Him, you need to have a clean heart concerning others; He places a high priority on *relationships*. 2) The sole responsibility of reconciliation is on you, not the one offended. 3) God expects you to act as soon as possible. 4) Clear up the offense first, then come back and worship Him.

When you carry this out, you are not only being obedient to the Lord, but you are bringing healing between you and your child. God works in both you and your child when confession is made and forgiveness given. It is supernatural!

✓ACTION PLAN

Take time and write out a prayer asking God for the strength to practice forgiveness daily.

_____

_____

_____

_____

_____

_____

_____

_____

Are you excused if your child is 18 months and barely talks? No. If you have failed by being angry, screaming or yelling in response to childish behavior, you need to say, "I'm sorry for _____, what Daddy/Mommy did was wrong. Please forgive me."

This process will become easier as you practice it and begin to experience the blessing of training your child God's way. As you confess sin, and repent, your conscience will become more sensitive, and your ability to walk in righteousness will increase. Following God's plan will give you power, and your sinful behavior will decrease as you gain self-control and learn to respond with Biblical love.

Ephesians 4:26, *"Be angry, and do not sin: do not let the sun go down on your wrath."*

Anger is natural, but does not necessarily lead to sin. And if it does, we need to practice the process of seeking forgiveness daily. To review: the process is simply going to the person offended, stating the offense(s) specifically, and asking for forgiveness (i.e. "Please forgive me for yelling; please forgive me for saying those harsh words; please forgive me for not being consistent.")

Angry outbursts are traumatic and often embarrassing. So we allow our sinful behavior, and growing bitterness, to continue because we do not want to revisit the problem. When God says *"do not let the sun go down"*, He means that we are not to even let our anger last longer than one day! This means we are to clear up the pain and havoc we create within that same day. By doing this, we set ourselves free as well as the offended person.

Every time you yell and scream at your kids, it is like slicing their hearts with a knife. If you do not ask for forgiveness, and apply the salve of healing (which is asking for forgiveness), infection will set in, then resentment, and then revenge. Many of you may have kids who are already angry, bitter and hurt because you have sliced them over and over and over again, and never applied the salve of forgiveness.

When you ask for forgiveness, you are giving the medicine God provides for their torn heart, and beginning the healing process. This is so very important. If we do not practice this daily with our children, it will hinder our own spiritual growth and transformation. If we *choose* not to, then we can become one of the Enemy's greatest tools to harden a child's heart. When this is true, the seeds of discipleship and discipline will not penetrate the heart and take root.

Remember, there is absolutely <u>no</u> justification for our sinful behavior. *We* must take full responsibility.

WEEK 10: DAY 3

STEP THREE: Forgive Others

Starting over begins with confession and asking for forgiveness, but how are we doing at forgiving others? We also need to forgive, and this definitely includes our children. You may be thinking, "Well, what about when my kids hurt me?" Dad says, "I'm still so angry at my son for taking the car on a joy ride that cost me $800. What do I do with that?" Mom says, "My daughter tells me I am ruining her life. She hates me."

DIG DEEPER: *FURTHER STUDY*

In the following Scriptures, what is God telling you to do? Is there any condition mentioned regarding your hurt feelings? Who is your example?

> **Colossians 3:12-13,** "*Therefore, as the elect of God, holy and beloved, put on tender mercies, kindness, humility, meekness, longsuffering; bearing with one another, and <u>forgiving</u> one another, if anyone has a complaint against another; <u>even as Christ forgave you</u>, so <u>you also must do</u>.*"

_____

_____

_____

_____

Ephesians 4:32 *"And be kind to one another, tenderhearted, forgiving one another, <u>even as</u> <u>God in Christ forgave you</u>."*

_____

_____

_____

_____

When it comes to how much we should forgive, the measuring device is how much Christ has forgiven us (*"even as Christ forgave you"*). You cannot put a price tag, or count up to how much He has forgiven and continues to forgive you.

Remember that you are Christ's minister to His children and, as such, you must have the mindset of *continuous* forgiveness. Just let it go today, whatever it is. Believe me, I realize some of the mistakes our kids make can be big ones, and they can be costly. But you have to let it go. It is a choice, an act of obedience to God; do not wait until you feel like it.

We must always remember that our kids have a fallen nature and are very capable of sin. Because we are their God-ordained authority, childhood rebellion is often directed at us. Because we love them and are responsible for their well being, their sin often hurts us. This being true, parents must daily apply the principle of forgiveness and reconciliation toward their children!

As we have seen, a child's disobedience must be corrected with training: rules/guidelines, corrective consequences and, when necessary, punishment. But we also face the challenge, as parents, of cultivating a loving parent/child relationship by forgiving them for their foolish, or rebellious behavior. And remember, love is the greatest motivator, and will *lead* a child to respond to your authority.

When a child learns to walk, you hold their hand, steady them, and cheer them on to success. When they fall, you pick them up and lovingly set them back on their feet. It would be absurd for a parent to resent a wobbly toddler for stumbling and falling! Imagine the parent of a one-year-old saying:

> *"He's falling down on purpose. He's doing that just to irritate me or embarrass me in front of the other parents. He's not trying hard enough. If he loved me, he would walk!"*

A sane parent would never be so foolish. Yet, when we take our children's failures *personally*, when we *refuse* to forgive and *forget* their mistakes (even if they have made the *same* mistake dozens of times), we are being foolish. As parents of growing children, we must keep the right perspective and treat their failures in the same way as when they were *learning to walk*. They need to be supported, steadied, and encouraged.

We must remember that our home is a training ground and **_parenting is a ministry_**. We are serving God as we minister and train up *His* children; forgiving is a non-negotiable requirement. Some kids are naturally more sensitive and may seek your forgiveness, while others plow through life with no apparent concern for the feelings of others. No matter the personality, your actions and instruction can lead either type of child to godly maturity. And remember, as we are training our children, God is training us! Our transformation is sometimes a painful process! If we trust in Him, God will use the disappointments and challenges that we experience from our children's failures and mistakes to conform us to His image.

DIG DEEPER: *FURTHER STUDY*

Read the following Scriptures and briefly write out what is being presented concerning forgiveness.

> **Mark 11:25–26,** *"And whenever you stand praying, if you have <u>anything against anyone</u>, <u>forgive him</u>, that your Father in heaven may also forgive you your trespasses. But **if** you <u>do not</u> forgive, neither will your Father in heaven forgive your trespasses."*

_____

_____

_____

_____

> **1 Peter 4:8,** *"And <u>above all</u> things have fervent love for one another, for love will <u>cover</u> a multitude of sins."*

_____

_____

_____

_____

Four Essentials of Forgiveness

 # One: *Forgiveness does not keep a record of wrongs.*

Once you forgive others, including your children, you cannot keep a record of the wrongs you suffered.

> **1 Corinthians 13:5,** *"Love. . . keeps no record of wrong."*

This means you cannot continuously bring up your children's failures. Unfortunately, many parents constantly bring up things that happened in the past. That is *very destructive* and not true forgiveness. If you have that bad habit, it is important that you get rid of it. And now that you have new perspectives, tools, and strategies, you are going to discipline in the moment and not drag up the past as part of your training plan.

SELF-EXAMINATION

Has this been a practice of yours? If so: write out a prayer of confession and asking God to change your heart and to convict you when you bring up the past.

_____

_____

_____

_____

_____

_____

Two: *Forgiveness eliminates gossip.*

Do not gossip to others about your children's failures or sins. Obviously it is acceptable to discuss discipline issues between husband and wife, but not in front of your kids. It would also be appropriate to talk privately with your pastor, or a counselor who is helping you.

Say a child has been misbehaving throughout the day, and Mom greets Dad at the door and immediately begins to blurt out, "You won't believe what happened today. . . blah blah blah." That is not appropriate. It is important to establish a time for Mom to share how the day went with the children, but not in front of them.

One day, my wife and daughter had a bad day homeschooling together. I came home that night, and I could tell it had been a rough day. Later that evening, my wife explained all the details of what had taken place, and how she had handled the problems.

At bedtime that night, as I prayed with Katie, she said to God, "I pray that Mommy and I have a good day tomorrow." I kissed her and said, "Yeah, I heard you had a rough day." She was surprised, "You know?" I said, "Of course I know." I could see her thinking, "Is he mad?" I merely said, "I bet you're going to have a better day tomorrow. I love you, Honey," gave her a kiss, and walked out.

The situation was handled, and Katie never felt the embarrassment of hearing her mom lay out all her shortcomings.

SELF-EXAMINATION

Do you share your children's faults and failures with friends or other family members, seeking self-pity or to expose their sin (**Gossip**)? If so write out a prayer to God asking His forgiveness, then ask those who you gossiped to, to forgive you, that it was wrong for you to share those things.

_____

_____

_____

_____
_____
_____

Write down what the following Scriptures say about what we are to speak.

Proverbs 8:8, *"All the words of my mouth are with righteousness; Nothing crooked or perverse is in them."*

_____
_____
_____
_____
_____

Proverbs 21:23, *"Whoever guards his mouth and tongue keeps his soul from troubles."*

_____
_____
_____
_____
_____

Proverbs 15:4, *"A wholesome tongue is a tree of life, but perverseness in it breaks the spirit."*

_____
_____
_____
_____
_____

 # Three: Forgiveness does not dwell on offenses.

Philippians 4:8, *"Finally, brethren, whatever things are <u>true</u>, whatever things are <u>noble</u>, whatever things are <u>just</u>, whatever things are <u>pure</u>, whatever things are <u>lovely</u>, whatever things are of **<u>good report</u>**, if there is any virtue and if there is anything praiseworthy—<u>meditate on these things.</u>"*

Someone has offended you; do not let it fester into a bitter feeling toward them. Let it go, and if you cannot, God says go to them in humility, seeking reconciliation. This also applies to our children; do not allow their past mistakes to create your current attitude. True forgiveness produces a parental attitude of hoping for, praying for, even expecting the best from a child, not anxiously waiting for the next mistake to occur.

> **Romans 12:18,** *"If it is possible, as much as depends on you, live peaceably with all men."*

Your children may sometimes express, or harbor, deep-seated bitterness and anger toward you. You may have to face a very angry teenager and, despite your best intentions, when you ask for forgiveness they may not cooperate. You need to reach out to your children, but do not expect them to always say, "OK, thanks," and embrace you. They are going to watch you; they are going to test you. This is normal. Seek God's grace to be patient and loving.

✓ACTION PLAN

If you have a child who is harboring bitterness or resentment toward you, write out an intercessory prayer to God that He would soften their heart and bind the work of the enemy.

_____
_____
_____
_____
_____
_____
_____
_____
_____
_____

Commit this to daily prayer.

Four: *Forgiveness is granted without limitation.*

> **Matthew 18:21–22,** *"Then Peter came to Him and said, "Lord, how often shall my brother sin against me, and I forgive him? Up to seven times?" Jesus said to him, "I do not say to you, up to seven times, but up to seventy times seven."*

As ministers, when can we stop forgiving our children? Never!

We must have a mindset that we will continuously forgive them, no matter what they do, even when they deliberately hurt us. Our job is to love and train them. Yes, it is hard. Standing on God's Word and calling on the power of the Holy Spirit is essential, and the only way we will succeed.

Parenting is difficult; it is certainly not for cowards.

WEEK 10: DAYS 4 & 5

Conducting the First Family Meeting

Make Reconciliation

Now, it is time to sit down with your kids and explain to them the things you have learned. In a two-parent family, the husband and wife should meet first and pray over and agree upon the rules, corrective consequences, appropriate punishments, and chores for each child, **AND WRITE THEM OUT.**

Remember, you are not doing this out of frustration with your children's behavior and attitudes, or because you are sick of the chaos. You are doing this because it is God's will. He has revealed truth and His desire for your family, so you are making changes in response to what you have learned.

Please note: if one of your children has a serious relationship problem with either parent, both should meet individually with that child before the family meeting takes place. Otherwise, if you sit down with the whole group first, and begin explaining what you are going to do, that particular child may have the attitude of, "Yeah, right," which may dampen the response of the other children.

Open this one-on-one meeting with prayer, then humbly acknowledge the past problem, and seek reconciliation with that child by asking for their forgiveness for the mistakes that you have made. Be specific. Dad, you start. Mom, you're next. Once you have said your piece, it is important that you give your child an opportunity to respond. However, do not be upset if they remain silent.

The Family Meeting

I have had many reconciliation meetings in my office; I love seeing the tears and unity that God brings in those meetings, how the Holy Spirit blesses them. But it does not always go down that way. Many times the child does not respond positively right away. And that is OK.

Make sure you have your rules, corrective consequences, appropriate punishments, and chore lists written out before you set up a family meeting. Provide a copy to each of your children, with the exception of kids that cannot yet read. Simply show your younger kids the lists. Later, you can post them in their rooms; I will return to that idea later in the chapter.

Again, begin the meeting with prayer, asking God for His help and guidance in your home. Fathers, I exhort you to be the one to lead the prayer, even if you have never prayed in front of your kids before. Yes, you will probably freak them out, but do it anyhow. *Prove* to them that *you* are asking for God's help to make these changes.

Then, apologize to your children as a group. Ask them to forgive you for your mistakes, your sins, and your lack of understanding of proper parenting thus far.

Even if you have already said these things to one of the children individually, it is important that your other children see what went on between you and this child. Asking forgiveness again, collectively, shows *humility*. That one child knows the other kids saw you hurt them by your behavior; your acknowledgement of this in front of all the kids emphasizes your *sincerity*.

It may sound something like this: "Some things have been brought to Mom's and my attention, things that we've been doing wrong as parents. And we already sat down with Johnny and asked for him to forgive us for what we've been saying and doing to him. But we want to say this to all of you kids, for the yelling and the screaming and the inconsistency, we're sorry."

Again, give your children an opportunity to voice their feelings, but do not require it. I strongly suggest, Dads, you continue by asking forgiveness for any specific sins the Lord has revealed to you and, Moms, be willing and ready to ask for forgiveness also. Remember, Dads, you are leading this discussion and keeping things peaceful.

Roll Out the Plan

And now, you come to the point where you introduce your child/children to the new plan for discipline, fully explaining the reasons and your motives for this new way of parenting. Explain the rules, the purpose of corrective consequences, and the how and why punishment will take place. Also review the chore lists along with the consequences. Make sure you communicate that these changes are *not* taking place because they have been bad and you are now forcing marshal law upon them. Review chapters 8 and 9.

Guidelines for Understanding Discipline:

First, explain that *discipline is **Biblical**,* and that God is holding you accountable for the way you train up your children.

Second, explain the ***difference*** *between corrective consequence and punishment* and the reasons behind each (see **Week 8: Day 4** for clarity).

Third, give them the definition of a ***mature adult***, and explain that your God-given responsibility is to lovingly train them to become those mature adults (see **Week 8; Day 2** for clarity).

✓ACTION PLAN

Write bellow what the definitions are for **Morals and Values**, **Personal Responsibility**, and **Self-Control**. Familiarize yourselves with them so you can **thoroughly** discuss these with your children, if married do this together. Do NOT rush through this; take some time to show them from the Bible that this is God's plan. We have given you plenty of Scriptures (Week 8) to illustrate this.

_____

_____

_____

_____

_____

_____

_____

Fourth, explain that the *family is a **team**,* and everyone needs to work together so that the home will be a refuge and a place of peace for all family members.

Fifth, explain the need and your desire for ***weekly family Bible Study,*** and let them know the *day* and *time* it will take place (See pages **Week 7: Day 5, "Seven Simple Steps for a Weekly Bible Study,"** for clarity).

Regarding Bible Study, I recommend you have one for the kid's age's five to ten, and a different one for the older kids, if possible. In some homes, mothers work with the younger children while fathers do devotions with the older ones, which is just fine. But be careful, fathers, do not use this as an opportunity to pass the whole thing off onto Mom. You are the priest of your household. You must take that responsibility very seriously; fulfilling your role as the spiritual leader is one of your wife's companionship needs, and a command to you from God (Eph 6:4).

My wife home schooled our daughter and Bible study was part of their daily routine. I would go over the Bible study with her almost every day at our prayer time in the evening. I also did a weekly Bible study with my children up until they left our home.

Follow-Up is Important
Allow for Transition
Be forewarned that if you have had very little structure in your home prior to this, your children will not jump for joy. Allow some grace on enforcing your discipline for the first week or so. If you have allowed arguing and debating in the past, let them slide on completing chores, it will take some time to break some bad habits. Let them know, "I'm going to remind you once for the next five days, but after that, there will be no more reminding."

Example: If you have allowed this arguing to go on for a long time, now that you have defined "respect" and implemented appropriate corrective consequence, if the conversations become heated, you simply say, "Hold it, Honey. I know this is something we used to do, but remember this is an area of disrespect. So I'm warning you right now, pull it together." Then, if they continue, you need to follow through and give them the predetermined corrective consequence.

So, do allow that grace period but, after the five days is up, remind them, "OK, grace period is over. Now the warning will stop."

Be Sensitive
Once the new system is up and running for a while, you may discover that some of your rules and disciplines are unfair, or too harsh. Be sensitive to God's guidance as you *evaluate* how the system is working.

Parents contact me quite often, trying to decide what is appropriate and what is not. **Example:** In a counseling session a father of a seventeen-year-old wondered if a 9 pm bedtime was inappropriate, since his son was having a problem with it. I told him, "Yeah, I do think 9 pm is pretty early for a seventeen-year-old." I asked the boy, "How late do you want to be up?" He replied, "At least until 10 o'clock." "Dad, what do you think?" "I guess that's OK." "Good, then are you OK to change your rule."

If the kids are strenuously objecting, and you think the rule may be too harsh, seek the Lord and get some counsel. Fathers, be ready to listen and consider your wife's input; it will be important here. If you decide the rule is too harsh, change it. Remember, your family is a team.

Post the rules and discipline list in an essential area of your home, like the kitchen. No, I do not encourage putting it in plain sight on the refrigerator, especially if you have older kids. Their friends come over and cannot resist the refrigerator, then you have, "What's this?" Small kids do not care where you post it, but when they get older, they are more sensitive about such things.

Instead, put it inside a kitchen cabinet, a drawer, or closet, and give the kids their own copies as well. Your teenagers will probably not want to post it in their room. Do not force it, simply give them a copy. Of course, they will probably lose it or throw it away. That's why you post your own copy.

Hold Periodic Family Meetings
A follow-up meeting should be held *every two months* for the next *six* months. It is important that you sit down with the kids and get feedback. You might have to shore things up in areas that have begun to slide back into old habits. Come together as a family and discuss these things; however, do not make this a time of negotiation. You are still in charge.

It is also vitally important for husband and wife to communicate *regularly* about how things are progressing, as when my wife told me about her rough home schooling day with Katie, and how she had resolved it. But remember, Mom, do not blast Dad the minute he walks in the door with all the bad things that happened that day. The house is supposed to be a refuge for everyone. Discuss with him when is the best time to present the information.

Parents, Examine Yourself Often

Finally, parents need to continually evaluate personal progress. **First**: Is Jesus still the cornerstone of my strong foundation? Because, as you know, your spiritual foundation (daily devotional time) is the most important aspect of fulfilling your job as a minister.

Second, continue to be very aware of the *quality* of your relationship with each child. Remember, each is unique and requires assurance, discipline, etc. that is geared for their specific personality needs. And remember; never compare your child to anyone else. Here are some areas to keep in mind as you evaluate your progress:

- Are you responding in love, or in anger?

- Are you communicating love by giving time and proper affection?

- Are you discipling faithfully?

- Is your system of discipline based on God's management style? (See week 6.) Working as a team?

- Are you staying consistent with the training plan?

It is so important that you check on yourself because, if any one of these things gets out of order, the plan can start unraveling.

Remember that God blesses obedience, so, by consistently applying the principles you have learned, you will bring His intervention right into your home. You will begin to understand His ways, and be so tuned to God's will that you can hear Him speaking to you about how your home should work, what rules you should have, and about the specific needs of each child.

God so desires that you succeed in training up your children in the way they should go! It is my deepest hope and desire that the principles and tools you have learned in this study will assist you in achieving that goal. Remember: God does not do by miracle what He has called you to do by obedience.

Please visit our website, www.parentingministry.org, for additional information and material, or to contact us. There is a detailed video series, with a workbook, that can help you implement these principles, along with a leaders' guide to help you teach others.

Now, go and minister to your children; they truly are gifts given to you by God! Plus begin to pray about discipling others in the things you have learned.

A Leader's Guide for this book for small or large groups can be found at www.parentingministry.org.

Appendix

Appendix A
Parent Self-Evaluation Checklist
(REVIEW AND DISCUSS AS A COUPLE, IF MARRIED)

Now that you have established your parenting structure, which includes the *Four Tools of Training* enforced in love, you may experience times of defeat or frustration and begin believing that this parenting style does not work for your family. If this happens, don't panic and look to the world's methods! Don't fall back on old habits! Instead, use the following evaluation checklist to discern the true source of the problem.

Your Spiritual Foundation

- How is your devotional life? Read *Psalm 1:1-3*. Would you use words like worshiping, listening, thanking, confessing, interceding, etc. to describe your daily communication with God?

- Do you read and meditate upon God's Word in a daily quiet time?

- Are you trusting God with your finances and giving tithes regularly?

- Are your priorities in accordance with God's desires for you and your family? Is the fruit of the Spirit evident in your life?

Remember: You must depend upon The Lord! The key is not your parenting methods, but a relationship with God!

Communicating In Love

- Take the **Effective Listening Self-Evaluation** in Appendix and see how you are doing.

- Have you been reacting in the flesh to your children or responding to them in love?

- Take a moment and review *What Love Is Not* (**Week 3:Day 4 – Week 4**). Are there areas where you need to improve in your communication or apologize to your children?

Remember: Your communication with and toward your child reflects the value you have placed upon them.

Training Your Children Through Discipleship and Discipline

- The best way to train is by personal example. How are you doing?

- If married, are you and your spouse working together and supporting one another? How is your management style? Who is the main disciplinarian?

- Are you sticking to your rules and using **only** the *pre-determined* consequences and punishment, or has nagging, yelling, empty threats, and *inconsistency* crept back in?

- Are you praying regularly with your children? Have you followed through with your commitment to have a weekly family Bible study?

Remember: God loves you and He loves your children. You must trust Him. He did not give you the wrong children. He has not given you a task beyond your ability to accomplish as you trust in Him and obey His will.

Has God revealed areas in your family relationships where you have drifted off-course? If so, follow the steps outlined below to get your home back on course.

1. Confess to God, acknowledging your weaknesses, mistakes, or failures.

2. Receive God's forgiveness. Allow Him to embrace you in His arms of love and grace.

3. Repent by turning away from your error and commit to walk in obedience to His will.

Appendix B
Commitment to Christ

Perhaps you have struggled in some areas of parenting and have come to realize that your struggles are a result of a weak or inconsistent spiritual life. God promises to bless, encourage, and strengthen us as we submit to His lordship in our life.

Psalm 29:11 *"The LORD will give strength to His people; the LORD will bless His people with peace."*

Write a prayer of commitment to the Lord, to put Him first in your life, and asking Him to help you parent the *gifts* (children) He has given you.

_____

_____

_____

_____

Perhaps you have never surrendered your life to Christ. Know that God loves you and has provided the way for you to have a relationship with Him. You must simply,

1.　　**Recognize and admit that you are a sinner.**

Romans 3:23 *"...for all have sinned and fall short of the glory of God."*

John 3:3 *"Jesus answered and said to him, 'Most assuredly, I say to you, unless one is born again, he cannot see the kingdom of God.' "*

2.　　**Believe that Jesus paid for your sins.**

John 14:6 *"Jesus said to him, 'I am the way, the truth, and the life. No one comes to the Father except through Me.' "*

Acts 4:12 *"Nor is there salvation in any other, for there is no other name under heaven given among men by which we must be saved."*

3.   Confess your sins to Jesus.

Acts 3:19 *"Repent therefore and be converted, that your sins may be blotted out, so that times of refreshing may come from the presence of the Lord."*

Romans 10:9 *"...that if you confess with your mouth the Lord Jesus and believe in your heart that God has raised Him from the dead, you will be saved."*

4.   Receive the gift of salvation.

John 1:12 *"But as many as received Him, to them He gave the right to become children of God, to those who believe in His name:"*

Romans 6:23 *"For the wages of sin is death, but the gift of God is eternal life in Christ Jesus our Lord."*

Repeat the following prayer,

"Lord Jesus, I know that I am a sinner. I am sorry for my sin. Thank you for dying on the cross for me and paying the price for my sin. Please come into my heart. Fill me with your Holy Spirit and help me to be your disciple. Thank you for forgiving me and coming into my life. Thank you that I am now a child of God and that I am going to heaven." Amen

Appendix C
How to Lead a Child to Christ

John 1:12 *"But as many as received Him, to them He gave the right to become children of God, to those who believe in His name."*

The only requirement to become a child of God is to believe and receive the Lord Jesus Christ. The Bible does not designate a specific age a child must reach in order to experience salvation. Jesus urged parents to bring their little children to Him, and rebuked those who attempted to keep the children away.

Luke 18:16-17 *"But Jesus called them to Him and said, 'Let the little children come to Me, and do not forbid them; for of such is the kingdom of God. Assuredly, I say to you, whoever does not receive the kingdom of God as a little child will by no means enter it.'"*

Most small children will respond to an invitation to ask Jesus to come into their hearts. Their innocence, sense of wonder and trusting hearts provides fertile soul for the gospel. The following are truths that a child must receive and should be explained in simple, age-appropriate language. As they mature, they will grasp the deeper meaning of these truths.

1. God made us, and everything around us. He loves us and watches over us from heaven.

2. God is good. He has never done or thought anything bad.

3. All people are sinners.
   - Explain to the child that this means that every person has done naughty things.
   - Give the child examples of sin: lying, stealing from others, hitting others, etc.
   - Acknowledge to the child that you have done naughty things, and that you too are a sinner.
   - Ask the child if they have ever been naughty. You may need to remind them of something naughty that they did recently.

Romans 3:23 *"...for all have sinned and fall short of the glory of God..."*

4. God loves us even though we are sinners. He wants to forgive us.
    *   Explain to the child that to forgive means to not be angry and to not remember that we have sinned.

John 3:16 *"For God so loved the world that He gave His only begotten Son, that whoever believes in Him should not perish but have everlasting life."*

5. Jesus is God's Son. He lived in heaven with His Father. A long time ago Jesus came to earth. He came to tell everybody how much God loves us.
    *   Explain to the child that because all people are sinners Jesus died on the cross. Jesus did not stay dead. Three days later He came back to life!

6. Because Jesus died and rose from the dead, God will forgive us for all of our sins if we believe in Jesus.

Romans 10:13 *"...for 'whoever calls on the name of the Lord shall be saved.'"*

7. Jesus now lives in heaven with His Father. He also wants to live inside of our hearts.
    *   Explain to the child that if they invite Jesus, He will come to live in their hearts. They will become God's children.

John 1:12 *"But as many as received Him, to them He gave the right to become children of God, to those who believe in His name:"*

8. Ask the child if they want Jesus to forgive them for their sins and live inside of their heart. Tell the child that even though God is in heaven, He hears us when we talk to Him.

9. If the child is willing, ask them to repeat, sentence by sentence, the following prayer.

Dear Lord Jesus,
I know that I am a sinner. Thank you for dying on the cross for my sins. Please come into my heart and be my Lord and Savior. Thank you for forgiving me. Help me to live for you everyday. In Jesus' name, Amen.

Appendix D
How to Develop Intimacy with God Through Daily Devotions
HOMEWORK

- **Intimacy** – *Marked by very close association, contact, or friendship developing through long association; very familiar; suggesting informal warmth or privacy; of a very personal nature.*

1. Choose the best time of day (morning or evening) to commit to setting aside devotional time. Don't set yourself up for discouragement by setting a goal that you will not be able to keep. Start small, and then add time as you grow. Begin with 15 minutes.

2. Choose a book of the Bible. Read one chapter, or less if it is a long chapter or verses that you want to ponder. In addition, you may also want to read a daily devotional. See suggestions listed below.

3. Pray. Specifically pray over the truths you have read, asking God to speak to you about how you can obey; what you should do or what you should change in your life in order to obey.

4. Spend a few minutes in quiet listening. This may be uncomfortable for you at first. Living in a noise-filled world, most of us are not accustomed to sitting quietly. Persevere and God will be faithful to speak to you. Remember that the Holy Spirit is dwelling in your heart and mind and can minister to you in your thoughts!

5. Journal. Write out what these verses mean to you.

- **Journal** – *A record of experiences, ideas, or reflections kept regularly for private use.*

1. Pray. Use the following to help you pray effectively:

    Adoration – *Worship and praise God*
    Confession – *Confess and repent of any known sins*
    Thanksgiving – *Expressing gratitude for God's blessings in your life*
    Supplication – *Humbly make requests for your needs and the needs of others*

2. Pray that God will help you to know and acknowledge His presence throughout your day.

Suggested Devotionals

Biblical Principles for a Strong Foundation, by Craig Caster

Daily Experience with God, by Andrew Murray

Drawing Near: Daily Readings for a Deeper Faith, by John F. MacArthur

Every Day with Jesus: First Steps with New Believers, by Greg Laurie

Experiencing God, by Henry T. Blackaby and Claude V. King

Meet the Bible: A Panorama of God's Word..., by Philip Yancey and Brenda Quinn

My Utmost for His Highest, by Oswald Chambers

On the Other Side of the Garden, by Virginia Ruth Fugate (married women)

Streams in the Desert, by Mrs. Charles E. Cowman

The One Year Book of Psalms, by William J. Peterson and Randy Petersen

The Power of a Praying Wife, by Stormie Omartian (married women)

Appendix E
Recommended Devotional and Discipleship Books

Devotional and Discipleship Books
The Bible

Strong Foundation Discipleship Workbook, Family Support Foundation

Meet the Bible by Philip Yancey and Brenda Quinn. (ISBN #0-310-22776-3)

Everyday With Jesus by Greg Laurie. (ISBN #1-56507-309-6)

Self-Confrontation by John C. Broger. (ISBN #1-878114-01-8)

Experiencing God by Henry Blackaby. (ISBN #0-8054-9954-7)

Drawing Near by John F. MacArthur. (ISBN #0-891-07758-8)

My Utmost for His Highest by Oswald Chambers. (ISBN #0-916441-42-3)

The One Year Book of Psalms by William J. Petersen and Randy Petersen. (ISBN #0-8423-4372-5)

Streams in the Desert by Mrs. Charles E. Cowman. (ISBN #0-310-23011-X)

Devotional and Discipleship Books for Children and Adolescents
Favorite Bible Stories for 3rd & 4th graders, by Rainbow Books. (ISBN #0-937282-41-3)

Talksheets™ - Junior High by Youth Specialties. (ISBN #0-310-20941-2)

Talksheets™ - More Junior High by Youth Specialties. (ISBN #0-310-57481-1)

Talksheets™ - High School by Youth Specialties. (ISBN #0-310-20931-5)

Talksheets™ - More High School by Youth Specialties. (ISBN #0-310-57491-9)

Devotions for Girls, ages 2–5 by Legacy Press. (ISBN #2-885358-61-X)

Devotions for Girls, ages 6–9 by Legacy Press. (ISBN #1-885358-60-1)

Devotions for Girls, ages 10–12 by Legacy Press. (ISBN #1-885358-54-7)

Devotions for Boys, ages 2–5 by Legacy Press. (ISBN #1-885358-96-2)

Devotions for Boys, ages 6–9 by Legacy Press. (ISBN #1-885358-97-0)

Devotions for Boys, ages 10–12 by Legacy Press. (ISBN #1-885358-98-9)

Bad to the Bone by Miles McPherson. (ISBN #0-7642-2280-5)

Growing Little Women by Donna J. Miller with Linda Holland. (ISBN #0-8024-2185-7)

Youth Devotions by Josh McDowell. (ISBN #0-842-34301-6)

Appendix F
Essentials for Single Parents

God's original plan for the family was to bring the man and woman together in the love and commitment of the marriage relationship. He would then bless their love and commitment with the gift of children. In an environment of intimacy, love, and submission to their Creator, the parents would love and train their children in God's ways. God desired that the fruit of the marriage relationship would be godly offspring.

> **Malachi 2:14-15** *"... the LORD has been witness between you and the wife of your youth... she is your companion and your wife by covenant...did He not make them one...? And why one? He seeks godly offspring..."*

When the man and woman turned from their Creator and sinned in the Garden of Eden, their intimacy with God was destroyed, they were expelled from the garden, and God's original plan for the family was affected. The Fall resulted in disunity and contention between the man and the women, which continues to dominate and destroy male and female relationships and marriages today. In addition, the offspring from the marriage inherited their parent's sin nature, and suffered like consequences. Single parent families, resulting from death, divorce and children born to unmarried mothers were a consequence of the fall of man.

> **Matthew 19:8** *"...Moses, because of the hardness of your hearts, permitted you to divorce your wives, but from the beginning it was not so."*

The first single parent family recorded in Scripture was Hagar, Abram and Sarai's (Abraham & Sarah) Egyptian maid, and her son, Ishmael, fathered by Abram. Sarai was unable to bear children, therefore she urged her husband to father a child with Hagar. Sarai later changed her mind and resented Hagar and her son. On two occasions Hagar had personal encounters with God.

Hagar's first meeting with God was before the birth of her son. Having been harshly treated by Sarai, she fled to the wilderness. God met her there and confirmed to her that He heard her affliction. He then counseled her to return to her home, and instructed her to name her son Ishmael, which means *God hears*.

Her second visitation with God was a few years later when she and Ishmael, driven from Abraham's home, departed and wandered in the wilderness. Certain that she and her son would soon die, she lifted up her voice and wept. God proved to this single parent once again that He is the God who hears. God comforted her, counseled her and opened her eyes to His will for her and her family.

> **Psalm 10:17-18** *"LORD, You have heard the desire of the humble; you will prepare their heart; you will cause Your ear to hear, To do justice to the fatherless and the oppressed, that the man of the earth may oppress no more."*

Read the account of Hagar and Ishmael in Genesis 16:1-16 and 21:9-21. Our culture has changed drastically since this family lived several thousand years ago, but single parents today share many of the same struggles, needs, feelings and emotions. Though this biblical account centers on a woman, single fathers and mothers alike know the hurt of rejection, loneliness, and fear for their children, as well as financial crisis. Consider the following important principles we learn from Hagar's experience with the God who hears.

- The Angel of the Lord (an Old Testament appearance of Jesus Christ) found Hagar in the wilderness.
- The Angel of the Lord guided her in the midst of her distress.
- He gave her His promises.
- He gave her hope for her future and the future of her son.
- Hagar responded to Him with faith calling God, *Elroi*, the God who sees.
- God heard the cries of her son.
- He spoke to Hagar about the welfare of her son.
- God commanded Hagar to lift up her son and hold him by the hand.
- God opened Hagar's eyes to see His provision.
- God was with Ishmael.

The important lesson that we learn from this story is that God sees, hears, cares and is waiting to intercede in the single-parent family. He loves the children in these homes, children who have suffered loss through death, divorce, or abandonment by those who were called by God to love and train them. We learn that God not only hears, but He heals. God is waiting to demonstrate His faithfulness and power to you and your children. You must respond as Hagar, with trust and obedience.

PRINCIPLES FOR SINGLE PARENT FAMILIES
1. RECEIVE YOUR DAILY STRENGTH AND GUIDANCE FROM THE LORD.
Single parents must spend time daily with the Lord. If our busy lifestyles overrule our intimacy with Christ, we will soon find ourselves powerless and overwhelmed by our circumstances.

We need God's perspective, wisdom, hope and guidance everyday. Parents must set the example, showing their children what it looks like to live a godly life in the midst of difficult circumstances!

Psalm 10:14 *"...The helpless commits himself to You; you are the helper of the fatherless."*

2. ENCOURAGE YOUR CHILD TO HAVE A RELATIONSHIP WITH THE OTHER PARENT.
Even if the other parent is not fulfilling their role in a consistent and biblical manner, your children need to have a relationship with that parent. Never compromise your child's physical or emotional well being. As your child grows and matures they will make their own choices about their relationship with the other parent.

3. MAKE EVERY EFFORT TO PROMOTE UNITY WITH THE OTHER PARENT.
If possible, agree on your rules and methods of discipline. In order for this to happen, parents must set aside all selfishness and unforgiveness. Life can become very stressful and confusing for a child who routinely has to go back and forth between different homes. When parents are able to work together, it helps to eliminate some of this confusion. When children witness their parents working together, it is a blessing for them. In some cases this is not possible. Never put your child or yourself in an emotionally or physically dangerous or damaging situation.

Romans 12:18 *"If possible, so far as it depends on you, be at peace with all men."* (NAU)

4. ACCEPT YOUR CHILD'S DESIRE TO SEE THE OTHER PARENT.
You must not allow yourself to be overwhelmed that your children are spending time with their other parent. Your attitude can set the stage for behavior problems. This transition is hard enough on the children. Don't let a poor attitude on your part add to the confusion. Be sensitive to your child when they arrive home after visiting the other parent, ready to listen and express happiness if they had a good time. If necessary remind them that they are home where your rules are the standard.

5. ESTABLISH YOURSELF AND YOUR CHILDREN IN A BIBLE-TEACHING CHURCH.
While there is no perfect church, there is a perfect church for you and your children. God's Word exhorts us to,

Hebrews 10:25 *"...not forsake our own assembling together, as is the habit of some, but encouraging one another..."*

Psalm 92:13 *"Those who are planted in the house of the LORD shall flourish in the courts of our God."*

The church is God's family. Your children need the love, stability, mentoring and parenting of other members of the family of God. Children from single-parent families need to see how two-parent families function, and have healthy role models.

Psalm 68:5-6 *"A father of the fatherless, a defender of widows, is God in His holy habitation. God sets the solitary in families..."*

James 1:27 *"Pure and undefiled religion before God and the Father is this: to visit orphans and widows in their trouble, and to keep oneself unspotted from the world."*

6. PURSUE FRIENDSHIP, FELLOWSHIP AND FUN WITH OTHER CHRISTIAN FAMILIES.
Being unmarried, many single parents feel that they do not fit in with married couples. Although because they are parents, they also do not feel that they fit in with singles. The result can be loneliness and isolation. If parents are lonely and isolated, their children will either follow their example, or pursue a social life on their own. Take advantage of extended family, your children's school activities, as well as opportunities to participate in fellowship and social functions through your church.

I John 1:7 *"But if we walk in the light as He is in the light, we have fellowship with one another, and the blood of Jesus Christ His Son cleanses us from all sin.*

7. IF THE NEED ARISES, SEEK GODLY COUNSEL.
If you feel that there are issues and situations in your life or the lives of your children that need immediate attention and solutions, you may want to seek biblical counseling from your pastor or a qualified Christian counselor.

Proverbs 11:14 *"Where there is no counsel, the people fall; but in the multitude of counselors there is safety."*

Proverbs 12:15 *"The way of a fool is right in his own eyes, but he who heeds counsel is wise."*

Appendix G – Worksheet
Disciplining Behavior, Not Attitudes & Revenge versus Training
Parent Discussion Homework
(Review and discuss as a couple, if married)

There is a lot of confusion when it comes to how parents should deal with bad attitudes. As you read through the following worksheet, I believe you will get a better perspective on how you should deal with your children's bad attitudes. What to do and also what not to do.

Attitude – A posture or position; feeling; opinion or mood.

Behavior – The act or manner of behaving.

- Behavior is something we do or don't do, by either breaking a rule or not doing what is expected of us.

God gave us our emotions.

"Be angry, and do not sin…" Psalms 4:4

Attitudes stem from the heart. The heart of a child can only be changed through their willingness to accept our authority, to receive from us the love of Christ and God's instructions for them.

Behaviors are changed through discipline/training, which is a corrective consequence.

- A rebellious heart is a miserable heart. It has no peace, joy, contentment, or lasting pleasure – all by God's design.

- If you know that your child is harboring bitterness toward you, or is rebelling against God's plan for their life, it requires your commitment to prayer and patience, without compromise. To compromise means several things for parents:

A) You allow a child's bad attitude to make you angry or resentful. You misrepresent God in the way you treat your child.

B) You allow the child's bad attitude to rob you of your inner peace.

C) You allow the child's bad attitude to dictate how you follow through with your agreed corrective consequence or you add to it.

We must allow our children to feel the way they feel.

In many cases children use this as a form of manipulation or revenge.

Manipulation - to control or play upon by artful, unfair, or insidious means, especially to one's own advantage.

• Some children will try to manipulate parents with attitudes so the parents will not follow through with a corrective consequence. They will even premeditatedly attempt to set the parents up to guilt the parents into allowing them to do something they would not normally permit them do.

• When children know that if they exhibit a bad attitude and it bothers their parents, this often prompts them to continue this behavior. This is our sin nature to get revenge. When their pouty, moody, or bad attitude provokes you to anger or sadness, you can be the one encouraging them to continue in this childish, manipulative practice. It takes two to play this game.

When we become angry, this gives our children satisfaction that is very damaging to his/her character development, your faith, and your authority. It is important to not show any emotion when correcting our children or giving a corrective consequence. Stay to the overall discipline plan. If you don't respond in the way they want or, in other words, if you don't serve the ball back to them, they will eventually quit playing this game.

If you have been playing this sinful game for a while it may take some time to break the bad habit, for both of you. Be patient and stay the course and the Lord will have victory.

Remember: if the bad attitude turns into a poor behavior choice such as: yelling at you, a bad word, kicking the wall, slamming the door, etc. then you follow through with a corrective consequence for that behavior, not the attitude.

Revenge **means to inflict injury in return for an insult.**

The Lord has instructed us to train up our children, not inflict injury in reaction to their childish and foolish choices. Is our attitude one that wants to get even with them and/or hurt them in some way because they just won't do what we ask? This is our problem, not our children's fault. The Lord gave us these children and sometimes it is hard to raise them in the way He desires. If you have the wrong motive when giving a corrective consequence to your children, you should repent immediately and ask for forgiveness from both your child and the Lord.

- **Revenge does not train our children, but instead, causes them to become defiant.** This will lead to division between the parents and the children.

   Training **= Discipline (which is a corrective consequence)**

- Training teaches our children. It is fair and not motivated by anger or revenge. It transforms and shapes our children's character without destroying or bringing division.

Notes:

_____

_____

_____

_____

_____

_____

_____

_____

_____

_____

_____

_____

_____

Appendix H – Worksheet
Disciplining Behavior
PARENT DISCUSSION HOMEWORK

1. Discuss together (if married) the *Train Behaviors—Not Attitudes* section of Week 8:Day 5 along with this handout. Write out what you believe are the typical bad attitudes you see manifesting in each of your children (you may want to use a separate sheet of paper for this exercise). It is important for you, as a husband and wife, to be unified in your plan for dealing with this. Try to clarify the difference between their attitudes and what the behavior is that may stem from these attitudes.

Child's Name: _____

_____

_____

_____

Child's Name: _____

_____

_____

_____

Child's Name: _____

_____

_____

_____

Child's Name: _____

_____

_____

_____

Child's Name: _____

_____

_____

_____

2. Discuss together, as husband and wife, how what you have learned changes any of the rules you have listed in this lesson. Would you change any? Why or Why not?

_____

_____

_____

_____

_____

_____

_____

_____

_____

_____

_____

_____

_____

_____

_____

_____

_____

_____

_____

Appendix I – Worksheet
Effective Listening Self-Evaluation
HOMEWORK

Complete the *Effective Listening Self-Evaluation* to help you become more aware of your listening habits. Answer each question thoughtfully and honestly.

COMMUNICATING KNOWLEDGE AND ATTITUDES

#	Do You…	Most of the Time	Frequently	Occasionally	Almost Never
1	…tune-out your child when you don't agree with them or don't want to hear?				
2	…concentrate on what is being said even if you are not really interested?				
3	…assume you know what your child is going to say and stop listening?				
4	…repeat in your own words what your child has just said?				
5	…listen to your child's viewpoint, even if it differs from yours?				
6	…remain open to learning something from them, even if it seems insignificant?				
7	…find out what words mean when they are used in ways not familiar to you?				
8	…form a rebuttal in your head while your child is still talking?				
9	…give the appearance of listening when you are not?				

10	...daydream while your child is talking?				
11	...listen for main ideas, not just facts?				
12	...recognize that words don't always mean the same thing to different people?				
13	...listen to only what you want to hear, blotting out your child's whole message?				
14	...look at your child when they are speaking?				
15	...concentrate on your child's meaning rather than how he or she looks?				
16	...know which words and phrases you tend to respond to emotionally?				
17	...think about what you want to accomplish with your communication?				

COMMUNICATING KNOWLEDGE AND ATTITUDES

#	Do You...	Most of the Time	Frequently	Occasionally	Almost Never
18	...plan the best time to say what you want to say?				
19	...think about how the other person might react to what you say?				
20	...consider the best way to communicate (written, spoken, and/or the timing)?				
21	...always care about your child's emotional condition when speaking to them (if they are stressed, sad, worried, hostile, disinterested, rushed, angry, etc.)?				
22	...adjust your communication to each child's personality?				

23	...think, *"I assumed he or she would know that?"* Assuming that your child knows and understands what you are communicating and/or communicated to them?				
24	...allow your child to respectfully vent negative feelings toward you without becoming defensive?				
25	...regularly make efforts to increase your listening efficiency?				
26	...take notes when necessary to help you remember?				
27	...listen closely without being distracted by surroundings?				
28	...listen to your child without judging or criticizing?				
29	...restate instructions and messages to be sure you understand correctly?				
30	...have a concerned attitude why your child feels the way they do?				

HOMEWORK

EFFECTIVE LISTENING SELF-EVALUATION SCORING INDEX

Circle the number that represents the category you checked on each item of the
Effective Listening Self-Evaluation.

#	Most of the Time	Frequently	Occasionally	Almost Never
1	1	2	3	4
2	4	3	2	1
3	1	2	3	4
4	4	3	2	1
5	4	3	2	1
6	4	3	2	1
7	4	3	2	1
8	1	2	3	4
9	1	2	3	4
10	1	2	3	4
11	4	3	2	1
12	4	3	2	1
13	1	2	3	4
14	4	3	2	1
15	4	3	2	1
16	4	3	2	1
17	4	3	2	1
18	4	3	2	1
19	4	3	2	1
20	4	3	2	1
21	4	3	2	1
22	4	3	2	1
23	1	2	3	4
24	4	3	2	1
25	4	3	2	1
26	4	3	2	1
27	4	3	2	1
28	4	3	2	1
29	4	3	2	1
30	4	3	2	1
Total				

GRAND TOTAL _____

(Examine your scores on the next page.)

110-120:   **Excellent Listener**   _____

99-109:   **Above Average Listener**   _____

88-98:   **Average Listener**   _____

77-87:   **Fair Listener**   _____

<77:   **Poor to Very Poor Listener**   _____

Appendix J – Worksheet
Improve Your Loving Communication Habits
HOMEWORK
(IF MARRIED, REVIEW AND DISCUSS AS A COUPLE)

After completing the *Effective Listening Self-Evaluation* and totaling your score, write out, by priority the areas you need to change. Review and discuss as a couple, if married.

1. _____
2. _____
3. _____
4. _____
5. _____
6. _____
7. _____

Then review *What Love Is and Is Not* from **Week 3:Day 4 – Week 4** of your workbook and write out, by priority, any unbiblical communication habits you have been practicing in your home that you need God's strength to change.

1. _____
2. _____
3. _____
4. _____
5. _____
6. _____
7. _____
8. _____
9. _____
10. _____

If you believe that you have not been demonstrating loving communication to your children (or a particular child), I strongly recommend that you follow the steps below to reconciliation.

1) Confess this to the Lord and ask Him to forgive you for not communicating love to *His* child/children.

   1 John 1:9 *"If we confess our sins, He is faithful and just to forgive us our sins and to cleanse us from all unrighteousness."*

2) Ask God to fill your heart with renewed love for your child/children.

   Romans 5:5 *"Now hope does not disappoint, because the love of God has been poured out in our hearts by the Holy Spirit who was given to us."*

3) Go to your child/children and make an age-appropriate confession. For example, *"I love you, but I know that I have not been showing you that love with my words. I have been very impatient (unkind, etc.) and I need to apologize. Please forgive me. I love you and I am so glad to be your mom/dad."*

4) Pray with your child.

Write out a prayer of commitment to seek the Lord to empower you to change in these areas and to become the parent to your child that God desires you to be.

_____
_____
_____
_____
_____
_____
_____
_____
_____

Appendix K – Worksheet
Ways to Tell Your Child "I Love You" Without Saying the Words
(REVIEW AND DISCUSS AS A COUPLE, IF MARRIED)

1. Attend their sports events, music performance, school plays, etc.

2. Find opportunities to trust your child by granting him/her a new area of responsibility.

3. Have a family picnic on a Sunday afternoon.

4. Walk in the rain and jump puddles together.

5. Listen to your child with all your attention.

6. Sit down together and watch your child's favorite television show.

7. Skip rocks together on a lake, pond, or river.

8. Say, "I'm proud of you."

9. After your teenager comes in from an outing, have popcorn together by the fireplace.

10. Tell your child about the things that you appreciate most about your own parents.

11. Have a family water-balloon fight (without you as the prime target).

12. Take an evening walk together.

13. Let your child catch you bragging about them to a friend.

14. Hug your child just because.

15. Postpone an appointment and, instead, do something your child enjoys doing.

16. Surprise your child by giving them a day off from school and spend the day together.

17. Tell your daughter that she is beautiful.

18. Tell your son that he is handsome.

19. Give your child grace when he/she has made a mistake.

20. Pray with your child everyday!

21. Seize appropriate opportunities to ask your child for his/her opinion.

22. Accept your child's unique personality traits.

23. Write a note expressing your love for them.

24. Bake or buy their favorite cookies.

25. Make popcorn and enjoy an old movie together.

26. Take them out to a restaurant for breakfast or dinner.

27. Take up a hobby that they particularly like to do.

28. Start a new hobby together.

Positive Reinforcement Applied Correctly
(REVIEW AND DISCUSS AS A COUPLE, IF MARRIED)

Positive reinforcement is using charts, graphs, or some other system to record a child's behavior, accompanied with ongoing rewards for good behavior. It is not very effective for the strong-willed child or beneficial for the compliant child for the following reasons.

- Love, not gifts or gimmicks, is the most powerful motivator and the most powerful way to build self-worth.

- Parents should be daily complimenting and praising their children because they are a gift from God, not tied to performance.

- Good behavior is expected, not rewarded. Our love toward them and how we show it should not change because of their failures.

- It can be beneficial for parents to use *special incentives* for a child who is struggling to overcome a particular weakness or personal challenge, such as bedwetting or academic struggles in school. For example: a special outing with the child or a material reward if they put forth the effort and improve in a specific area, not an ongoing reward system for perpetual behavior.

- If you have a compliant child whose natural bent is to please mom and dad they will find this system very appealing. However, if they have a brother or sister who is not compliant, but has a strong-willed bent (the strong-willed child), they will begin to resent their compliant sibling and struggle with their own self-worth. They can easily become discouraged because their compliant sibling receives more gifts and/or affirmation than they receive from what they perceive comes more natural to the compliant sibling.

- A perpetual system of rewards for good behavior for even a younger compliant child can set the stage for an entitlement mentality within the compliant child as he or she grows older. Once the rewards are removed, or become unsatisfactory, the compliant child may rebel in an effort to manipulate the reinstatement or improvement of the reward system to his or her benefit. The child has learned to selfishly seek the reward first and the good behavior has become only a means to a reward. Simple chores may not get done if they are not accompanied by a reward. This is teaching the child to serve only when it has personal benefit for them.

The parent's attitude toward their child's failures should be similar to when the child first began to walk; proud and excited when they first stood on their own and took their first steps. When they fell, the parents lovingly picked them up and encouraged them to try again, confident that in time they would develop, mature, and learn to walk on their own.

Appendix M – Worksheet
Eliminating Inappropriate Entertainment
PARENT DISCUSSION HOMEWORK
(REVIEW AND DISCUSS AS A COUPLE, IF MARRIED)

1.   Make a list of the music, videos, video games, magazines, posters, television programs, books, and other forms of entertainment that you and/or your children are currently enjoying that need to be eliminated. A simple question that will help you sort through this exercise is: *If Jesus visited your home today, do you believe He would approve of these materials?*

_____   _____   _____

_____   _____   _____

_____   _____   _____

_____   _____   _____

_____   _____   _____

2.   Do you need to make some changes in your home in this area?   ❏ Yes ❏ No

3.   Write out your commitment to make changes where needed and to diligently disciple your children on the subject of appropriate forms and content of entertainment.

_____

_____

EFFECTING CHANGE
Parents should be careful **_not_** to act impulsively or like tyrants in an effort to make these changes. Parents should **_not_** go through their teen's bedroom with a vengeance, tearing posters off the walls and destroying music. Your children should be approached with love, humility, and without anger or arrogance.

If you have previously allowed inappropriate entertainment in your home, take the following steps:

- Pray and seek the LORD'S guidance and wisdom.

- Discuss and agree as a couple on what items should be discarded.

- If your child has purchased these items with their own money, with either your explicit or implied permission, you may, if applicable, offer to replace the inappropriate entertainment with reasonable appropriate entertainment of your child's choice.

4. Discuss together your plan of action on how, **together**, you are going to make these changes. Write out your plans.

_____

_____

_____

_____

_____

Appendix N
Parent's Questionnaire for Teenagers

Choose an appropriate time when your teen is in a relaxed mood, possibly at dinner or while playing cards or a board game together, to ask them the following questions. Be casual, not intense! Do not simply hand your children the questionnaire to complete on their own. You may have to *prod* them a little. For example, if they answer question #3, "*I don't know,*" press them a little by asking, "*What are you doing at your age right now and what is important to you?*" Remember to give them time to answer. Don't tell them what *you* think they should answer, and *absolutely* do not belittle them!

1.   **What does the term *adolescence* mean?**

_____

_____

2.   **When does adolescence begin and end?**

_____

_____

_____

_____

3.   **The years between the ages of 13 and 18 is a time to be doing what?**

_____

_____

_____

_____

4.   **What is your definition of a mature adult, and when does someone become a mature adult?**

_____

_____

_____

_____

5.   What do you think you are currently doing that is helping you become a mature adult?

_____

_____

_____

_____

6.   What role do your parents play in your life right now?

_____

_____

_____

_____

Appendix O
Parent's Questionnaire for Youth Turning Age 18
(REVEALING THE PARENTS' REALITY VS. THE CHILD'S POSSIBLE DELUSION)

The following questions are designed for discussion with your child just prior to his or her 18th birthday and/or for parents who have a child over 18 living at home. They are most effective when discussed in a relaxed setting, for the purpose of stimulating your child to think, and to encourage a more adult relationship with your child as they are entering adulthood. It will also reveal what they believe is going to change or has changed in their relationship with you and your support of them.

Give one copy to your child to fill out & one copy for you to fill out. Set a date and time when you will sit down with your child to discuss their answers and share your answers (reality) with them.

1.   At 18 what do mom and I owe you besides our love?

_____

_____

2.   Do you believe that the reason we help you the way we do is because we love you?
❑ Yes   ❑ No

_____

_____

3.   Should we be doing more for you than we are currently doing?
❑ Yes   ❑ No   if yes, what should we be doing?

_____

_____

4.   Do we have the right to require anything of you in return for you continuing to live in our home?
❑ Yes   ❑ No   Explain.

_____

_____

5. If you do not agree with something we ask or require of you what should you do?

_____

_____

6. If you ignore our request and do something that we have made clear not to do, what do you think we should do? What should you do?

_____

_____

Appendix P – Blank Worksheet

Chore List

HOMEWORK

Child's Name _____

Chore: _____ Day _____ Time _____

Consequence _____

Chore: _____ Day _____ Time _____

Consequence _____

Chore: _____ Day _____ Time _____

Consequence _____

Chore: _____ Day _____ Time _____

Consequence _____

Chore: _____ Day _____ Time _____

Consequence _____

Chore: _____ Day _____ Time _____

Consequence _____

Chore: _____ Day _____ Time _____

Consequence _____

Chore: _____ Day _____ Time _____

Consequence _____

Family Rules and Corrective Consequences
HOMEWORK

Child's Name _____

Rule 1: _____

Consequence: _____

Rule 2: _____

Consequence: _____

Rule 3: _____

Consequence: _____

Rule 4: _____

Consequence: _____

Rule 5: _____

Consequence: _____

Rule 6: _____

Consequence: _____

Rule 7: _____

Consequence: _____

Rule 8: _____

Consequence: _____

Rule 9: _____

Consequence: _____

Rule 10: _____

Consequence: _____

Appendix R
Parent's Commitment Letter

Dear Parents,

As you begin these lessons, I want to encourage you that God will bless you as you seek His guidance and wisdom for your family.

Hebrews 11:6 *"...He is a rewarder of those who diligently seek Him."*

I also want to challenge you to make a serious commitment to finish the workbook. If God has led you to begin, know that He desires you to finish. After reading the following commitment, please sign and date below.

I commit to seek the Lord's will and guidance for my family, to attend each parenting class, to complete my assigned homework, and to pray for the other parents in the class.

_____   _____

Father's Signature   *Date*

_____   _____

Mother's Signature   *Date*

Appendix S
Parenting & the Blended Family
ADDRESSING THE 5 BIG ISSUES OF BLENDING A FAMILY

1. STEP-FAMILIES ARE OFTEN CREATED FROM A PAINFUL LOSS EFFECTING BOTH PARENTS AND CHILDREN.

There are many reasons why a divorce takes place and no matter what the reason is, when it happens, one or both parents and children are hurt.

For the parent:

If there was a divorce, it is important to understand why it happened, which includes your participation in it, if any.

It is our nature to place blame on others and the truth is in most, NOT all, but most cases, both husband and wife had some input as to why the divorce happened.

If a person is ignorant to what God's will is as a husband, wife, or parent, how can they honestly examine their own part in the failed marriage?

> **Matthew 7:2-5,** *"For with what judgment you judge, you will be judged; and with the measure you use, it will be measured back to you. And why do you look at the speck in your brother's eye, but do not consider the plank in your own eye? Or how can you say to your brother, 'Let me remove the speck from your eye'; and look, a plank is in your own eye? Hypocrite! First remove the plank from your own eye, and then you will see clearly to remove the speck from your brother's eye."*

HERE ARE 4 IMPORTANT STEPS TO HELP IN THE HEALING PROCESS.

A. Spend Some Time Investigating what God's will is for a husband & wife.

If you did not have a good example and you were never discipled in how to be a husband, wife, or parent, then there is a good chance you made some mistakes and have some ownership in the discord of your previous marriage.

To be healed and also to learn not to repeat the same mistakes, you need to take some time and investigate what God's will is for you as a husband, wife, or parent as you are now going through these parenting materials.

Matthew 7:5 said *"Hypocrite! First remove the plank from your own eye, and then you will **see clearly** to remove the speck from your brother's eye."*

"...First remove the plank from your own eye..." means to know what your faults were; using the Word of God as your only measuring tool.

I strongly encourage you to take some time and go through a good biblically based marriage study such as our DVD series *Marriage is a Ministry* (www.parentingministry.org). You will learn what God's purpose is for marriage and His instructions in how to fulfill your spouse's companionship needs.

Remember: God created marriage and if we do not look to Him (His Word) for how to do it correctly and instead, lean on our own understanding and do it wrong – this is sin. You can't ask God to forgive you if you don't know what it is you did wrong. Also, you don't want to repeat, in your current marriage, what it is you did in the past marriage.

B. Find healing through Forgiveness:
Christ is the only one who can heal the hurts that are caused by a divorce and/or a spouse who hurt you.

If you want to be healed and move forward, you need to take these steps.

> **1 John 1:9,** *"If we confess our sins, He is faithful and just to forgive us our sins and to cleanse us from all unrighteousness."*

We need to confess our sins to the Lord; those things that His Word revealed that was your part in the failed marriage. Can we, as Christians, ever justify our sin because a person has hurt us? **NO**. Can we justify our sin due to ignorance? **NO**

> **Proverbs 28:13,** *"He who covers his sins will not prosper, But whoever confesses and forsakes them will have mercy."*

We are also instructed to confess our sins to the one we have sinned against.

James 5:16, *"Confess your trespasses to one another, and pray for one another, that you may be healed. The effective, fervent prayer of a righteous man avails much."*

Let me ask you – Do you want to be healed from the pain of the divorce? Remember *James 5:16*. If we do this we will be healed.

You can do this in a phone call, a letter, or an email. The Word of God is clear – you must ask them to forgive you. If remarried, it is very important to involve your current spouse in this process. You don't want to promote any jealousy.

C. You also need to be willing to forgive them.

Mark 11:25, *"And whenever you stand praying, if you have anything against anyone, forgive him, that your Father in heaven may also forgive you your trespasses."*

You can do this in the same letter or email where you are asking them to forgive you. To tell them you forgive them does not mean what they did was ok or right. The purpose for forgiving them is for Christ's sake, to do *His* will and for your own healing (see **Forgiveness & Reconciliation** in the Appendices).

D. Seeking Reconciliation with ex-spouse is not always possible.

Matthew 5:23-24, *"Therefore if you bring your gift to the altar, and there remember that your brother has something against you, leave your gift there before the altar, and go your way. First be reconciled to your brother, and then come and offer your gift."*

Reconciliation with ex-spouse or the child's other bio-parent means:

    a.   To agree not to speak evil of each other, especially in front of the children.

    b.   To not discuss certain subject matters in front of the children (financial issues, child support, etc.).

    c.   To try and cooperate in the rules and disciplining of the children to minimize the child's confusion and increase the effectiveness of raising them toward maturity.

    d.   Work together and cooperating where the children are concerned, spending time with other parents, vacation, etc.

Abuse, violence, drugs, alcohol, or they are living a very unhealthy lifestyle; all can contribute to reasons why reconciliation may not be possible.

By not attempting to do this when possible, not only will you not experience this healing from the Lord, in many cases, bitterness will come out in ways that will hurt your children — bad-mouthing the other parent, unwilling to work with other parent and so on. There is no guarantee the other parent will cooperate and/or be reasonable. Your part is to be open to working on it but without compromise.

> **Hebrews 12:15,** *"...looking carefully lest anyone fall short of the grace of God; lest any root of bitterness springing up cause trouble, and by this many become defiled..."*

Those roots of bitterness will spring up and spew poison upon those around you.

- Speaking in an un-honorable way toward the other parent.

- Unwilling to work with them for the children's sake in scheduling time with the other parent, or setting the rules, and disciplines.

- Your unwillingness to forgive will also make a mockery of your faith. Hypocrisy is Satan's tool to push our children away from trusting God and breeds rebellion in our children.

When you come to Christ to praise Him, to receive from Him, to ask for His help and blessings, do you want Him to hear you and respond to you?

Remember **Matthew 5:23-24** *"...go your way. First be reconciled to your brother..."* Trusting the Lord means you are willing to obey Him and do what He asks of you. Are you ready? Pray and ask for His grace to help you.

Helping the Children — Important Considerations

Divorce is one of the most devastating things a child can experience. **Most children in blended families have experienced some very difficult trials and deep wounds that are all too often not dealt with before they are asked to accept a step mom or dad and maybe step sisters and/or brothers** – often the parent seeks out their own emotional support through a relationship before the children had time to adjust and find some healing themselves.

It is very common for children to believe they are responsible in some way; that they are the reason why the divorce took place. They believe if they could have just acted better or helped more in some way then the divorce wouldn't have happened. It is very important for you to reassure them often that this is not the case.

You need to reassure them that their normal misbehaving had nothing to do with the divorce and/or they could not have done anything more to stop the divorce. This reassurance needs to be given with gentleness and the utmost empathy for your child. Some children struggle more and/or longer than others in this area. So if one of your children is taking a longer time working through this, be patient with them and be willing to listen and reassure them with love and truth.

It is also very common for children to be confused over why God would let this happen. The child can not understand that if *they* love and need both of their parents so much, *why* is God not stopping this from happening?

Helping your child work through this.

A.   *Help them see things from an eternal perspective.*

They need to understand how God's sovereignty and His providential permission work for His ultimate purpose – even in painful situations. Many parents feel their children need to be at least 12 or older to be able to grasp and understand this truth but I have witnessed young children at the age of 6 be able to grasp this and accept it. The truth is that children can grasp the truth much easier than adults. Yes – the way you explain it to them is very important. A parent needs to present this truth at the child's level and believe it for themselves.

The word Sovereign means - *Possessing supreme power, unlimited wisdom, absolute authority, All-knowing past, present, and future.*

Daniel 4:35 (The Message), *"At the end of the seven years, I, Nebuchadnezzar, looked to heaven. I was given my mind back and I blessed the High God, thanking and glorifying God, who lives forever: "His sovereign rule lasts and lasts, his kingdom never declines and falls. Life on this earth doesn't add up to much, but God's heavenly army keeps everything going. No one can interrupt his work, no one can call his rule into question.*

Psalm 139:1-18 *"O LORD, You have searched me and known me. You know my sitting down and my rising up; You understand my thought afar off. You comprehend my path and my lying down, And are acquainted with all my ways. For there is not a word on my tongue, But behold, O LORD, You know it altogether. You have hedged me behind and before, And laid Your hand upon me. Such knowledge is too wonderful for me; It is high, I cannot attain it. Where can I go from Your Spirit? Or where can I flee from Your presence? If I ascend into heaven, You are there; If I make my bed in hell, behold, You are there. If I take the wings of the morning, And dwell in the uttermost parts of the sea, Even there Your hand shall lead me, And Your right hand shall hold me. If I say, "Surely the darkness shall fall on me," Even the night shall be light about me; Indeed, the darkness shall not hide from You, But the night shines as the day; The darkness and the light are both alike to You. For You formed my* *inward parts; You covered me in my mother's womb. I will praise You, for I am fearfully and wonderfully made; Marvelous are Your works, And that my soul knows very well. My frame was not hidden from You, When I was made in secret, And skillfully wrought in the lowest parts of the earth. Your eyes saw my substance, being yet unformed. And in Your book they all were written, The days fashioned for me, When as yet there were none of them. How precious also are Your thoughts to me, O God! How great is the sum of them! If I should count them, they would be more in number than the sand; When I awake, I am still with You."*

These verses teach that God knows each of us intimately. All of our days were fashioned or created by Him. Before you knew God, or accepted Him as Lord and Savior He knew you and predestined all the days of your life. God gave all of us the gift of freewill. He chose you that you might follow Him, and gave you the freedom to accept or reject Him.

Psalm 139:1-6 (The Message), *"GOD, investigate my life; get all the facts firsthand. I'm an open book to you; even from a distance, you know what I'm thinking. You know when I leave and when I get back; I'm never out of your sight. You know everything I'm going to say before I start the first sentence. I look behind me and you're there, then up ahead and you're there, too—your reassuring presence, coming and going. This is too much, too wonderful—I can't take it all in!*

God has given mankind freedom to do good and the freedom to do evil; that includes doing things their own way. Therefore, the reality is that God's children live in a fallen world and are often touched by the evil around them that others have caused. If God shielded His children from all evil, allowing only good, the unsaved would only be motivated to turn to Him for the guarantee of an easy life.

You can give your child an example using your own relationship with them. You can say to your child, "If you only told me you love me and do what I ask of you if I give you something like a toy or candy, then you are only doing it for what you can get. That's not love."

So, it's not God who made these bad things happen, but God promises to help you through it.

James 1:13-14 (The Message), *"Don't let anyone under pressure to give in to evil say, "God is trying to trip me up." God is impervious to evil, and puts evil in no one's way. The temptation to give in to evil comes from us and only us. We have no one to blame but the leering, seducing flare-up of our own lust. Lust gets pregnant, and has a baby: sin! Sin grows up to adulthood, and becomes a real killer.*

God does not make bad things happen, but when they do happen, He does want to help us.

God is the only one who can heal the broken hearts, so if the child is questioning God, "Why did You make this happen." Or they are mad at God for this happening; blaming Him, then they are not allowing God to help them and heal their broken hearts.

> **Matthew 13:15,** *"For the hearts of this people have grown dull. Their ears are hard of hearing, And their eyes they have closed, Lest they should see with their eyes and hear with their ears, Lest they should understand with their hearts and turn, So that I should heal them."*

The child needs to be praying for the faith to trust God in His perfect plan in giving all people free will. They also need to pray for God to help them through this difficult time and for Him to heal their broken heart; to respond to those thought that they are to blame in some way with, "No, I am not to blame. God loves me and I did not cause this to happen".

Reassure your children that God knows the pain they are experiencing and it is His will to help them through this painful ordeal.

B.   It is important that they also don't become bitter at you or the other parent.

> **Hebrews 12:15,** *"...looking carefully lest anyone fall short of the grace of God; lest any root of bitterness springing up cause trouble, and by this many become defiled..."*

This teaches us that if we become bitter at someone this will cause us to become bitter ourselves. We will feel sad, angry, and confused as well as treat others in a bad way.

A good analogy: say there was a berry bush in the back yard and it was poisonous and every time you ate of it, it made you feel really sick. You wouldn't eat those berries yourself if you wanted someone else to become sick.

It's the same with anger and bitterness. If they were mad at someone, would they eat those berries themselves, hoping the person they were mad at would suffer in some way? NO – that would be foolish. That's why God teaches us not to be bitter at others, even if they hurt us, but we are to forgive them because the only one we are hurting is ourselves if we do not.

Becoming bitter and being angry at someone and not forgiving them is like eating those poisonous berries.

> **Mark 11:25,** *"And whenever you stand praying, if you have anything against anyone, forgive him, that your Father in heaven may also forgive you your trespasses."*

Just like God forgiving us for our sins, He tells us we must forgive those who hurt us.

You might have to help them with this prayer: *Lord, help me not to be bitter at my dad/mom. Lord, please help me to forgive them and not become angry. In Jesus' name – Amen*

Share with them that forgiveness is the only means of breaking the cycle of blame and suffering, and in many cases destructive, sinful behaviors that stem from these hurts.

Forgiveness offers the way out! It does not settle all questions of blame and fairness, and often evades those questions altogether. It can allow a relationship to start over, and begin anew if possible and heals the wounds caused by others.

The story in the Bible about Joseph found in Genesis is a great Bible Study to help your children see how God works in these painful trials.

This truth is demonstrated in the life of Joseph in *Genesis chapters 37-45*. Though he was mistreated, betrayed, abandoned by his brothers, sold into slavery, and imprisoned – not because he did anything wrong; all these hurtful things that touched Joseph's life happened because of bad choices that his father and brothers made. However, He refused to allow the root of bitterness to take hold of his life. Shortly before being reunited with his brothers, he testified of the healing work that God had done in his life during the years of separation, as demonstrated in the naming of his sons. In *Genesis 41:51-52* we read:

> *"Joseph named the firstborn Manasseh, 'For,' he said, [which means] 'God has made me forget all my trouble in all my father's household.' "*

> *"He named the second Ephraim, 'For,' he said, [which means] 'God has made me fruitful in the land of my affliction...' "*

To <u>forget</u> in this sense does not mean to cease to remember, but *to <u>let go</u>,* to cease to let the memory of hurtful things control your present life. Joseph's blessed life and *fruitfulness* was directly related to his *trusting God and not harboring bitterness.* The word resentment means *to feel again.* Joseph chose to trust God with these painful experiences and his past.

UNFORGIVENESS IMPRISONS US TO THE PAST HURTS AND HINDERS THE POTENTIAL FOR A FRUITFUL LIFE.

During Joseph's years alone in Egypt, he allowed God to heal his heart, which had been broken by his own brothers. Later, when given the opportunity, Joseph extended love, forgiveness, and grace to his brothers. Joseph speaks to them in *<u>Genesis 45:5, 7, & 15</u>*.

"Now do not be grieved or angry with yourselves, because you sold me here, for God sent me before you to preserve life...and to keep you alive by a great deliverance...He kissed all his brothers and wept on them, and afterward his brothers talked with him."

JOSEPH TRULY BELIEVED:

Genesis 50:20, *"But as for you, you meant evil against me; but God meant it for good, in order to bring it about as it is this day, to save many people alive."*

"...meant it for good..." means God will, as He did with Joseph, take these painful experiences in our life and use them to make us stronger in our faith to Christ.

There was no blaming, no explanations demanded, only the voice of mercy and forgiveness. The way was cleared for Joseph and his brothers to be reunited and begin a new relationship.

Romans 8:28, *"And we know that all things work together for good to those who love God, to those who are the called according to His purpose."*

2. HELPING THE CHILD WITH A NEGATIVE PRE-EXISTING DISPOSITION TOWARD STEPPARENT.

When a child is still hurting over their parents getting a divorce and/or were hoping that their parents would get back together, many of these children struggle with accepting the new marriage, the stepparent, their authority, or their siblings.

This is why it is so important to help the children work through the forgiveness and healing prior to moving ahead into another marriage relationship.

In some cases, especially with children that are 12 and up, if they don't want any help and/or choose to hang onto the hurt or bitterness, there is little a parent or parents can do other than pray, be patient, and continue to fulfill their role as a parent.

NOTE: I don't believe a child should be able to hold their parents hostage and keep them from moving forward into a relationship with someone and getting remarried. However, a parent should allow enough time for a child to work through these things. I suggest a minimum of 1 year.

After you are re-married, exercising patience without compromising your authority and the discipline is very important.

As a step in Dad or Mom, God has called you to be the authority over your children.

Ephesians 6:1-2, *"Children, obey your parents in the Lord, for this is right. "Honor your father and mother," which is the first commandment with promise:"*

As a step-parent, you needed to accept your God given role in this family when you said, "I Do." When you got married, you did not only say that to your spouse, you said it to God also. "I do" means, "I take this spouse to tend to him/her according to Your will God." "I do accept the responsibility as a husband/wife and parent in this family." "I do accept the authority role to the children that dwell within our home; to love and train them according to Your will."

When a husband and wife embrace this and together manifest this before their children, this will create the correct reality within the home and the children will eventually yield and embrace it.

Helping the children understand God's perspective in raising children.

It is important for you, as the parents, to explain to your children the following: As Christians, we are here to do the Lord's will. God is the Creator of the family and we are looking to Him for how to run our family. His Word teaches that both parents are to work together in the training of the children.

God has defined the authority in the home.

Colossians 3:18-21, *"Wives, submit to your own husbands, as is fitting in the Lord. Husbands, love your wives and do not be bitter toward them. Children, obey your parents in all things, for this is well pleasing to the Lord. Fathers, do not provoke your children, lest they become discouraged."*

The fathers are the head over the homes but the mother is also part of that authority structure over the home. They are to work together in the training up of **_all_** the children in the home.

Romans 13:1-2, *"Let every soul be subject to the governing authorities. For there is no authority except from God, and the authorities that exist are appointed by God. Therefore whoever resists the authority resists the ordinance of God, and those who resist will bring judgment on themselves."*

God is the one who establishes the authority within the home and we need to trust Him. If we don't, verse 2 says, *"...those who resist will bring judgment on themselves."* It's not talking about damnation but more of God's disciplines, which means; a parent who does not accept this authority or a child who will not yield to it will experience inner turmoil: no joy, no peace, and no contentment. Feelings of confusion, anger, and frustration will fill their hearts and minds; depression will follow.

God's Word says in ***1 Peter 5:5-7*** *Likewise you younger people, submit yourselves to your elders. Yes, all of* *you be submissive to one another, and be clothed with humility, for "God resists the proud, But gives grace to the humble." Therefore humble yourselves under the mighty hand of God, that He may exalt you in due time, casting all your care upon Him, for He cares for you.*

1) *"...Submit yourself to your elders..."* includes the stepparent.

2) *"...God resists the proud..."* He allows the internal misery and depression to continue until they yield to Him.

3) *"...But gives grace to the humble..."* Those who accept God's will; His authority and yields to it, He will bless them and give them the strength to walk according to His will.

4) *"...casting all your cares upon Him..."* If they turn to God, asking for the strength to be healed from the pain of the divorce and accept their parents' decision, God will give them that inner peace and joy that comes only from Him.

Both parents need to exercise patience.

2 Timothy 2:24-26, *"And a servant of the Lord must <u>not quarrel</u> but <u>be gentle</u> to all, <u>able to teach</u>, patient, <u>in humility correcting those</u> who are in opposition, if God perhaps will grant them repentance, so that they may know the truth, and that they may come to their senses and escape the snare of the devil, having been taken captive by him to do his will."*

God gives parents some clear instructions here on how to respond to those children who are struggling in this area:

1) *"...Not quarrel..."* means don't argue. It takes 2 to argue – use His Word as your defense.

2) *"...Gentle..."* means not being harsh, mean, or in anger; but in love.

3) *"...Able to teach..."* means bringing clarity to the situations. This includes helping them understand why you are an authority within the home. Helping them to understand why they are struggling. Making it clear for them how to find healing from the trials that have touched their life. Also, why their wrong behavior and breaking a particular rule must be disciplined.

4) *"...Patient..."* it's a process – not in your time. You need to press on & stay consistent.

5) *"...In humility..."* with a humble heart, not acting like you are better than them, but you are equal in God's sight. You've been called & anointed by God to this position; you did not earn it.

6) *"...Correcting..."* means not retreating; you need to accept your authority; follow through and implement the discipline. Not letting the child's bad attitude or the threat of going to live with the other parent, dictate if you follow through or not. It also means not <u>Disengaging, becoming solitude, or giving up.</u>

NOTE: doing the will of God as a husband, wife, and parent is one of the most powerful things you can do to help them work through this negative pre-existing disposition toward either of you.

Very Important: These principles are not something you cover once. Life's situations will give you many opportunities to revisit these important biblical principles and apply them toward your parent/child relationship.

3. MAKE SURE THAT THE 'NO HOME SYNDROME' DOESN'T HAPPEN TO YOUR CHILDREN

After the divorce, many children find they are living in two separate home environments whereby they are essentially shuffled back and forth between the homes of the biological parents on a weekly, monthly, or bi-monthly schedule.

This can create some difficulty for the child to feel settled and secure in one or both homes. If both parents have remarried and their new step-parents have children, this adds to the difficulty for them to adapt and feel like either of their homes feel like 'home'.

HERE ARE SOME PRACTICAL SUGGESTIONS TO HELP THESE CHILDREN THROUGH THIS.

A. *Unity in Leadership within the Blended Family Home*

It is critical that the leaders (husband & wife) of the blended family are unified and working together according to God's management style in the home. Biology does not supersede God's command for the man to lead and the woman to be his helpmate in leading, loving, and training all the children dwelling in the home.

> **Ephesians 5:30-33,** *"For we are members of His body, of His flesh and of His bones. "For this reason a man shall leave his father and mother and be joined to his wife, and the two shall become one flesh." This is a great mystery, but I speak concerning Christ and the church. Nevertheless let each one of you in particular so love his own wife as himself, and let the wife see that she respects her husband."*

B. *Cooperative Parenting*

Make a sincere attempt at developing a cooperative parenting plan between your home and the home of the other biological parent. Pray and ask the Lord to impress upon the heart of the other biological parent the long term importance of cooperative parenting with a plan to help in the child's weekly or monthly transitions between homes.

Don't let the enemy influence the way you communicate with your ex-spouse in developing and managing the cooperative parenting plan, or any other matter that is better served by both parties participating cooperatively. Do not attempt to dominate your ex-spouse or control all of the decisions you think are important. Make room for cooperation, without compromise.

> **Ephesians 4:29,** *"Let no corrupt communication proceed out of your mouth, but that which is good to the use of edifying, that it may minister grace unto the hearers."*

> **Ephesians 5:21,** *"Submitting yourselves one to another in the fear of God."*

C.   *Home Coming: When the Child Returns from the Other Parents' Home*

Especially with younger children it is important to give particular attention to the child returning from the other home. They may want to share about their adventures, challenges, and disappointments. It is important that you fight the temptation to be jealous of any wonderful adventures they had or to belittle their disappointments. Be a good listener. Rejoice with them when they are rejoicing about special opportunities they were able to experience even if there is unresolved conflict between you and the other parent. Don't let the unresolved issues between ex-spouses infect your relationship with your children. Be careful to speak only what will edify your child and impart grace to them about the other parent, their habits, their spoiling the child or their mistakes with the child.

If your child reveals that he lives by less godly standards while in the home of the other parent, I suggest you not try and discipline them for something the other parent permitted. Instead, be wise about when and how to disciple your child on these matters as a part of your regular discipleship time with your child. Another helpful thing is to consider a little extra grace for a very short period of time when the child first arrives back in your home. If there is no or very little structure at the other home, you can expect the child to need some time to adjust. For the first day you should use a gentle reminder (once – not two or three times) or warning before you discipline them.

> **Ecclesiastes 3:1-8,** *"To everything there is a season, A time for every purpose under heaven: A time to be born, And a time to die; A time to plant, And a time to pluck what is planted; A time to kill, And a time to heal; A time to break down, And a time to build up; A time to weep, And a time to laugh; A time to mourn, And a time to dance; A time to cast away stones, And a time to gather stones; A time to embrace, And a time to refrain from embracing; A time to gain, And a time to lose; A time to keep, And a time to throw away; A time to tear, And a time to sew; A time to keep silence, And a time to speak; A time to love, And a time to hate; A time of war, And a time of peace.*

Different seasons in the life of the child require different approaches to managing the reconnecting of your relationship with your child after they return from their time with their other parent. You are learning in this study some important insights on how to always communicate in a loving way to your children.

D.   *Not a Weapon*

Your child is not a weapon to fight the battles between you and your ex-spouse. Except for extreme circumstances of imminent serious danger to the health of your child, do not use your child as a weapon against your ex-spouse to achieve any of your own goals.

> **Matthew 5:43-48,** *"You have heard that it was said, 'You shall love your neighbor and hate your enemy.' But I say to you, love your enemies, bless those who curse you, do good to those who hate you, and pray for those who spitefully use you and persecute you, that you may be sons of your Father in heaven; for He makes His sun rise on the evil and on the good, and sends rain on the just and on the unjust. For if you love those who love you, what reward have you? Do not even the tax collectors do the same? And if you greet your brethren only, what do you do more than others? Do not even the tax collectors do so? Therefore you shall be perfect, just as your Father in heaven is perfect."*

> **Remember:** your ex-spouse is not the enemy. Satan is the enemy. How you interact with your ex-spouse should reflect the will of God, not your own will.

> **Romans 12:21,** *"Do not be overcome by evil, but overcome evil with good."*

> **Ephesians 6:12,** *"For we do not wrestle against flesh and blood, but against principalities, against powers, against the rulers of the darkness of this age, against spiritual hosts of wickedness in the heavenly places."*

There can be many reasons and/or situations why you can bad-mouth or be tempted to use your child as leverage either against or to get something from your ex-spouse, but it is important that you do not do this. It is not only sin, it also hurts your child and fosters these feelings of not belonging.

E.   *Being Fair in Your Parenting*

> Many homes of blended families have the presence of step-siblings. In these cases it is important to make certain there are no favorites played on a day-to-day basis. You have made a commitment to God to love and train all of the children He gives to you either through biology or remarriage with no partiality.

1 Timothy 5:21, *"I charge you before God and the Lord Jesus Christ and the elect angels that you observe these things without prejudice, doing nothing with partiality."*

James 2:1 (NIV), *"My brothers, as believers in our glorious Lord Jesus Christ, don't show favoritism.*

4.   FINANCIAL IMPACT

The financial impact of divorce can be significant. Divorce can impact the resources of one parent differently than the other parent. No matter what the reasons for your financial condition, you should employ a financial strategy that protects the child from playing any role in resolving financial differences between you and your ex-spouse.

Also, do not permit any pressure from either your ex-spouse or child to influence you to make unwise financial decisions and deter you from following your financial expense budget you and your spouse have agreed to. Make sure you are employing proper financial planning and maintaining your financial boundaries for the long term financial health of your family.

1 Peter 5:6-9, *"Therefore humble yourselves under the mighty hand of God, that He may exalt you in due time, casting all your care upon Him, for He cares for you. Be sober, be vigilant; because your adversary the devil walks about like a roaring lion, seeking whom he may devour. Resist him, steadfast in the faith, knowing that the same sufferings are experienced by your brotherhood in the world."*

When circumstances arise that impact your budget such as sports, trips, special events, planning for education, cars, and many other possible considerations, it is good practice to prayerfully consider inviting your ex-spouse to participate in a manner that is reasonable. Remember, this is an invitation, not an expectation.

Before you extend the invitation you should have already established a plan for making the final decisions on financial matters based upon factors such as your blended family's financial condition, the financial practices with the other children in your home, the plan you and your current spouse have agreed upon, and other possible criteria.

In some cases your ex-spouse will not participate for financial, personal, or selfish reasons. This is not a time to inform your child that they will miss the opportunity because of some failure of the other parent. Your communication with your child should not imply anything negative about the other parent or project fault on your ex-spouse for a failure to meet your expectations for financial participation.

Simply communicate your family's decision regarding the matter without casting dispersion or blame on others.

If a financial situation arises and it is beyond your ability to pay for it entirely, it is ok to let your child know what you can do toward helping and let them (your child) talk with their other biological parent to see if they can pay the rest. Open, honest, and fair is the key to helping your child in these situations.

Warning:

If the step-father is the primary bread winner in the family and his children are living in the home, it is very important to make sure all the children are treated fairly when it comes to these financial decisions. Those items mentioned above, inheritances, and trusts for your biological children are handled differently and I strongly suggest you seek out good financial planning advice in this area.

5. NEEDING MORE AFFIRMATION DURING ADOLESCENCE FROM THE SAME GENDERED PARENT

Different seasons of emotional growth in the life of the child may bring very natural desires in the child to spend more time with the same gender parent. This is very normal between the ages of 12 and 17 years old. Don't be offended and/or allow the enemy to cause you to become bitter and treat your child or ex-spouse in a sinful way.

It is very normal for a young man to desire more time with his father and a young woman to desire more time with her mother. This should not be discouraged. Even if the living arrangements dictate a specific amount of time in each home, be flexible to meet the desires of your child to spend extra time with the other parent as the child grows into adolescence. Resist the temptation to use this change as a bargaining tool against your ex-spouse and become jealous or turn it into a money issue. NOTE: Not if it is a toxic and/or dangerous environment for your child.

> **Proverbs 22:6,** *"Train up a child in the way he should go, and when he is old he will not de-part from it.*

This is not a guarantee but an idiom that means: we are to adapt to our children's needs to love and raise them without compromising the truth.

Remember *Ecclesiastes 3:1-8*? To everything there is a season...

Be conscious of your child's sensitivities regarding the ways affection is given to them as they develop into young men and women. The God ordained changes they will experience during the season of adolescence will possibly impact the child in their need to spend more time with a particular parent. Good communication and loving responses to the child's requests should be the standard here. Don't be offended. This is a natural season for this change to take place. Instead, look for ways to reinforce your love to the child and be willing to adjust the visitation, if necessary.

> **Philippians 2:3,** *"Let nothing be done through selfish ambition or conceit, but in lowliness of mind let each esteem others better than himself."*

Appendix T
Glossary of Words and Terms

Abide — means, *"To stay, remain, to continue in a place, to endure without yielding."*

Accountability — means subject to giving an account, answerable, a statement explaining one's conduct.

Admonition — (Eph. 6:4) *nouthesia* (Greek), warning, exhortation, any word of encouragement or reproof, which leads to correct behavior. It is the idea of having a corrective influence on someone by imparting understanding.

Affectionately longing or fond affection — (1 Thes 2:8a) *homeiromai* Geek means to long for someone passionately and earnestly, and, being linked to a mother's love, is intended here to express an affection so deep and compelling as to be unsurpassed. Ancient inscriptions on the tombs of dead babies sometimes contained this term when parents wanted to describe their sad longing for a too-soon-departed child.

Approve — means to continually put to the test, examine prior to the approval of your action.

Arrogant or proud — means to be conceited; feeling or showing self-importance, disregard for others. Prideful; giving oneself high rank, or an undue degree of significance.

Attitude — is a posture or position; a feeling, opinion or mood.

Bears all things — bears, *stego* (Greek), means to hide, to conceal. Love hides the faults of others, or covers them up. It keeps out resentment as the ship keeps out the water, or the roof the rain.

Behavior — on the other hand, is "the act or manner of behaving.

Believing — is *pisteuo* (Greek), and means having faith in, or to be firmly persuaded in something. It indicates that there is an attitude of expectant hope.

Blamelessly — means faultless, able to stand a critics' scrutiny. As you move along in obedience to God's will, you are transformed into the image of Christ, and your Godly behavior becomes evident to others.

Brag — to talk about oneself, or things pertaining to oneself, in a boastful manner; to boast.

Bring them up — (Eph. 6:4) *ektrepho* (Greek), to nourish, rear, feed. To nurture, rear, to bring up to maturity such as children, in the sense of to train or educate.

Charged, Implore, Urging — *martyromenoi* (Greek), implies the "delivery of truth" and was likely meant to convey the more directive functions of a father. A good father encourages and provides guidance, not that the mother doesn't also.

Chastening or discipline — is the same Greek word used in Ephesians 6:4 (*paideia),* and means correction or training. In other words, there is a consequence for every offense; some type of training/correction will follow.

Cheat — (take you captive NASB, Col 2:8) means to plunder or rob as when plunder is taken in war. In this case it is to rob believers of the complete riches that they have in Christ as revealed in the Word, plus His power and intervention.

Communication — the act of communicating is the exchange of thought, message, or information.

Confess — is to agree with God that what you did ignorantly or deliberately was a sin.

Controlling — To exercise power over, to dominate or rule, to restrain, a restraining force.

Countenance — *paniym* (Hebrew), does have the literal meaning of *face* (Gen. 43:31; 1 Kings 19:13), but also means the reflection of a person's mood or attitude, such as being defiant (Jer. 5:3); ruthless (Deut. 28:50); joyful (Job 29:24); humiliated (2 Sam. 19:5); terrified (Isa. 13:8). The Scripture gives us examples of a bad countenance in (Matt. 6:16), and a good one in (Psalm 4:6).

Defiance — is when a child rebels against the authority and the *discipline that follows* their foolish act of immaturity.

Defile — means to pollute, render impure; or corrupt.

Devoutly — Holy, pious, sacred, dedicated to God. This describes your abiding relationship with Christ. When you are devoted, or dedicated to God, that relationship is the source of a sacred life, and the following two behaviors normally follow.

Diligently — Perseveringly attentive; steady and earnest in application to a subject or pursuit; prosecuted with careful attention and effort; not careless or negligent.

Disciple — (verb) Instilling God's Word into our children's hearts through example and instruction, teaching them to pray, and how to have a relationship with God (spiritual training of morals and values).

Disciple — (noun), Greek, *mathētēs*, is a student, learner, or pupil, but it means much more in the NT. It is a follower who accepts the instruction given to him and makes it his rule of conduct. In Classic Greek, *mathetes* is what we would call "an apprentice," one who not only learns facts from the teacher, but other things such as his attitudes and philosophies. In this way the *mathetes* was what we might call a "student-companion," who doesn't just sit in class listening to lectures, but rather, who follows the teacher to learn life as well as facts and progressively takes on the character of the teacher.

Discipling/Discipleship — Discipling is an intentional relationship in which we walk alongside other disciples in order to encourage, equip and challenge one another in love to grow toward maturity in Christ. This includes equipping the disciple to teach others as well.

Discipleship/Direct — instruction-discipleship is the time that you set aside to have devotionals (a Bible study) with your children. It is a planned activity that involves the family.

Discipleship/Indirect — instruction-discipleship occurs when God presents an opportunity for an informal, or unplanned discussion of spiritual things. This means that a parent is paying attention, seeing those opportunities.

Discipline — (Eph 6:4) of children, instilling the character traits of a mature adult, which are morals and values, personal responsibility and self-control, into our children (training behavior).

Discouraged — *athumeo* (Greek), is a very insightful word. The root of this word is *thumos*, which means violent motion or passion of mind, such as anger, wrath or indignation. By putting the "*a*" (alpha) in front of the word, it becomes a negative, means "without". So it means without passion, despondent, disturbed in mind, and indicates loss of courage. **Colossians 3:21** says, *"Fathers, do not provoke your children, lest they become **discouraged**."*

Edification — *oikodome* (Greek), means to build up for the spiritual profit or advancement of someone else, and also used to indicate building up a house or structure.

Encourage, or Comfort — means to inspire, support; console in time of trouble or worry, soothing encouragement designed to cheer up and to inspire correct behavior.

Endure all things — to endure, *hupomeno* (Greek), means to abide under, to bear up under, suffer, as a load of miseries. It is also patient acquiescence, holding its ground when it can no longer believe nor hope.

Envy — this is discontent or uneasiness at the sight of another's excellence or good fortune, accompanied with some degree of hatred and a desire to possess equal advantages; malicious grudging.

Exhort — *parakleo*, (Greek), to call to one's side, to aid, to encourage, admonish or exhort someone to do something. We are to come alongside our children and help them grow in the things of the Lord.

Faith — *pisteuo* (Greek), means to have faith in, trust; particularly, to be firmly persuaded as to something. This is more than just giving a mental assent; it means to act on what is believed.

Foolishness — means, "lack of character," deficient in understanding, unwise, brainless, irrational, ludicrous, a lack of judgment.

Forsake — means to deny, telling us to daily align our priorities to God's Word, which places His will over ours.

Gentle — denotes seemly, fitting; hence, equitable, fair, moderate, forbearing, not insisting on the letter of the law; it expresses that considerateness that looks humanely and reasonably at the facts of a case.

Genuineness — *dokimion* (Greek), means something that has been tested and approved. It was used of metals that had been through a purifying process to remove all impurities.

Cherish — (tender care, NAS 1 Thes 2:7c) - To give heed to, to pay attention to, to minister, to soften by heat, to keep warm as of birds covering their young with feathers (Deut. 22:6), to cherish with tender love, to foster with tender care.

Glorify — To reflect, to honor, praise, to give esteem or honor by putting him into an honorable position.

Consequences — that which follows from breaking a rule. In other words, when you have a rule there *must* be a corrective consequence for breaking that rule.

Head — means the chief or lead person to whom others are subordinate. Metaphorically of persons, i.e., the head, chief, one to whom others are subordinate, e.g., the husband in relation to his wife (1 Cor. 11:3; Eph. 5:23) insofar as they are one body (Matt. 19:6; Mark 10:8), and one body can have only one head to direct it; of Christ in relation to His Church which is His body, and its members are His members (cf. 1 Cor. 12:27; Eph. 1:22; 4:15; 5:23; Col. 1:18; 2:10, 19); of God in relation to Christ (1 Cor. 11:3). In Col. 2:10 & Eph. 1:22, God the Father is designated as the head of Christ

Heart — Hebrew *lebab*, meaning heart, mind, inner person (mind, will, emotions). The primary usage of this word describes the entire disposition of the inner person. Greek *kardia*, is the seat of the desires, feelings, affections, passions, impulses, i.e., the heart or mind.

Hurts — harboring bitterness toward parents, an ex-spouse, children, current spouse, or whomever, blocks the transformation of character that God desires for you. Bitterness cuts us off from the grace of God needed to walk and grow spiritually, and causes us to contaminate others. Hebrews 12:15 says, "… *looking carefully lest anyone fall short of the grace of God; lest any root of bitterness springing up cause trouble, and by this many become defiled.*"

Hypocrite — is someone who acts phony, or is a counterfeit; a man who assumes and speaks, or acts, under a pretend character.

Impart — this verb has the idea of sharing something, which one already retains in part.

Integrity — indicates singleness of heart, not double-minded - one who walks according to His will and exemplifying God's righteousness.

Justly — means with integrity and honesty, just, uprightness of character and behavior, daily desiring to live life according to what pleases God. When you know the Word of God, you are able to judge what is right and wrong.

Kind — *chrestos (Greek)*, to do good; denotes being gentle, merciful, sympathetic, gracious and good natured in contrast to harsh, hard, sharp, bitter or cruel. The term also expresses the idea of moral excellence.

Knowledge — is *epignosis* (Greek), which means thorough participation in acquiring knowledge, but then applying it.

Longsuffering, or patience — means to be long-tempered, the opposite of hasty anger, instead it involves exercising understanding and patience toward people. It also requires that we endure circumstances, not losing faith or giving up.

Love — *Agape* (Greek), the response of God's heart toward unworthy sinners. Agape is God's love demonstrated in self-sacrifice for the benefit of the objects of His love. God's essential quality that seeks the best interests of others regardless of the others' actions, it involves God doing what He knows is best for man and not necessarily what man desires…His son to bring forgiveness to man. It is choosing to love.

Love — *Phileo* (Greek), *The response of the human spirit to what appeals to it as pleasurable. "Phileo seems to be clearly distinct (from agape) and speaks of esteem, high regard, and tender affection and is more* *emotional." Phileo is friendship love, determined by the pleasure that one receives from the object of that love. Phileo is conditional love.*

Make Disciples — (verb) Greek, *matheteuo*, is to make a disciple (Matt 28:19; Acts 14:21); to instruct (Matt 13:52) with the purpose of making a disciple. It is not exactly the same as "make converts," though it is surely implied. The term "make disciples" places somewhat more stress on the fact that the mind, as well as the heart and the will, must be won for God by instructing new believers on how to follow Jesus, to submit to Jesus' lordship, and to take up his mission of compassionate service. It also involves bringing people into relationship with Jesus as pupils to teacher and getting them to take His yoke of instruction upon themselves as authoritative (Matt 11:29), accepting His words as true, and submitting to His will as what is right.

Manipulation — means to control or play upon by artful, unfair and insidious means, especially to one's own advantage.

Meditate — in the Biblical world meditation was not a silent practice; it meant to moan, utter or growl. It had the idea of muttering sounds like reading half aloud or conversing with oneself so that you would so interact with the text that it would soak into your mind. As a tea bag soaking in water permeates the liquid, so meditating on Scriptures permeates our minds.

Minister — *(noun) A servant or waiter, one who oversees, governs and fulfills.*

Minister — *(verb) To adjust, regulate and set in order; to serve, render service to another; to labor for the Lord as a servant.*

Morals and Values — for the Christian, *morals* are defined by what is right and wrong from God's perspective. *Values* are the principles, or actions you live by, meaning that your behavior shows what you value most.

Not rejoicing in iniquity — this means that when you see someone fall into sin, or make a mistake, you are not happy and/or vindictive toward him or her.

Nurse — (1 Thes 2:7b) The act of nursing, suckle, nourish, train, something that nourishes, to supply with nourishment, to educate or foster, to further the development of someone or something.

Perfectly trained — *katartizo* (Greek), means is to put a thing in its appropriate condition, to establish, equip so it is deficient in no part.

Perfect/Mature — (Eph 4:13) *teleios* (Greek), meaning goal, or purpose; finished, that which has reached its end, term, limit; hence, complete, full, wanting in nothing.

Persecute — To pursue in a manner to injure, grieve, or afflict; to oppress; to set upon with cruelty; to cause to suffer.

Personal Responsibility — the ability to take care of oneself; to follow through on things you have committed to do, or the things required, without anyone else having to prompt you; taking ownership, being accountable and accepting responsibility for your actions.

Power — is *dunamis* (Greek), which translates as dynamic strength, or ability to do what only God can do.

Punishment — A measured amount of pain to motivate, or the infliction of a penalty. Punishment is part of the overall discipline plan, but it is different from a corrective consequence. Punishment motivates a child to yield to parental authority and accept the corrective consequence.

Purpose — means an intended, or desired, result or goal.

React — The dictionary defines the word *react* in the following way: to act in response to a stimulant or to stimulus, to act in opposition.

Reacting in the Flesh — can be defined as a Christian reacting to a situation in a sinful manner, in the habit of their old fallen nature, or reacting in their strength and understanding rather than the power and wisdom of the Holy Spirit.

Rebuke — means to convict, to prove one in the wrong.

Rejoicing in the truth — this means that you have great joy, or you are able to rejoice at what is true, based on God's promises.

Repent — to resolve; to amend one's life as a result of contrition for one's sins; to feel regret for one has done or omitted to do before God. To turn around and go another direction; to change one's mind, will and life, resulting in a change of behavior; to do things another way.

Revenge — means to inflict injury in return for an insult.

Scourges — entails all and any suffering, which God ordains for His children, which is always designed for their good. Also it includes the entire range of trials and tribulations, which He providentially ordains and which work to mortify sin and nurture faith.

Self-seeking — means doing things in our own way, using ours, or this world's wisdom in making choices.

"Shut Down," — meaning room restriction with no friends, phone, radio, computer, games, or iPods.

Respond — According to the dictionary, when we *respond* to someone, we react positively or favorably.

Responding in Love — A Christian responding to a situation with the inward guidance, love, wisdom and power of the Holy Spirit.

Reward — a great precious value.

Rightly dividing — has the idea of cutting something straight as you would in carpentry, masonry or with cutting a piece of cloth to be sewn together.

Rude — characterized by roughness; harsh, severe, ugly, indecent, or offensive in manor or action.

Rule — To rule, manage, lead, shepherd and guide. By implication this means to take care of something, to be diligent, to practice.

Seek first — is a command to do and never stop. (Matt 6:33)

Seek and **Set your mind** — are imperative verbs, indicating the action is a continual process. *"Seek"* means to look for and strive to find. *"Set your mind"* refers to the will, affections and conscience. (Col 3:1-2)

Seek your own way — this is a person who pursues what best fits their own interests, without any concern of how their actions or ways affect others. This person is unwilling to receive input, which includes instruction from God's perspective.

Self-control — the ability to govern oneself emotionally, physically, and spiritually; the ability to not always yield to the path of least resistance.

Sin of Commission — which means that we sin acting out of our own authority. God says no do not do that, and we do it anyway. Example: God says don't steal (Eph 4:28), but we steal.

Sin of Omission — which means that we sin by not doing what is right by God, He commands us to do something, and *we* decide not to do it or, out of ignorance we treat our children according to what *we* feel is best, NOT doing God's will. Another example: God says to forgive, but we refuse to.

Steward — Overseer; manager; one who acts as a custodian, administrator or supervisor.

Study — this word is an imperative verb, meaning it is a command to do and to continue to do. The word denotes a zealous persistence in accomplishing a goal.

Submissive — *hopotasso* (Greek), means a voluntary attitude of giving in, cooperating, assuming responsibility, and carrying a burden.

Thinks no evil — *logizomai* (Greek), is used as an accounting term, meaning to put things together in one's mind, to count or add up, to occupy oneself with calculations.

Train up — (Prov 22:6) in the original Hebrew is *chanak,* which means to dedicate or set aside for Divine service.

Training — (Eph. 6:4) *paideia* (Greek), means chastening, because all effectual instruction for the sinful children of men includes and implies discipline, correction...as the Lord approves. Discipline that regulates character.

Training — To cause to grow as desired; to make or become prepared or skilled.

Thoroughly equipped for every good work — means it is God's intention for us to both understand His will and be empowered to follow through in obedience.

Transformed — *metamorphóō* (Greek), from which we derive our English word metamorphosis: to change into something entirely different, as a caterpillar to a butterfly.

Voids — something that has been left out. For example, a child has certain developmental emotional needs that must be nurtured through loving authority, with consistent proper discipline. If these needs are compromised and/or not provided, a void is created within the child. This often occurs because parents do not understand their God-given responsibilities, or the extent of their influence for good or bad. Most children cannot identify what is missing, what the void is, but they will instinctively try to fill it with something. For example, a lack of real love and proper discipline can make a child vulnerable to addictions and/or emotional and psychological problems that lead to destructive behavior. As you move through these lessons, you will receive biblical instruction which, *when followed*, can produce a healthy relationship with your child and also an emotionally healthy person in your child.

Wiles — is *methodia* (Greek), which comes the English word *method*, indicating craftiness, cunning, and deception. The term was often used of a wild animal that cunningly stalks and then unexpectedly pounces on its prey. Satan's evil schemes are built around stealth and deception.

Appendix U
Biblical Principles For Forgiveness & Reconciliation

The Sovereignty of God

The word **Sovereign** means - *Possessing supreme power, unlimited wisdom, and absolute authority.*

> **Daniel 4:35,** *"All the inhabitants of the earth are accounted as nothing, but He does according to His will in the host of heaven and among the inhabitants of the earth; and no one can ward off His hand or say to Him 'What have You done?'"*

> **Psalm 139:1-4,** *"...You have searched me and known me. You know when I sit down and when I rise up; You understand my thought from afar. You scrutinize my path and my lying down, and are intimately acquainted with all my ways. Even before there is a word on my tongue, Behold, O Lord, You know it all."*

Psalm 139:1-18 teaches that God knows each of us intimately. <u>All</u> of our days were fashioned or created by Him. Before you knew God, or accepted Him as Lord and Savior He knew you and predestined all the days of your life. God gave you and others the gift of freewill. He chose you that you might follow Him, and gave you the freedom to reject Him.

God has given mankind freedom to do good and freedom to do evil. Therefore, the reality is that God's children live in a fallen world and are often touched by the evil around them. If God shielded His children from all evil, allowing only good, the unsaved would only be motivated to turn to Him for the guarantee of an easy life. In fact, this is the very argument that began the historic showdown in heaven between God and Satan in the life of Job.

Satan said to God,

> **Job 1:9-11,** *"Does Job fear God for nothing? Have You not made a hedge about him and his house and all that he has, on every side? You have blessed the work of his hands, and his*

possessions have increased in the land. But put forth Your hand now and touch all that he has; he will surely curse You to Your face."

God then *allowed* Satan to bring evil upon Job through the loss of his possessions, his children, and finally his health. God is a loving Father and does not *bring* evil into our lives, however for His purpose and for our ultimate good, He *allows* us to be touched by evil. The outcome of Job's suffering was trust and intimacy with God.

Job did not understand *why* God was *allowing* him to suffer (God had declared in Job 2:3 that Job was a righteous man), therefore Job asked God, "W*hy?*" For several chapters Job agonizes over this question, seeking a satisfactory answer. God never answers the question, instead He directs Job's attention to His power and glory, which is displayed in His creation. Job is satisfied with a newfound understanding of the greatness of God. When we suffer we, like Job, want an explanation. *"Why, why, why?"* One of the many lessons we learn from Job is that *"Why?"* is the wrong question. We should instead ask God, *"What?"*

- **What are You trying to teach me?**

- **What is Your will for me in this season of suffering?**

   James 1:13,14, *"…God cannot be tempted by evil, and He Himself does not tempt anyone. But each one is tempted when he is carried away and enticed by his own lust."*

   Job 42:1-6, *"Then Job answered the Lord and said, 'I know that You can do all things, and that no purpose of Yours can be thwarted…I have heard of You by the hearing of the ear; but not my eye sees You…'"*

- **This being true, what part of your life is beyond God's power, wisdom, or authority?**

_____

_____

- **What day or circumstance has touched you that God did not know beforehand?**

_____

_____

   Ephesians 1:11, *"In Him we were also chosen, having been predestined according to the plan of Him who works everything in conformity with the purpose of His will."*

- **How should you respond to life's disappointments, difficulties, suffering, and trials?**

We can choose to either harbor bitterness toward parents who disappointed us, a spouse who deserted us, friends who failed us, or a drunk driver who killed a loved-one, or we can place our faith in a sovereign God.

When we come to Christ, we trust Him with our eternal destiny. We must also trust Him with our past and present circumstances. He alone can comfort and strengthen us in and through our trials. He alone can bring good out of bad. Our obedience to God's Word <u>will</u> give us peace, and bring praise, honor, and glory to our Lord Jesus Christ.

Read the following verses and write out in your own words what it is saying to you.

> **1 Peter 1:3-7,** *"...In this you greatly rejoice, even though now for a little while, if necessary, you have been distressed by various trials, so that the proof of your faith, being more precious than gold which is perishable, even though tested by fire, may be found to result in praise and glory and honor at the revelation of Jesus Christ."*

_____

_____

_____

Trials and Tribulation

GOD'S WORD TEACHES THAT TRIALS AND TRIBULATIONS ARE PART OF THE CHRISTIAN LIFE.

> **John 16:33,** *"These things I have spoken to you, that in Me you may have peace. In the world you will have tribulation' but be of good cheer, I have overcome the world."*

Just as the refiner places the crude gold into the crucible, and administers heat in order to bring the dross to the surface, God places His beloved children in the crucible of suffering in order to refine us, and transform us into the image of our Redeemer.

> **Malachi 3:3,** *"He will sit as a smelter and purifier of silver, and He will purify the sons of Levi and refine them like gold and silver, so that they may present to the Lord offerings in righteousness."*

If we trust Him our very lives will permeate with the love, hope, and confidence of Jesus Christ. Those around us will see the righteousness of Jesus Christ being worked out in us.

Romans 8:28, 29, *"And we know that all things work together for good to those who love God, to those who are the called according to His purpose. For those whom He foreknew, He also predestined to become conformed to the image of His Son..."*

God did not say *some things*, but *all things*. The key is faith. If we choose to believe God's promises and trust Him in all of our trials and tribulations, we will be victorious and God will be glorified in our life.

2 Corinthians 2:14, *"But thanks be to God, who always leads us in triumph in Christ, and manifests through us the sweet aroma of the knowledge of Him in every place."*

- Are you willing to trust God with the pain that others have caused in your life?

- Are you willing to allow God to transform your life through your trials?

"...to those who love God", means those who have received Him as Lord and trust Him with their past, present, and future; to trust His instructions, His Word, in how to live and deal with life's trials.

- Are you willing to trust God in how to deal with your hurts and trials in your life?

"There are times, says Jesus, when God cannot lift the darkness from you, but trust Him. God will appear like an unkind friend, but He is not; He will appear like an unnatural Father, but He is not; He will appear like an unjust judge, but He is not. Keep the notion of the mind of God behind all things strong and growing. Nothing happens in any particular unless God's will is behind it, therefore you can rest in perfect confidence in Him."
                                                      My Utmost for His Highest Oswald Chambers

The Cost of UnForgiveness

The word *forgive* means literally, *to give away*. When a debt is forgiven, the rights to payment are *given away*. If someone injures me and I forgive them, I *give away* the freedom to continue being angry and resentful towards the one who wronged me. This includes breaking of the strongholds of many emotional and psychological problems that can stem from these hurts. To trust God and forgive others is giving our hurts to God to take away from us. The word *pardon* is derived from the Latin word, *perdonare*, meaning to *grant freely*. True forgiveness is undeserved, unmerited, and free. It is not *just* or *fair*. In the Scriptures, to *forget* means, *to let go from one's power.*

When we refuse to grant forgiveness, choosing rather to maintain our *right* to demand payment for wrongs done to us, we must be willing to absorb the cost incurred by that choice. Forgiveness is free, however unforgiveness carries with it a costly price tag. Unwillingness to forgive produces many negative consequences for us, the most common one is *resentment*. Resentment means, *to feel again*. **Resentment clings to the past, reliving it over and over**. Resentment, like *picking a scab*, prohibits our wounds from healing.

> **Hebrews 12:15,** *"See to it that no one comes short of the grace of God; that no root of bitterness springing up causes trouble, and by it many be defiled."*

- In Hebrews 12:15 we learn that bitterness, like a deep root, takes a firm hold in the human heart, then grows, and produces *fruit*. However, rather than nourish others, this fruit is bitter, causes trouble, and defiles ourselves and others.

- Most of us do not readily admit that we have been harboring unforgiveness. However, Ephesians 4:31 teaches that there is undeniable evidence in an individual's life that the bitter tree of resentment is growing within their heart.

> **Ephesians 4:31,** *"Let all bitterness and wrath and anger and clamor and slander be put away from you, along with all malice."*

> **Wrath** – *An outburst of a strong, vengeful anger or indignation, seeking retribution.*

> **Anger** – *A state of mind marked by fretfulness and reacting to life's challenges with frustration.*

> **Evil speaking** – *Unkind words, verbal abuse against someone, clamor/slander, wounding someone's reputation by evil reports, backbiting, insult and defamation.*

> **Malice** – *Hateful feelings that we nurture in our hearts. A desire to see another suffer and/or to separate ourselves from that person, not wanting to work toward reconciliation.*

Ask yourself, *"Are any of these common in my life?"*

• Pride • Self-righteous • Self-pity • Emotional disturbances • Anxiety, tension & stress • Health problems • Eating Disorders • An unhealthy sense of self-confidence • Lack of trust in relationships • Lack of intimacy in marriage • Sexual Dysfunction • Judgmental & critical of others • Ultra-sensitive & easily offended • Absence of peace & joy • Broken fellowship with Jesus • Afraid to lead as a husband • Afraid to follow as a wife

Why Forgive?

Besides the before mentioned devastation that results from unforgiveness, we are indebted to forgive because:

GOD COMMANDS IT

Obedience to God the Father is not optional. If we pick and choose when we will and will not obey God's commands, we will live unfruitful, ineffective, and spiritually barren lives.

> **Luke 6:35,36,** *"But love your enemies, and do good...and you will be sons of the Most High; for He Himself is kind to ungrateful and evil men. Be merciful, just as your Father is merciful."*

> **Mark 11:25,** *"And whenever you stand praying. If you have anything against anyone, forgive him, that your Father in heaven may also forgive you your trespasses."*

IN FORGIVING, WE RESEMBLE JESUS, AND BEAR THE FAMILY LIKENESS

The term *Christian* means *little Christ*. As Christians, we are called to carry the name of Christ to a lost world. We must be willing to bear His image; to be like Him. Christ demonstrated forgiveness. He came to this earth to bring forgiveness to the guilty. He gave the commission to the church to continue proclaiming forgiveness. We must, if we are to rightly bear His name, forgive those who have offended us!

> **Luke 23:34,** *"Then Jesus said, 'Father, forgive them, for they do not know what they do.' "*

> **1 John 2:6,** *"...the one who says he abides in Him ought to walk in the same manner as He walked."*

IT IS THE ONLY MEANS OF BREAKING THE CYCLE OF BLAME, PAIN, AND MANY STRONGHOLDS

Forgiveness offers the way out; an antidote to be healed! It does not settle all questions of blame and fairness, often evading those questions altogether. It does allow a relationship to start over, to begin anew, if applicable.

This truth is demonstrated in the life of Joseph in Genesis chapters 37-45. Though he was mistreated, betrayed, abandoned by his brothers, and sold into slavery, he refused to allow the root of bitterness to take hold of his life. Shortly before being reunited with his brothers, he testified of the healing work that God had done in his life during the years of separation, as demonstrated in the naming of his sons.

In Genesis 41:51,52 we read:

> "Joseph named the firstborn Manasseh, "For," he said, "God has made me forget all my trouble in all my father's household."

> "He named the second Ephraim, "For," he said, "God has made me fruitful in the land of my affliction..."

To *forget* in this sense does not mean to cease to remember, but *to let go*, to cease to let the hurtful things control your present life. Joseph's *fruitfulness* was directly related to his putting his trust in God's sovereignty and forgiving others. Remember that resentment means *to feel again*. Joseph chose to trust God with his past.

Unforgiveness imprisons us to the past and locks out all potential for a fruitful life.

During Joseph's years alone in Egypt, he allowed God to heal his heart, which had been broken by his own brothers. Later, when given the opportunity, Joseph extended love, forgiveness, and grace to his brothers. Joseph speaks to his brothers in Genesis 45:

> "Now do not be grieved or angry with yourselves, because you sold me here, for God sent me before you to preserve life...and to keep you alive by a great deliverance...He kissed all his brothers and wept on them, and afterward his brothers talked with him."

There was no blaming, no explanations demanded, only the voice of mercy and forgiveness. The way was cleared for Joseph and his brothers to be reunited and begin a new relationship.

- Forgiveness loosens the stranglehold of guilt in the offender

    Ephesians 2:7 *"...in the ages to come He might show the surpassing riches of His grace in kindness toward us in Christ Jesus."*

Joseph's brothers would have carried their grief to their graves if they did not have an opportunity to ask for forgiveness to Joseph. Forgiveness, undeserved and unearned, can cut the cords and let the oppressive burden of guilt roll away.

If Jesus had not extended kindness and forgiveness to sinners, we would remain in the stranglehold of guilt. He made the first move toward us that made it possible for us to be reconciled to Him.

Reconciliation

To reconcile is to restore to friendship or harmony, or to settle or resolve differences. It is the doing away of an enmity, the bridging over of a quarrel. Reconciliation implies that the parties being reconciled were formerly hostile to and/or separated from one another.

NOTE: there are many cases or situations where reconciliation is not necessary, possible, or even needed. Such as:

- An emotionally or physically abusive parent or ex-spouse.

- A random person that hurt you or a loved one: a rapist, a drunk who hurt or killed a loved one, an old teacher or coach that verbally hurt you, etc.

Reconciliation is to be sought out for family members and other believers in our life. In all of our relationships outside of our immediate family setting, respectful boundaries and maintaining a healthy relationship is important.

> **Ephesians 4:31,32,** *"Let all bitterness and wrath and anger and clamor and slander be put away from you, along with all malice. Be kind to one another, tender-hearted, forgiving each other, just as God in Christ also has forgiven you."*

The Scriptures instruct us to "Let all bitterness... be put away from you... be kind... tenderhearted, forgiving..." It guides us and instructs us in each of these questions.

- How do we put away bitterness?

- How do we reconcile with someone that we have offended?

- How do we repair the hurt we have caused others?

- How do we forgive someone who has offended us?

- How can we change our own feelings about a wrong done?

If You Need To Be Forgiven

As an act of the will, you must:

1. Confess your sin to God and ask Him to forgive you and, by His Holy Spirit to fill your heart with His love.

>**Psalm 32:1,3-5,** *"Blessed is he whose transgression is forgiven, whose sin is covered...When I kept silent, my bones grew old through my groaning all the day long. For day and night Your hand was heavy upon me; my vitality was turned into the drought of summer. I acknowledged my sin to You and my iniquity I have not hidden. I said, "I will confess my transgressions to the Lord," and You forgave the iniquity of my sin."*

>**1 John 1:9,** *"If we confess our sins, He is faithful and just to forgive us our sins and to cleanse us from all unrighteousness."*

>**Psalm 103:12,** *"As far as the east is from the west, so far has He removed our transgressions from us."*

- Take a moment right now to cry out to God, asking Him to forgive you and to fill you with His Holy Spirit to strengthen you to obey.

- God alone forgives sins. He forgives and He forgets. By faith, accept God's absolute forgiveness and cleansing.

>*"Forgiveness is not an emotion...Forgiveness is an act of the will, and the will can function regardless of the temperature of the heart."*
>
>**-Corrie ten Boom**

2. If possible, go to those you have wronged, humbly make confession, and ask for their forgiveness.

>**Matthew 5:23-24,** *"Therefore if you bring your gift to the altar, and there remember that your brother has something against you, leave your gift there before the altar, and go your way. First be reconciled to your brother, and then come and offer your gift."*

Write out your commitment to obey Matthew 5:23,24.

_____

_____

_____

Write out the names and a brief description of what you are asking forgiveness for.

_____

_____

_____

_____

SIX OF THE MOST POWERFUL WORDS IN THE ENGLISH LANGUAGE, "I WAS WRONG. PLEASE FORGIVE ME."

If possible, do this face to face. However, due to logistics or possible confrontation, you may have to communicate with the person by telephone or in writing.

Note: Don't let distractions or other obstacles delay this act of obedience. In our modern society, the telephone system, postal service, emails, and texting can put us in touch with others in a moment or a day or two.

Share your decision with a trustworthy Christian friend, asking them to prayer partner with you and hold you accountable to follow through on your commitment.

Note: If the person you have wronged has passed away, you need simply go to God with your confession.

3. Spend time daily with the Lord in His Word, and in prayer.

One of the many negative consequences of not asking for or giving forgiveness toward others is a hindered relationship with God. Praise the Lord He never leaves us or forsakes us! But our heart is what grows cold and feels separated from God, therefore, affecting our intimacy with Him. I believe this is a consequence God designed within us to motivate us to practice forgiveness in our life.

> **Matthew 6:33,** _"But seek first the kingdom of God and His righteousness, and all these things shall be added to you."_

Verbalize your decision to the Lord to spend time with Him daily in prayer, reading of His Word, and meditation.

_____
_____
_____
_____
_____
_____

4. Ponder the meaning of the cross and the sacrifice Jesus made for your sins.

Titus 3:3-5, *"For we ourselves were also once foolish, disobedient, deceived, serving various lusts and pleasures, living in malice and envy, hateful and hating one another. But when the kindness and the love of God our Savior toward man appeared, not by works of righteousness which we have done, but according to His mercy He saved us, through the washing of regeneration and renewing of the Holy Spirit."*

Take a moment right now and thank Jesus for all that He has done for you, for forgiving you for all of your sins, for His perfect plan of transforming you into His image, and for the gift of His Holy Spirit.

If You Need To Forgive

1. Pray and ask God for the strength to obey and forgive the person or persons.

Matthew 21:21, *"So Jesus answered and said to them, "Assuredly, I say to you, if you have faith and do not doubt...if you say to this mountain, 'Be removed and be cast into the sea,' it will be done."*

God promised to give us the strength to move mountains. This may be your Mt. Everest!

"Whenever I see myself before God and realize something of what my blessed Lord has done for me at Calvary, I am ready to forgive anybody anything, I cannot withhold it. I do not even want to withhold it."

—Dr. Martyn Lloyd-Jones

We know that it is God's will that we forgive others, so we can be confident that if we ask for this strength, it will be granted.

2. Communicate your forgiveness to the person or persons.

1 John 5:14, *"Now this is the confidence that we have in Him, that if we ask anything according to His will, He hears us."*

Romans 14:19, *"Therefore let us pursue the things which make for peace and the things by which one may edify another."*

Get Motivated!

In Matt 22:36-40 the Lord Jesus told us what is the greatest command from Him. "Teacher, which is the great commandment in the law?" Jesus said to him, "'You shall love the Lord your God with all your heart, with all your soul, and with all your mind.' This is the first and great commandment. And the second is like it: 'You shall love your neighbor as yourself.' On these two commandments hang all the Law and the Prophets. Jesus Himself said that our love for others is equally as important as our love for Him.

This verse is NOT saying our love for others is to put other peoples desires above Gods. For we are to love Jesus supremely and put His will above anyone else's including our self.

Matt 5:22 says, "But I say to you that whoever is angry with his brother without a cause shall be in danger of the judgment. And whoever says to his brother, 'Raca!' shall be in danger of the council. But whoever says, 'You fool!' shall be in danger of hell fire.

Let's bring some clarity to these words in this verse. To be "angry with his brother means; treating someone in thought, word or deed in an unloving way. How common is this among believers today to treat their spouse, children, employee, a person in a business deal or even a stranger in an unloving way and excusing their behavior and not seek reconciliation?

The word Raca means to hold someone in contempt, to judge, or believe they are worthless or less than you are in some way. The word 'fool' means one who is morally worthless and undeserving of salvation. These are serious charges that many believers are practicing toward others for one reason or another. The Lord says in 1 Corinthians 6:20 "for you were bought at a price; therefore glorify God in your body and in your spirit, which are God's".

We are to glorify or in other words, reflect, Christ likeness to all, no exception. So any lingering thoughts or behavior toward others that is unloving or un-Christ like, we must not excuse it and repent to both God and the person. This grieves the Lord and has consequences.

That's why in Matthew 5:23-24 it says, "Therefore if you bring your gift to the altar, and there remember that your brother has something against you, leave your gift there before the altar, and go your way. First be reconciled to your brother, and then come and offer your gift".

Why do we go to the altar? This is talking about our fellowship with Jesus, our time in prayer, thanksgiving and asking of Him. It is our daily devotion and abiding in Him.

John 15:5-6 says, "I am the vine, you are the branches. He who abides in Me, and I in him, bears much fruit; for without Me you can do nothing". To abide means to dwell with; to live in a constant awareness of being the temple of the Holy Spirit. This includes our prayer and devotion toward Him. And it says **IF** we do, we will bear much fruit for without His grace we can do **NOTHING**. So going to the altar means our fellowship with Jesus and our receiving His grace to bear fruit or to obey His will.

When we owe someone forgiveness be it, giving it, or asking for it, this is a prerequisite God says we first must do before we can expect His blessings and grace. He said first go and get things right with those who we were unloving toward and that includes forgiving those who have hurt us.

What are the gifts Matthew 5:23 is talking about when it says, "Therefore if you bring your gift to the altar...". We know that bringing sacrifices to the temple was a common practice as part of their atoning for their sins. Today, our gifts are our praise, tithes, worship, obedience, and our service to Him. Yet Jesus said these gifts will not be received by Him if you owe a person reconciliation.

I Samuel 15:22 says, "Has the Lord as great delight in burnt offerings and sacrifices, as in obeying the voice of the Lord? Behold, to obey is better than sacrifice, and to heed than the fat of rams." Our service and work for Him will not fix this problem.

In 1 Corinthians 11:26-32 we are exhorted to examine our self even before we take communion. It says, "For as often as you eat this bread and drink this cup, you proclaim the Lord's death till He comes. Therefore whoever eats this bread or drinks this cup of the Lord in an unworthy manner will be guilty of the body and blood of the Lord. But let a man examine himself, and so let him eat of the bread and drink of the cup. For he who eats and drinks in an unworthy manner eats and drinks judgment to himself, not discerning the Lord's body. **For this reason many are weak and sick among you, and many sleep. For if we would judge ourselves, we would not be judged. But when we are judged, we are chastened by the Lord, that we may not be condemned with the world.**"

How often do Christians come to church and partake of communion and never first examine their heart to see if they are harboring bitterness and/or have sinned against someone and do not repent or plan on being reconciled with that person/s?

The word reconcile means to make things right; to change ones feelings or perspective toward another or to pay a debt owed.

Romans 13:8 tells us, "Owe no one anything except to love one another, for he who loves another has fulfilled the law.

As Christians we have a debt to pay that God Himself has placed upon us that we owe others: to love them in thought, word, and deed. This also includes forgiving those who have hurt us. Today, many Christians are harboring bitterness, resentment, or un-forgiveness toward someone because they have hurt them in some way. Their justification for harboring these feelings is because this person has not yet paid any deserved consequences, nor have they taken any responsibility for what they have done. This is also considered un-loving or being angry with a brother. A fact of life for all Christians is: we will be hurt by others even from those who are supposed to love us. Our parents, siblings, uncles, aunts, friends, pastors, teachers, etc. can hurt us both ignorantly and/or deliberately.

The word forgive *is a* verb, *or an* action word. *To truly forgive requires you to* take action. *God is using His Word to speak to you right now, revealing truth for you to obey and* act upon.

Edify – *To* build up, *or* encourage.

NOTE: Matthew 5:23-24 also applies to us to forgive others. God's Word says we owe every person love.

Forgiveness is not an easy thing to do, therefore you must not try to stand alone, but seek the support and accountability of a mature Christian friend, spouse, or prayer partner.

Write out your commitment to forgive the person or persons, and give yourself a date to contact them by, so you won't let yourself put it off!

_____
_____
_____
_____

Matthew 6:14, *"For if you forgive men their trespasses, your Heavenly Father will also forgive you."*

In some cases, due to logistics, cost of travel, safety to you, or the ability of the other person to be quiet long enough to let you say what you need to say, a letter, email, text or telephone call may be the best way for you to accomplish this.

Keep these points in mind when either speaking or communicating in writing:

1. ***You are doing this out of obedience to your Heavenly Father who loves and cares for you.***
   He wants you to be free from the bondage and oppression you have been experiencing as a result of unforgiveness.

2. ***You do not have to rehearse every detail or act of the offense against you.***
   Many times, especially when forgiving parents, they are completely unaware of what they may have done that hurt you. In other cases, it may have been blatant sin against you, for example, sexual, physical, or emotional abuse, rape, abandonment by a parent, friend, or spouse, slander spoken against you, etc. In these cases, you can be more specific as to why you need to forgive.

3. ***Do not try to compel others to own up to their offenses.***
   God has called you to obey, not to be a prosecuting attorney, jury, judge, or to try and make them confess that what they did was wrong!

4. ***Keep it short.***
   In most cases, due to the high level of emotions, we can find ourselves saying things we did not plan on saying that may undermine the purpose of the meeting, letter, or conversation.

5. ***Finally (if applicable), ask them to forgive you for harboring bitterness toward them.***
   Remember that what they may have done was wrong and offensive, but bitterness and unforgiveness is equally wrong.

   Romans 2:16, *"In the day when God will judge the secrets of men by Jesus Christ, according to my gospel."*

   Romans 2:1, *"Therefore you are inexcusable, O man, whoever you are who judge, for in whatever you judge another you condemn yourself; for you who judge practice the same things."*

"The degree to which I am able and willing to forgive others is a clear indication of the extend to which I have personally experienced God my Father's forgiveness for me."

—Phillip Keller

Maintaining Your Commitment to Forgive

The person you have forgiven may continue to be a regular part of your life; possibly a parent, father/mother-in-law, a child, or a spouse. When this is the case you may encounter a spiritual and fleshly battle after you have asked for forgiveness or forgiven them.

> **Galatians 5:22-26,** *"But the fruit of the Spirit is love, joy, peace, longsuffering, kindness, goodness, faithfulness, gentleness, self-control. Against such there is no law. And those who are Christ's have crucified the flesh with its passions and desires.If we live in the Spirit, let us also walk in the Spirit. Let us not become conceited, provoking one another, envying one another."*

The forgiveness experience has changed you, but it does not necessarily change them. God has had a major victory in your life in bringing you to this place of surrender and obedience, however, their position and/or their brash personality may not have changed! They may continue to hold onto bitterness toward you. If this is the case you need to seek God daily for His strength to extend mercy and compassion to them without compromising.

For example, if you forgave a parent for being harsh and unloving, and asked them to forgive you for harboring bitterness, yet the next time you see them, they continue to be harsh and unloving, your flesh may want to react in the way you formerly reacted. God will be faithful to produce His fruit in your life as you surrender to Him moment by moment.

> **Ephesians 6:12,** *"For we do not wrestle against flesh and blood, but against principalities, against powers, against the rulers of the darkness of this age, against spiritual hosts of wickedness in the heavenly places."*

You must keep in mind that your obedience in forgiving was not so that the other person or persons would change. Unless they surrender their lives and experiences to the Lord, they cannot change. Only God can change our hearts and renew our minds, and only if we surrender to Him.

We are involved in a spiritual battle everyday. The enemy, Satan, does not want you to obey God or have victory over sin or hurts. Therefore, he will attack your mind with past memories, evil thoughts, lies, temptations, and condemnation. You must exercise mental self-control and remember what and whom you are battling!

> **Ephesians 4:26,27,** *"Be angry, and do not sin; do not let the sun go down on your wrath, nor give an opportunity to the devil."*

This is the reality in which we live! Satan hates to lose ground in your life. He does not like the idea that he has lost the ability to continue to rob you of God's peace and joy.

How do I stop giving the devil opportunities to work his destruction in my life?

1. *Take each thought that enters your mind and measure them by God's Word to see if they are from God, from your flesh, or from the enemy.*

> **2 Corinthians 10:3-5,** *"For though we walk in the flesh, we do not war according to the flesh. For the weapons of our warfare are not carnal but mighty in God for pulling down strongholds, casting down arguments and every high thing that exalts itself against the knowledge of God, bringing every thought into captivity to the obedience of Christ, and being ready to punish all disobedience when your obedience is fulfilled."*

> **Philippians 4:8,** *"Finally brethren, whatever things are true, whatever things are noble, whatever things are just, whatever things are pure, whatever things are lovely, whatever things are of good report, if there is any virtue and if there is anything praiseworthy – meditate on these things."*

2. *Pray in each instance, asking for God's power to do His will.*

> **Romans 12:21,** *"Do not be overcome by evil, but overcome evil with good."*

> **Romans 15:13,** *"Now may the God of hope fill you with all joy and peace in believing, that you may abound in hope by the power of the Holy Spirit."*

3. *Resist and rebuke the devil in the name of Jesus – FIGHT!*

> **Jude 1:9,** *"Yet Michael the archangel, in contending with the devil...dared not bring against him a reviling accusation, but said, "The Lord rebuke you!"*

1 Peter 5:6-9, *"Therefore humble yourselves under the mighty hand of God...casting all your care upon Him, for He cares for you...your adversary the devil walks about like a roaring lion, seeking whom he may devour. Resist him, steadfast in the faith..."*

2 Corinthians 2:9-11, *"... I have forgiven that one for your sakes in the presence of Christ, lest Satan take advantage of us; for we are not ignorant of his devices."*

God wants you to be aware of the devil's devices so that you can have victory. Unforgiveness is one of Satan's most powerful tactics to keep God's people in bondage!

You May Need to Establish Boundaries.

It is important to know that just because we asked for or gave forgiveness toward a person, it does not give that person the right to treat you with disrespect and/or harshly. *Example:* If you had a mother that was very harsh or manipulative toward you when you were growing up and she continued after you moved out, got married, etc. After you forgive her, you can set boundaries in your relationship. "Mom, I want a relationship with you but I need to establish some boundaries so I am not being hurt by you." "Mom, I need you to speak to me in a loving way and I promise to do the same toward you. If either of us say something unkind to each other and we say, 'that hurt' and/or 'I wish not to talk about that subject, we need to apologize and/or stop talking about the subject'. If those boundaries are not respected then I will hang up and we won't talk for a few days. Mom, the only way we can truly know if we desire to have a relationship is by the way we love and respect each other."

What if the person I need to forgive is deceased? Can I still forgive them?

Bitterness in the human heart lives on long after the object of that bitterness has died. It is so important to view forgiveness as a powerful antidote to heal the human soul of many unhealthy human conditions. If a person chooses to trust God and receive this "antidote" God will bring healing and even fill those voids that are in your soul. The death of the offender does not nullify God's Word. True, biblical forgiveness requires us to take action. We must do more than agree in our minds or hearts that we should forgive. The Bible does not command us to merely feel forgiveness. We must exercise our will and follow through with our actions!

You must begin with confession to the Lord. To confess means to acknowledge or disclose one's misdeed, fault or sin. It is helpful if you speak your confession out loud and verbalize your forgiveness of the deceased person, in the presence of a trusted friend, spouse, pastor, counselor, etc.

Use the following prayer to help guide you:

"Lord Jesus, thank you for dying on the cross and forgiving me for all of my sins. I agree with Your Word that I must forgive this person for the hurt they caused me. I ask You for the strength to obey and speak these words of forgiveness.

I forgive…for…(you may say out loud, if you wish). I ask you to take away my hurts and forgive me for holding onto this for so long. In Jesus Name I pray. Amen"

What if the person that I am forgiving does not want to reconcile the relationship?

You must keep in mind that you are only responsible for your part of reconciliation. Regardless of the position the other person takes, you must obey God by asking for forgiveness and giving forgiveness. If the other person refuses to grant you forgiveness or if they do not acknowledge their wrong toward you, God will still bless you for your obedience and pour out His peace, grace, and mercy upon your life. You will still experience His freedom from your bondage.

You cannot place any expectations or requirements upon what the other person may say or do, but surrender all to the Lord and trust Him to work in the midst of your circumstances. This is a major inner personal battle that many people face with this act of obedience.

We must not lean on our own understanding, but obey and surrender to God and His will. He has given us spiritual laws to govern, protect, and set us free. His Word gives us understanding and instructions in how to follow these laws. Our flesh, our pride, and fear will keep us from trusting and obeying God in these situations, but through the power of the Holy Spirit, we can overcome.

Proverbs 3:5,6, *"Trust in the Lord with all your heart, and lean not on your own understanding; in all your ways acknowledge Him and He shall direct your paths."*

Pray this prayer:

"Lord Jesus, I pray for the strength to trust You in these circumstances. Help me to remember that I am doing this for You. I do not look to… for anything, but place my life in Your hands. I pray for reconciliation with this person, but I know that I can only do my part. I pray for…to surrender to You that You might be glorified. I trust you entirely with the results. In Jesus Name I pray. Amen"

Conclusion

At times it can be awfully hard to forgive. But the truth is…it is harder not to forgive. If we do not forgive, we deny what Jesus has done for us on the cross. Our experience of God's forgiveness is directly related to our ability to forgive. A readiness to forgive others is part of the indication that we have truly repented, surrendered our life, and received God's forgiveness. A surrendered heart toward God cannot be a hard heart toward others.

Pride and fear keep us from forgiveness and reconciliation. Refusing to give in, or be broken, insisting on our rights, and defending ourselves are all indications that our selfish pride is ruling our life, rather than the Lord. If fears of 'what-ifs' are consuming and controlling you, you need to pray for the faith to trust and obey God. Enemies are very expensive to keep. Matthew 18:21-35 warns that an unforgiving spirit will put us in an emotional prison.

> *"The first and often the only person to be healed by forgiveness is the person who does the forgiving… When we genuinely forgive, we set a prisoner free and then discover that the prisoner we set free was us."*
>
> *—Lewis Smedes*

CPSIA information can be obtained at www.ICGtesting.com
Printed in the USA
BVOW10s0832210114

342520BV00004B/5/P